T5-BAR-989

Latin America's New Internationalism

edited by

Roger W. Fontaine
James D. Theberge

Published in cooperation with the Center for Strategic and International Studies, Georgetown University

The Praeger Special Studies program—utilizing the most modern and efficient book production techniques and a selective worldwide distribution network—makes available to the academic, government, and business communities significant, timely research in U.S. and international economic, social, and political development.

Latin America's New Internationalism

The End of Hemispheric Isolation

PRAEGER SPECIAL STUDIES IN INTERNATIONAL ECONOMICS AND DEVELOPMENT

Praeger Publishers New York Washington London

Library of Congress Cataloging in Publication Data
Main entry under title:

Latin America's new internationalism.

(Praeger special studies in international economics and development)
"The papers were originally presented at the Center's conference 'Latin America in the World System,' April 11-13, 1975."
Includes index.
1. Latin America—Foreign economic relations—Congresses. 2. Latin America—Foreign relations—Congresses. I. Fontaine, Roger W. II. Theberge, James Daniel.
HF1480.5.L3855 327.8 76-14779
ISBN 0-275-56750-8

PRAEGER PUBLISHERS
111 Fourth Avenue, New York, N.Y. 10003, U.S.A.

Published in the United States of America in 1976
by Praeger Publishers, Inc.

Printed in the United States of America

PREFACE

Today there are still only two dominant, but quite conventional schools of thought about Latin America and its relations with the United States. One believes the region should be a special concern of the United States, but finds it deplorably neglected by American officialdom. This interpretation, however, is still essentially benign about U.S. attitudes and actions. The second view stresses Latin America's dependence on the United States, which by means of a sphere of influence mentality exerts a malign control over the fortunes of its hemispheric neighbors.

Each school has produced a small library of volumes dedicated to proving its principal thesis. Despite their obvious differences, however, both share one extremely important assumption: the western hemisphere is much more than a geographic expression; this has been true for some time; and will continue to be so in the future. More precisely, it is assumed that the political and economic life of the Latin American republics will continue to be ordered (in whatever fashion) by the United States of America.

This collection of essays offers another much needed perspective on Latin America's contemporary role in the world arena. The papers prepared by leading scholars came out of the Second Williamsburg Conference held in Williamsburg, Virginia, in April 1975 and sponsored by the Center for Strategic and International Studies, Georgetown University. The essays are not a frontal assault on conventional analysis, but they are a most useful corrective to it. Moreover, they are not intended to be a fresh prescription for the ills that plague United States-Latin American relations. But they most certainly provide new information and insights that American policy so badly needs.

Therefore, the purpose of the conference was to assess Latin America's current political and economic position in the world, and not simply the hemisphere alone. Contemporary relations with Western Europe, Japan, and the Socialist bloc, as well as Canada and the Third World nations, are examined. Other essays look at the region's resources necessary to carry out the new and expanded role: oil and other minerals as well as its growing military capability. Our objective was to review that role without exaggerating its importance. Therefore, while it may not be the end of the New World as a geopolitical given, Latin America can no longer be considered an isolated backwater, well out of the mainstream of world politics.

The editors would like to thank the Tinker Foundation, and the DeWitt Wallace Foundation, and Readers Digest Foundations for their financial assistance in making Williamsburg II possible. We would also like to thank Mary Park for typing and retyping the essays and for the no less heroic task of keeping track of thirteen separate manuscripts.

CONTENTS

Chapter | Page

LIST OF TABLES

Table Page

LIST OF FIGURES

Figure		Page

LIST OF ABBREVIATIONS

ACP	African, Caribbean, Pacific
AEC	Atomic Energy Commission (U.S.)
CALA	Canadian Association for Latin America
CALAS	Canadian Association for Latin American States
CACM	Central American Common Market
CAP	Common Agricultural Policy
CBTN	Compania Brasilena de Tecnologica Nuclear
CCD	Conference of the Committee on Disarmament
CDC	Canada Development Corporation
CECLA	Special Economic Coordinating Commission for Latin America
CEP	Comision Ejecutivo Permanente
CEPAL	Economic Commission for Latin America
CFE	Comision Federal de Electricidad
CIAP	Inter-American Economic and Social Council
CIDA	Canadian International Development Agency
CIEN	Inter-American Nuclear Energy Commission
CIES	Consejo Inter Americano Economico y Social
CIPEC	Intergovernmental Council of Copper Exporting Countries
CNEA	Argentine National Commission of Atomic Energy (Comissao Nacional de Energia Nuclear)
CNEN	Comision Nacional de Energia Nuclear

CPE	Centrally Planned Economies
CUSO	Canadian University Service Overseas
CVP	Venezuelan Petroleum Corporation (Corporacian Venezolana de Petroleo)
DAC	Development Assistance Committee
EEC	European Economic Community
ECLA	Economic Commission for Latin America
ERDA	Energy Research and Development Administration (U.S.)
FIRA	Foreign Investment Review Agency
FLQ	Front de Liberation du Quebec
FNV	Fabrica Nacional de Vagoes
GATT	General Agreement on Tariffs and Trade
IAEA	International Atomic Energy Agency
IADB	Inter-American Development Bank
ILPES	Instituto Latinoamericano de Planificacion Economica y Social
IMF	International Monetary Fund
INEN	Instituto Nacional de Energia Nuclear
IOEC	Iron Ore Exporting Countries
JEN	Junta de Energia Nuclear
LAFTA	Latin American Free Trade Association
LME	London Metal Exchange
MAP	Military Assistance Program
NATO	North Atlantic Treaty Organization

NPT	Non-Proliferation Treaty
OAS	Organization of American States
ODA	Official Development Aid
OECD	Organization for Economic Cooperation and Development
OLAS	Organization of Latin American Solidarity
OPANAL	Organization for the Prohibition of Nuclear Weapons in Latin America
OPEC	Organization of Petroleum Exporting Countries
SELA	Latin American Economic System
UNCTAD	United Nations Conference on Trade and Development
UPEB	Union de Paises Exportadores de Banano
WDC	World Disarmament Conference

CHAPTER

1

LATIN AMERICA'S NEW INTERNATIONALISM: AN HISTORICAL OVERVIEW

Roger W. Fontaine

It seems to be the nature of regional and country specialists to deplore current American policy toward the region or country they are concerned with. In the case of Latin America, specialists have been criticizing official policy since the early nineteenth century. The government, meanwhile, has reacted with anything from healthy contempt to vague unease. Rarely has academic special pleading resulted in any grand design for Latin America, the Alliance for Progress being the most notable exception.

But whatever the official reaction—indifference, concern, or interest and a sense of adventure—rarely were the bedrock assumptions conventionally accepted by all specialists, questioned by the skeptics. Almost no one asked whether Latin America had ever really occupied a special place in U.S. foreign policy or, more important, whether it should, and why? No one asked whether cooperation with Latin America was increasing or whether it would if the United States abandoned its narrow and shortsighted policies.

These questions, which would have been considered radically revisionist a few years ago, are now being asked and answered in ways that cut across the path blazed by an earlier generation of Latin America experts. Today it is fashionable to regard Latin America's drawing together, without help or hindrance from the United States, as an agreeable development. Similarly welcomed is the spirit of internationalism that pervades the political and economic agreements Latin American countries have made recently with nations which diplomats hardly took seriously only a decade ago. Quite clearly the supremacy, even the partnership, of the United States in the hemisphere is being challenged. Are these developments welcome? And are they actually novel?

The first of these questions requires serious thought and is beyond the scope of this essay. The second, which requires serious historical investigation, is the theme of this chapter. Because of space limitations, only two periods that found the United States confronted with a "Latin American problem" will be examined. Both date from the nineteenth century, which has hardly been touched upon, even by specialists, in the last fifty years. In fact, the nineteenth century presented a series of problems similar to those that currently confront the hemisphere, or at least that part of the hemisphere that is south of the forty-ninth parallel.

The two periods considered here are the first and last quarters of the nineteenth century. This nation's Latin American policy in each case was dominated by a single individual: John Quincy Adams in the first instance and James G. Blaine in the second. Adams, on balance, serves as a positive example; Blaine, a negative one. Both confronted issues—the character of the special relationship, hemispheric security, diplomatic recognition, and trade policy—that have a contemporary ring. Yet, especially in the earlier period, no assumptions went unexamined, no policy went into effect without strenuous debate, and, for the most part, sharp differences were drawn between sentiment and national interest.[1]

It is also important to realize that the first generation of North American policymakers (many of whom were Founding Fathers) did not subscribe to the premises of latter-day Pan-Americanism, although such ideas already had been advanced. Now-forgotten men like William Duane, William Thornton, and Henry M. Brackenridge all pressed for heavy U.S. involvement in South American affairs on the basis of common aspirations as well as geography.[2] But the first leaders of the United States—Jefferson and even Clay eventually, and, more forthrightly, the Adamses—resisted their ideas.

THE FOUNDING FATHERS AND LATIN AMERICA

What are the major questions, still relevant today, that the first generation of American leaders asked regarding South America? Broadly speaking, they were concerned, first, with whether or not the western hemisphere was unique, and, if it was, whether or not a special relationship existed between North and South America. North America had achieved independence first; did it then have a special obligation to assist its "Southern brethren"? What kind of specific policies flowed from that obligation? Were there common security interests, and how were they to be coordinated? Was a special trade policy indicated? Was the United States to encourage democratic and republican institutions in South America, and, if so, by what means?

The question of the uniqueness of this hemisphere is the broadest and at the same time the most crucial the student can ask. Yet, at first glance, the specialness of the Americas, the New World, seems obvious to us (and how much more so to men who were caught up in the process of freeing themselves from a monarchical Europe) that we are startled to find upon preliminary investigation that few Americans have found it worthy of discussion or even casual speculation. One could hardly argue that Franklin, Washington, and Hamilton, for example, were ignorant provincials who knew nothing beyond their immediate world. Yet these men never entertained the notion that the Americas were a unique whole. Franklin confined his interest in South America to scientific topics. Washington was concerned chiefly with maintaining good relations with Spain and took firm measures against the Yankee adventurers who wished to "liberate" adjacent Spanish territory from the chains of absolute monarchy.[3]

The first American who took the matter at all seriously was Thomas Jefferson. His earliest known concern with South America is reflected in a series of letters written in France between 1786 and 1788. South America (as the first generation preferred to call it, not Latin America, a term invented later by the French) was still under the control of Spain. Jefferson believed it was in the United States self-interest that Spain, "not forever, but very long retain her possessions in that quarter."[4] Why? Jefferson did not want the vast Spanish territories to fall under the more secure domination of another European power. His greatest concern was that Spain remain "too feeble to hold them [its possessions in North America] till our population can be sufficiently advanced to gain it from them piece by piece." As far as South America was concerned, he knew of the uprisings that had already taken place there, and feared they would only provoke a Spanish alliance with France.[5]

Jefferson's earliest concern with South America developed from national self-interest. His clearest articulation of the idea that the western hemisphere was a place set apart, comes in two letters. The first was to Alexander Humboldt and the other to James Monroe, who was seeking Jefferson's advice on a presidential message that later became known as the Monroe Doctrine.[6] Nowhere else in the literature of the early national period is this idea entertained.

The Humboldt letter is often quoted, but usually in a highly selective and misleading manner. To be correctly interpreted, the passage must be considered as a whole, even if this makes lengthy quotation necessary. Jefferson is discussing the emerging countries of South America:

> But in whatever governments they end they will be American governments, no longer to be involved in the never-ceasing broils of Europe. The European nations constitute a separate division of the globe; their localities make them part of a distinct system; they have a set of interests of their own in which it is our business never to engage ourselves. America has a hemisphere to itself. It must have its separate system of interest, which must be subordinated to those of Europe. The insulated state in which nature has placed the American continent, should so far avail it that no spark of war kindled in the other quarters of the globe should be wafted across the wide oceans which separate us from them. And it will be so. In fifty years more the United States alone will contain fifty millions of inhabitants, and fifty years are soon gone over. The peace of 1763 is within that period. I was then twenty years old, and of course remember well all the transactions of the war preceding it. And you will live to see the epoch now equally ahead of us; and the numbers which will then be spread over the other parts of the American hemisphere, catching long before that the principles of our portion of it, and concurring with us in the maintenance of the same system.[7] (Author's italics.)

The first sentence of this passage has been interpreted as evidence of Jefferson's primitive or even unqualified Pan-Americanism![8] Taken as a whole, however, the passage is a sophisticated elaboration of the American self-interest. It is clear that Jefferson was talking about an American continent that embraced the hemisphere, that is, not just United States territory. But it is equally clear that he saw the hemisphere as a distinct unit only in terms of its relations with Europe; that is to say, the fact of Europe itself defined as the American continent. Thus, the only common interest of the New World (a term Jefferson does not use) was to avoid any entanglement with Europe that would involve it in European broils. This, of course, was no remote contingency, but a situation Jefferson himself remembered. The colonial wars that ended in 1763 were fought in America as well as in Europe, but the American colonists, North and South, had little or no say in their conduct.

Therefore, as long as South America, that is, the area from Mexico (which then consisted of large parts of the North American continent) and Florida to the Strait of Magellan, belonged to the Spanish monarch, this vast area would perpetually be involved in the dynastic conflicts of Europe and would thus endanger U.S. interests, including national survival. A European struggle for Florida or Cuba would directly threaten this nation's well-being, and Jefferson knew it. Furthermore, even if the United States could remain free from war while the rest of the hemisphere was a battleground, there would be no way of avoiding costly disruptions of trade mounted by the navies and privateers of the belligerents. Therefore, for Jefferson, the hemisphere's interests were maintaining peace and commerce and avoiding the kind of relationship with Europe that would threaten it.

Ten years later, in the 1823 letter to Monroe, Jefferson repeated himself in a compressed form. Europe and the Americas have separate interests, and the "fundamental maxim" for Americans is never to "entangle ourselves in the broils of Europe." Furthermore, America (both North and South) "*should* therefore have a system of her own, separate and apart from that of Europe." (Author's italics.) And he adds: "While the last is laboring to become the domicile of despotism, our endeavors should surely be, to make our hemisphere that of freedom."[9]

Jefferson's use of the conditional must be noted. The hemisphere did not have a system of its own, although Jefferson hoped it would. The hope that the protonations of South America would be free and republican was not a purely altruistic notion. If most of the New World were controlled by monarchies fearful of republican subversion, the chances for the United States remaining at peace would be far less.

But how likely was it that an independent South America would share the United States political principles? This question is important because it hinges on the substance of the bond between North and South. Was the hemisphere more than conveniently isolated from Europe? Could it realistically become a successful example of stable, nondespotic government?

It must be said that, in general, Jefferson approved of the South American revolution. For him, at least at first, it was "another great field of political experiment."[10] He exclaimed to Kosciusko:

> And behold! another example of man rising in his might and bursting the chains of the oppressors, and in the same hemisphere. Spanish America is all in revolt. The insurgents are triumphant in many of the States, and will be so in all.[11]

But, along with this early enthusiasm, Jefferson harbored doubts about the viability of these countries and, therefore, their commonality with the United States. In the same letter to General Kosciusko, he added, immediately after his initial republican trumpet blast:

> But there the danger is that the cruel arts of their oppressors have enchained their minds, have kept them in the ignorance

> of children, and as incapable of self-government as children. If the obstacles of bigotry and priest-craft can be surmounted, we may hope that common sense will suffice to do everything else. God send them safe deliverance.[12]

Jefferson's pessimism gradually increased. His mature reflections on South America were best expressed in a letter to Humboldt written in 1817:

> The issue of [South America's] struggles, as they respect Spain, is no longer matter of doubt. As it respects their own liberty, peace and happiness, we cannot be so certain. Whether the blinds of bigotry, the shackles of the priesthood, and the fascinating glare of rank and wealth, give fair play to the common sense of the mass of their people, so far as to qualify them for self-government, is what we do not know. Perhaps our wishes may be stronger than our hopes. The first principle of republicanism is, that the lex majoris partis is the fundamental law of every society enounced by the majority of a single vote, as sacred as if unanimous, is the first of all lessons in importance, yet the last which is thoroughly learnt. This law once disregarded, no other remains but that of force, which ends necessarily in military despotism. This has been the history of the French Revolution, and I wish the understanding of our Southern brethren may be sufficiently enlarged and firm to see that their fate depends on its sacred observance. . . .[13]

Jefferson saw South America's political culture as already corrupted with the spirit of religious intolerance and the inability to compromise. In a letter to Lafayette November 30, 1813 (P. L. Ford, op. cit., vol. 9, pp. 435-436), he was even blunter, and in a style reminiscent of John Adams: ". . . the result of my enquiries does not authorize me to hope they are capable of maintaining a free government. Their people are immersed in the darkest ignorance, and brutalized by bigotry and superstition. Their priests make of them what they please, and though they may have some capable leaders, yet nothing but intelligence in the people themselves can keep these faithful to their charge." Also, he felt that the great inequalities in wealth and social rank were sure to provoke endless disputes, especially in a culture that did not even pay lip service to egalitarianism.

Given an ignorant mass, a wealthy but provincial elite, and a lack of legitimacy in any institution, the last remaining thread was a respect for majority rule—a thread easily broken and replaced with rule by force. Jefferson, it should be added, was not writing a gloomy post-mortem; he made these observations seven years before the last Spanish troops were driven from South America.

How could the South Americans escape this problem? Jefferson, although an ardent republican, was not eager to impose American institutions on anyone. Instead, he advocated South America's gradual separation from Spain. He explained this best in a letter to the Marquis de Lafayette:

> No one, I hope, can doubt my wish to see them and all mankind exercising self-government, and capable of exercising it. But the question is not what we wish, but what is practicable? As their sincere friend and brother then, I do believe the best thing for them, would be for themselves to come to an accord with Spain, under the guarantee of France, Russia, Holland, and the United States, allowing to Spain a nominal supremacy, with authority only to keep the peace among them, leaving them otherwise all the powers of self-government, until their experience in them, their emancipation from their priests, and advancement in information, shall prepare them for complete independence.[14]

Five years later he was still recommending a special relationship, not with the United States, but with Spain:

> Yet as they wished to try the experiment, I wished them success in it; they have now tried it, and will possibly find that their safest road will be an accommodation with the mother country, which shall hold them together by the single link of the same chief magistrate, leaving to him power enough to keep them in peace with one another, and to themselves the essential power of self-government and self-improvement, until they shall be sufficiently trained by education and habits of freedom, to walk safely by themselves.[15]

The moderate course that Jefferson hoped Latin America would take did not emerge, of course, and, as he predicted, the South Americans were unable to establish orderly and free government.

THE FIRST GENERATION AND DIPLOMATIC RECOGNITION OF LATIN AMERICA

Was the hemisphere more than a geographic entity? The first generation had its doubts, and articulated them clearly. Nor was this a mere exercise in wide-angle public diplomacy. The broad issue quickly narrowed to a very difficult question: Under what circumstances would the United States recognize the new states in Latin America? For archrepublicans the matter was simple: the United States should extend recognition and even military aid to the struggling South American regimes and rid the largest part of the hemisphere of monarchy forever.

For the men who actually dealt with the problem, the matter was not so simple. Jefferson, for example, linked the issue with that of war. His earliest statement on recognition is in an 1816 letter to then Secretary of State James Monroe.[16] It reveals a tension between morality ("justice" according to Jefferson) and expediency (self-interest). On the one hand, the South Americans were demonstrating their ability to be independent, and therefore the United States should show them "every kindness, . . . every friendly office and aid within the limits of the law of nations . . . without fearing Spain or her Swiss auxiliaries. For this is but an assertion of our independence." On the other hand, Jefferson argued that such friendliness does not mean joining in their war, "to which even some members of Congress seem to squint."

And what was the U.S. interest in South American independence? Jefferson did not hesitate to balance the pluses and minuses. On the one hand, a free South America would damage United States trade relations: ". . . they will drive every article of our produce from every market, by underselling it, and change the condition of our existence, forcing us into other habits and pursuits." Some commerce, of course, would develop, but in which products, Jefferson professed ignorance. "We shall have nothing to offer which they cannot raise cheaper," he warned, foreshadowing the cheap labor argument. The other cost would be the "everlasting enmity of Spain."[17]

But for Jefferson there were compensating advantages also, mostly involving national security. Spain "from her jealousy" was a natural enemy, and as long as South America remained part of the Spanish Empire, she would use it as a base of operations against the United States in war. In peace Spain would continue to close the South American ports to North American merchants. Summing up, Jefferson found that "interest . . . would wish their independence, and justice makes the wish a duty." The injection of an obligation beyond the immediate self-interest of his country brings Jefferson to the Good Samaritan metaphor: "They have a right to be free, and we a right to aid them, as a strong man has a right to assist a weak one assailed by a robber or murderer."[18]

Unfortunately, Jefferson did not spell out the exact nature of the right the United States possessed in this matter. For, in fact, the Spanish Americans were not mere innocent travelers suddenly and without provocation attacked by the Spanish thug. They were in open revolt against their government—good or bad does not make a difference in this case—and could hardly be compared with the innocent victim in the parable.

And what of the consequences of our acts of assistance? Jefferson faced them squarely:

> That a war is brewing between us and Spain cannot be doubted. When that disposition is matured on both sides, and open rupture can no longer be deferred, then will be the time for our joining the South Americans, and entering into treaties of alliance with them. There will then be but one opinion, at home or abroad, that we shall be justifiable in choosing to have them with us, rather than against us. In the meantime, they will have organized regular governments, and perhaps have formed themselves into one or more confederacies; more than one I hope, as in a single mass they would be a very formidable neighbor.[19]

In this fascinating passage, Jefferson almost seemed to welcome war with Spain. This is remarkable since Jefferson himself had warned against entangling alliances that did not support immediate self-interest. But no matter how he qualified the above statement, it was a departure from his basic theme.

Four years later, however, Jefferson had become more cautious. He argued in a letter to Destutt de Tracy that war for South American independence was out of the question, but immediate recognition was also. Europe, he claimed, was on the point of bursting into flame, and it was the first duty of American leaders to avoid that conflagration. Formal recognition would mean war with Spain and possibly England. Furthermore, war would be costly and would burden the succeeding generation with an enormous debt.

In the meantime, American policy should continue on its previous course; that is, maintain neutrality that recognized the South American revolutionaries as belligerents in a civil war. That naturally meant American ports would be open to their commerce (as well as Spain's), and when their claim to independence was irrefutable the United States would at least be the second nation to recognize them.[20]

By 1824, Jefferson repudiated entirely the suggestion of war for South America. Branding this a "quixotic adventure," Jefferson saw war with Spain as leading to war with Russia and France, which together had 140 ships of the line. He concluded:

> It is not for the interest of Spanish America that our republic should be blotted out of the map, and to the rest of the world it would be an act of treason. . . . We feel strongly for them, but our first care must be for ourselves.[21]

But Jefferson, whose views on recognition remained sketchy, was a retired senior statesman. The man who wrestled with this difficult question on a daily basis was John Quincy Adams.

The demand for recognition even at the risk of war was commonplace in the United States after 1808. For example, Adams writing from England, said "There seemed to be too much of the warlike humor in the debates of Congress—propositions even to take up the cause of the South Americans; predictions of war with that country to the end of time, as cool and as causeless, as if they were talking of the expense of building a lighthouse, or of adding five cents to the salary of the Secretary of State, which you see they have had the magnanimity to refuse."[22] The fundamental assumption of South America enthusiasts like William Duane was that the Latin Americans were experiencing what the United States had already gone through, namely, a revolution for independence. Thus, fellow feeling alone should prompt the United States to offer special assistance.

John Quincy Adams very early questioned this easy assumption. In a letter to Alexander Hill Everett, Adams expressed skepticism about the similarities, pointing out that the Buenos Aires regime was actively seeking a European prince, and that Bolivar's sudden emancipation of Venezuelan slaves was drastically different from our own social policy. Adams also made several distinctions between the North and South American revolutions. The former came in two distinct stages in ". . . the first of which we contended for our civil rights, and in the second for our political independence."[23] The Americans only fought for the second because it became the only method to secure the first. In other words, war was the last resort in order to gain what had always belonged to Americans. In South America such rights were not the issue, because they had never existed. The proof of this was that they were, according to Adams, "equally disregarded and trampled upon by all parties."[24] In Buenos Aires no constitution restricted the regime from the arbitrary use of force. Venezuela "has been constantly alternating between an absolute military government, a capitulation to Spanish authority, and guerrillas black and white, of which every petty chief has acted for purposes of war and rapine as an independent sovereign."[25] The indictment is severe, but no student of the

Spanish-American wars of independence can deny the facts, even if he denies Adam's conclusions.

It was Adams, too, who most clearly laid down the principles of recognition. In an aide-memoire to President James Monroe (written in August 1818), Secretary of State Adams, after outlining the military situation in South America, took up the delicate problem of recognition:

> But there is a stage in such contests when the party struggling for independence has, as I conceive, a right to demand its acknowledgment by neutral parties, and when the acknowledgment may be granted without departure from the obligations of neutrality. It is the stage when the independence is established as a matter of fact, so as to leave the chance of the opposite party to recover their dominion utterly desperate.[26]

Adams was convinced that the South Americans had a just claim to independence. But a mere claim to independence, even if legitimate, did not impose a duty upon the United States to accept it. For one thing, the claim itself had to be based on fact, and, furthermore, the act of recognition must not endanger the United States. But if the United States should not intervene directly, as many people were demanding, then at least the U.S. government could publicly express support for Latin American independence.

John Quincy Adams, however, made it clear that the United States should do no such thing. Good wishes without recognition would only dissatisfy both parties and would bring upon the United States a justifiable charge of duplicity. To the Spanish, such sentiments would violate the United States' policy of neutrality, while to the revolutionaries they would be hollow words—"contradicted by the refusal to do the only act which they ask of you, and which could manifest your friendship for them and your sympathy with their cause."[27]

James Monroe showed the same mixture of prudence and interest in South American affairs that Adams did, especially in regard to independence. Of all the early Americans leaders, Monroe showed the warmest personal interest in the South Americans and their cause. He alone referred to them as neighbors and brothers,[28] and in his public utterances expressed sentiments of concern that Adams thought useless, and possibly dangerous. This sympathy can be found, for example, in Monroe's third annual message to the Congress:

> This contest has from its commencement been very interesting to other powers, and to none more so than to the United States. A virtuous people may and will confine themselves within the limit of a strict neutrality; but it is not in their

> power to behold a conflict so vitally important to their neighbors without the sensibility and sympathy which naturally belong to such a case.[29]

But as openly sympathetic as Monroe and many of his countrymen were, Monroe felt compelled to add immediately this admonition:

> It has been the steady purpose of this Government to prevent that feeling leading to excess, and it is very gratifying to have it in my power to state that so strong has been the sense throughout the whole community of what was due to the character and obligations of the nation that very few examples of a contrary kind have occurred.[30]

The interplay of sympathy and self-interest in Monroe's thought is possibly the most complex to be found in the record of any of the early policymakers. It is best illustrated by two letters he wrote, one to Andrew Jackson and the other to Albert Gallatin, in late spring 1820. In the first place, he outlined the objective of American policy. It was, in his words, "to throw into their scale, in a moral sense, the weight of the United States, without so deep a compromitment as to make us a party to the contest."[31] What Monroe meant by moral support was that America "openly and frankly" wished success to the South Americans. Moreover, it meant their status was raised in American eyes to that of coequal belligerent. That is, the South Americans were not merely rebels mounting an insignificant insurrection, but acknowledged contestants in a civil war that had a recognized international status. This was precisely the position that Great Britain and France later adopted in regard to the American southern states after 1861.

But was Monroe's policy wise? After all, the republican experiment was not popular in Europe, much less Spain, and an angry Spain with its monarchical allies could mean serious danger to the United States. Monroe replied that the environment was not all that hostile and therefore the policy not that risky. Why? Because Europe was absorbed in its own difficulties; South America was really peripheral. In Monroe's words:

> Most of the governments of Europe are unsettled. The movement has assumed a more marked character in Spain, but a like spirit exists in Great Britain, France, Russia, and many parts of Germany, and in Italy. Where this will terminate, or what will be its immediate course, is uncertain, as it likewise is what effect it will produce on the contest between Spain and the Colonies.[32]

Monroe had a point. Revolutions and revolts had broken out in Naples, Greece, and Spain, among other places. In England the Cato Street Conspiracy, led by the unfortunate Henry Thistlewood, had involved the assassination of the entire Tory cabinet and the seizure of power, and in France the Duc de Berri, nephew of the king, Charles X, had been assassinated.[33] But Europe's instability was not to be counted on very far. Therefore, Monroe argued that recognition could well bring on a war with Spain and its allies. Avoiding war, of course, was in the United States interest, but Monroe was anxious to make clear that it was in South America's interest also:

> We have thought that we even rendered them more service in that way than we should have done by taking side with them in the war, while we secured our own peace and prosperity. Our ports were open to them for every article they wanted; our good offices are extended to them, with every power in Europe, and with great effect. Europe has remained tranquil spectators of the conflict, whereas had we jointed the Colonies, it is presumable that several powers would have united with Spain.[34]

Monroe quite rightly saw that wise policymakers did not go into the world looking for a fight or flaunting principles that would invite conflict. Thus, unlike other statesmen who mixed ideals and self-interest, Monroe and Adams did spell out the issues with a clearheaded, reasonable conception of the duty and self-interest of the United States regarding Latin America's struggle for independence.

When the United States finally extended diplomatic relations to some of the newly independent countries of South America in 1822, Monroe delivered a characteristic message. In a brief essay free of any hint of stridency, the president outlined the reasons for the new policy. He noted that Buenos Aires, Colombia, Chile, and Mexico (although he admitted that the evidence was not completely clear with regard to this last) had all declared their independence and had been able to maintain it for a period of at least three years. All Spanish forces in South America had been eliminated or reduced to impotence. Furthermore, Spain "has not sent a single corps of troops to any part of the country, nor is there any reason to believe it will send any in future."[35] Therefore, it was apparent that the former colonies were enjoying their independence. At the same time, Monroe was eager to assure Europe that the United States wished to cooperate in the reconciliation of Spain with her former possessions, and he expressed the hope that the European powers, too, would join in a policy of recognition, although he frankly admitted that Europe had not made clear its policy in regard to South America.[36] Perhaps, as he suggested, its interest was inversely proportional to the distance between Europe and South America.

In the meantime, the American recognition of the fact of South American independence in no way changed U.S. policy toward neutrality. That policy would not change in the slightest, and the "friendly disposition" toward Spain would be reaffirmed—hardly a policy to satisfy the ardent Hispanophobes who hated Spain as much as latter-day liberals revile the Franco regime.

Monroe, if he had wanted to, could have taken this opportunity to put forth a hemispheric doctrine, a statement of common ties vis-a-vis the rest of the world, but it is important (as well as obvious) that he did not wish to do any such thing. He made it clear that recognition was a matter of accepting a reality (in this case, he played down as much as he could the justice of the insurgents' cause) and asked for European cooperation and looked forward to conciliation between Spain and Spanish America. It was hardly the war cry of a Pan-Americanist and, therefore, received few plaudits from the supporters of the South American cause.

It actually enraged one ardent supporter, Henry Shaw, a former congressman from Massachusetts, who communicated his feelings in a letter to Henry Clay: "The day has long ago passed by in which our acknowledgment of Southern Independence could have shed a lustree on our name forever—There was time when <u>recognition</u> would have looked like a noble and chivalrick defense of the principles of Freedom—It now flows from the calculations of sordid interest alone. There was a time when <u>recognition</u> would have stayed the desolations of war, lifted up the broken spirits of a brave and generous people, and bound together our Hemispheres, by the facination of a glowing and ardent sympathy—That moment it was your fortune to distinguish—but the Evil Genius of our Country forbade its improvement—But after I should, nay, I do rejoice sincerely at this late and halting and reluctant step, so far as the South are concerned—but I regret it for the honor of our Name—we had far better have never recognized—negotiating with the Holies of Europe for a simultaneous recognition—Uniting our character with theirs—fearing to advance in our own Course and moreover so managing as to have our conduct in regard to Spain wear the aspect of duplicity—for so it will appear in after time—we could do nothing 'till we got Florida—and then—well let it go—it is humiliating to see the fair form of our Empire daubed by---. And after all England, yes, England will have the Glory of atchieving the Independence of the South . . . but I write to you as though you were a stranger to the subject—forgive me—the feelings, like Truant schoolboys will sometimes run wild."[37] Indeed they do, and though the language seems a bit quaint, that choking kind of outrage, that self-righteous condemnation of others who consider only "sordid self-interest" is still common, especially to those who are in the habit of mounting one and only one policy horse. To Clay's credit, he did not endorse Shaw's sentiments.

Within the broader context of the special relationship is the practical question of whether North and South have or will have similar political institutions. It is, of course, the staple idea of Pan-American rhetoric that this is the case. When Latin governments obviously fail to establish representative democracies (or even political order), their failures are considered pathological, certainly temporary departures from some imagined norm.

Was this doctrine subscribed to by an earlier generation of American leaders? We have already noted the hopes and doubts of Thomas Jefferson. John Quincy Adams also had opinions on that subject and expressed them most succinctly to the arch-South American sympathizer in the United States Congress, Henry Clay. After jousting with the speaker of the house on domestic political matters,[38] and after listening to Clay's criticisms of the Monroe administration's South American policy,* Adams again asserted his belief in the inevitability of the region's independence, along with the need for American neutrality. But after that, Adams, as secretary of state, proceeded in short, sharp strokes to demolish any kind of special relationship:

> So far as they were contending for independence, I wished well to their cause; but I had seen and yet see no prospect that they would establish free or liberal institutions of government. They are not likely to promote the spirit either of freedom or order by their example. They have not the first elements of good or free government. Arbitrary power, military and eccelesiastical, was stamped upon their education, upon their habits, and upon all their institutions. Civil dissension was infused into all their seminal principles. War and mutual destruction was in every member of their organization, moral, political, and physical. I had little expectation of any beneficial result to this country from any future connection with them, political or commercial. We should derive no improvement to our own institutions by any communion with theirs. Nor was there any appearance of a disposition in them to take any political lesson from us.[39]

---

*Clay's views will be considered separately. See below.

It was, of course, obvious that if there were no such similarity, it would be foolish for the American government to spend any effort in promoting democracy where none existed or, in negative terms, to penalize regimes that did not measure up to some American political standard.

We have already noted that James Monroe possessed an uncharacteristic optimism about South American institutions, but he, too, opposed the United States actively imposing its own standards. In his eighth annual message, he made it clear that we "ardently wish them to persevere" in perfecting republican institutions, and hastened to add:

> In this, their career, however, we have not interfered, believing that every people have a right to institute for themselves, the government which, in their judgment, may suit them best. Our example is before them, of the good effect of which, being our neighbors, they are competent judges, and to their judgment we leave it. . . .[40]

The first generation of leaders who dealt with Latin America, primarily Jefferson, Quincy Adams, and Monroe, expressed at one time or another varying degrees of sympathy for the South Americans and their cause. Direct support of their effort, however, was never seriously considered. Despite the high moral purpose one could attach to such a crusade, a prudent regard of the United States' welfare came first and necessarily canceled any claims on the United States based on an alleged commonality between it and the protoregimes of Latin America.

The Congress at Panama: Genesis of Pan-Americanism?

It would be wrong to suggest that the first leaders would have nothing at all to do with Latin America. Indeed, the United States did finally extend recognition once the new regimes had met the minimum tests of sovereignty. After recognition was extended, the United States, under the leadership of President John Quincy Adams, maintained its previous course. There is no better illustration of this continuity than Adams's attitude toward the Panama Conference of 1826.

Pan-Americanists have always viewed this conference, despite its failure to achieve very much, as "the beginning of the movement for inter-American cooperation"[41] on the historicist assumption that history progressively unfolds a certain inevitable design, in this case, "regional cooperation." Other specialists have been less charitable and have criticized Adams's lukewarm support for the conference. Unfortunately, the reasons behind Adams's actions never have been examined seriously. In fact, as we have seen, Adams was no stranger to Latin American matters. It was not ignorance that made him cautious about the conference. Caution was the result of a carefully wrought argument that has relevance today.

Before examining the United States position, it would be wise to clarify the nature of the Panama Congress. In the first place, it was not an inter-American conference as Pan-Americanists would have it. Among the invited guests were England and Holland, and the former played an extremely active role at the conference. In addition, many of the South American nations did not attend, Brazil, Argentina, and Chile, for example. As for the four who did attend, Arthur Whitaker has claimed they embraced territory subsequently divided into twelve states. Unfortunately, the four (Mexico, Central America, Colombia, and Peru) did not represent any such number. Venezuela was already independent of Colombia and Ecuador was virtually independent. Bolivia no longer belonged to Peru. In the meantime, it is incorrect to say that only three stayed away, since Argentina (again nominally) also included Paraguay and Uruguay. Thus, it is far more realistic to say that eight states stayed away, and of the nine remaining, six were the tiny republics of Central America (including Panama).[42]

Finally, little is made of the fact that Simon Bolivar, who originally extended the invitations (including the one to England), did not invite the United States. Whether this was an expression of enmity for America (which Pan-Americanists have always sought to disprove) is immaterial.[43] The important consideration is that Bolivar did not think the United States belonged to any regional grouping he had in mind. His view simply was that the Spanish-American states should confederate and that they should have a special relationship with Great Britain, not the United States.

The United States was eventually invited through Colombia, specifically Vice-President Santander, who thought the Americans could be induced to sign a regional defense pact, albeit with the British navy serving as the primary shield. In the meantime, the Latin American ambivalence over a United States presence was more than reciprocated by the U.S. Congress. Debate went on in the House and Senate for over four months with the Senate Foreign Relations Committee actually refusing to approve the nominations of the proposed U.S. envoys. When the nominations were finally approved, along with the appropriations necessary to pay for the delegation, it was too late. The conference adjourned before one of the representatives, John Sergeant, arrived; the other, Richard Anderson, died en route.

Adams sent three messages to the Congress dealing with Panama. The first, dated December 6, 1825, announced the president's determination that the U.S. delegates would only take part "so far as may be compatible with that neutrality from which it is neither our intention nor the desire of the other American states that we should depart."[44] In his message to the Senate December 26, 1825,[*] he stressed first that the United States did not intend to take part in any deliberations "of a belligerent nature; that the motive for their attendance is neither *to contract alliances* nor to engage in any undertaking or project importing hostility to any other nation."[46] (Author's italics.) The primary purpose, instead, was to advance the United States commercial interests. These, in turn, would be protected if the United States could show the South American nations how to avoid neocolonial links with other countries. More specifically, the new nations "in the infancy of their independence have manifested dispositions to reserve a right of granting special favors and privileges to the Spanish nation as the price of their recognition."[47] Whatever positive construction Adams might put upon them, such arrangements were detrimental to U.S. trade interests. And in case any congressman had missed the point, Adams said bluntly:

> At others they have actually established duties and impositions operating unfavorably to the United States to the advantage of other European powers, and sometimes they have appeared to consider that they might interchange among themselves mutual concessions of exclusive favor, to which neither European powers nor the United States should be admitted. In most of the cases their regulations unfavorable to us have yielded to friendly expostulation and remonstrance. But it is believed to be of infinite moment that the principles of a liberal commercial intercourse should be exhibited to them and urged with disinterested and friendly persuasion upon them when all assembled for the avowed purpose of consulting together upon the establishment of such principles as may have an important bearing upon their future welfare.[48]

Adams's fear, then, was twofold. The nonparticipation of the United States would give the European powers a decided advantage in winning South American markets, especially those powers that attended

---

[*]In Richardson, the Senate message takes up two pages; the message to the House, which is dated March 15, 1826, runs twenty pages. It reflects the concern over the sharp debate Adams's proposal had engendered in Congress.[45]

the conference, namely, England, already the greatest trader in the southern half of the hemisphere, and Holland, a leading commercial power in its own right. The second concern was South America forming a common market and thus shutting out both the United States and Europe. Thus, Adams's rationale for sending representatives to the Panama Congress was to protect U.S. interests.

Adams reiterated in his message to the House (March 15, 1826) that the United States would make no alliance even of a defensive character because it would inevitably "import hostility to Europe or justly excite resentment in any of her States."[49] The most to which Adams would agree, then, was no more than "a mutual pledge . . . to maintain the principle in application to its own territory. . . ."[50] And what of the Monroe Doctrine? Adams appears to retreat from it. According to him, each country itself is responsible for resisting "colonial lodgments or establishment of European jurisdiction upon its own soil. . . ."[51] Here the United States no longer seems to be willing to declare unilaterally against European intrusion outside its own territory.[52] Finally, in regard to "obtrusive interference from abroad," Adams suggested that a "joint declaration of its character and exposure of it to the world" would be sufficient, but added the proviso that U.S. participation in such a declaration would not be automatic, but a matter for deliberation.[53]

Another security problem revolved around the Spanish occupation of Cuba and Puerto Rico. Adams knew full well that both Mexico and Colombia had been contemplating expeditions against these possible jumping-off points for future Spanish moves against independent South America, and he outlined the dangers to the United States of any such expedition:

> The convulsions to which, from the peculiar composition of their population, they would be liable in the event of such an invasion, and the danger therefrom resulting of their falling ultimately into the hands of some European power other than Spain, will not admit of our looking at the consequences to which the congress at Panama may lead with indifference. It is unnecessary to enlarge upon this topic or to say more than that all our efforts in reference to this interest will be to preserve the existing state of things, the tranquility of the islands, and the peace and security of their inhabitants.

Adams used elliptical language. By "peculiar composition" he meant the large number of Negro slaves on the island. Thus, his scenario predicted an invasion by outside forces, the collapse of authority in Cuba and Puerto Rico, and a slave revolt followed by European intervention. Neither a slave revolt similar to the one that had taken place in Haiti nor a major-power occupation of these islands was in the security interests of the United States. It became obvious to Adams that the Panama Conference would be a convenient forum from which to discourage any such plans.

So far, the objects of the conference as defined by Adams had been within the national interest of the United States. What then of the earlier proposition, that Adams had caught the Spanish-American fever? Had Adams now claimed that Latin America stood "in a different and closer relation" to the United States than it did to Europe?[54]

The basis for this argument is found in half a dozen paragraphs at the end of the message to the House. Characteristically, Adams confronts the question head-on. Does U.S. participation change the policy "of avoiding all entangling alliances and all unnecessary foreign connections"? His answer is not a simple one, nor is it a surrender to internationalism. First, he reminds us that Washington's advice was that, in expanding foreign trade, the United States should avoid "political connections" as much as possible. The reason for this was that Europe had a "set of primary interests" that had little to do with the United States and that involved it in constant controversies. Because of the United States' distance from Europe, it could follow a different course.

After thirty years, Adams attempted to recast Washington's arguments. First, Europe still retained its primary interests, which had little in common with those of the United States. In the meantime, the United States was no longer alone, that is, the only independent nation on the continent:

> Those colonies have now been transformed into eight independent nations, extending to our very borders, seven of them Republics like ourselves, with whom we have an immensely growing commercial, and must have and have already important political connections; with reference to whom our situation is neither distant nor detached; whose political principles and systems of government, congenial with our own, must and will have an action and counteraction upon us and ours to which we can not be indifferent if we would.[55]

Furthermore, in that thirty years, the United States had grown stronger: wealth, territory, and population had tripled. If this was the case, then it was true that America (and it is not clear whether Adams meant only the United States or the hemisphere) had a set of primary interests that precluded European interference. If Europe did meddle, then "we might be called in defense of our own altars and firesides to take an attitude which would cause our neutrality to be respected, and choose peace or war, as our interest, guided by justice, should counsel."[56]

Adams's argument fell in two parts. First, the United States had increased in strength to a point where it could resist any European intrusion. The second change was the appearance of eight new nations in the hemisphere, seven of them republics. The United States could not remain entirely uninvolved with these nations. Their political principles were similar to those of the United States and in contrast to those of monarchical Europe. This statement reveals a change in his thinking. Nevertheless, the closeness of South America (closer at least than Europe) would not put an end to United States neutrality nor would it imply a kind of hemispheric confederation. The altars and firesides Americans would defend would be those of their own nation.

What can be distilled from Adams's argument is that closer but carefully circumscribed relations with weak republican governments of South America did not present the same kind of threat that relations (entanglements) with monarchical, strong, and perpetually quarrelsome European governments did. Furthermore, South America presented an opportunity for trade that could not be ignored if the United States were to grow even stronger.

Nevertheless, even given this ambiguity, Adams did shift from a position of relative aloofness from the South Americans to a policy of warmer relations with them in contrast to Europe. What accounted for this shift? Contemporary critics suggested it was the work of Henry Clay. Today, it is impossible to tell how much influence Clay exerted, as there are no accounts of his discussing the issue with Adams. Adams did keep an enormous correspondence as well as a personal journal, but only two references are available regarding the Panama Conference. In May 1825, that is, six months before the first message to Congress, Adams talked to Richard Anderson about Anderson's being a delegate "to consult, deliberate, and report, rather than to contract any positive engagements."[57]

The second private reference came nearly a year later when Adams noted in his journal the earnest debate in the Senate over the nominations. In this brief passage, one cannot detect the slightest zeal for the project. Adams seems completely detached from the debate, although he adds that Henry Clay is confident of a positive role in the Senate and a large majority in the House where the ex-speaker still had many friends.

Clay (who was Adams's secretary of state) possessed a hearty enthusiasm for the project from the beginning. In the spring of 1825, the ministers of both Colombia and Mexico made "separate, but nearly simultaneous" communications to Clay requesting informally the presence of the United States at the Panama Congress. Formal invitations were to be offered to the Americans if that seemed agreeable. Clay convinced Adams that it would be, and replied favorably to the Latin American ministers.

Clay's enthusiasm for the project remained until well after the congress, but in March 1827, he wrote to Joel Poinsett, the American minister to Mexico, that "well-founded intelligence" had it that Bolivar had lost interest in the congress and viewed with disfavor the treaty drawn up by the delegates. Clay's information was correct, and while he still favored American participation in the second conference scheduled to be held at Tacubaya, Mexico (in fact this meeting was canceled), it was clear that his enthusiasm had diminished.[58]

The U.S. delegates, of course, did not make an appearance in Panama. The conventional Pan-Americanist interpretation of this "misfortune" is merely to blame the partisan U.S. Congress and regret a missed opportunity.[59] But what if the United States had participated in the congress? Of course, one cannot conjure up an alternative history with any certainty. But one can surely trace both sides' documented perceptions as to what the Panama Conference was all about. How much these perceptions varied can be gathered first from the preliminary negotiating between the United States and the South American ministers. Adams and Clay agreed that before the congress assembled there were

> . . . several preliminary points, such as, the subjects to which the attention of the Congress should be directed, the nature, and the form, of the Powers to be given to the Ministers, and the mode of organizing the Congress. If these preliminary points could be adjusted in a manner satisfactory to the United States, the Ministers from Mexico and Colombia were informed that the United States would be represented at the Congress.[60]

The South American ministers were unable to answer the secretary of state, but promised to communicate with their respective governments. In the months that passed no reply was made, and Poinsett was urged to get some answer from the Mexican government.[61] Finally, on November 3, 1825, Pablo Obregon, the Mexican minister, was happy to report his government's pleasure over the U.S. response, but with masterful evasiveness, did not answer Adams's questions. Clay, in his response to Obregon, registered the administration's disappointment:

> In your note there is not recognized so exact a compliance with the conditions on which the President expressed his

> willingness that the United States should be represented at Panama, as could have been desired.[62]

But Clay, in view of the great time delay and his own personal eagerness to go to Panama, informed Obregon that no further satisfaction would be required, and none was given. This meant that the United States would go to Panama with only the vaguest idea of what would be discussed and of who would be there. The United States seems to have been unaware that England and Holland, two of its great commercial rivals, also had been invited.

Even without those assurances, the United States was prepared to participate. We have seen what it was willing to discuss; it was also specifically unwilling to undertake certain involvements. As one scholar sympathetic to Pan-Americanism put it:

> The United States would take no part in an assembly whose object was to legislate for the whole continent; would form no alliance with the new powers for the purpose of maintaining their independence, nor for the purpose of preventing European interference in their affairs; would enter into no arrangement by which its freedom of action in any contingency might be restricted; and finally, would not lend its aid to the formation of a powerful neighboring confederation, which might become a menance to republican institutions, or which might succeed in assuming the position of leadership which the United States desired to retain for itself.[63]

Yet the formal discussions, which lasted three weeks, and the preliminary discussions between the Peruvian and Colombian delegations, were focused almost entirely on the very issues that the United States had no intention of discussing. The four conventions that were signed dealt with the establishment of a confederation that would have provided for the common defense. This included a commitment to defend the territorial integrity of each member state and to coordinate the members' armed forces and the surrender of control of troops aiding an endangered ally. In the meantime, the projects that Adams had in mind either were never discussed (Cuba and Puerto Rico) or postponed (trade relations).

It must be pointed out, too, that the congress nearly broke up before it began. The earliest arrivals were the delegates from Peru and Colombia. The Peruvians immediately presented a treaty of confederation that went beyond even what Bolivar had in mind. The Colombians rejected it. Undaunted, Peru presented another, less radical plan, but that, too, was rejected. At this point, Mexico's representatives arrived and formal discussions began and ended with an even more moderate scheme for confederation and common defense.

It is hard to see how the U.S. delegates could have taken any of these proposals seriously even if they had arrived on time. (The Peruvians also made it clear that unless the United States became a party to the treaty it should not be allowed to participate in any regional gatherings.[64]) Either they would have taken no part in the discussions or they would have resisted each proposal—and rightly so. The South American states, in varying degrees, were threatened by Spain, but the United States faced no such threat, and being dragged into a war without clear purpose or profit was and is now unthinkable. In the meantime, U.S. interests would have been ignored since an increase in trade between North and South America was never even a moderately important issue for the South Americans.

The Panama Congress was neither an inter-American gathering nor the seedbed for a unique regionalist experiment. But it was the beginning of a myth that survives today, namely, that profound interests bind the Americans together. What, in fact, existed were two different perceptions of the common interest: for the United States, a liberal trade policy and isolation from Europe; for the South Americans, despite their disagreements, alliance and treaty commitments for the common defense.

For the North Americans the congress was a convenient forum in which to advance national interests that would benefit other nations too. For the South Americans, the Panama Congress was an attempt to shape a grand regional confederation, an attempt that was hopelessly premature since two of the participating nation-states would collapse in civil war within a year, but nonetheless zealously pursued to the exclusion of the less heroic but far more practical matter of adjusting competing national policies.

JAMES G. BLAINE AND AMERICAN CONTINENTALISM

For half a century after 1830, U.S. statesmen took little interest in Latin America as a region. There was, in Arthur Whitaker's words, "a very perceptible slowing down in the process of expansion in its various aspects—in the extension of knowledge and of commercial and cultural relations, and in the development of policy."[65] The United States was experiencing a kind of political and economic continental drift.

Of course, Latin America did not become entirely terra incognita for policymakers during this period. James K. Polk fought and won a war with Mexico while ignoring an Anglo-French intrusion in the

Plate River region. James Buchanan suggested in all seriousness in his annual message of 1859 that, as a good neighbor, the United States ought to occupy Mexico.[66] President Grant proposed to the Senate a scheme that would have incorporated the Dominican Republic into the union. But in no case did an American chief executive or his secretary of state work out a broad strategy that dealt with the area, as the first generation had done.

And the separation was mutually, if tacitly, agreed upon. The South American nations held three "congresses" after Panama, in 1847, 1856, and 1864. The United States was not invited; indeed, the second conference in Santiago, Chile, dealt with collective measures to be taken in case of U.S. attack. Furthermore, there is not the slightest evidence that the United States was interested in attending, even though two of the congresses dealt with European intrusions into South American affairs.

Various explanations have been offered and need only be mentioned. Both Anglo- and Latin Americans were preoccupied with internal problems. After 1830 political leaders (including Henry Clay) struggled to balance (or advance) sectional claims, then wage a civil war, and then argue over the route of reconstruction. Latin nations experienced similar problems with "nation-building," but for the most part (Chile is an exception) never quite solved them in as clear-cut a fashion as their northern neighbor.

Moreover, in North America the great task of economic development continued, focused not on international trade but on industrialization and internal improvements. Meanwhile, Latin America continued and expanded its trade relations with Europe, which always seemed more natural to them than with the United States. By 1880, the hemisphere had lost the unity that an earlier generation of American policy makers had claimed was natural.

But in 1881, American policy toward Latin America switched from "neglect" to almost frenzied preoccupation. There is no need for deep socioeconomic explanations of this phenomenon. Its cause was James G. Blaine, secretary of state under President James A. Garfield. Blaine was the dominant political figure of the quarter century that followed the Civil War. Once presidential nominee and a serious candidate for the nomination five times, Blaine was also speaker of the house, a senator, and twice secretary of state. But, more important, he was the only genuinely charismatic American politician of the period. While even presidents were men of few genuine followers, Blaine inspired men to band together year-in and year-out in Blaine clubs across the nation.[67]

Characteristically, Blaine felt a secretary of state should be much more than the president's first adviser on foreign affairs. He was supposed to be the first adviser of the president on all questions. His enemies accused Blaine of wanting to be premier to the supposedly weak and vacillating Garfield. That particular charge, however, need not concern us, for it is clear that Blaine did consider himself the shaper of the nation's foreign policy, subject only to the president's approval. And Garfield, with little experience in the subject, and overwhelmed with patronage matters, gladly let his new secretary take command.[68]

James Blaine did not begin his tenure as secretary of state with a full-blown doctrine for Latin America, although elements of his interest were already apparent in the shipping subsidy speech of 1878 in which he cast England as our chief rival for vital South American markets.[69] But strategy or no, Blaine plunged into the area with a great deal of vigor (one of his favorite words). His first opportunity was the diplomatic morass in Central America.

This area, which had been united under the Spanish, included the provinces of Guatemala, Chiapas, Honduras, El Salvador, Nicaragua, and Costa Rica. Independence was declared from Spain in 1821, and almost immediately Central America fell under the rule of Augustin Iturbide, self-proclaimed emperor of Mexico. Two years later, Central America (except the province of Chiapas) revolted against Mexican rule and established a confederation in 1824, but that broke apart fourteen years later. From then until Blaine's assumption of office, some or all of the Central American states tried to reestablish a union no less than six times—each attempt, of course, a short-lived failure.[70]

Despite these repeated failures, Blaine made it official policy of the United States to support vigorously any scheme of confederation. According to a dispatch from Blaine to the U.S. minister in Guatemala City:

> There is nothing which this government more earnestly desires than the prosperity of these states, and our own experience has taught us that nothing will so surely develop and guarantee such prosperity as their association under one common government, combining their great resources, utilizing, in a spirit of broad patriotism, their local power, and placing them before the world in the position of a strong, united, and constitutionally governed nation.[71]

Blaine continued by pointing out that Central America, with its population of 3 million, was similar to our thirteen colonies in 1776. Growth had been due to our union, and Central America would be wise to imitate our example.

A united Central America was important to the United States, he argued, for four reasons. First, our trade would increase. Second, we would have the pleasure of helping create another sturdy republican regime in the hemisphere. Third, a Central American government would provide an opportunity to construct an interoceanic canal. Fourth, European powers would have fewer opportunities to intervene.[72]

Blaine's support of the chimerical Central American confederation led him into other difficulty, but the original idea was bad in itself. Since all policymakers tend to be fascinated by large-scale projects, it is worth scrutinizing Blaine's arguments. First, it is apparent that Blaine was not aware of the previous failures at confederation. A study of these unsuccessful efforts would have revealed to him the enormous divisions that existed within the region and the enmities that had developed among its components.[73] Even more disturbing was his misuse of historical analogies. Central America was not a proto-United States. It possessed few resources, had no room for expansion, and contained a population that hardly matched that of the United States in skills and political habits. While union had enormously increased the North American states' chances of political and economic success, it was hardly the single cause that Blaine implied. Furthermore, the union of five impoverished provinces would not improve the military strength of the area, certainly not its ability to resist a decent power like England. With its disparate populations and poor communications, a Central American union could scarcely hold off a third-rate power like Mexico for very long.

Blaine's greatest mistake, however, was a complete disregard for the conditions necessary for a political union. He talked hopefully of republican government, but any workable confederation would have had to be held together by sheer force. And the only source of power sufficient to maintain it would have been Guatemala, the largest of the old provinces. Moreover, since Guatemala had been run for a decade by dictator Justino Rufino Barrios, any such union would have been the result of a tyrant imposing his will by force of arms. There was no alternative, whatever Blaine's wishes were. Support for a Central American confederation, although it sounded progressive and rested on the assumption that much was shared between the United States and Central America, was, in practice, support for the ambitions of a provincial warlord.

Blaine's propensity for action led him to an even more foolish enterprise. On June 15, 1881, the Guatemalan minister to the United States, A. Ubico, wrote the secretary asking his assistance in the settling of a boundary dispute with Mexico. Like most boundary problems in the Third World today, this dispute had originated in confusion over colonial jurisdiction. The territory in question, the province of Chiapas, almost three quarters the size of Guatemala itself, had been under the jurisdiction first of New Spain (Mexico) and later of the Captaincy-General of the Reino de Guatemala. After independence, the confusion had grown. At first independent from Mexico, Chiapas later was absorbed by Iturbide's Mexican Empire, and then lost again. But in 1823 when the rest of Central America broke irrevocably from its northern neighbor, Chiapas returned to Mexican control, more or less by consent. And although Guatemala chose (after the dissolution of the Central American confederation in 1838) to maintain the old claim to Chiapas, it was ignored by the Mexicans.

To complicate the matter further, a district within Chiapas, Soconusco, declared its independence from everyone and maintained it until Mexican troops moved into the district in 1842. Guatemala, at the time, did not protest this move, nor did it contest the claim actively until 1877, when it got Mexico to agree to a mixed commission, but that project ended abruptly with the arrest of the Guatemalan surveyors by Mexico.[74]

The immediate reason for Guatemala's refurbishing an old claim was that its dictator, President Barrios, was in deep political trouble. After ten years in power, he had accumulated enough enemies to make up a powerful and thoroughly disloyal opposition.[75] By seeking a foreign confrontation, Barrios seemed to be engaging in the classic tactic of the ruler in domestic trouble. In fact, he was shrewder than that, for defeat, military or diplomatic, could have been the coup de grace for his regime. Barrios's strategy called for the involvement of the United States. Thus armed, he would have been in a far better position to win the contest with Mexico.

Some of Barrios's attempts to influence the United States were subtle, some crude. In the latter category was his offer to the United States of a naval base in Chiapas (which, of course, he did not possess).[76] Blaine, although enthusiastic about acquiring bases in the hemisphere, quite properly ignored the bribe, but he proved susceptible to less blatant methods of persuasion employed by Guatemala's clever representative in Washington. In that message of June 15, Senor Ubico, after recounting a highly one-sided history of the dispute, pleaded that his country had exhausted all "peaceful means of conciliation." Therefore, he argued:

> . . . my government sees no recourse left but to appeal to that of the United States as the natural protector of the integrity of the Central American territory. The Government of Guatemala, from which I have special instructions on the subject, and the people of Central America will see with profound gratitude any demonstration that the Government of the United States may find fit to make to that of the Mexican Republic, that may induce the latter to respect the integrity of Central American territory, and also lead to the cessation of an abnormal state of affairs which unfortunately has lasted too long already.[77]

Having flattered Blaine once, Ubico did it again four days later, stating in a letter that Guatemala would submit the matter to U.S. arbitration "because it considers that it is the mission of that government [the United States] to settle the disputes that unfortunately arise on this continent."[78]

While maneuvering Blaine into accepting responsibility for arbitration, Ubico pursued the task of getting specific U.S. support for Central American confederation under Guatemalan leadership. First, he argued, such a union was "a popular and accepted principle with all well-meaning and honest patriots in that country," and, second, Guatemala, with half the population of Central America and the support of the Salvadorean and Honduran governments, was the natural leader of such a union. Third, despite its obvious benefits, certain elements will oppose such a project, and therefore it needs the support of a "strong foreign government," that is, the United States. Ubico, once again, sang the siren song:

> The United States are the the most powerful and best constituted nation on the American Continent; they uphold the flag of the republican principles which they vindicate before the world by their prosperity; besides, their highest political authority proclaimed more than a half century ago the principle of the integrity of the American continent against any attempt at usurpation from foreign powers. They are, therefore, the natural protector of all the American sister republics, where principles identical to their own are sustained, if not with as great a success, until the present at least with an equal faith in their final beneficial results.[79]

The appeal must have been irresistible. Blaine was asked to further a cause he already believed in—Central American unity—and to assume the responsibility of a great republican power by preventing foreign, that is, nonhemispheric intervention. He did not resist. On June 16, in a letter to Ubico, Blaine agreed that peace between the Spanish-American republics was in the common interest of South and North America. He added that while the United States would not choose sides in this dispute or consider itself "the arbiter of the destinies, in whole or part, of its sister republics," it would "tender frank and earnest council touching anything which may menace the peace and prosperity of its neighbors. . . ."[80] "Above all," Blaine added, the American government is anxious "to do any and everything which will tend to strengthen the indispensable and natural union of the republics of the continent in the face of tendencies which operate from without to influence the internal affairs of South America," especially Central America.*[81]

To carry out this self-imposed duty, Blaine informed the Guatemalan envoy that the United States had instructed its minister in Mexico:

> . . . to set before that government his conviction of the danger to republican principles which must ensue should international boundaries be disregarded, or force resorted to in support of rights not made clear by recourse to the peaceful procedures recognized by the modern code of intercourse.[82]

Of course, directly stating that Mexico's rights to Chiapas were not clear went a long way in support of the Guatemalan claim.

In a preamble to that dispatch to Philip M. Morgan, Blaine stated that since the United States was the "guarantor and guardian of republican principles on the American continent," it was proper to bring up the boundary dispute as an interested party.[83] Blaine then proceeded to outline virtually a duplicate of the Guatemalan brief. After portraying Guatemala as the wronged party, Blaine presented his credentials as mediator. The United States, he argued, was "the natural protector of the rights and national integrity of the republican forms of government so near our shores and to which we are bound by so many ties of history and of material interest."[84] Thus, an American secretary was claiming unilaterally a special relationship with the republics of the hemisphere. By implication, he had assumed for the United States the role of protector of small countries against the larger. Blaine clinched his argument by warning Mexico that "establishment of rights over territory which they claim" by force would be considered "by the President as an unfriendly act" damaging the cause of "building republican governments in South America. . . ."[85]

On the whole, it is an odd argument. Blaine, with only the Guatemalan brief before him, accepted its "facts" and assumed that Mexico had no clear authority over Chiapas (which, in fact, had never belonged to Guatemala proper). Yet Mexico had had possession of Chiapas longer than the United States had owned the territory it had taken from Mexico in 1848. And although a treaty had been signed, the U.S. right to California, for example, had been established by conquest.

---

*Since Great Britain by treaty had an interest in any isthmian canal (which Blaine tried unsuccessfully to renegotiate), plus territory (British Honduras), plus a protectorate over the Mosquito Indians on the Honduran coast, it is quite clear whom Blaine, with an already developed case of Anglophobia, meant.

Moreover, Mexico had had no real opportunity to sign a definitive agreement on Chiapas with Guatemala because of the latter's penchant for revolving-door governments. To appreciate the Mexican reaction to Blaine's mediation, one need only ask if Blaine would have resented a demand by Mexico that the United States reopen the boundary question with an impartial counselor to supervise "the negotiations."

Blaine's assumption that fostering republican government in South America was an important interest of the United States led to more problems. That interest was rooted in Guatemala's claim to Chiapas, and how resolution of a dormant border dispute could advance the cause of republicanism was never made clear by Blaine.

But Blaine did not leave the issue there. Five days later, after hearing reports that fresh Mexican troops had been sent to the border,* Blaine sent another message to the Mexican government via Minister Morgan in which he expressed his alarm over Mexico's alleged attempt "to precipitate hostilities with Guatemala, with the ultimate view of extending her borders by actual conquest."[86] And since "a continental policy" had developed favoring "fixity of boundaries and abstention from territorial enlargement," any violation of that principle menaced the interests of all.

As a part of the continental system, and as a firm supporter of nonacquisition, the United States, according to Blaine, had a primary responsibility to use its good offices for "our sister republics" in the "discouragement of any movement on the part of neighboring states which may tend to disturb the balance of power between them."[87] He continued:

> More than this, the maintenance of this honorable attitude of example involves to a large extent a moral obligation on our part, as the strong but disinterested friend of all our sister states, to exert our influence for the preservation of the national life and integrity of any one of them against aggression, whether this may come from abroad or from another American republic.[88]

But on what did this moral commitment rest? Why were we concerned with boundary disputes in far-off jungles? How were American interests (or for that matter the interests of Argentina) directly affected? Blaine spun out the worst-case scenario for the benefit of the Mexicans, who, by this time, were asking these very questions.

---

*Blaine was totally dependent on his information from C. A. Logan, who was close to the Barrios regime.

> As long as the broadened international diplomacy of our day affords peaceable recourse to principles of equity and justice in settlement of controversies like that between Mexico and Guatemala, the outbreak touches farther-reaching results than the mere transitory disturbance of the entente cordiale so much desired by the United States Government between all the American republics. Besides the transfers of territory which might follow as enforced compensation for the costs of war, it is easy to foresee the serious complications and consequent dangers to the American system, should an opening be afforded to foreign powers to throw their influence or force into the scale in determination of the conquest. . . . The peaceful maintenance of the status quo of the American commonwealths is of the very essence of their policy of harmonious alliance for self-preservation, and is of even more importance to Mexico than to the United States.[89]

The "American system," in short, was asserted to be an integrated whole, and any sudden breach within it would invite "foreign," that is, hostile intervention.

Having made this extraordinary case for American diplomacy, Blaine reiterated that Mexico must cooperate in a peaceful solution to the problem, and further requested that Morgan press the matter.[90] Mexico, not surprisingly, resisted the good offices of its northern neighbor on a matter that did not (according to them) need arbitration. Even in the face of hints by the U.S. envoy that American investment would begin to dry up if the matter were not settled, Foreign Minister Ignacio Mariscal agreed only to presidential arbitration of the exact boundary, provided that everyone agreed that Chiapas belonged to Mexico.[91]

But soon the matter was out of the hands of the diplomats. By September both countries were sending troops to the border, and Morgan was warning his superior that war would begin unless the United States was prepared to use force. Otherwise, he concluded, "it would be the part of wisdom on our side to leave the matter where it is."[92] In the same dispatch, Morgan detailed an acrimonious anti-American campaign conducted by the semiofficial Mexican press which called for, inter alia, the limiting of American enterprise in the country, and the need to counter-balance its influence with European capital and labor. In short, Blaine's prime rationale for intervening, the limitation of extracontinental influence, resulted in a stimulation of that influence within his nearest neighbor. That peculiar phenomenon of approach-rejection will be seen again.[93]

Blaine, however, did not act until Garfield died on September 19. But as he looked for a way out, the Guatemalans continued their furious lobbying. In June, President Barrios asked for a $2 million loan for war materiel, and Minister Ubico showered the State Department with notes of appreciation.[94] In September, Guatemala's foreign minister visited Washington, and in a series of personal interviews and letters to Blaine, pressed his country's claim against Mexico and asserted Guatemala's leadership of Central America. In doing so, he incidentally rewrote the history of the western hemisphere when he informed the secretary of state that, without American support, the South American states would not be independent. Indeed, the United States was the "natural protector of the integrity of the continent, and history shows how nobly and worthily they have fulfilled their high mission."[95]

Perhaps, but Blaine now wanted out of this messy situation, although he was as yet unwilling to bite the bullet Morgan offered to him: "To leave the matter where it is, you must perceive, is simply impossible, for it will remain there."[96] Blaine then repeated the familiar rationale for American intervention, adding that a refusal of Guatemala's request by the United States would have been "a violation of confidence in the purposes and character of the Mexican Government which we could not entertain."[97] (The argument is not convincing. Blaine is clearly fabricating rules of protocol ad hoc, and showing sensitivity to feelings the Mexicans quite obviously did not have.) Blaine requested Morgan to pursue the offer of good offices, but it is clear that he no longer expected them to accept. He therefore urged Mexico to join the United States in an effort to persuade "the independent governments of North and South America to aid in fixing this policy of peace for all the future disputes between the nations of the western hemisphere."[98]

This examination of Blaine's attempts at peaceful settlement of disputes shows, first, that Blaine's indignation over Mexico's inability to accept his protestations of impartiality were naive. No prudent man responsible for his country's interests can take the fair words of a foreign leader at face value, especially when that leader is an ignoramus. Second, in promoting the Central American confederation, Blaine made the mistake of supporting an idea that seemed flawless in the abstract, but in fact served as an added impetus to the imperialist schemes of a Guatemalan tyrant.[99] Finally, Blaine, in confusing the weak with the virtuous, managed to damage relations with his near neighbor Mexico.

Meanwhile, the crisis sputtered on, but Blaine played no further direct role in the affair. The Guatemalans, sensing the United States withdrawal, redoubled their efforts.[100] They offered bases and port facilities in December 1881. In May 1882, it was canal rights and a low tariff schedule. Later that month Montufar suggested to Blaine's successor that he become Guatemala's negotiator with Mexico.[101]

Blaine's activism and confusion over the United States role in Latin America got him into more trouble when he tried to sort out a Costa Rican-Colombian border dispute. Uninvited, he turned a small boundary adjustment problem into a major international issue, ignoring the wishes of the Latin American states involved and enraging the British, who were on solid legal ground in the matter. Even more serious was Blaine's attempt to end the War of the Pacific between Chile and Peru. By the time the American secretary intervened, Peru had lost the war. But Blaine succeeded in at least appearing pro-Peruvian, which enraged the Chileans, encouraged the Peruvians, and thus (as in the case of Chiapas) prolonged the conflict. The issue was only resolved after Blaine's retirement, which was followed by American withdrawal from the conflict.

These failures, however, did not chasten Blaine. Indeed, in retirement he posited an even more extravagant role for the United States in the hemisphere. In September 1882, Blaine composed his most coherent statement on his foreign policy in a letter to the Chicago Weekly magazine. It is important to note that, while this letter was supposedly a review of President Garfield's foreign policy, it discussed only relations with Latin America. In general, the former secretary presented a picture of decline and drift in our relations with the region: ". . . from ardent friendship with South America we have drifted into indifference if not into coldness."[102] And this contrasted sharply with U.S. attitudes of only sixty years before. Blaine conjures up a heroic and intimate past:

> The present tendency in those countries is towards Europe, and it is a lamentable fact that their people are not now so near to us in feeling as they were sixty years ago when they threw off the yoke of Spanish tyranny. We were then a weak republic of but ten millions, but we did not hesitate to recognize the independence of the new Governments, even at the risk of a war with Spain. Our foreign policy at that time was especially designed to extend our influence in the Western Hemisphere, and the statesmen of that era—DeWitt Clinton and the younger Adams, of Clay and Crawford, of Webster and Calhoun, . . .—were always courageous in the inspiring measures which they advocated for the expansion of our commercial dominion.[103]

This passage, of course, was replete with exaggerations, especially the remark on rising war with Spain; not even the young and aggressive Henry Clay had wished that. But the myth of the special relationship served the purpose of an activist who was attempting to rally the nation around his particular grand design.

Blaine not only dwelt on lost opportunities but also sounded the alarm over alleged dangers. Europe had made great inroads into Latin American markets, and some countries had been invited to guarantee the proposed interoceanic canal. The latter Blaine labeled "one of those dangerous movements."[104] But the most dangerous development, he argued, would be America's refusal to offer its aid in making peace between warring brothers. Refusal, in fact, would be tantamount to giving Europe a free hand to intervene, opening the way for "a practical destruction of the Monroe doctrine, and an unlimited increase of European influence on this continent."[105]

Before outlining Blaine's prescription for winning back the region, we must ask, did Blaine consider the possibility that Latin America's drift toward Europe was a matter of choice, not circumstances? Blaine, in fact, did consider this explanation and rejected it:

> They are at the same time generous and chivalrous, and though tending for years past to estrangement and alienation from us, they would promptly respond to any advance made by the Great Republic of the North, as they have for two generations termed our Government.[106]

Blaine did not produce any evidence to support this claim, although the flattering correspondence he received from Guatemalan and Peruvian diplomats might have been the basis for his conclusion.

Blaine's strategy contained two interlocking proposals. First, measures must be sought to guarantee peace in the hemisphere. Second, with the coming of peace, trade will flourish between North and South America and, incidentally, the former's negative balance of trade will be corrected.[107] Promoting peace meant convoking a peace congress. The purpose of that congress was to achieve "a well-digested system of arbitration, under which all future troubles between American States could be promptly and satisfactorily adjusted."[108] There was no doubt in Blaine's mind that out of the morass of conflict, such a system of arbitration would "have raised the standard of their civilization."[109] Furthermore:

> It would have turned their attention to the things of peace; and the Southern continent, whose undeveloped wealth amazed Humboldt, might have received a new life, might have seen a new and splendid career opened to its inhabitants.[110]

That underdeveloped wealth mesmerized Blaine as it once had Henry Clay (although not his more astute contemporaries). How that wealth could be tapped was Blaine's next concern. After the peace conference, a commercial conference would be held, and from that closer trade relations would follow.[111] Again, the heroic past is invoked. Trade had been extensive; it had been a central concern of our forefathers. But by the 1880s the United States had come to a negative balance with South America of some $120 million per year. There was no economic reason for this imbalance. Blaine cited a long list of products, everything from harnesses to kerosene, that were manufactured more cheaply in the United States than in Europe.

What was wrong? Blaine avoided placing blame on anyone in particular, but argued that American exports would increase "whenever the United States desires it and wills it, and is ready to take the steps necessary to secure it."[112] Willing it meant having the courage to reinvoke the peace and commercial congresses. As Blaine summarized it:

> If these tendencies are to be averted, if Spanish-American friendship is to be regained, if the commercial empire that legitimately belongs to us is to be ours, we must not lie idle and witness its transfer to others. If we would reconquer it, a great first step is to be taken. It is the first step that costs. It is also the first step that counts. Can a wiser step be suggested than the Peace Congress of the two Americas, that was devised under Garfield and had the weight of his great name?[113]

Blaine's interest in Latin America was in 1881. Five years later, however, Latin America was an oddity fashionable once more: academics, journalists, and congressmen began repeating the themes that Blaine had outlined in the Chicago Weekly. In 1882 the New York Evening Post coined the term Pan-Americanism, which soon gained wide currency in this country.[114] And in 1884 a special commission was sent by Congress to Latin America to study problems, the first such mission since 1817.

The mission had two tasks: first, to interview merchants and manufacturers in New York, Philadelphia, Baltimore, New Orleans, and San Francisco; next, to talk with presidents and cabinet ministers in Mexico and Central America and then proceed to South America, traveling down the west coast and returning via the River Plate countries and Brazil.[115] Their report, along with accompanying statements and letters, was submitted to Congress in the spring of 1886.[116] In general, all three men glowed with enthusiasm upon their return from El Dorado, and, unlike their three predecessors of 1817, they all came back convinced Pan-Americanists.

Quite properly, S. O. Thatcher began the commission's report by testifying to a subcommittee of the Senate Foreign Relations Committee. He opened on an ominous note: "The question before the committee is one whose magnitude and far-reaching importance can not be too earnestly considered."[117] That "ever-urgent" problem turned out to be the American economy's penchant for producing more than the American public could consume.

> In some branches of productions, there is a slight reaction from the paralysis of the past, but on the whole, as never before, our future growth, peace, and tranquility depend on finding more consumers for what we have to sell. In this measure there is an effort to open to our producers of agricultural and manufactured wealth an adequate market.[118]

How was America to cope with this crisis? Thatcher supplied the answer in the next paragraph of his testimony.

> In vain do we turn our eyes to any other part of the world for a people who at once need and are willing to take from our farms, looms, forges, and wells of mineral oils what we are able to produce and spare. The nations of Central and South America offer not alone the most alluring and most profitable markets whereby to relieve our excessive productions, but there is no other field.[119]

But Thatcher also argued that while the United States was solving this crisis, it could hardly be content with mere commercial relations. We must move beyond the material level and establish close political rapport.[120] Yet what had we done in the past? Sounding a familiar theme, Thatcher chastised American officials for remaining indifferent to Latin America. "The wonder remains," Thatcher concluded, "that, notwithstanding all this neglect to cultivate and encourage those nations, they still admire our greatness and long for a nearer bond of union and fellowship."[121]

Yet, for Thatcher, there was hope for the United States as long as it followed through on arranging a continental conference and thus exercised its leadership over the community of constitutional republics. Happily, too, an inter-American congress with its "benign objects" would contrast sharply with other international conferences "where the repression of human liberty and progress were the bonds of the confederating potentates."[122] It would be a sublime gathering, where the United States, "the greatest Republic on earth—if not the greatest nation," would exercise a moral power and be guided by the truth "that no nation with a republican form of government can live to itself alone." Nevertheless, its specific objects seemed embarrassingly mundane, to wit: the adoption of a common silver coin and the establishment of trans-American steamship lines. The latter would be the vital links in the newly expanded trade between North and South. The mere facts of the United States overabundance of industrial goods and Latin America's "want of manufactured products" would naturally lead to "the permanence of the demand for our goods."[123]

The apparently perfect complementarity of North and South had but one flaw: European competitors were already long established in South America. England, of course, presented problems, but even more worrisome to the commissioners was the specter of Germany, "intrenched behind encouraging and protecting legislative walls" and seeking with "unflagging energies" choice markets in the western hemisphere.[124] Thatcher continued his description of the industrious Teuton in terms made familiar by later experience:

> They are clever imitators of every new invention, of every improved machine, and of many of the most useful and popular goods produced in the United States. They send out counterfeits of the famous "Collins" wares, even to the very brand; they make mowers and agricultural implements as nearly like ours as possible. Our sewing machines are copied by these people, and the imitations are palmed off on the South American trade as coming from the United States.[125]

Yet, once proper lines of communication were open, the United States could easily compete with the Europeans since its "superior material, workmanship, and fidelity of our goods would defy all competition."[126]

The silver coin that was to circulate freely throughout the hemisphere also played its part in prying Latin America away from Europe. The continental powers (including England) were generally on the gold standard, while most countries in the Americas were either bimetallic or relied on silver alone.

There was, to be sure, an element of political fallout from a conference concerned chiefly with trade. The conference's delegates, for one thing, would experience the United States way of life firsthand. Freedom of religion, thought, and enterprise would "profoundly impress our visitors and they would carry back to their own lands, new views and purposes."[127] In addition, increased trade would encourage the prospects for peace and would make unnecessary military tyrants. Thus, governments "founded on universal and intelligent suffrage" would come about among all Latin American nations.[128] Thatcher, like all Pan-Americanists, while forced to admit the existence of political irregularities south of the Rio Bravo, firmly insisted that those countries were close to genuine republicanism. It has been a long twilight for the tyrants.

Thatcher's themes were repeated by the other commissioners; William Curtis was possibly even more enthusiastic. Nevertheless, it took almost two years before a bill was favorably reported out of both Senate and House committees and finally passed in May 1888.

The distortions contained in the commissioners' report were not simply a matter of artless exaggeration or excessive enthusiasm. There was also a certain amount of plain deceit. The most blatant example deals with the proposal of a common silver coin. The commission had lobbied energetically on this point in Latin America and reported great success.

> This proposition has been favorably entertained by all the Governments advised with as one which would add value to the silver product and prove a potent factor in promoting commerce between the countries adhering to it.[129]

Curtis, now speaking for himself, elaborated further:

> The reports of the commission show that the suggestion for a common currency was favorably received by all the Governments visited, <u>including Chile</u>. All the Spanish-American countries are now under a system of monometalism. There is no gold to be seen. Silver is not only the current coin, but the legal tender everywhere. These countries have paper money, but its value is regulated by the silver coin that prevails in each. They do not even coin their own production of gold. (Author's emphasis.)[130]

If one proceeds to read through the lengthy (and more honest) country-by-country report, however, the universal acclaim for the silver coin becomes somewhat abridged. Of the nine republics analyzed, only six favored the project and some of them none too enthusiastically. The three dissenters were Venezuela, Costa Rica, and Ecuador. Nevertheless, the U.S. Congress, and later the U.S. delegation to the first Pan-American conference, were convinced the idea had widespread support. They would discover otherwise at the conference itself.

James G. Blaine: The Second Term of Office

By a stroke of political fortune, Blaine had another chance as secretary of state, this time under President Benjamin Harrison, which allowed him to take advantage of the Pan-Americanist ferment of the late 1880s.

The Pan-American Conference held its first session in October 1889 with all the hemisphere's nations in attendance except Canada and the Dominican Republic. The first was not invited; the second refused to come. This first gathering of American nations including the United States since 1826 has been depicted as a commercial congress. Indeed, economic determinists see it as nothing more than an attempt by the United States to carve out new markets in its sister republics. The conference did deal in trade, but not exclusively. The delegates also considered arbitration. Thus, Blaine's twin goals—a hemisphere at peace and united by close commercial ties—was at least to be discussed by North and South Americans.

Secondary accounts of this first meeting have tended to be sketchy, even a bit vague. In a few paragraphs the reader is given the impression that the agenda was modest, dealing with highly abstruse questions of diplomacy and commerce. In fact, what could be more "technical" than discussion of a common silver coin, weights and measures, and an intercontinental railroad? The commentaries suggest that the meeting was not a complete success, but, at least, in Samuel Flagg Bemis's words, "it was the harbinger of a memorable movement that was to yield richer results in riper times. . . ."[131] Unfortunately, this cheerful historicism, which runs rampant through the literature, implies two assumptions that are quite false. First, there is the feeling that the meeting was a success because it happened at all, which in turn rests on the premise that Pan-Americanism is viable. The second assumption, closely related, is that the meeting was important because it was the genesis of a movement that would develop in the coming decades. In fact, to accept that a relationship did develop, rather than that past mistakes were repeated, is probably wrong. Indeed, this conference, like the Panama Congress, deserves careful analysis. For far from being a harbinger of happier times, it was, in fact, an early warning system that should have revealed to prudent men the enormous gap that separated U.S. and Latin American interests.

Blaine, of course, was oblivious to any such difficulties. In his opening address to the delegates he quite clearly laid out the proposition that the western hemisphere was a special place. The nations of the new world, he argued, would not tolerate an "artificial balance of power" or secret understandings or "the spirit of conquest" or large standing armies. Instead, the American republics would meet "on terms of absolute equality" at a conference in which "there can be no attempts to coerce a single delegate against his own conception of the interests of his nation."[132]

Besides genuinely hoping that developments of real substance would take place at the conference, Blaine also believed that the style of this conference would be different from its European version. Blaine felt that a gathering of American republics was a family affair, and therefore a certain informality should highlight the proceedings. The rules of protocol should be relaxed a bit. Unfortunately, this, too, revealed his misperception of the Latin American sensibility. The matter came to a head with an argument over the rules involving the agenda. The American delegation thought the agenda should serve as a convenient beginning point from which the delegates could move to in far-ranging discussions of practically anything they liked. The Argentines objected and demanded a strict construction of the agenda originally outlined by the U.S. Congress. Why had the Argentines acted so vigorously? According to one student of Argentine diplomacy:

> The Argentine effort to bind the conference to limits may be attributed to a fear that the restless power of the United States would influence the other delegates to exceed the bounds which had been indicated, and that thus the United States would emerge from the conference claiming the role of arbiter of the western hemisphere.[133]

But Blaine's problems hardly ended with the quarrel over the agenda (followed by another, over the lack of Spanish interpreters; Blaine had naively thought the conference could be conducted in English alone). The very substance of the discussions would involve a painful shedding of illusions. It had been an article of faith with James Blaine that there existed large untapped areas of agreement among the American republics. Unfortunately, this view was based on self-generated illusion. This can be demonstrated by a closer look at three issues: the monetary convention, the arbitration agreement, and the customs union. The congressional commission had reported hemispheric unanimity on the first and Blaine himself had asserted that the last two had great support among the sister republics.

The first substantive controversy came over the silver coin scheme, which supposedly had received wide support in Latin America. At the Pan-American Conference, the matter was referred to the Committee on Monetary Convention. The committee had seven delegates including two Americans, Thomas Jefferson Coolidge, a New Englander, and Morris Estee of California. The five Latin American delegates proposed delicately that the matter should be discussed later at a special conference. The Americans managed to submit two minority reports. Coolidge, a defender of the gold standard, saw the coin as the thin edge of the wedge of free silver. Moreover, as he explained over thirty years later in his memoirs:

> . . . as long as we remained on a gold basis the States of South America being on a silver or paper one, the legal tender dollars they were allowed to coin would go to the United States and gold be taken in exchange at a profit to them of thirty-three percent and the same loss to us.[134]

In the meantime, Morris Estee, a Westerner, favored free silver and quibbled with the other delegates only on the amount of legal tender issued by means of the coin.[135]

But in plenary session, the Argentines would not let the matter be held over for consideration at another conference. They argued that while a common coin might be acceptable, it should not be restricted to silver. With its surplus trade position (and ample gold reserves), Argentina argued for gold. (A gold coin would also mesh with European monetary practice; Argentina traded largely with that continent and therefore was satisfied with the arrangement.)

The Americans, having made the earlier volte-face, were shocked, but other delegations joined the Argentines and the matter was voted back to committee. Ten other delegations voted with Argentina on this, with the United States supported by only three small Central American and Caribbean states.[136] The following day, April 2, 1890, the monetary committee recommended the creation of an inter-American commission that would discuss the coin (metal this time unspecified). The vote was fifteen to one, with Guatemala alone opposed. That commission did meet a year later, but no further recommendations were made and the project was abandoned.[137] Thus ended a proposal that "was favorably received by all the Governments visited, including Chile."

Much closer to James Blaine's heart was a system of compulsory arbitration that would be a bulwark against European intervention and a firm foundation for growing hemispheric trade. But before the United States was able to submit its peace plan, Brazil and Argentina proposed a voluntary arbitration scheme. The Argentines especially were anxious to avoid compulsory arbitration since that bit so deeply into national sovereignty. They argued that no regime could place major questions of national policy in the hands of men who were not accountable to anyone and remain in power and indeed responsible to its own people.[138] Faced with this opposition, Blaine left his post as conference chairman and entered the debate from the floor. But his eloquence could not head off support for the Argentine-Brazilian plan. The final resolution, which was approved unanimously, specifically excluded compulsory arbitration and a permanent board of arbiters.[139] The smaller Latin American nations, acutely aware of their inferior power position, refused to surrender what control they had over their destinies, especially when the arbitration board might consist of "neutral" North Americans. The controversy thus was only one more issue that divided the powerful from the weak.

Blaine's final pet project dealt with the establishment of an American customs union. It is true that the secretary did not have a blueprint outlining precisely instructions to the U.S. delegates. "Full freedom of discussion" was invited, but the central assumption remained: the hemisphere's nations were agreed on drawing closer into some kind of commercial union.[140] Certainly, the congressional commission had led those who read it to that conclusion.

But Blaine's political sense betrayed him again. The expansion of American markets in South America was not looked upon by many South Americans as mutually beneficial. In fact, the proposal for a customs union was rejected in committee unanimously as utopian and possibly dangerous to the smaller countries. A far milder resolution favoring reciprocity treaties, however, was signed by six committee members (including the United States) with two, Chile and Argentina, opposing.

But defeat in committee did not discourage the Argentines. In four weeks of debate they delivered sixteen speeches criticizing any special inter-American trade arrangements. Any move toward a customs union would benefit only the powerful, they argued. Furthermore, countries with European trade partners did not wish to jeopardize their relations by adhering to risky Pan-American schemes. An American Zollverein, no matter how it was disguised, would:

> . . . be a war of one continent against another—eighteen sovereignties allied to exclude from the life of commerce that same Europe which extends to us her hand, sends us her strong arms, and complements our economic existence, after apportioning to us her civilization.[141]

The Argentine delegate Saenz Pena concluded with a famous argument that contradicted the Pan-Americanist premises of Clay, Blaine, and similar enthusiasts:

> I have terminated my official declaration. Permit me now to make a most personal statement. Let no one see in what I have said anything but fraternal affection for all the nations and governments of this continent. . . . I do not lack affection or love for America, but I lack ingratitude or distrust

> toward Europe. I do not forget that Spain, our mother, is there, and that she watches with earnest rejoicing the development of her ancient domains. . . . I do not forget that Italy, our friend, and France, our sister. . . who has just called the world together on the Champs de Mars, are also there.
>
> The nineteenth century has put us in possession of our political rights, and affirmed those which her elder sister brought with her. . . . Let the twentieth century, already called by many the century of America, behold our trade with all the nations of the earth free, witnessing the noble duel of untrammeled labor, of which it has been truly said, God measures the ground, equalizes the weapons, and apportions the light.
>
> Let America be for humanity.[142]

Eloquence aside, the Argentines could not convince a majority to vote against reciprocal treaties, but they did defeat decisively (and apparently for all time) a hemisphere-wide customs union. South America would not follow the south German states, which had joined a Prussian-dominated customs union and then found themselves drawn into one empire. It might be added that the Argentines, who were trying to keep their ties with Europe intact, won still another victory. Thus, despite a number of reciprocal treaties that were signed after 1890 (with Blaine's hearty support), U.S.-Latin American trade relations remained unchanged until the disruption of traditional European-Latin American ties caused by World War I.

This first Pan-American conference was not merely a case of negative Latin reaction to North American proposals based on the assumption that the hemisphere was somehow a special place. The southern republics did argue, for example, that there existed an American international law that differed on a number of vital points from (European) international law. The U.S. delegation opposed this interpretation of the hemisphere, however. The weaker Latin American nations saw the issue as one involving power. The root of their argument was that all nations should be made as equal as possible. One area that challenged that equality was the legal position of the foreigner in Latin America. Was there a minimum standard of treatment he could expect from a regime even when that minimum standard did not exist for the regime's own nationals? If a standard did exist, would the resident alien's government have a right to intervene to see that if was enforced?

The Latins argued (as they have continued to argue) that American law does not permit unequal treatment of foreigners and nationals, and emphatically does not allow foreign intervention. The result was a proposal that stated:

> . . . a nation has not, nor recognizes in favor of foreigners, any other obligation or responsibilities than those which in favor of the natives are established, in like cases, by the constitution and the laws.[143]

The resolution passed with only one negative vote: that of the United States.

On this issue, the U.S. argument was advanced by the delegation's only experienced diplomat, William H. Trescott. "There can no more be an American international law than there can be an English, a German, or a Prussian international law."[144] Since international law was the common law of the civilized world, it reflected the long and settled experience of nations familiar with every conceivable situation that involved two or more nations and its citizens. Furthermore, Trescott argued:

> We accepted it as one of the conditions of our recognition, and we have no right to alter it without the consent of the nations who really founded it and who are and must be today, notwithstanding our increasing power and consequence, large and equal factors in its maintenance.[145]

Additions or amendments to international law could be suggested unilaterally, but they needed the consent of all civilized nations before they could take effect. Turning to the specific problem of treatment of foreigners, Trescott agreed that under ordinary circumstances, the alien can lay claim to no special privileges, assuming "substantial justice" is done to native and alien alike. Of course, that assumption loomed large in the conclusion of Trescott's argument:

> If under any peculiar law, under any absolutism of procedure, under any habit or usage of traditional authority to which natives are accustomed and willing to submit, the native process or judgment does not afford this substantial justice, the right of the foreigner to such substantial justice would be nevertheless complete, and how can it be assured to them? But if this be so even in cases of private contention, how is it with the cases where the reclamation of the foreigner is against the Government itself?
>
> Into what court will the Government allow the sovereignty of the nation to be called to answer its responsibilities to the

> claimant and how is its judgment to be enforced? (Author's emphasis.)[146]

Trescott did not directly answer the question, and the issue would bedevil U.S. policymakers in the future. For the Latins, however, there was a clear answer. Thus, they possessed not only the advantage of numbers but also the certainty of purpose when the issue came up again.

The conference closed on April 19, 1890, the first and longest of inter-American gatherings. In view of the unexpected and largely successful opposition to most of Blaine's ideas, he was left to make this hopeful benediction:

> The extent and value of all that has been worthily achieved by your Conference can not be measured today. We stand too near it. Time will define and heighten the estimate of your work; experience will confirm our present faith; final results will be your vindication and your triumph.[147]

The unpleasant truth was that both the Pan-American Conference and the Panama Congress revealed vast differences in interests between Anglo and Latin America. Those differences have largely remained, although in the twentieth century the attempts to paper them over have been far more numerous.

Present-day American policymakers can learn from the past. First, difficulties owing to conflicting interests are nothing new. There is no golden age of United States-Latin American relations that somehow should be attempted to be revived. Nor are differences exclusively caused by neglect, paternalism, or whatever catchword strikes the fancy of the latest commission dedicated to telling us what's wrong with U.S. policy in Latin America.

Second, those different sets of interests held by most Latin America nations have led them in the past to seek closer ties with other countries outside the hemisphere. They often have resisted stoutly the idea that the hemisphere should in any way be an exclusive community.

Third, U.S. policymakers have gotten into difficulty when they have exaggerated the degree of commonality within the hemisphere.

Fourth, having said that, a prudent Latin American policy is not simple neglect of the region, but a policy carefully fashioned around self-interest and a skeptical attitude toward grant designs—the kind of prudence best exemplified by the first generation of American leaders in their dealings with the emergent nations of South America.

NOTES

1. The best book on this very neglected subject is Arthur Whitaker's The United States and the Independence of Latin America: 1800-1830 (Baltimore: Johns Hopkins Press, 1941; republished by W. W. Norton, 1964). Although the work is over thirty years old, it is still the best (and nearly the only) serious examination of U.S.-Latin American relations in that period. Nevertheless, it does have serious lacunae, and I have felt free to reexamine primary sources, that is, the letters, speeches, and pamphlets of the men most concerned with South America.

2. William Duane was an ardent Republican and publisher of the Aurora in Philadelphia; William Thornton is better known as the architect of the U.S. Capitol; H. M. Brackenridge was the secretary of the first U.S. fact-finding mission sent to Latin America in 1818. On his return, he wrote and published a two-volume study of South America. His convictions are readily seen in a portion of a letter he sent to Henry Clay after the commission's arrival in Venezuela: "The yeomanry of the country are represented as a hardy, independent race of people and sufficiently intelligent for all the purposes of self-government. A love of liberty is zealously inculcated among the rising generation; and a martial spirit infused into their minds, which will be capable, if necessary, of seasonable application." From James F. Hopkins, ed., The Papers of Henry Clay, vol. 2, The Rising Statesman, 1815-1820 (Lexington, Ky.: University of Kentucky Press, 1961), pp. 584-585. Letter written July 13, 1818. It might be noted that even so romantic a temperament as Bolivar's did not lead the Liberator to such rash conclusions. He knew his llaneros too well for that.

3. See Franklin's letters to James Bowdoin, May 31, 1788, and to Dr. Arthaud, July 9, 1786, in Albert Henry Smyth, ed., The Writings of Benjamin Franklin, vol. 9 (New York: Macmillan, 1907), pp. 526-527. Like many of his contemporaries, Franklin feared that Spain would attempt to keep the United States "cooped up" behind the Alleghenies; he expressly hoped that the U.S. Congress would insist on the Mississippi as the boundary and would obtain free navigation of that river. Ibid., vol. 8, Letter to Robert Livingstone, from Passy, France, August 12, 1782, pp. 576-580. See Washington's "Proclamation Against Forces to be Enlisted in Kentucky for the Invasion of Spanish Territory," issued in Philadelphia, March 18-19, 1794 and found in Harold C. Syrett, ed., The Papers of Alexander Hamilton, vol. 16 (New York: Columbia Press, 1972), pp. 162-163. Hamilton approved of Washington's move without reservation.

4. Paul Leicester Ford, ed., The Writings of Thomas Jefferson, vol. 5 (New York: G. P. Putnam, 1895), p. 23. Letter to William Carmichael June 3, 1788.

5. Adrienne Koch and William Peden, eds. Life and Writings of Thomas Jefferson (New York: Modern Library, 1944), p. 391. Letter to A. Stuart, Esq., January 25, 1786; Andrew A. Lipscomb, ed., The Writings of Thomas Jefferson, Memoral Edition, vol. 6, (Washington, D.C., Thomas Jefferson Memorial Association 1903), p. 373. Letter to Colonel William Smith, November 13, 1787. This last letter contains the famous metaphor of the "tree of liberty" being refreshed occasionally "with the blood of patriots and tyrants." It is most important to note that while Jefferson took this seriously for his country he did not apply it to South American events.

6. The letter to Humboldt, dated December 6, 1813, can be found in P. L. Ford, op. cit., vol. 9, pp. 430-433. The letter to Monroe, dated October 24, 1823, is in Koch and Peden, op. cit., pp. 708-710.

7. P. L. Ford, op. cit., vol. 9, pp. 430-433.

8. See, for example, the interpretation of Wilfrid H. Callcott, The Western Hemisphere (Austin, Tex.: University of Texas Press, 1968), p. 14.

9. Koch and Peden, op. cit., p. 708.

10. Lipscomb, op. cit., vol. 13, p. 1.

11. Ibid., p. 43. Letter to General Thaddeus Kosciusko, April 13, 1811.

12. Ibid.

13. Koch and Peden, op. cit., p. 681. Letter to Humboldt, June 13, 1817.

14. P. L. Ford, op. cit., vol. 10, p. 85. Letter to Lafayette, May 14, 1817. Note that Jefferson left out England in this joint power guarantee. Why? ". . . because her selfish principles render her incapable of honorable patronage or disinterested cooperation; unless, indeed, what seems now probable, a revolution should restore to her an honest government, one which will permit the world to live in peace."

15. P. L. Ford, op. cit., vol. 10, p. 187. Letter to John Adams, January 22, 1821. Jefferson, like Adams, was no friend of Spain (see, for example, his letter to James Madison, August 16, 1807, in Lipscomb, op. cit., vol. 11, p. 326), but his practical statesmanship led him to this inescapable conclusion he repeated on other occasions. See P. L. Ford, op. cit., vol. 10, p. 108. Letter to 1818.

16. P. L. Ford, op. cit., vol. 10, p. 19. Letter to James Monroe, February 4, 1816. Jefferson's pessimism (which Quincy Adams was in agreement with) is in contrast to the great hopes Henry Clay attached to his "American system."

17. Ibid., p. 19.

18. Ibid.

19. Ibid., pp. 19-20.

20. P. L. Ford, op. cit., vol. 10, p. 175. Letter to A. C. V. C. Destutt de Tracy, December 26, 1820. In the same letter, Jefferson again expressed his pessimism over South America's political future. "What that independence will end in, I fear is problematical. Whether in wise government or military depotisms. But prepared, however, or not, for self-government, if it is their will to make the trial, it is our duty and desire to wish it cordially success, and ultimate success there can be no doubt, and that it will richly repay all intermediate sufferings."

21. P. L. Ford, op. cit., vol. 10, pp. 316-317. Letter to James Monroe, July 18, 1824.

22. Worthington Chauncey Ford, ed., The Writings of John Quincy Adams, vol. 6 (New York: Macmillan, 1913), p. 45. Letter to George Erving, June 10, 1816.

23. W. C. Ford, op. cit., vol. 6, p. 282. Letter to Alexander Hill Everett, December 29, 1817.

24. Ibid.

25. Ibid.

26. Report dated August 24, 1818; W. C. Ford, op. cit., vol. 6, p. 442.

27. C. F. Adams, ed., Memoirs of John Quincy Adams, vol. 4 (Philadelphia: Lippincott, 1875), p. 167. Entry dated November 7, 1818.

28. For a reference to the "Southern Brethren," see Monroe's letter to Joel Barlow, November 27, 1811, S. M. Hamilton, ed., The Writings of James Monroe, vol. 5 (New York: Putnam, 1900), p. 364; regarding our neighbors, see his third annual message, December 7, 1819, Hamilton, op. cit., vol. 6, p. 112.

29. Ibid., p. 112.

30. Ibid.

31. See Hamilton, op. cit., vol. 6, p. 132. Letter to Albert Gallatin, May 26, 1820. He uses nearly identical language in his letter to Jackson, May 23, 1820. Ibid., p. 128.

32. Ibid., p. 128.

33. The details can be found in Frederick B. Artz, Reaction and Revolution (New York: Harper and Brothers, 1934), pp. 149-183.

34. See Hamilton, op. cit., vol. 6, pp. 128-129. Letter to Jackson. In the letter to Gallatin (pp. 132-133), Monroe even more clearly expressed the United States relationship to Europe. By not entering into the fray, he argued, "we have given to other powers an example of forbearance, and retained the right to communicate with them as

friends on that interesting subject—a right we should have lost with change of attitude."

35. Hamilton, op. cit., vol. 6, pp. 208-209. March 8, 1822.

36. Ibid. pp. 209-210.

37. Hopkins, op. cit., vol. 3, pp. 184-186. Letter from Henry Shaw, April 4, 1822.

38. Clay asserted that President Monroe as a lame-duck president would not have the slightest influence in Congress. Indeed, Clay went on, according to Adams, to say that "there was and would not be a man in the United States possessing less personal influence over them than the President." Adams understood Clay to be building up his own importance, and the secretary later, in describing Clay's character, found him "half educated"; "impetuous" in temper; ambitious; and a man of loose morals, public and private. Yet he was "an eloquent man, with very popular manners and great political management"—a quality Adams admired and lacked. See Adams, op. cit., vol. 1, pp. 324-325. (Author's emphasis.)

39. Ibid., p. 325.

40. Hamilton, op. cit., vol. 7, p. 47.

41. Samuel Guy Inman, Inter-American Conference, 1826-1959 (Seattle: University of Washington Press, 1965),p. 20.

42. Whitaker, op. cit., pp. 581-582.

43. Inman, op. cit., p. 13.

44. James D. Richardson, ed., Messages and Papers of the Presidents, vol. 2, (New York: Bureau of National Literature and Art, 1903), p. 302.

45. Richardson, vol. 2, op. cit., pp. 318-319, 320-340.

46. Ibid., p. 319.

47. Ibid., vol. 2, p. 318.

48. Ibid.

49. Ibid., p. 335.

50. Ibid.

51. Ibid.

52. For a similar but not identical interpretation, see Dexter Perkins, A History of the Monroe Doctrine (Boston: Little, Brown and Co., 1955), p. 71.

53. Richardson, op. cit., p. 35.

54. The expression and thought are Whitaker's. See Whitaker, op. cit., p. 574.

55. Richardson, op. cit., p. 338.

56. Ibid.

57. Adams, op. cit. vol. 7, pp. 15-16. May 27, 1825.

58. Joseph Byrne Lockey, Pan-Americanism: Its Beginnings (New York: Macmillan, 1926), p. 353. Clay's earlier enthusiasm for Bolivar is also apparent in this New Year's (1825) toast in which he

saluted General Bolivar as the "Washington of South America and the Republic of Colombia" and contrasted him and South America to "wretched and miserable" Spain. For the secretary of state to refer to a nation with whom the United States was at peace as "wretched and miserable" does show a remarkable lack of discretion. Hopkins, op. cit., p. 1. January 1, 1825.

59. See Inman, op. cit., pp. 15-16, and his quote from John Bassett Moore, described as a "careful student" of American foreign policy. Moore called U.S. nonparticipation an "unfortunate omen."

60. See Hopkins, op. cit., vol. 4, pp. 684-685. Instructions to Joel R. Poinsett, Envoy Extraordinary and Minister Plenipotentiary to Mexico, September 24, 1825.

61. Ibid., p. 685.

62. Ibid., p. 869.

63. Lockey, op. cit., p. 426.

64. See Lockey, op. cit., p. 338; for a full discussion of the events, see pp. 316-354.

65. Whitaker, op. cit., p. vii.

66. Buchanan said in part that Mexico was "a wreck upon the ocean, drifting about as she is impelled by different factions. As a good neighbor shall we not extend to her a helping hand? If we do not it would not be surprising should some other nation undertake the task, and thus force us to interfere at last, under circumstances of increased difficulty, for the maintenance of our established policy." See Samuel Flagg Bemis, The Latin American Policy of the United States (New York: Harcourt, Brace, 1943), p. 110. (Earlier Buchanan as Minister to Great Britain drew up, with the aid of two other American diplomats, the so-called Ostend Manifesto, which stated baldly that if Spain did not sell Cuba to the United States, the latter had the right "by every law human and Divine," to take it by force. Ibid., p. 403n.) Lincoln, who was as much interested in American security as Buchanan, took a much more relaxed attitude toward Mexico, which by 1863 had actually been occupied by French troops. Maximilian's empire, he thought, was "a pasteboard concern on which we won't waste a man or dollar. It will soon tumble to pieces and, may be, bring the other down with it." The "other" referred to Louis Napoleon, and indeed the inglorious end of the Mexican adventure was a major blow to his prestige. See William M. Armstrong, E. L. Godkin and American Foreign Policy, 1865-1900 (New York: Bookman Associates, 1957), p. 59.

67. David M. Fletcher, The Awkward Years (Columbia, Mo.: University of Missouri Press, 1962), p. 268. Fletcher characterizes Blaine as "brilliant, . . . witty, a magnetic orator and conversationalist, a thoughtful, courteous man, and a crafty parliamentarian who had dominated the unruly House of Representatives for years through the force of his personality." (p. 14.) We will meet this kind of man

again—capable of dominating "unruly" and powerful legislators by his charm and immense energy—in Lyndon Johnson.

68. Details can be found in Gail Hamilton, Biography of James G. Blaine (Norwich, Conn.: Henry Bill Publishing Co., 1895), pp. 486-487. Gail Hamilton was the pseudonym of Mary Dodge, a niece of Blaine's.

69. See James Blaine, Political Discussions (Norwich, Conn.: Henry Bill Publishing Co., 1887), p. 187. Speech June 5, 1878. Blaine, of course, refused to consider the possibility that England, a highly industrialized island-state, needed an extensive world commerce in order to survive, and thus would naturally surpass in ocean tonnage, and go on a continental state on the verge of industrialization (and incidentally one that was extremely protective of its large home market—a policy that Blaine himself enthusiastically endorsed).

70. Edward Perry, "Central American Union," Hispanic American Historical Review (February 1922): 30-51, especially 30-33.

71. Blaine's dispatch to C. A. Logan, May 7, 1881, in Foreign Relations, 1881 (Washington, D.C.: Government Printing Office, 1882), p. 102.

72. Ibid., pp. 102-104.

73. Blaine need not have consulted any academic source on the unlikelihood of a Central American union. His own minister in Guatemala City, C. A. Logan, wrote: "Nothing but the strong arm of an absolute monarchy, supported by ample resources of money, ships, and men, could tie them into a single government. When railroads and telegraphs are built so that quick communication can be had from Mexico to Costa Rica such a project may be entertained. At present it is impracticable, and operating upon a smaller scale; the difficulty mentioned constitutes the chief obstacle against a federal union of the Central American states, as heretofore stated to the Department in my dispatches; but a single agency—the protectorate of a powerful country—can make such a union possible in Central America." Dated May 24, 1881 in Foreign Relations, 1881. A staunch republican like Blaine would hardly approve the notion of a monarchy, but Logan points to the principal obstacle to union, and that is order.

74. Fletcher, op. cit., pp. 34-35; Russell M. Bastert, "A New Approach to the Origins of Blaine's Pan American Policy," Hispanic American Historical Review (August 1959): 381.

75. Blaine was informed of this, at least in part, by Logan in a dispatch received only two days after the Ubico letter. Logan stated that Barrios was in serious trouble, that his government was "a very weak one. . . . His old opponents . . . are held down with an iron hand, made up, so to speak, of muskets and brass bands. By themselves they can do nothing, but if Mexico, with a few thousand men, were to call away the Guatemalan troops from the capital to defend the border,

twenty-four hours would not elapse before the clericals would be massed into an aggressive army, and, being in the majority, Barrios would be soon crushed." Dispatch, Logan to Blaine, May 24, 1881, in Foreign Relations, 1881. This, then, was the nature of Barrios's gamble. He must unite the nation against Mexico without being forced to commit his troops (that is, his bodyguard) against Mexico and be left defenseless against his internal enemies.

76. Fletcher, op. cit., p. 35.

77. Foreign Relations, 1881, p. 598. Ubico to Blaine, June 15, 1881.

78. Ibid., p. 600. Ubico to Blaine, June 19, 1881.

79. Ibid., p. 601. Ubico to Blaine, June 22, 1881.

80. Ibid., p. 599. Blaine to Ubico, June 16, 1881.

81. Ibid., p. 599.

82. Ibid.

83. Ibid., p. 766. Blaine to Morgan, June 16, 1881.

84. Ibid.

85. Ibid.

86. Foreign Relations, 1881, p. 768. Blaine to Morgan, June 21, 1881.

87. Ibid.

88. Ibid., pp. 768-769.

89. Ibid., p. 769.

90. Ibid., pp. 769-770.

91. Fletcher, op. cit., p. 37.

92. Foreign Relations, 1881, p. 809. Morgan to Blaine, September 22, 1881.

93. Ibid., pp. 807-808.

94. Fletcher, op. cit., p. 38.

95. Foreign Relations, 1881, p. 613. Montufar to Blaine, November 7, 1881.

96. Ibid., p. 600. Blaine to Morgan, November 28, 1881 in Blaine, op. cit., p. 382.

97. Ibid., p. 815.

98. Ibid., p. 816.

99. In that last dispatch to Morgan, he professed to be ignorant of the "personal ambitions" of General Barrios, and stated flatly that the United States "would deem any inquiry into or consideration of such a subject both unworthy and improper in any discussion of the great interests which concern the people of Central America, and their relation to the kindred republics of this continent." (Ibid., p. 816.) It might be added that three years later, "President" Barrios would be killed in an unsuccessful attempt to force El Salvador into the confederation.

100. Blaine resigned in December 1881, and several weeks earlier informed Foreign Minister Montufar that he was politically dead. His successor, Fredrick Frelinghuysen, was chiefly noted for his caution. Fletcher, op. cit., p. 106

101. Ibid., pp. 106-108.

102. Blaine, op. cit., pp. 418-419.

103. Ibid., p. 418.

104. Ibid., p. 419.

105. Ibid., p. 414. Why couldn't the South American nations settle their differences among themselves? Blaine answers: "They require external pressure to keep them from war; when at war they require external pressure to bring them to peace. Their outbreaks are not only frequent but are sanguinary and sometimes cruel. The inhabitants of those countries are a brave people, belonging to a race that has always been brave, descended of men that have always been proud. They are of hot temper, quick to take affront, ready to avenge a wrong whether real or fancied." (Ibid., pp. 413-414.) Our grand designers of today, of course, would gag on Blaine's patronizing attitude, but is it very different to assert that Latin American nations are essentially helpless to develop themselves and thus need large quantities of cheap capital?

106. Ibid., p. 414.

107. Ibid., p. 411.

108. Ibid., p. 419.

109. Ibid., p. 414.

110. Ibid.

111. Ibid., p. 415.

112. Ibid., p. 417.

113. Ibid., p. 419.

114. Arthur P. Whitaker, _The Western Hemisphere Idea_ (Ithaca, N.Y.: Cornell University Press, 1954), p. 74.

115. Fletcher, op. cit., p. 340.

116. _Compilation of Reports of the Committee on Foreign Relations_, U.S. Senate, 1789-1901, vol. 6 (Washington, D.C.: Government Printing Office, 1901).

117. Ibid., p. 279.

118. Ibid. To the economist it may seem strange that the author had ignored completely the truth of Say's law. However, by the 1880s, the notion of overproduction had become an idée fixe after the depression of 1873. To the general reader, the idea that Americans believed nearly a century ago that they were saturated with goods and services sounds utterly fantastic. Yet that idea was seriously entertained by many people only a few years ago, when the truth was that a vast majority of their countrymen did not feel especially overprivileged in material goods.

119. Ibid., p. 279.
120. Ibid., p. 280.
121. Ibid., pp. 280-281.
122. Ibid., p. 283.
123. Ibid., p. 284.
124. Ibid., p. 285.
125. Ibid.
126. Ibid.
127. Ibid., p. 283.
128. Ibid.
129. Ibid., p. 301.
130. Ibid.
131. Bemis, op. cit., p. 126.
132. James W. Gantenbein, ed., The Evolution of our Latin American Policy: A Documentary Record (New York: Columbia University Press, 1950), p. 55.
133. Thomas F. McGann, Argentina, The United States and the Inter-American System, 1880-1914 (Cambridge, Mass.: Harvard University Press, 1957), p. 139.
134. Thomas Jefferson Coolidge, The Autobiography of Thomas Jefferson Coolidge (Massachusetts Historical Society, 1923), p. 128.
135. Ibid., pp. 127-128.
136. McGann, op. cit., p. 144.
137. Coolidge, op. cit., p. 128.
138. Ibid., pp. 145-146.
139. Ibid., p. 147; Alice Felt Tyler, The Foreign Policy of James G. Blaine (Minneapolis: University of Minnesota Press, 1927), pp. 179-180. The watered down resolution got unanimous approval, but no governments ratified it. This has frequently been the fate of measures approved at inter-American gatherings.
140. Tyler, op. cit., p. 182.
141. McGann, op. cit., p. 156.
142. Ibid., pp. 157-158.
143. Lloyd J. Mecham, The United States and Inter-American Security, 1889-1960 (Austin, Tex.: University of Texas Press, 1963), p. 54. See also Bemis, op. cit., p. 233.
144. Bemis, op. cit., p. 233.
145. Ibid.
146. Ibid.
147. Gantenbein, op. cit., p. 58.

CHAPTER

2

LATIN AMERICA AND THE PACIFIC REGION: TRADE, INVESTMENT, AND TECHNOLOGY ISSUES

Miguel S. Wionczek

GROWING LINKS ACROSS THE PACIFIC

For the purposes of this paper the Pacific region has been defined as Oceania and all the countries bordering on the Pacific Ocean in Asia and the western hemisphere. While the western United States is clearly part of that region, the United States has been excluded from our analysis because its relations with Latin America are the subject of other chapters in this volume.

Although the Pacific region still seems to belong to the realm of geopolitical and strategic concepts, rather than, at least as far as Latin America is concerned, to exist as a politico-economic community, over the past ten years growing trade, investment, and technology links have developed between the southern part of the western hemisphere and Oceania, the Far East, and Canada. The nature and the future of these links will be discussed below.[1]

The only major economic link, the commercial exchange between Latin America and the rest of the region (which excludes the United States), is still of marginal importance to all parties concerned. It did not exceed 10 percent of Latin America's foreign trade in 1970. About two thirds of these commodity flows represented trade with Japan and another 30 percent with Canada. Trade between Latin America and the rest of the Pacific region over the past decade has consisted of the following flows: Latin America exported primary industrial commodities—minerals from Chile and Peru, mainly to Japan, oil from Venezuela, and bauxite and alumina from the Caribbean to Canada—and tropical agricultural products, including coffee and cotton from Brazil, Central America, and Mexico principally to Japan and

Canada. Moreover, some products of temperate zone agriculture, such as grains and meat, were exported to Japan and smaller Far Eastern countries.

In the opposite direction, there have been imports of wool and tin from Australia and Malaysia, respectively; of capital goods by major Latin American countries from Japan and Canada; and of consumer durables and nondurables by the less developing Latin American republics, particularly Central America, Panama, and Venezuela, from Japan and, in negligible quantities, from Hong Kong. As one might have expected, Latin American trade with New Zealand, the Far East, and Southeast Asian developing countries, such as South Korea, Taiwan, the Philippines, Indonesia, and Thailand, and with China and Soviet Asia has been practically nonexistent. Very recently, however, some Latin American countries (Brazil, Mexico, Peru, and Venezuela) have begun trade relations with China.

In brief, the major part of the expanding commercial exchange between Latin America and other countries located within the Pacific basin as defined here involves almost exclusively Japan and Canada and conforms to the overall patterns of Latin American foreign trade. This should be kept in mind when one approaches the main subject of this chapter—the potential contribution of the major Pacific countries other than the United States to Latin America's capital and technology.

ECONOMIC NATIONALISM VERSUS TRANSNATIONAL CORPORATIONS

The general lack of knowledge in Latin America of the economic, resource, and technological developments taking place in Australia, Canada, Japan, and lesser western Pacific countries is the single most important obstacle to the expansion of the region's present tenuous economic, financial, and technological relations with the Pacific region, and makes very difficult any preliminary prognosis for rapprochement. This lack of knowledge, which has historical and political roots, impairs the Latin American vision of the rapid changes occurring in an area whose role in the world economy is increasing very swiftly.

Judging by the rates of gross national product (GNP) growth, the expansion of their external trade, and their technological progress, today Japan, Australia, and Canada together are the third most dynamic subsector of the world economy, after the European Socialist bloc and the European Economic Community. Taken individually, Japan, the fastest growing industrial economy in the world, occupies second place in terms of the GNP after the United States. According to Japanese estimates, within the next fifteen to twenty years, Japan will overtake most of its industrial rivals in terms of GNP, per capita income, and share of the world's trade, and well before the end of the century will have the highest per capita income in the world. Even if one takes into consideration the most recent slowdown in the growth of the Japanese economy, and the doubts expressed by large segments of Japanese society about the need for accelerated growth, few experts question the validity of Japanese long-term economic projections.

While in comparison with Japan, both Canada and Australia seem to be second-class industrial powers because of their relatively small populations, their resource bases have expanded during the sixties and the early seventies at an unprecedented pace. Moreover, these two economies have grown in the past ten years at a considerably higher average rate than the economies of most older, industrial, free market countries. This growth, both in terms of GNP and of newly discovered natural resources, is prompting the two leading members of the British Commonwealth in the Pacific region to search for new international economic alignments, particularly as a result of their somewhat disappointing experiences with traditional economic and financial links with North Atlantic countries and with the U.S.- and U.K.-based transnational corporations that increasingly dominate both the extractive and the manufacturing industries of Australia and Canada.

If any common denominator can be found in these three Pacific countries, it is economic nationalism. It has been present in Japan since its opening to the West about a century ago. It seems to be gaining strength in Canada, which lives in the shadow of the United States's power,[2] and to be emerging in Australia, whose historical dependence on U.K. capital and technology recently has been broken by the forceful entry of U.S. competition. The impression that economic nationalism is gaining the upper hand in these two countries is confirmed by most of the economic development studies and reports that have appeared over the last fifteen years in Canada and about the last ten years in Australia.[3]

Most of the literature discusses the prospects for the future growth of the Canadian and Australian economies within the framework of the increasing domination of the world economic scene by a few hundred transnational corporate giants, mostly U.S. and U.S.-based. The growth of transnational corporations has been one of the most outstanding features of the past twenty years. Since 1968 their total annual sales, both in the markets in which parent companies operated and through exports, exceeded in value the GNP of every country except the United States and the Soviet Union. Fifty-five percent of the assets of these corporate bodies, whose number does not exceed 500, are owned by U.S. interests, 20 percent by British, and the rest largely by Japanese and European corporate groups. The output of parent companies was expanding at some 10 percent annually over the period 1950-70, twice the rate of growth of world GNP and 40 percent faster than world exports. Their technological expertise and economies of scale lead to estimates that by the turn of the century the largest 200 or 300 transnational concerns will account for more than 50 percent of world output. One of the features of these corporate giants is their concentration in certain fields. In 1971 some 85 percent of the plant and equipment expenditures of overseas subsidiaries of U.S. manufacturing concerns was in four sectors: transport equipment, chemicals, mechanical engineering, and electrical equipment. The geographic distribution of the transnational corporations differs widely and is particularly heavy in Australia and Canada. More than 50 percent of Canada's industrial capital assets were owned in 1971 by U.S. or U.K. corporations. The proportions seem to be similar, although somehow lower, in Australia.

Political leaders, economists, and large sectors of public opinion in Canada and Australia show growing preoccupation with the impact of these corporate structures—horizontally and vertically integrated, concentrated in the extractive industries and manufacturing, and operating worldwide—upon the national development of Australia and Canada. These countries, at the same time, are searching for ways and means to impose national economic and social objectives upon those giants without necessarily closing the door on the capital and technology they control.

If the Japanese do not complain about the real, potential, or presumed dangers of transnational foreign-based corporations, it is because their policies diverge fundamentally from neo-classical trade and investment theories. Japan never really has opened itself to foreign capital. Two of the factors that have contributed to the Japanese economic miracle of the past quarter-century have been the country's ability to mobilize an extremely high internal saving rate (up to one third of the national income) and its ability to adapt to Japanese conditions technology developed elsewhere, while rejecting the traditional proposition that the only way to develop a free market economy is through the package transfer of capital/technology/managerial skill involving the direct participation of foreign private investment.

Since the Meiji period, Japan has developed its own capital and managerial resources base. It copied foreign technology first, and started buying selectively afterward—at internationally competitive prices. Only now is Japan opening itself to the outside world by lifting slowly, and again selectively, its restrictions upon the entry of foreign private capital. The present policy change, however, does not seem to endanger Japan's economic independence, since it occurs only when Japan is becoming an increasingly important exporter of its own capital, technology, and managerial skills, not only to neighboring countries but also to other developing parts of the world, including Soviet Asia.

The demand for raw materials in what might be called the giant Switzerland of the Far East grows by leaps and bounds, and Japan's attempts to diversify its natural resource availability have already overstepped the boundaries of the Asian continent, which had been providing Japan with practically all its primary commodities before and during the Second World War. In the late sixties, Australia became Japan's principal supplier of raw materials, and the two countries' interdependence has been increasing. In iron ore, alumina, copper, coal, titanium, zinc, wool, wheat, sugar, and meat, Australia is far and away the biggest single exporter to the Japanese market. Moreover, there is little doubt that Australia will become, during the late seventies, the world's largest exporter of a whole range of minerals, particularly of iron ore, aluminum, coal, copper, lead, and zinc.

If the rate of discovery of natural resources in Canada is less impressive than that in Australia, it is by no means negligible. Whereas the Canadian GNP and foreign trade are growing more slowly than those of Japan and Australia, one would suspect that this is not necessarily due to the resources base, which is enormous, but to other factors.

The most important ones are perhaps Canada's continuing dependence upon slowly growing primary commodity markets, such as the United States and Great Britain, and its difficulties in accelerating its manufacturing exports because of restrictive policies followed by the large number of U.S.-owned industrial transnational corporations that play a decisive role in the manufacturing sector and are the major source of Canadian technology.

The structure of the Canadian economy, however, is also undergoing a rapid change. Between 1950 and 1965, a technological revolution took place in agriculture, with the proportion of people working in that sector falling from 21 to 9 percent, while farm output doubled. Moreover, somewhat belatedly, Canada decided to undertake a major scientific and technological effort, largely financed by government. Federal expenditures on research and development, which were increasing at an average rate of 10 percent in the past decade and reached $600 million by 1968, jumped considerably in the early seventies. Total research and development expenditure should reach close to 3 percent of the Canadian GNP by the end of the present decade, twice as much percentagewise as in 1960.

Thus, in the Pacific area, Latin America faces three major countries engaged in constant efforts at expanding their resources base (by worldwide joint mining and other ventures in resources-poor Japan), improving their intake of technology (divorced from foreign private capital in Japan), and strengthening their domestic research and development base through generous state support. Despite the recent difficulties concomitant to the worldwide economic recession, all these countries are enjoying fairly rapid economic growth. Such a performance would have not been possible without the presence of well-designed educational systems, particularly on the middle technical level, which permit both a continuous increase in labor productivity and the relatively easy shift of labor from agriculture to more research-and-development-based productive sectors. Their impressive growth proves that the quality of education, technology, and resource exploration, together with the quality of managerial skills, whose presence is patent in Japan and growing in Australia and Canada, are more important tools for the achievement of economic growth than the traditional economic policy followed by the earlier industrializers, such as the United States and Great Britain.

The pace of resource development in the Pacific area, accompanied by rapid economic growth, has helped to destroy myths still circulating in Latin America about the limited availability of natural resources throughout the world; about the impossibility of acquiring technology from outside other than in neatly organized packages of capital/technology/managerial skills, sold to Latin America by U.S. transnational corporations; and about the allegedly secondary relevance of major education and research and development efforts for rapid growth.

It is important to note that in two out of the three major Pacific countries that found themselves as yet unable to unravel the knot of the capital/technology/managerial skills package, Australia and Canada, the role of foreign private investment and, in particular, of transnational corporations is the most sensitive political and economic issue. There is considerable evidence that many actions of these transnational companies are contrary to the long-range interests of the host countries.[4] But it is only fair to add that such actions originate not as much in the wickedness of the giants, per se, as in the absence of clearly defined public policy toward this particular form of business organization. Recent government actions, both in Australia and Canada, have proved that, once a government decided to take upon itself the task of policing transnational corporations, it could eliminate their worst excesses, alleviate the negative effect of others, and even turn the presence of foreign private capital to the host country's advantage.*

The degree of success of public policy in this field will depend, however, on many factors. No government can undertake such difficult tasks if, in its day-to-day operations, it is entirely dependent upon the

---

*See, for example, the Canadian legislation on the review and assessment of acquisition and control of domestic business enterprises by foreign interests (1972) and the Australian law to control foreign takeovers of certain companies (1972).

goodwill and financial support of a big power in which transnational corporations have their headquarters if it represents the national interest in words only, does not have a reasonable long-term economic policy, finds itself unable to demand minimum efficiency from local vested industrial interest groups, and, finally, shows little willingness to launch and finance major education, science, and technology efforts. This is, unfortunately, still the case of many Latin American republics.

Only if these mostly internal obstacles are eliminated can the host country be even partially successful in ensuring that transnational corporations do not discriminate against nationals in employment; do not swallow up domestic firms through mergers and acquisitions; accept the necessity of decentralizing the parent companies' decisions affecting its national interests; eliminate practices of market division and the tied-in purchase of imported inputs from the parent, which results in great foreign exchange losses through the overpricing of imports; sell technology to the subsidiaries at prices relatively in line with those prevailing under international competitive conditions; and, finally, limit excessive borrowing from local sources.

According to some recent Canadian and Australian experiences with transnational corporations, both in the extractive and the manufacturing sectors, the policing measures taken by the respective governments decreased abuses considerably.[5] If this is so, it suggests that the nature of relations between transnational corporations and the host countries depends largely upon the bargaining power of the latter. If most of the excesses of foreign private corporations enumerated above are common practice in Latin America, it only means that Latin American bargaining power vis-à-vis the outside world is still very low, for reasons largely known to serious students of the sociopolitical situation prevailing in our part of the world.

LATIN AMERICA AND THE THREE PACIFIC MIDDLE POWERS: JAPAN, CANADA, AND AUSTRALIA

At this point the question arises as to what extent Latin America's bargaining power vis-à-vis transnational corporations, the major holders of capital, technology, and managerial skills in the world of the seventies, might be strengthened by the diversification of their commerical, financial, and technological ties with the three major Pacific powers other than the United States. The answer depends upon a definition, first, of what these three major powers can offer Latin America and what, in turn, Latin America can offer Japan, Australia, and Canada. At the risk of separating artificially what are traditionally components of a single package, we will treat the problem of possible new intra-Pacific relations under five separate headings: development aid, trade, private capital, technology, and information.

Development Aid Prospects

Together with the Scandinavian countries, Japan, Australia, and Canada belong to a small group of advanced countries whose contribution to official development aid flows, if measured by the aid-GNP ratio, has been decreasing in the past few years much less rapidly than those of the United States, the United Kingdom, and most countries of continental Europe. Measured in absolute terms, the net flow of resources from Japan, Australia, and Canada to developing areas under official development assistance increased from $240 million to $680 million between 1960 and 1968 and to $1,800 million in 1973. At the end of the period it represented about 20 percent of the total official aid of the Development Assistance Committee (DAC) countries, as compared with only 5 percent in 1960 and 10 percent in 1968.[6]

All this does not mean, however, that Latin America may count on a considerable increase in official aid from Japan, Canada, and Australia. At the moment, most of Japan's official capital and technical assistance continues going to its Asian neighbors, followed as a rule by considerable amounts of export credit and private capital investment. No substantial change in the distribution patterns of rapidly growing Japanese official capital aid can be expected in the future. As in the case of most other advanced countries, Japanese development aid has two major objectives: the widening of access to additional primary resources and the creation of new export markets.

The recent increase of Australian official development aid is due mainly to the urgent need to help New Guinea-Papua, which, in 1970, absorbed 70 percent of Australia's total capital aid and technical assistance. The rest of Australian development aid goes to South and Southeast Asia under the Colombo Plan. Economic assistance to these areas will consume most of the increases in total Australian development aid in the seventies.

The distribution of Canada's growing official aid probably reflects less immediate economic and political aims than those of Japan and Australia. Some two thirds of Canadian development aid and technical assistance goes to India, Pakistan, and Ceylon. Other priority areas are ex-British Africa (particularly Nigeria and Ghana) and the former British West Indies. In these two last areas, Canada has strong commercial and financial interests. Moreover, they provide that country with a considerable part of its demand for tropical agriculture commodities.

Total Canadian aid to non-Caribbean Latin America amounted in 1973 to some $20 million, one third of which was export credits. No considerable expansion of official aid from this source can be expected by Latin America either, although the "1970 White Paper on Canadian Foreign Policy for the Seventies" gave high priority to the expansion of economic relations with this part of the world, without Canada formally joining hemispheric organizations, such as the Organization of the American States. The white paper mentioned, however, only the possibility of setting up bilateral aid and technical assistance programs for some Latin American republics, with subsequent private investment in mind.

Trade Relations

Some remarks on the nature of the trade between Canada, Australia, and East Asia, including Japan, on the one hand, and Latin America, on the other, were made at the beginning of this chapter. It is particularly difficult to project future trade trends from past performance in view of dynamic changes in the patterns of intra-Pacific trade and the rapid growth of the three major economies (Japan, Australia, and Canada). Much of the new trade in the Pacific basin, particularly in the case of Australia, is due to the spectacular expansion of the Japanese economy. Since the trade between Canada and Japan is also growing rapidly, there is no reason why trade between Latin American Pacific countries and their more developed counterparts in the region should not expand as well. The obstacles, however, are formidable.

It is generally assumed that distance is the single major obstacle to trade, but this is not necessarily so, as growing worldwide exports of Japanese capital and consumer goods demonstrated during the sixties.

On the one hand, we are witnessing the resource-base "explosion" in the western Pacific (Australia, New Guinea, Indonesia, and elsewhere) and in Canada, and, on the other, the intensification of economic nationalism in Latin America, deeply involving attitudes toward exploitation, management, and international commercialization of raw materials, particularly mineral resources. Under these conditions it is difficult to foresee the expansion of traditional exchange of Latin American materials against manufactures from Australia and Canada, countries well endowed in raw materials, or even against industrial goods produced in raw-material-hungry Japan, unless these three major Pacific industrial powers decide to invest heavily in export-oriented industrial joint ventures in Latin America. The rapid growth of trade between Brazil and Japan points in that direction.

If Brazil allows its minerals to be shipped in growing quantities to the Japanese market, it is because Japan, in association with local interests, invests in Brazil in both mining and industry. The presence of Japanese enterprises, not only in the mineral sector but also in export-oriented manufacturing, makes it politically palatable for Brazil to accept that a considerable part of its natural wealth is exported with little processing. Other Latin American countries would like to see the kind of foreign investment strategy followed by Japan in Brazil applied to them as well. In the longer run this may occur, particularly if the Latin American countries neighboring the Pacific Ocean integrate into a common market. At present, their industrial and technological backwardness and the size of their individual economies make them less attractive than Brazil for the new foreign investment cum foreign trade policies.

Thus, in some more distant future the Japanese policy patterns that include technical assistance to the state-owned heavy industries, and even participation in joint investment ventures with local state enterprises, may be adopted by Canada and perhaps by Australia, helping the expansion of intra-Pacific trade relations in the framework of economic nationalism.

One may add that recent developments in Southeast Asia and the victory of radical nationalism in Indochina will have a double effect on relations in the Pacific basin. While political and economic nationalism in all developing parts of the region will be strenthened by the demonstration effect of the events in Indochina, relatively "soft" Latin American nationalism may become more palatable to industrial market economy countries, including the United States. The recent economic policies of Japan, Australia, and Canada toward China and Canada's policy toward Cuba strongly suggest that all these major Pacific countries are capable of considerable nonideological economic policy adjustment to new political situations. Consequently, one may expect that U.S. trade and investment relations with Indochina will be quickly superseded by new trade links between that part of the Pacific area and the three Pacific industrial powers, which studiously avoided any direct involvement in the Indochina conflict. What may represent economic loss to the United States may become commercial gain to Japan and Australia and perhaps even to Canada. On the whole, however, contrary to some opinions, it is difficult to envisage that the developments in Southeast Asia will negatively affect trade relations in the Pacific region.

New Modes of Private Capital Investment

Since prospects for official aid from the developed Pacific economies are very poor, once Latin America finally realizes that financing imports through acceptance of expensive export credits only postpones the day of judgment, only two avenues will be left for trade expansion: increased purchases of Latin American primary commodities by major Pacific countries and the appearance of non-U.S. Pacific capital in Latin America. This capital might enter Latin America in the form of joint ventures for producing raw materials for the investor countries and some manufactured goods for sale in third markets. These measures might be the only solution acceptable to all parties concerned and offer a medium-term stimulus to the growth of intra-Pacific trade and the Latin American economies.

As we have noted, Japan, the most innovative society of all, is taking exactly this route. The Far Eastern industrial superpower is conscious of Latin America's marginal importance as a resource base and potential export market, yet the number of Japanese ventures in Latin American mining and manufacturing is on the increase. While all Japanese official resources flows to Latin America until 1970 took the form of export credits, Japanese private direct investment in the region lately has been increasing considerably. While it amounted to a total of slightly over $60 million during the whole decade of the fifties, it increased to about $55 million annually in the mid-sixties and exceeded $200 million in 1973. Already in the mid-sixties Japanese private investment in Latin America represented close to one third of the total Japanese private investment abroad, a larger proportion than in Southeast Asia, presumably because of the earlier Japanese preempting of attractive investment opportunities in that part of Asia and the persistence of war conditions in Indochina.

Japanese direct investment in Latin America, which had reached a total of perhaps $1,200 million by the end of 1972 and jumped to $2,000 million in 1974, takes three major forms: (1) participation in the equity capital of new enterprises, mainly in mining and manufacturing, with the Japanese providing not only some capital but also technology and management; (2) credits for the acquisition of capital equipment and technology by local enterprises, a technique followed in Latin American extractive industries with repayment taking the form of discounts on the prices of minerals produced for export to Japan; and (3) direct private investment in enterprises fully owned by Japanese interests. This last type of investment is of secondary importance, and applies mostly to land acquisition for Japanaese agricultural emigrants in Brazil. As Japanese sources stated in the late sixities, while the "aim of investments in Latin American extractive industries is to assure the supply of mineral resources needed by Japanese industries," that of manufacturing investments is "to promote Japanese exports through assistance to new industrial enterprises interested in the use of Japan-made complete plants, capital goods, raw materials and intermediate goods; in this way Japan is able to protect its participation in export markets or to open new ones."[7] Most investment in manufacturing is concentrated in the automotive and steel industries, although recently some Japanese investments have been made in chemicals and other nondurables, such as textiles in Central America.

Moreover, the large Japan-based transnational corporations are present in growing numbers in Latin America as contractors for state-owned projects, particularly steel mills, oil refineries, and port facilities. The number of Japanese private missions interested in surveying national resources in our part of the world and eventually exploiting them, preferably in joint ventures, has also been on the rise lately. Brazil, Chile, and Peru seem to offer particular attractions to Japan. Thus, Japanese interests in Latin America increase steadily and involve relatively small outlays of foreign capital, sales of technology embodied in capital goods, technical assistance, and the export of newly exploited raw materials to Japan.

The same cannot be said about Canadian investment, which originally entered Latin America in the first quarter of this century, mainly in public utilities. Latin America is the single largest area of Canadian direct private investment abroad. In addition to public utilities, Canadian private investment is concentrated in banking and mining in the Caribbean and Central America and in mining and related metal processing in the Andean countries. The present picture is one of disinvestment in public utilities and some expansion in mining, manufacturing, and ancillary activities, particularly in wood and paper industries. It is estimated that the flow of direct investment from Canada to Latin America averages some $30 million a year, accounting for only a fraction of the total Canadian capital exports, which go mainly to the United States and Great Britain. Some of this investment in Latin America would be encouraged by negotiation of double taxation treaties, efforts to combine joint ventures with export potential for Canadian industry, and dissemination of investor information in Canadian business circles.

While there are no Australian investments in Latin America, New Zealand occasionally grants the area medium-term credits aimed at financing its agricultural surplus exports. Since Australia, New Zealand, and Canada are capital-importing countries, it is hard to expect very large flows of their private capital to Latin America even in the long run, unless such investment were necessary to balance growing exports to our region.

There is, however, one powerful reason why this prognosis may turn out to be incorrect. The entry of Great Britain into the European Common Market involves a gradual fading out of the complicated system of preferences that previously existed with the Commonwealth. This development might force Australia and Canada to reorient their trade patterns. Australians seem to be giving some thought to this possibility. Their success at creating new trade flows outside the Commonwealth, together with the disappearance of Commonwealth preferential trade arrangements, has fomented a national debate among economists and private business people about the need to revise Australian international trade and financial policies in their entirety.*

It may well be that this debate will lead to some rapprochement with the Latin American countries in the Pacific region. Some signs of rapprochement have emerged very recently in the area of mineral resources export policy. It was reported that Australia has joined a large group of major iron ore producers in establishing an international consultative agency for the purpose of stabilizing world iron ore export prices. The initiative for such action originated in 1974 in Venezuela and Brazil.

Technology Transfers

Assuming that the prospects for the inflow of capital to Latin America from the major non-U.S. countries of the Pacific region other than Japan are limited, and that increasing dependence upon transfers of capital, technology, and managerial skills in the traditional package from involving full or majority control of the package by the capital exporters is not the best political and economic solution for Latin America, what are the region's chances for importing untied technology from Japan, Australia, and Canada?

Endowed with growing economic power, Japan, which itself mastered the art of importing technology separately from capital, does not seem willing to part with its present technology without capital and

*For the evidence, see the impressive volume of studies on the future economic relations of Australia with the outside world, sponsored by the influential private Committee for Economic Development of Australia. While these publications note the basic shift in Australian trade patterns from the United States and Europe toward Japan and the Southeast Asian and Pacific regions, they demonstrate a deep interest in diversifying Australia's external economic relations with other parts of the world as well.

managerial participation. As a matter of fact, complaints heard in Southeast Asia about the "invasion" of Japanese transnational corporations echo exactly the complaints of Latin America, Australia, and Canada about the growing predominance of U.S. transnational corporations in their respective economies. Yet Latin America's limited experience with Japan so far suggests that both Japanese public- and private-sector attitudes toward providing Latin America with capital, technology, and management are much more flexible than those that seem to prevail in the U.S. corporate world. This flexibility may well be owing to the fact that Japan does not consider it worthwhile to commit too much in the way of capital resources to a region of secondary importance. But, whatever the reasons, the Japanese performance seems to coincide to some extent with the exigencies of Latin American economic nationalism. Moreover, because of the whole tradition of adapting foreign technologies in Japan, Japanese technology may, in turn, prove more adaptable to Latin American conditions than U.S. technology.

The literature on transfer of technology to developing countries on the enterprise-to-enterprise level suggests strongly that U.S. corporately owned technology is the least adaptable to conditions prevailing in the developing regions. At best, U.S. transnational corporations adapt technology to the market size, but they practically never adjust it to local factor proportions as postulated by most economists. In Latin America, which is divided into highly protected markets, this may be a more rational approach on the part of U.S. investors in the short run than it seems on the surface. There are few reasons why a foreign private enterprise should mess around with its technology and complicate its own operational problems if it can receive practically any level of protection despite the low degree of economics of scale resulting from the investor's refusal to adapt technology to the remaining production factors.

If this is so and if, as one might assume, Japanese technology is cheaper than U.S. technology and the Japanese were willing to enter into joint ventures with practically anybody, including the public sectors because of the absence in Japanese culture of prejudice against state-owned or joint ventures, then Latin Americans should actively foster the entry of Japanese technology cum capital into their region. They might also try to obtain more Australian and Canadian technology, since the U.S.- and British-originated technology used in Australia and Canada presumably has already gone through a certain degree of adaptation to smaller markets and different production factor mixes.

Information Flows

Whatever advantages might accrue to Latin America from an additional trickle of official development aid from the major Pacific countries other than the United States, from the creation of new intra-Pacific trade, from the entry of foreign private capital from the Pacific region under conditions more flexible than those traditionally prevailing in the hemisphere, and from some injections of technology originating in Japan, Australia, and Canada with or without capital participation of these countries, very tangible benefits could be had just from greater awareness of the Pacific region on the part of Latin American economic policymakers, technical experts, and social scientists.

This chapter has attempted to demonstrate that many of the problems connected with the import of capital and technology, which Latin America now faces and finds difficult to resolve, have already been faced in recent decades by the three major Pacific countries. Unlike Latin America, these countries, however, have found it possible to design and implement policy measures that diminish to manageable proportions friction between the owners of foreign capital and technology and the host countries.

There seem to be five major fields of conflict between foreign private capital, particularly giant transnational corporations, and nationalist societies:

1. The size of profits from Latin American operations accruing to transnational enterprises through manipulation of intracompany transactions
2. The transnational corporations' lack of interest in fostering local research and development expenditures in the countries where their subsidiaries operate
3. Foreign takeover of domestic enterprises for the purpose of eliminating competition or creating a comfortable base for new operations
4. The concentration of foreign capital in key sectors of the economy, which, in accordance with nationalist thinking and feeling, should be left to the state or to domestically owned interests
5. The excessive use of local financial resources by foreign enterprises.[8]

Leaving aside the particular case of Japan, the two remaining major Pacific countries, Australia and Canada, progressively have developed countermeasures to curb these objectionable practices of foreign private capital. Against strong protest from the parties affected, the public disclosure of financial information by all corporate business has been enforced, while the problem of monopolistic intracompany pricing has been taken care of with some success through more efficient tax administration. While not much could have been done to increase the research and development effort of the foreign subsidiaries, the state, particularly in Canada, has started extending considerable financial support to local research and development, both at the domestic enterprise level and as a part of the general effort to improve educational levels.

The issue of foreign takeovers proved particularly difficult to handle, but Australia linked its solution in 1969 with the curtailment of foreign corporations' access to local financial resources. Although no efforts were made in either country to define which "key economic sectors" should be left to nationals, the fact that in Australia and Canada financial intermediaries have long been considered one of the sectors reserved to nationals was of considerable help. In fact, the banking laws in many Latin American countries are much more permissive toward foreign banking activities than Australian and Canadian legislation.

The use of this information for the purpose of defining coherent policies toward imports of capital and technology in Latin America would bring considerable benefits to this part of the world. At least it would prove that lack of enthusiasm for granting unlimited privileges to the capital/technology/managerial skills package transfer from the advanced countries is not the result of some peculiarly Latin American "perversion" or "irrationality."

In brief, while some possibilities can be envisaged for opening Latin America to the so-called Pacific market for capital and technology, perhaps the most urgent and most beneficial step for Latin America in the short run might be to widen communication and information channels between itself and the far-away strangers in the Pacific basin.

Latin America has a lot to learn, and must learn rapidly, if it wants to avoid a sociopolitical crisis of unpredictable proportions. One of the conclusions of this chapter is that, in the present-day multipolar world, there is more than one fountain of wisdom for Latin American economic development.

NOTES

1. For a detailed analysis of economic and technological relations between Latin America and the Pacific basin countries at the end of the sixties, see Miguel S. Wionczek, "The Pacific Market for Capital, Technology and Information and Its Possible Opening in Latin America,"

Journal of Common Market Studies 10, no. 1 (September 1971): 78-95.

2. See the "White Paper on Canadian Foreign Policy in the Seventies," released by the External Affairs Ministry of Canada, June 1970, and reportedly highly influenced by the thinking of Canada's present prime minister, Pierre Elliot Trudeau. The white paper declared that Canadian foreign policy in the seventies must diligently pursue national aims and interests, including the protection of Canada's independence and cultural identity when dealing with the United States. For the latest developments, see the January 1975 statement by Allen J. MacEachem, the Canadian secretary of state for external affairs, reported by Robert Trumbull, "Canada Says Policy Aim Is Independent Economy," New York Times, January 25, 1975, p. 1.

3. The starting point in the case of Canada has been the multivolume Report of the Royal Commission on Canada's Economic Prospects (known also as the Gordon Commission Report), published in Ottawa in the mid-fifties; in Australia, the officially sponsored Report of the Committee of Economic Inquiry (Vernon Committee Report) appeared in Canberra in 1965.

4. See, among others, The Impact of Multinational Corporations on the Development Process and on International Relations (New York: United Nations, 1974).

5. For evidence, among others, see A. E. Safarian, The Performance of Foreign-owned Firms in Canada (Washington, D.C.: National Planning Association and Montreal: Private Planning Association of Canada, 1970); see also Committee for Economic Development of Australia, Overseas Investment in Australia: Capital Inflow Guidelines, Memorandum for Trustees, Melbourne, February 1970.

6. See Development Assistance—1974 Review (Paris: OECD, November 1974).

7. Japan Economic Research Center, "Experience and Problems of Latin American Investments of the Private Japanese Sector," a document elaborated for the Sixth Annual Meeting of the Inter-America Economic and Social Council, Port-of-Spain, Trinidad, June 1969.

8. The first four issues, (illustrated by) Australian and Canadian experiences, were treated at some length in Harry G. Johnson, "Direct Foreign Investment: A Survey of the Issues," in Direct Foreign Investment in Asia and the Pacific, Peter Drysdale, ed. (Canberra: Australian National University Press, 1972). On similar Latin American experiences, see Constantine V. Vaitsos, Intercountry Income Distribution and Transnational Enterprises (Oxford: Clarendon Press, 1974).

CHAPTER

3

JAPAN'S ECONOMIC RELATIONSHIP WITH LATIN AMERICA

Hiroya Ichikawa

Until very recently, Japan's relationship with Latin America has been rather remote politically and economically as well as culturally. The presence of large Japanese communities in Latin America, particularly in Brazil has not had any significant influence over Japan's policy, and, while many Japanese are enthusiastic about Latin American music, such as the tango, Japanese interest in Latin American culture still amounts to little more than curiosity. Political contact has never developed to the point where serious discussions or careful diplomacy would have been necessary to maintain friendly relationships. And, although diplomats occasionally have emphasized the complementary nature of the two economies, Japan's economic interests in Latin America have been limited.

No doubt, the distance—geographic, cultural, and historical—that separates Japan and Latin America has been the main obstacle to close relations between these heterogeneous economies. In recent years, however, Japan's interests in Latin America, as well as Latin America's interests in Japan, have been rapidly increasing. This chapter will attempt to identify some of the main characteristics of an economic relationship that now commands the serious attention of many observers of Latin America.

JAPAN'S ECONOMIC POLICY TOWARD LATIN AMERICA

It is unlikely that Japan has ever formulated an official economic policy to be applied particularly to the Latin American nations, apart from its policy on immigration. Instead, Latin America fits into

Japan's overall policy of economic cooperation, which is based on the assumption that the development and prosperity of the Japanese economy are closely related to the state of the world economy. Since it must depend on overseas sources for virtually all important energy resources and raw materials, Japan is eager to develop smooth economic relations on a broad front. Thus, the Japanese government stresses the "need to make more strenuous efforts to achieve balanced developmental economic relations with all countries."[1]

Geographic Distribution of Japan's Bilateral Aid

In spite of this frequently repeated government statement, however, only 4.6 percent of Japan's official foreign aid went to Latin America in 1973, compared with 88.1 percent in Asia. And this was a radical improvement over the previous years, when as much as 98.2 percent of Japan's bilateral aid had gone to Asia. Aid channeled via multilateral agencies is not considered here. It is often said that "the poorer developing countries have come to rely upon official aid even more, while those slightly better off have been financed increasingly by private capital."[2] Indeed, Latin America, with one sixth of the population of all the developing countries, in the past has received more foreign private long-term capital than Africa or Asia. In this context, it is of some interest to know that the Japanese government seems to consider the Latin American economies to be "mid-developing," and government policy is that "economic cooperation to mid-developing countries should be extended through private resources rather than on an official basis."[3]

Setting aside the argument that the private investment is not economic aid, the Japanese government's policy of extending bilateral Official Development Assistance (ODM) to Latin America has been a restrictive one. However, there is no rule without exceptions, and the Japanese government allows exceptions in "cases where cooperation on a private basis alone cannot cope with projects which require the preparation of the massive infrastructure in the development of natural resources, large scale regional comprehensive development or agricultural development or even mining and industrial development."[4]

Table 3.1 contains a complete list of Japan's official loan commitments to Latin America since 1959.

TABLE 3.1

Japan's Loans to Latin America Through Japanese Government Agencies, 1959-74 (as of July)

Time of Loan Commitment	Recipient Country	Value (in millions)	Purpose
1959	Paraguay	$ 1,368	Seven river ships
1962	Brazil (BNDE loan)	6,317	Capital for USIMINAS steelworks
1965	Brazil	2,776	Refinancing of general commercial debts
		8,952	Refinancing of USIMINAS commercial debts to Japan
	Chile	2,248	Refinancing of general commercial debts
	Argentina	3,681	Refinancing of general commercial debts
1966	Latin American Development Bank	3,600	Current operation funds
	Brazil	4,794	USIMINAS debt to Japan
	Mexico (first loan)	3,600	Electric power expansion plan
1968	IDB[a]	3,600	Current Operation funds
1969	Mexico	4,180	Second electric power expansion plan
1969	Colombia	924	Bogota electric power project and national power distribution network project
	BCIE[b]	2,304	Microwave construction
1970	BCIE	1,800	General loan
	IDB	3,600	Current operation funds
1971	Mexico	7,916	Heavy electric machinery
	Brazil	590	Hydroelectric power project
	IDB	7,200	Current operation fund
	Peru	5,400	Electric power distribution network
1972	Peru	13,600	Fertilizer plants
	Peru	4,000	Microwave construction project
	BCIE	610	Microwave construction project
	Brazil	55,000	USIMINAS expansion project
	Paraguay	3,900	Microwave construction
	Chile	2,700	Mining machinery, electric equipment, etc.
1973	Mexico	25,500	Steel plant project
	Costa Rica	4,300	Port facility construction
1974	Guatemala	2,680	Electric power plant project

[a]Inter-American Development Bank

[b]Banco Centroamericano de Integracion Economica

Source: "White Paper on the Current State of Japan's Economic Cooperation", Ministry of International Trade and Industry (MITI).

Long-term Export Credit by Government Financial Agencies

Long-term export credit on a public basis has been extended to various countries since 1958. (A distinction is made here between private and official export credit.) The total long-term export credit extended by the Japanese government in 1973 amounted to about $254 million, of which 43.1 percent was extended to Latin America, compared with 47.7 percent extended to Asia in the same year. Over the past few years, Latin America's share has been increasing rapidly, while the total amount of long-term export credit extended by the Japanese government has been declining. Table 3.2 shows the trends in the geographic distribution of Japan's long-term export credit on an official basis.

TABLE 3.2

Geographic Distribution of Long-Term Export Credits
(percent)

	1971	1972	1973
Asia	55.0	56.1	47.7
Latin America	17.2	37.5	43.1
Africa	15.0	15.5	5.7
Europe	6.0	-12.1	3.2
Oceania	2.4	3.0	1.1
Middle East	3.7	0.04	-0.3
Total (in millions)	$271.7	$266.3	$254.0

Source: "White Paper on Current State of Japan's Economic Cooperation," MITI, 1972, 1973, and 1974 editions.

In 1973, 25.4 percent of the total long-term export credit was extended to Brazil, followed by Bermuda, with 5.4 percent, and the Dominican Republic, with 5.1 percent. Latin America's share was increased in 1973, and Asia's reduced, in line with the government policy known as the "globalization of Japan's economic cooperation."[5] Aside from broadening the geographic distribution of official long-term export credits, the new policy stresses the role of private enterprise in meeting the needs of the recipient countries.

Total Flow of Japan's Economic Aid to Latin America

The Development Assistance Committee (DAC) of the Organization for Economic Cooperation and Development (OECD) has defined flows of economic cooperation to include aid, export credits, and private funds. The total flow of Japan's economic cooperation thus defined rose from $2,725 million in 1972 to $5,844 million, that is, 1.44 percent of Japan's GNP, in 1973. This, however, is largely due to the surge in private capital flows in the form of direct investment and portfolio investment. Thus defined, Latin America's share of Japan's total economic cooperation rose sharply to 46.1 percent in 1973, while Asia's share fell to second place with 39.1 percent. Trends in the geographic distribution of total flows of Japan's economic cooperation are shown in Table 3.3.

TABLE 3.3

Geographic Distribution of Total Flows of Japan's Economic Cooperation (percent)

	1971	1972	1973
Latin America	16.6	33.4	46.1
Asia	64.1	53.6	39.1
Africa	8.6	6.5	7.6
Europe	3.1	1.1	3.0
Oceania	1.9	1.2	1.3
Middle East	5.6	4.1	2.7
Total (in millions)	$2,140	$2,725	$5,844

Source: "White Paper on Current Status of Japan's Economic Cooperation," MITI, 1972, 1973, and 1974 editions.

Bilateral aid accounted for 13.1 percent of the total flow of Japan's economic cooperation in 1973, while other official development flow, including export credits, direct investment loans, and loans to multilateral organizations, accounted for 20.2 percent. Private flows accounted for as much as 62.4 percent of Japan's total economic cooperation. Here, again, the basic government philosophy on economic cooperation is that "private enterprise should play an important role." This basic posture stems from the following considerations, set out in the 1974 White Paper:

1. For economic cooperation to be truly meaningful, it is essential that financial assistance be extended only after adequate technical preparation (such as appropriate comprehensive economic development programs or project identification and feasibility surveys) has been made.

2. Accordingly, mere provision of the necessary funds is not sufficient.

3. In order to achieve the ultimate purchase of economic cooperation, it is necessary to consider comprehensive and consistent implementation of measures for stable management and for the development of related infrastructure, the transfer of technology and managerial know-how vital to the operation of the projects, the supplying of raw materials, the marketing of products, and so on.

4. Mere construction of factories, then, is not adequate either. Private enterprise, of course, should play an important role in improving the quality of economic cooperation.[6]

An important function of government in the area of economic cooperation is deemed to be the provision of proper guidance to private enterprise, although the term "proper guidance" is used without elaboration. In others words, the government's current posture is to let private capital flow freely to those areas where the investing industries have the comparative advantage, but where it is possible for the recipient countries to gain the advantage later on. In the latter part of this chapter, Japanese private investment in Latin America will be briefly reviewed.

JAPAN'S TRADE RELATIONS WITH LATIN AMERICA

Latin America as an Export Market for Japan

Over the period 1960-73, Japan's exports to Latin America increased sharply from $303 million to $2,761 million. Over the same period, however, Japan's total exports to the world increased equally sharply, from $4,054 million to $36,930 million. Thus, one relative importance of the Latin American market for Japanese export products has remained fairly stable, fluctuating between 5.9 and 8.1 percent of Japan's total exports. Coincidentally, Latin America received 7.5

percent of Japan's total exports in both 1960 and 1973, the two end years of the period under consideration (see Table 3.4).

Another interesting figure is Japan's share in world export trade with Latin America (see Table 3.5). In 1960, Japanese exports to Latin America accounted for about 3.5 percent of the world's export trade with Latin America. In the same year, Japan's total exports accounted for about 3.6 percent of the world's total export trade. While Japan exported 7.5 percent of its total exports to Latin America in 1960, Japan's share in the world export trade with Latin America was almost proportional to Japan's market share in the total world export trade. Japan's share of the world export trade increased from 3.6 percent in 1960 to 7.8 percent in 1972. Similarly, Japan's share in world export trade with Latin America was 7.4 percent in 1972, an increase from 3.5 percent in 1960. Here we can see a proportional improvement in Japan's competitiveness in the world export market as well as in the Latin American market.

The implications of these trends are that, while Japanese products are becoming more important in the Latin American market, the relative importance of Latin America as an export market for Japanese products has remained more or less the same over a little more than a decade, even though the growth rate of Japan's exports to Latin America has been exceeding the overall growth rate of Japan's exports in the last five years (see Table 3.4).

Japan's Export Commodity Structure and Latin America's Import Demand

Industrialization has proceeded on the basis of import substitution in many Latin American countries, and the introduction of more sophisticated industries has created the need for complex machinery. As is well known, the process of industrialization itself makes large imports necessary. As Table 3.6 shows, Latin America's large import items have been machinery and transport equipment, accounting for 42 percent of Latin America's total imports in 1971. Other industrial products, including chemicals and manufactured goods, accounted for about 35 percent of the continent's imports. This import demand pattern is indeed complementary to the Japanese export commodity structure. In 1971, nearly 48 percent of Japan's total exports to the world were in the form of machinery and transport equipment, and another 47 percent were in the form of chemicals and other manufactured products (see Table 3.7).

Of Japan's $2.8 billion exports to Latin America in 1973, 92 percent was chemical and heavy industrial products. Light industrial

TABLE 3.4

Japan's Exports to Latin America

Year	Japan's Total Exports (FOB) (A) Value (in millions)	(B) Growth Rate (%)	Japan's Exports to Latin America (FOB) (C) Value (in millions)	(D) Growth Rate (%)	Latin America's Share in Total Japanese Exports $\frac{(C)}{(A)}$ x 100 (%)
1960	$ 4,054	—	$ 303	—	7.5
1961	4,236	4.5	345	13.9	8.1
1962	4,916	16.1	354	2.6	7.2
1963	5,452	10.9	360	1.7	6.6
1964	6,673	22.4	471	30.8	7.1
1965	8,451	26.7	482	2.3	5.7
1966	9,776	15.7	556	15.4	5.7
1967	10,442	6.8	612	10.1	5.9
1968	12,972	24.2	742	21.2	5.7
1969	15,990	23.1	943	27.1	5.9
1970	19,318	20.8	1,187	25.9	6.1
1971	24,019	26.3	1,592	34.1	6.6
1972	23,591	16.3	1,980	24.4	6.9
1973	36,930	29.2	2,761	39.5	7.5

Source: "The Summary Report: Trade of Japan," compiled by the Ministry of Finance, and published by the Japan Tariff Association.

TABLE 3.5

Japan's Export Market Shares in World Export Trade
(percent)

Year	Japan's Share in World Export Trade	Exports to North America	Exports to Latin America	Exports to Western Europe	Exports to Asia (excluding Japan)	Exports to Communist Bloc
1960	3.59	6.07	3.46	0.88	13.66	0.49
1965	5.14	9.48	4.40	1.30	17.07	2.27
1966	5.42	9.69	4.47	1.42	18.50	2.73
1967	5.52	9.30	4.72	1.51	20.10	2.26
1968	6.14	10.41	4.93	1.59	23.11	2.28
1969	6.62	11.56	5.47	1.68	26.07	2.74
1970	6.96	12.86	5.82	2.03	26.98	3.32
1971	7.75	14.14	7.05	2.14	30.31	3.20
1972	7.80	12.39	7.43	2.51	25.28	5.79

Source: Bureau of Statistics, Bank of Japan.

TABLE 3.6

World Import Trade Commodity Structure
(percent)

Year	Foodstuffs (SITC 0.1)*	Raw Materials (SITC 2.4)	Fuels (SITC 3)	Chemicals (SITC 5)	Machinery Transport Equipment (SITC7)	Other Mfg. Steel and Textiles (SITC 6.8)
Developing countries						
1960	18.9	20.0	10.2	5.5	18.1	26.6
1965	16.9	15.1	10.0	6.1	21.9	28.6
1970	13.5	11.6	9.8	6.5	26.9	30.1
1971	13.1	10.4	11.1	6.5	28.2	29.2
Underdeveloped countries						
1960	16.4	7.5	10.2	7.7	28.2	28.4
1965	15.7	6.8	8.6	8.5	30.5	27.0
1970	12.8	5.9	8.1	9.0	33.6	26.7
1971	12.8	6.0	8.8	8.9	34.7	26.2
Latin America						
1960	11.3	5.9	7.9	10.1	38.4	25.1
1965	11.7	7.1	6.4	11.7	36.6	24.7
1970	8.8	6.4	5.3	12.0	41.8	23.7
1971	8.9	6.1	6.3	12.1	42.2	22.6

*Standard International Trade Code (SITC).

Source: UN Monthly Bulletin of Statistics.

TABLE 3.7

Japan's Export Commodity Composition
(percent)

	1960	1965	1970	1971
Foodstuffs (SITC 0.1)	6.6	4.1	2.8	2.3
Raw Materials and Fuels (SITC 2.3.4)	4.2	3.3	2.2	2.0
Chemicals (SITC 5)	4.2	6.5	6.2	6.2
Machinery Transport Equipment (SITC 7)	22.9	31.3	44.1	47.8
Other Manufacturing (SITC 6.8)	61.8	54.3	43.9	40.8

Source: Bureau of Statistics, Bank of Japan.

products accounted for only 7.8 percent. The major export items were iron and steel products and ships (including ships exported to Panama in order to take advantage of the expedient nationality transfer available then). This predominance of chemical and heavy industrial goods was even greater than it has been in Japan's trade with Africa (87 percent), the European Common Market (80 percent), West Africa (73 percent), and Southeast Asia (73 percent). Japan's exports by commodity and by region are shown in Table 3.8.

Latin America as Japan's Import Source

In 1960, Japan's share in the world import trade was 3.8 percent (C.I.F. basis), compared with 6.2 percent in 1972. During the period 1960-72, the world import trade increased by 320 percent, while Japan's imports expanded by more than 520 percent. Over the same period, the world's imports from Latin America (or Latin America's exports to the world) increased by only 160 percent, while Japan's imports from Latin America increased by 290 percent. As a result, Japan bought about 5 percent of Latin America's total exports in 1972, compared with 2.8 percent in 1970.

As we have seen, Japan did not expand its imports from Latin America as fast as it did its import trade with the world as a whole. Here, again, the relative importance of the Japanese market for Latin

TABLE 3.8

Japan's Exports by Commodity and by Region, 1973
(FOB) (millions of dollars)

	Total (A)	Light Industrial Products (B)	Textiles (C)	Heavy Chemical Products (D)	D/A (percent)
Total	36.9	6.0	3.3	29.3	79.4
Southeast Asia	8.9	1.9	1.4	6.5	73.0
West Asia	1.6	0.4	0.3	1.3	75.0
Western Europe	4.4	0.6	0.1	3.5	79.5
North America	10.4	1.6	0.6	8.4	80.8
Latin America	2.3	0.2	0.1	2.5	92.0
Africa	3.1	0.3	0.2	2.7	87.1
Oceania	1.6	0.4	0.2	1.1	68.8
Communist Bloc	2.0	0.2	0.2	1.7	85.0

Source: "White Paper on Japan's International Trade, 1974," MITI.

American exportable products has been increasing as Latin America's export share in the world market has shrunk. At the same time, the relative importance of Latin America for Japan's imports has not changed. In fact, Latin America's share has been on a slightly declining trend in recent years (see Table 3.9), although the effects of changes in exchange rates and the recent drastic price increase of imported oil should be taken into consideration to some extent.

Japan relies heavily on foreign sources of energy, metal, textiles, and other raw materials for its industrial production. About 73 percent of Japan's total imports in 1974 was industrial supplies, including crude materials (21 percent), mineral fuels (40 percent), and so on, and about 15 percent was food and consumer goods. In 1974, Latin America supplied about 11 percent of Japan's food imports, 9 percent of Japan's imports of crude materials, 11 percent of its total imports of metals, and 3 percent of its total textile imports. Latin America's supplies of capital equipment are almost negligible at this time; Japan, meanwhile, must import most of its raw materials. Japan depends upon imports for approximately 90 percent of its iron ore, 76 percent of its copper ore, 55 percent of its lead ore, 55 percent of its zinc ore, 100 percent of its bauxite and nickel ore, 79 percent of its coal, 99 percent of its crude oil, and so on. Chile and Peru supply 6 and 4 percent, respectively, of Japan's total consumption of copper ore; Brazil,

TABLE 3.9

Japan's Share in World Import Trade

	1960	1965	1970	1971	1972	1972/60
(A) World Imports (CIF) ($ billions)	119	174	292	325	380	3.19
(B) Japan's Exports (CIF) ($ billions)	4.5	8.2	18.9	19.7	23.5	5.22
(C) Japan's Share in World Imports B/A (percent)	3.76	4.69	6.46	6.06	6.17	—
(D) World Imports from Latin America (FOB) ($ billions)	8.6	11.1	12.8	12.5	13.9	1.64
(E) Japan's Imports from Latin America (FOB) ($ billions)	0.24	0.48	0.78	0.67	0.69	2.88
E/D (percent)	2.79	4.34	6.10	5.34	4.97	—
Latin America's Share in World Exports (FOB) (percent)	7.6	6.8	4.6	4.0	3.8	—

Source: Bureau of Statistics, Bank of Japan.

Chile, and Peru supply 8, 6, and 6 percent, respectively, of its total consumption of iron ore. Mexico and Brazil supply 15 and 7 percent of Japan's total consumption of raw cotton, and Argentina provides 5 percent of Japan's total consumption of foodstuffs (see Table 3.13).

Future Trade with Latin America

As we have seen, Japan's international trade—its share in both the world export market and the world import market—has been increasing very rapidly over the last decade. In 1972, Japan's share in the world export market was 7.8 percent; its share in the world import market, 8.2 percent. These two shares imply that Japan's participation in the world export trade was slightly greater than its participation in the world import trade. Japan's participation in world export trade can be conveniently compared with its participation in world import trade by calculating the ratio of Japan's export market

TABLE 3.10

Japan's Share in World Import Trade by Region
(FOB) (percent)

Year	In World Import	From North America	From Latin America	From Western Europe	From Asia	From Communist Bloc
1960	3.86	6.26	2.79	0.70	9.92	0.73
1965	4.69	6.70	4.34	0.78	12.70	2.00
1966	4.97	6.89	4.55	0.88	13.66	2.54
1967	5.82	7.66	5.04	1.17	14.40	2.73
1968	5.81	7.46	4.91	1.09	15.00	2.56
1969	5.90	7.89	5.50	1.13	15.20	2.29
1970	6.47	9.14	6.10	1.22	17.48	3.11
1971	6.06	7.88	5.34	1.10	17.33	3.27
1972	6.17	8.55	4.97	1.12	17.24	3.67

Source: Bureau of Statistics, Bank of Japan.

TABLE 3.11

Japan's Imports from Latin America

	Japan's Total Imports (CIF)		Japan's Imports from Latin America (CIF)		Latin America's Share in Japan's Total Imports
	(A)	(B)	(C)	(D)	
Year	Value ($ millions)	Growth Rate (percent)	Value ($ millions)	Growth Rate (percent)	$\frac{C}{A}$ x 100 (%)
1960	$ 4,419	—	$ 310	—	6.9
1961	5,810	29.4	481	55.2	8.3
1962	5,636	-3.0	477	-0.8	8.5
1963	6,736	19.5	564	18.2	8.4
1964	7,937	17.8	692	22.7	8.7
1965	8,169	2.9	707	2.2	8.7
1966	9,523	16.6	781	10.5	8.2
1967	11,663	22.5	855	9.5	7.3
1968	12,987	11.4	960	12.3	7.4
1969	15,025	15.7	1,162	21.0	7.7
1970	18,881	25.7	1,373	18.2	7.3
1971	19,771	4.4	1,338	-2.9	6.8
1972	23,471	19.1	1,418	6.0	6.9
1973	38,313	63.2	1,955	37.9	5.1

Source: "The Summary Report: Trade of Japan," compiled by The Ministry of Finance and published by the Japan Tariff Association.

TABLE 3.12

Value of Japanese Imports from Latin America by Major Commodity, 1974
(millions of dollars)

Country	Grand Total	Food-stuffs	Textile Mate-rials	Metal Ores Scraps	Iron Ore	Soybeans	Wood	Nonmetallic Mineral Ores	Mineral Fuels	Chemicals	Machine Equipment
Mexico	308	45	132	14	—	—	1	36	—	8	7
Guatemala	42	8	32	—	—	—	—	—	—	—	—
El Salvador	46	29	15	—	—	—	—	—	—	—	1
Nicaragua	36	—	28	—	—	—	—	—	—	1	—
Cuba	443	438	—	—	—	—	—	—	—	5	—
Venezuela	46	4	—	—	—	—	—	—	42	—	—
Peru	297	8	3	206	92	—	—	—	—	1	—
Chile	404	—	—	269		—	—	—	1	4	—
Brazil	657	187	35	269	265	21	2	5	14	24	43
Argentina	229	167	11	—	—	—	—	—	1	19	12
Total	62,110	8,122	1,861	5,328	2,076	882	3,682	683	24,895	2,668	4,748

Source: The Summary Report, Trade of Japan, Ministry of Finance.

TABLE 3.13

Ratios of Japan's Export Shares to Japan's Import Shares by Region

Year	A/B*	North America	Latin America	Western Europe	Asia (excluding Japan)	Communist Bloc
1960	0.955	0.970	1.240	1.257	1.377	0.671
1965	1.096	1.415	1.014	1.667	1.344	1.135
1966	1.091	1.406	0.982	1.614	1.354	0.828
1967	0.948	1.214	0.937	1.291	1.396	0.828
1968	1.057	1.395	1.004	1.459	1.541	0.891
1969	1.122	1.465	0.995	1.487	1.715	1.197
1970	1.076	1.400	0.954	1.664	1.543	1.068
1971	1.279	1.794	1.320	1.945	1.749	0.979
1972	1.264	1.449	1.495	2.241	1.466	1.578

*A, Japan's export market share in the world; B, Japan's import market share in the world.

Note: Ratios by region are ratios of Japan's exports shares in the region to Japan's import shares in the world import trade from the region concerned.

Source: Bureau of Statistics, Bank of Japan.

share in world export trade to Japan's share in world import trade. This ratio is set out, by region, in Table 3.14.

As the table shows, Japan's participation in world export trade has been slightly greater than its participation in world import trade over the period 1960-72, except in two years, 1960 and 1967. In particular, in 1971 and 1972, Japan's export trade participation compared with import trade participation increased sharply. It is of some interest to investigate the movements in these ratios by region.

With North America, this ratio was below unity in 1960, but since then it has been always over unity. In 1971, this ratio registered 1.8, meaning that Japan's export market share in North America was four fifths greater than its import market share from this area, a source of considerable tension between Japan and the United States, in particular. Similarly, the ratios of Japan's export market shares and its import market shares have been greater than unity with Asia and Western Europe. In 1971, this ratio reached a peak of 1.9 with Western Europe and 1.7 with Asia. For Latin America, these ratios were smaller than unity in some years and greater than unity in others, indicating no clear trend until 1970. After 1971, the ratio increased to more than unity and registered 1.5 in 1972, indicating a greater Japanese presence in exports than in imports.

Japan has been a modest trading partner for Latin America. While Latin America's share in the world export trade has been declining, Japan has been buying from Latin America at a faster rate than the rest of the world. This has made Japan seem to be a good candidate for even closer economic partnership with Latin America. One of the problem areas ahead for Japan will be living up to the expectations that have arisen concerning its future role in Latin America.

Recent sudden changes in world economic conditions implied a sharp increase in Japan's economic interests in Latin America. Latin America can supply large and increasing amounts of the primary products required by Japan. Thus, Japan has turned with increasing interest to Latin America as a logical supplier of the raw materials required to feed Japanese industry, as well as an outlet for some of the products of this industry. Japanese investment in resource development projects with the collaboration of national governments in Latin America certainly will have "trade creation effects," promoting both Japanese exports and the industrial development of these economies. Japan's economic aid to agricultural development in the form of joint-venture projects or government assistance will also serve the mutual interests of these two heterogeneous economies. Thus, the trade flow between Japan and Latin America is expected to grow in the long run.

However, owing to Japan's efforts to diversify supply sources as well as export markets, Latin America's shares of Japan's total exports and imports may not change drastically. One of the leading

TABLE 3.14

Japanese Direct Overseas Investment
(millions of dollars)

Country	1951-67	1968	1969	1970	1971	1972	1973	As of March, 1974	
								Accumulated Total Value	Number of Investment Projects
North America	406	185	129	192	230	406	914	2,462	2,977
Latin America	380	40	100	46	140	282	822	1,811	1,133
Asia	310	78	197	167	237	402	1,001	2,391	3,694
Middle East	240	28	38	28	36	236	110	716	66
Europe	58	153	93	335	85	936	338	1,217	979
Africa	18	43	18	14	21	34	106	254	229
Oceania	39	31	89	123	110	42	208	640	429
Total	1,451	557	665	904	858	2,338	3,497	10,270	9,507

Source: 1974 White Paper on Current Status of Japanese Overseas Investment, Japan External Trade Organization (JETRO).

economic research institutes in Japan, the Japan Economic Research Center, projects that by 1985 Japan will be importing 5.9 percent of its total imports from Latin America and will be exporting 7.4 percent of its exports to the region; in other words, this trade relationship will change very little.

JAPAN'S PRIVATE CAPITAL FLOW INTO LATIN AMERICA

The Surge in Japanese Investment in Latin America

One of the developments that have made observers of Latin America pay more attention recently to the Japan-Latin America relationship is a sharp increase in Japanese private capital flow into the region. This surge, however, has taken place not only in Latin America but in other regions as well. Between 1951, when Japanese overseas investment activities resumed, and 1960, the annual outflow of Japanese investment was rather moderate, and it remained below the $100-million level during the period 1961-65. Japanese overseas investment has grown more rapidly since then, and in 1972 alone $2.3 billion was invested abroad. This trend continued into 1973, and the accumulated total of Japanese direct overseas investment reached $10 billion in March 1974. The annual outflow of Japanese investment into Latin America was below the $100-million mark before 1969, but it has increased since 1971, and over $800 million was invested in the region during fiscal year 1973.

Latin America ranks fourth in relative importance to Japan in terms of the geographic distribution of Japanese investment overseas (accumulated total on approval basis): it holds 17.6 percent of Japanese investment, after North America (23.9 percent), Asia (23.2 percent), and Europe (19.4 percent), followed by Oceania (6.2 percent), the Middle East (6 percent), and Africa (2.4 percent). During fiscal year 1973, Latin America received the third largest flow of Japanese overseas investment (23.5 percent of total Japanese overseas investment), almost as large as those received by Asia (28.6 percent) and North America (26.1 percent) (see Table 3.15).

As of March 1974, the accumulated total of Japanese investments in Latin America reached $1.8 billion. Brazil, by far, was the largest beneficiary of Japanese investment, with $1.04 billion of the accumulated total. Out of $822 million invested in Latin America by Japanese during fiscal year 1973, as much as $435 million was invested in Brazil. Because of the unique position of Brazil, a separate, detailed examination of its Japanese overseas investments will be undertaken.

TABLE 3.15

Japan's Overseas Investments in Latin America by Industry

	(A) Accumulated Total			(B) All Regions			A/B
	Amounts ($ millions)	Percent	Cases	Amounts ($ millions)	Percent	Cases	Percent
Manufacturing							
Food	$ 40	2	30	$167	1.6	236	24.0
Textiles	183	10	83	742	7.2	545	24.7
Lumber & pulp	19	1	17	362	3.5	166	5.2
Chemicals	343	19	42	538	5.2	322	63.8
Iron & nonferrous metals	159	9	42	486	4.7	269	32.7
Nonelectric machinery	93	5	55	217	2.1	337	42.9
Electric machinery	69	4	52	328	3.2	538	21.0
Transportation machinery	125	7	23	222	2.2	91	56.3
Others	26	1	42	197	1.9	641	13.2
Subtotal	1,056	58	336	3,260	31.7	3,145	32.4
Nonmanufacturing							
Agriculture & forestry	24	1	38	152	1.5	251	15.8
Fishery	15	1	27	77	0.7	164	19.5
Mining	189	10	50	3,061	29.8	319	6.2
Construction	41	2	25	67	0.7	132	61.2
Commerce	120	7	193	1,232	12.0	2,888	9.7
Finance & insurance	211	12	58	917	8.9	413	23.0
Others	150	8	336	1,504	14.6	2,195	10.0
Grand Total	1,808		1,113	10,270		9.507	17.0

Source: 1974 White Paper on Current Status of Japanese Overseas Investment, JETRO.

Main Features of Japanese Investments in Latin America

The main features of Japanese private investment in Latin America can be briefly summarized:

1. Recent sharp increases in Japanese investment in Latin America have been largely concentrated in the manufacturing sector. About 58 percent of the accumulated total of Japanese investment in the region has gone to the manufacturing sector, amounting to about \$1.1 billion, or about 33 percent, of Japan's total overseas investment in the manufacturing sector.

2. Among the manufacturing industries, chemicals, textiles, iron and nonferrous metals, and transportation machinery predominate. About 19 percent of the Japanese investment in the region has been in the chemical industry, 10 percent in textiles, 9 percent in iron and nonferrous metals, and 7 percent in transportation machinery. Nearly 64 percent of Japanese overseas investment in chemicals went to Latin America, as did 25 percent of the investment in textiles, 33 percent of the investment in iron and nonferrous metals, and 56 percent of the investment in transportation machinery. Also, about 43 percent of Japanese overseas investment in the nonelectric machinery industry went to Latin America (this was only 5 percent of the total Japanese investment in the region).

3. While Japanese investment in manufacturing and commerce is concentrated in Brazil and Mexico, Japanese investment in resource development is more typical in other countries. Investment in the mining sector accounts for 10 percent of Japanese overseas investment in Latin America and about 6 percent of Japan's total world investment in the mining sector. Lately, agreements have been reached with Chile and Peru on copper development projects. Furthermore, aluminum projects in Venezuela and Brazil have also been agreed upon. It is expected that Japanese investment in resource development projects will increase.

4. According to a survey conducted by the Japanese Ministry of International Trade and Industry, a simple average of the capital participation ratios of 1,788 Japanese companies investing abroad was 74.7 percent in fiscal year 1972 (see Table 3.16). The capital participation ratio in commerce was 91.2 percent, which is much higher than the simple average ratio of the manufacturing sector, 60.8 percent. In the manufacturing sector, the simple average of the capital participation ratios in Latin America was 71 percent, second highest after the North American ratio of 79.2 percent. Table 3.17 shows Japanese overseas investment capital participation ratios by region for the manufacturing sector.

TABLE 3.16

Capital Participation Ratios of Japanese Overseas Investments, FY 1972 (simple average in percent)

Investment	Percent
Industries	74.7
Commerce	91.2
Manufacturing sector	60.8
Mining	68.4
Textile	55.8
Pulp & paper	69.9
Chemicals	50.7
Iron & nonferrous	50.2
Electric machinery	66.3
General machinery	87.7
Transportation machinery	57.6
Precision	69.8
Agriculture & fishing	65.3

Source: "A Survey of Japanese Enterprises Overseas Operation 1974," Japanese Ministry of International Trade and Industry.

TABLE 3.17

Capital Participation Ratios in Manufacturing Sector by Region, FY 1972

Region	Percent
Average	60.8
Latin America	71.1
Africa	43.8
Middle East	34.0
Asia	58.3
Oceania	64.1
North America	79.2
Europe	64.5

Source: "A Survey of Japanese Enterprises Overseas Operation 1974," Japanese Ministry of International Trade and Industry.

5. Of the 203 Japanese companies in Latin America that were included in the survey by the Japanese Ministry of International Trade and Industry, 125 reported that their capital participation ratios were more than 95 percent. Table 3.18 shows the distribution of the capital participation ratios of Japanese subsidiaries in Latin America by major industries. Although the survey does not cover all Japanese subsidiaries in the region, it does provide some useful information.

TABLE 3.18

Distribution of Capital Participation Ratios of Japanese Subsidiaries in Latin America by Industry, FY 1972
(Number of Companies)

Capital Participation Ratios (in percent)	Agriculture, Forestry, & Fishery	Mining	Manufacturing	Commerce	Total
More than 95	3	8	37	64	125
51 to 94	1	1	18	8	31
50	1	0	7	5	14
25 to 49	1	1	18	4	24
Less than 25	0	0	8	1	9
Total	6	10	88	82	203

Source: "A Survey of Japanese Enterprises Overseas Operation 1974," Japanese Ministry of International Trade and Industry.

6. Among 88 Japanese subsidiaries in the manufacturing sector in Latin America (covered by the survey), 16 have capital exceeding 1 billion yen and 40 between 0.1 and 1 billion yen. The regional distribution of the Japanese subsidiaries abroad according to size is shown in Table 3.19.

Factors Accelerating Japanese Overseas Investment in Latin America

One of the basic factors that have accelerated the pace of Japanese overseas investment in the past few years has been a sharp increase in Japan's foreign exchange reserves, which continued until the outbreak of the oil crisis. Since October 1969, the Japanese government has

TABLE 3.19

Distribution of Japanese Subsidiaries Abroad by Size of Capital and by Region (in yen)

	Less than 100 million	Between 100 million and 1,000 million	Over 1,000 million	Total
Europe	11	16	3	30
North America	26	18	7	51
Oceania	6	17	4	27
Asia	310	250	34	594
Middle East	0	4	1	5
Africa	5	19	3	27
Latin America	32	40	16	88
Total	390	364	68	822

Source: "A Survey of Japanese Enterprises Overseas Operation 1974," Japanese Ministry of International Trade and Industry.

accelerated the liberalization of capital transactions. Other factors that have stimulated overseas investment from both domestic and external economic conditions are as follows:

Domestic Factors

Finding suitable factory sites in Japan is becoming increasingly difficult because of environmental considerations. The chemicals, iron, and nonferrous industries are facing these problems. Worsening labor shortages and soaring wage costs are becoming serious constraints to the textiles and electric industries, in particular. In the face of these domestic constraints, the textiles, chemicals, iron, nonferrous, and electric-machinery industries, notably, felt that they had to be more internationally oriented in order to maintain and develop their business activities. Furthermore, the upward float of the yen lowered Japanese overseas investment costs.

External Factors

Growing difficulties in securing raw materials from abroad and the worldwide shortage of energy have affected in particular energy-consuming and iron and nonferrous industries and raw-material-consuming industries, such as the pulp and paper industries, all of which increasingly felt the need to invest abroad.

The worsening export climate for Japanese products is also being felt by many electric-machinery, textiles, and chemicals industries. These industries are investing abroad in order to build up overseas production and maintain their market shares in the recipient countries.

During the period when Japan was accumulating foreign exchange reserves very rapidly, there were many economic missions to Japan, from developing as well as developed countries, whose purpose was to encourage Japanese investment in their countries. Reverse investment missions from the United States, Canada, some European countries, and many Latin American countries gave Japanese potential investors further incentive. In particular, there have been strong requests from many developing nations for Japanese economic assistance in the form of private capital inflow in order to facilitate industrialization and regional development. These requests coincide with Japanese government policy on economic cooperation. Many missions from developed countries, too, have emphasized their need to create job opportunities and solve regional unemployment problems.

All of these factors are closely interrelated, and each decision to invest abroad is, no doubt, the result of various combinations of them.

The choice of a location for investment is also heavily influenced by the various investment incentives, such as tax exemptions, provided by host countries. Government policy toward foreign capital inflow played an important role in attracting Japanese capital into Latin America. For instance, the Andean countries' common policy toward foreign capital and Mexico's new law regulating foreign capital inflow were designed to invite on a select basis that kind of foreign capital in order to facilitate their industrialization, regional development, and export promotion. Yet the restrictive character of some of these regulations certainly has made potential investors more cautious.

In this connection, it is interesting to note that Brazil alone among Latin American nations has had a very liberal policy toward foreign capital. The fact that many more Japanese manufacturers have invested in Brazil than in other Latin American country is largely the result of the host countries' attitudes towards foreign capital. (However, there are some indications that under the new Geiser government, Brazil is becoming more selective in its policy toward foreign capital.)

In addition to government policy, political stability and general economic conditions, including the rate of inflation, the availability of energy, natural resources, manpower, and raw materials, as well as overall future prospects, are also important factors. All of these, too, attracted Japanese investment to Brazil, which has recently experienced more rapid economic growth, slower inflation, and greater political stability than most of its neighbors and which has abundant natural resources and energy. The presence of the Japanese-Brazilian community may have helped further to induce the Japanese to invest in Brazil. What's more, after a certain point, existing investments invite new investment, so we are witnessing a "Brazil boom in Japan" and a "Japan boom in Brazil."

The Pattern of Japanese Overseas Investment

It may be useful to review the pattern of Japanese overseas investment briefly here, since it is quite different from the investment patterns of major Western capital-exporting countries. For instance, nearly one half of Japan's direct investment overseas has gone to developing regions. This can be sharply contrasted with the U.S. figure of 26 percent and West Germany's 29.9 percent (Table 3.20). However, Japanese investment in developed areas has been increasing recently.

TABLE 3.20

Outstanding Direct Overseas Investment in Developing Countries by Main Countries (millions of dollars)

	United States	United Kingdom	West Germany	Japan
End of 1960	11,129	1,087	1,304	265
	(34.9%)	(36.8%)	(43.1%)	(74.2%)
End of 1965	15,177	1,395	2,216	667
	(30.7%)	(33.1%)	(26.6%)	(72.7%)
End of 1970	21,448	1,907	0,212	1,808
	(27.4%)	(33.1%)	(29.0%)	(5.03%)
End of 1973	27,867	—	9,649	4,862
	(26.0%)	—	(29.9%)	(50.8%)

Source: "White paper on Current Status of Japanese Overseas Investment," 1974, Japan External Trade Organization (JETRO).

In the past, Japanese overseas investment was subject to the criticism abroad that Japan was only interested in natural resource development projects that would meet the needs of Japanese industries. Recent sharp increases in manufacturing investment, however, have made this sector as important as raw material and resource development, each accounting for about 32 percent of Japanese overseas investment. Even so, U.S., British, and West German overseas investment is even more heavily weighted toward the manufacturing sector. About 74 percent of West German, 54 percent of British, and 42 percent of U.S. investments had gone to the manufacturing sector by 1972 (see Table 3.21).

TABLE 3.21

Principal Countries' Direct Overseas Investment by Industry (millions of dollars)

	Japan (1974)	United States (1973)	United Kingdom (1971)	West Germany (1972)
Total (accumulated)	10,270	107,268	17,495	8,253
	(100%)	(100%)	(100%)	—
Natural resource development	3,290	37,050	—	—
	(32%)	(34.6%)	—	—
(Mining)	3,061	7,483	1,266	483
	(29.8%)	(7.0%)	(7.2%)	(5.3%)
(Petro)	—	(29,567)	—	—
	—	(27.6%)	—	—
Manufacturing	3,260	45,791	9,419	6,107
	(31.7%)	(42.7%)	(53.8%)	(74.0%)
Other	3,270	24,427	6,810	1,708
	(36.2%)	(22.8%)	(38.9%)	(20.7%)

Source: 1974 Report on Japanese Overseas Enterprises Activities, MITI, and 1974 white paper on overseas market, JETRO.

Japanese overseas investment in commerce and banking, insurance, and other services generally goes to developed regions, while investment in mining, agriculture, forestry, fishing, and marine-product industries tends to go to developing countries. Many Japanese investments in the manufacturing sector center on labor-intensive industries, aimed at building up overseas bases for exports to third countries.

The average investment scale per project is comparatively small, and the rate of return on investments relatively low.

In terms of its stock outstanding per capita and as a percentage of GNP, Japan's direct overseas investment has remained small compared with those of countries like the United States and the United Kingdom. Japan is still a young overseas investing nation (see Table 3.22).

JAPANESE OVERSEAS INVESTMENT IN BRAZIL

A Brief History

As of March 1974, there had been 1,133 Japanese overseas investment projects in Latin America, valued at an accumulated total of $1.8 billion. But more than half of this investment, $1.04 billion, had gone to a single country, namely, Brazil. In fiscal year 1973, Japanese investment in Latin America was $822 million, out of which $435 million was invested in Brazil. Japan's investments in Brazil include the USIMINAS steelworks, one of Japan's three big overseas investments after World War II. (The two others were the development of offshore oil resources in the Persian Gulf and the production of pulp in Alaska.) In addition, large-scale investments have been made in such industries as shipbuilding, automobiles, and textiles.

The Japanese firms that pioneered investment in Brazil suffered from unexpectedly severe inflation and the devaluation of the Brazilian currency. More recently, however, the remarkable economic surge known as the "miracle in Brazil" has attracted the Japanese investors' attention.

In the 1950s, there were only 36 Japanese enterprises in Brazil, and during the 1960s, only 38 new ones arrived. Since then, the number of Japanese enterprises in Brazil has increased sharply. During the period 1970-73, as many as 135 Japanese enterprises, more than 60 percent of the present total, established themselves in Brazil (Table 3.23).

Until the end of the 1960s, Japanese private investment in Brazil grew very slowly; the annual rate of growth was 2 percent in 1967, 5.4 percent in 1968, and 6 percent in 1970. After 1970, however, Japanese investment in Brazil accelerated, increasing to 12.1 percent in 1970, 27.2 percent in 1971, 33.8 percent in 1972, and 90.5 percent in 1973. Before 1970, Japanese investment in Brazil had been concentrated in small-scale projects, producing import-substitution goods destined for the domestic market. After 1970, however, a change in the Brazilian government's policy encouraged the Japanese to

TABLE 3.22

Direct Overseas Investment Outstanding by Main Countries (as of the end of 1972)

	Investment Outstanding ($ millions)	Share in DAC Member Countries (percent)	Ratio to GNP (percent)	Ratio to Exports (percent)	Outstanding Per Capita ($ millions)	Average Increase Rate of Investment Outstanding, 1967-72 (percent)
Japan	6,773	3.9	2.3	23.7	63	36.0
United States	94,031	53.8	8.1	191.0	450	9.6
United Kingdom	25,511	14.6	16.5	104.6	457	7.8
France	10,062	5.8	5.1	38.6	195	10.8
West Germany	8,253	4.7	3.2	17.9	134	22.3
Canada	6,319	3.6	6.1	30.1	289	11.1
Total DAC member countries	174,883	100.0	6.9	62.2	275	10.9

Source: White Paper on Japan's International Trade, 1974. MITI.

TABLE 3.23

Number of Japanese Enterprises Established in Brazil

Year	Number	Percentage
1950s	36	17.2
1960s	38	18.2
1970-73	138	64.6
Total	209	100.0

Source: Japanese Chamber of Commerce and Industry in Brazil, 1974.

undertake more joint ventures with Brazilian enterprises and more investments oriented toward the production of exportable products.

Japanese Capital Investment in Brazil

Brazilian government policy has encouraged the inflow of foreign capital into Brazil. Foreign direct investments in Brazil increased 17 percent in 1971 and 35 percent in 1973, according to the Central Bank of Brazil. Japan's share of the total foreign capital in Brazil also has increased very rapidly, rising from 4.3 percent in 1971 to 6.9 percent in 1973. The largest investor in Brazil is the United States, which accounts for about 38 percent of the total foreign investments, followed by the European Common Market, with about 30 percent. Japan was the sixth largest investor in Brazil in 1973, after the United States, West Germany, Canada, Switzerland, the United Kingdom and France (see Table 3.24).

Foreign capital is being widely invested in many sectors of the Brazilian economy. The chemicals and petrochemicals industries account for about 17 percent of total foreign capital invested in Brazil, followed by the transport equipment industry (14 percent) and the electric and telecommunications equipment industries (7.0 percent). This is the area where the introduction of foreign capital and technology can best contribute to the development of the recipient economy. The fourth largest foreign-capital-dominated sector is real estate and the construction industry (6 percent), followed by machinery (5.1 percent), finance (4.1 percent), and iron and steel (3.1 percent). Nearly 20 percent of the Japanese investment in Brazil went into iron and steel, 14 percent into machinery, 11 percent into finance, 9.0 percent into

TABLE 3.24

Shares in Total Foreign Direct Investments in Brazil
By Major Investing Countries

	Percentage		
	1971	1972	1973
U.S.	37.7	37.4	37.5
West Germany	11.4	10.9	11.4
Canada	10.1	9.0	7.9
U.K.	9.4	8.2	7.1
Switzerland	6.6	7.5	7.8
France	4.5	4.8	4.5
Japan	4.3	5.7	6.9
Other	16.0	16.5	16.9
Total	100.0	100.0	100.0

Source: Central Bank of Brazil. Quoted in Keidanren Pamphlet on the "First Japan-Brazil Businessmen's Economic Joint Meeting in Rio de Janiero," January 1975.

textiles, 9 percent into shipbuilding, and 8.9 percent into the trading sector (Table 3.25).

A breakdown of Japan's share of the foreign investment in Brazil, by industry, may give a somewhat clearer picture (Table 3.26). In the shipbuilding industry, about 81 percent of foreign capital is from Japan. About 44 percent of foreign investments in the Brazilian steel industry is Japanese, 31 percent in the timber industry, 23 percent in textiles, 19 percent in machinery, 18 percent in finance, etc.

Considering major investment projects that are currently under discussion between Brazil and Japan, Japanese investments in Brazil will further increase, in particular, in the pulp, iron and steel, aluminum refinery, and shipbuilding industries. There will be also a remarkable expansion in the area of chemical fertilizers, metal industry, and machinery industry, on which the current Brazilian government has placed priorities.

In 1974 the first meeting of Japan (Brazil's businessmen's joint meeting) was held in Rio de Janeiro. At this meeting, the Brazilian businessmen explained a role of foreign capital in Brazilian economy, their government's priority on investment fields. In particular, they indicated their reluctance to accept foreign capital investments in the real estate business in Brazil. The Brazilian government explained to the Japanese delegation about its priority industries (such as steel,

TABLE 3.25

Japanese Enterprises Established in Brazil by Industry and Period of Time of Investment

Industry	1950s	1960-64	1965-69	1970-73	Total	Percent
Mining				2 (2)	2	1.0
Manufacturing	(19)*	(9)	(12)	74	(114)	(54.5)
Iron & steel		1 (1)		4 (4)	5	2.4
Pulp, paper, timber				3 (2)	4	2.0
Fertilizer, chemicals				5 (5)	7	3.3
Heavy machinery	6 (3)	3 (1)	3 (1)	12 (7)	23	11.0
Light machinery	1			7 (3)	8	3.8
Electronics & electronic appliances	1	1 (1)	1 (1)	9 (5)	14	6.7
Textiles	5 (2)	2	2	24 (13)	32	15.3
Food	4	1 (1)	3 (1)	5 (3)	13	6.2
Printing	1 (1)			1 (1)	2	1.0
Other	1			4 (2)	6	2.9
Agriculture		4 (1)	1 (1)	1 (1)	6	2.9
Real estate	1		1	19 (4)	21	10.0
Trading companies	11	1	2 (2)	10 (4)	30	14.3
Finance & insurance	5 (4)	1	3 (2)	10 (9)	19	9.0
Transportation		1			1	0.5
Branches		1	2	13	10	7.0
Total	36 (10)	17 (6)	21 (10)	135 (65)	209	100.0
	17.2%	8.2%	10.0%	64.6%	100%	

*Numbers in parentheses indicate number of joint ventures with local firms.

Source: Japanese Chamber of Commerce in Brazil, quoted in Keidanren pamphlet on the "First Japan-Brazil Businessmen's Economic Joint Meeting in Rio de Janeiro," January 1975.

TABLE 3.26

Japan's Share in Foreign Capital Invested in Brazil by Industry

	(A) Value of Foreign Capital Invested (in millions)	(B) Japanese Investment (in millions)	B/A
Mining	$ 76.7	$ 8.8	11.5
Nonferrous	124.5	3.3	2.6
Iron and steel	143.8	62.5	43.5
Metal industry	216.6	9.5	4.4
Machinery	234.0	43.5	18.6
Electrical telecommunication	335.8	17.4	5.2
Shipbuilding equipment	39.4	28.5	80.5
Transport equipment	13.9	4.5	2.3
Timber	18.6	5.8	31.2
Pulp & paper	88.8	—	—
Rubber	116.3	2.5	—
Chemicals & Petrochemicals	794.7	5.2	0.7
Fertilizer	20.1	3.1	15.5
Medical	197.2	0.4	0.2
Textiles	122.6	28.6	23.4
Clothing	18.1	3.1	17.2
Food	191.5	6.9	3.6
Public service sector	190.9	—	—
Agriculture	31.7	3.3	10.5
Real estate & construction	279.0	6.9	2.5
Finance	186.9	33.5	18.0
Trading	173.4	28.2	16.3
Total	4,579.2	318.3	

Source: Japanese Chamber of Commerce in Brazil, quoted in Keidanren pamphlet on the "First Japan-Brazil Businessmen's Economic Joint Meeting in Rio de Janeiro," January 1975.

nonferrous metal, chemicals, chemical fertilizers, pulp and paper, cement, general machinery industries). At the same time, the Brazilian government showed an interest in the introduction of antipollution technology in Brazil. After the Japanese businessmen's meeting, then Japanese Prime Minister Tanaka visited Brazil, reflecting the Japanese government's increased interests in Brazil.

All these recent trends indicate that the relationship between Japan and Brazil will become closer. Yet the closer their economic relations become, the greater the need for cultural exchanges between the two countries. "Specific guidelines on doing business in Brazil" drawn up by the Japanese Chamber of Commerce and Industry in Brazil (which will be briefly explained in the final section) reflect the difficulties Japanese businessmen have had in maintaining smooth economic relations with Brazil, and their efforts to overcome them. The Japanese increasingly are interested in Brazil, meanwhile, but still from a distance. Essentially, the cultural gap remains to be bridged.

PROSPECTS FOR THE FUTURE

As its direct overseas investments have grown, Japan gradually has become aware of the possibility of serious friction with recipient countries. Recently, for example, great resentment was expressed about the Japanese economic presence in Southeast Asia.

It is hoped that this will not happen in Latin America, where Japanese capital is considered to have contributed to the development of the local economies. Furthermore, the Japanese seem to have a reasonable degree of acceptability in Brazil and many other Latin American countries. They are eager to maintain it. In June 1973, a set of "Guidelines for Investment Activities in Developing Countries" was issued in Japan by the five major Japanese business organizations, including Keidanren, the Japanese Chamber of Commerce and Industry, the Japan Committee for Economic Development, and the Japan Foreign Trade Council. These guidelines were prompted by the recognition that Japanese investment in the developing countries must be made acceptable and welcome to the host countries on a long-term basis, and were not drawn up with any single nation in mind.

The Japanese Chamber of Commerce and Industry in Brazil released its own declaration based upon these guidelines, entitled "Specific Guidelines on Doing Business in Brazil." Drawing upon past experience, these include practical advice on doing business in Brazil and advice on achieving cooperation and harmonious relations with the local economy and community, organized around nine points: basic posture of trust; enlargement of personnel for overseas assignments, and transfer of authority from the home office to the local offices; education and training for local employees; fostering related industries by utilizing the locally supplied products; promotion of reinvestment; cooperation with Brazilian industry by preventing disturbance of the local economy; and maintenance of a harmonious relationship in Brazil.

Both sets of guidelines are useful, but further improvements in government policy may also be necessary. Japan should study the possibility of modifying the preferential tariff scheme that was implemented in August 1971 to achieve economic cooperation through trade. In order to maintain sound and balanced economic relations with Latin America in particular, the Japanese government should expand its assistance in such fields as social infrastructure and agricultural development. Although Japan has become the second largest donor country in the world, after the United States, of high quality economic cooperation, there is still much room for improvement. For instance, private flows and official financial flows in the form of export credits account for a large part of Japan's economic cooperation. The level of official development aid is low, both as a share of the total flow of resources to developing countries and as a percentage of Japan's GNP. Furthermore, Japan has offered aid on comparatively stringent terms, and bilateral assistance has tended to be concentrated in the Asian countries. No doubt, future Japanese-Latin American economic relations can be improved through various institutional channels. A new Japanese-Latin American relationship is just beginning, but both sides must work toward a higher degree of mutual trust and understanding.

NOTES

1. "1974 Kezai Kyoryoku No Genjo To Mondai-Ten" ("The 1974 White Paper on the Current State of Japan's Economic Cooperation"), Ministry of International Trade and Industry, p. 163.

2. John H. Dunning, Studies in International Investment, (London: Allen and Unwin Ltd., 1970), p. 34.

3. Japanese Ministry of International Trade and Industry, "The 1974 White Paper on the Current State of Problems of Economic Cooperation."

4. 1974 White Paper.

5. Ibid.

6. Japan Economic Research Center, "Japan's Future in the World Economy," February 1975.

CHAPTER

4

CANADA DRAWS CLOSER TO LATIN AMERICA: A CAUTIOUS INVOLVEMENT

John D. Harbron

ROOTS OF CANADA'S LIMITED INVOLVEMENT IN LATIN AMERICA

For too long, indeed throughout the history of its public policy, Canada has denied its place among the nations of the western hemisphere. Membership in the old Pan-American Union, predecessor to the Organization of American States, and in the OAS itself, was not for Canada. In fact, the concept of pan-Americanism has had far less to do with Canada's national development than its strong European roots, or so Canadian political leaders and intellectuals reasoned. The "inter-American system," that phrase beloved of many generations of U.S. congressmen and continentalist Latin American intellectuals, was too much for the Canadians. They preferred to remain more European than American and to emphasize their ties with two global commonwealths, neither indigenous to this hemisphere, the British Commonwealth and the recently restructured Francophone community.

Canadian nineteenth- and twentieth-century suspicion of pan-Americanism and the inter-American system had deep historical roots. Better that Canada work within the British Empire it knew and which had eased Canada into full nationhood (by permitting separate Canadian signatures to the great powers' peace treaty in 1919 and through the Statute of Westminster in 1931) than to try to join forces with the "American Empire," whose republicanism it still mistrusted, or with the more distant Latin American republics, which had once been constitutionally structured as the "sister republics" of the United States. Moreover, Canada was a new nation compared to nearly all the Latin American republics, proclaimed only in 1867. (Cuba was the exception in Latin America, achieving some degree of independence only after the American military conquest of the island in 1898.)

The "Undefended Border"

The oldest cliche of Canadian-U.S. relations is the "undefended border 3,000 miles long," on either side of which the two countries have lived in perpetual peace. True for this century perhaps. But at the beginning of the nineteenth century, Canada, as a British colony, and the United States fought each other in the War of 1812, a war that is still being won by the Americans in their history books and by the British and Canadians in theirs. Many times during the last century—in 1837, 1865, 1866, 1894, and 1903—the two countries (Canada was still a cluster of British possessions—British North America—until 1867) were close to war. Although any open conflict technically would have been between Britain and the United States, presumably a Canadian militia would have participated as it did in the War of 1812 and in the South African British colonial war, 1899-1901.

The post-Civil War clamor for "manifest destiny," which brought Russian Alaska into the emerging U.S. commercial and geographic empire, made British North America uneasy. An Anglo-British conflict might have been touched off by the pressure tactics that President Theodore Roosevelt, fresh from wrestling the new Republic of Panama from Colombia, used to secure the Alaska Panhandle for the United States in 1903. The story is that the British chief negotiator, lukewarm to Canadian claims, made a behind-the-scenes deal with Roosevelt's delegation.

As late as 1925, a contingency plan to counter an American military invasion of Canada was prepared by a senior Canadian army intelligence officer for the Canadian Department of National Defence, and between 1919 and 1921 the U.S. Army War College, in a series of studies of potential conflict in the hemisphere, dealt with three scenarios: another war against the Mexicans, the sea defense of Hawaii, and the invasion of Canada.

A major scholarly paper was published in 1974 by Richard Preston, a Canadian history professor at Duke University, North Carolina, who was once on the academic staff of the Royal Military College, Kingston, Ontario, Canada's equivalent to West Point.[1] Preston's study, based on surviving records of both the U.S. War Department and the Canadian National Defence Department, indicates lingering interest in studying a military attack on Canada as recently as 1938, although Admiral W. D. Leahy, as chief of naval operations, recommended that such plans be scrapped as "wholly inapplicable to present conditions."[2]

When war broke out between Canada and Nazi Germany on September 10, 1939, the Canadian army, about to accept a few very old World War I "whippet"-style tanks from the United States, was embarrassed to have coastal defense guns on the Canadian side of Lake Ontario near

Toronto still pointing across the lake in the direction of the American shoreline about thirty-five miles away. Those guns are long gone, removed early in World War II, but not the many forts and related defense installations close to Canada's land and water borders with the United States built by the British after the War of 1812. They have been restored as major tourist attractions and historical centers; such cities and towns as Kingston, Ontario, and Niagara-on-the-Lake are veritable museums of a time when an American invasion was very much feared. Fort William Henry at Kingston, completed in the early 1830s, is one of the largest surviving fortresses of its kind in North America.

Preston suggests that the latent emnity between the two nations, one born of revolution against the British crown and the other through allegiance to it, ended relatively recently:

> It was not until . . . experience had been gained with machinery for the settlement of disputes, not until Canada had assumed control of her own external affairs and not until the alliance of the First World War, that the people of the two countries began to accept the idea that they could, "sleep on arms that can never be aimed inwards at America."[3]

CANADA'S TUPAMAROS: THE FRONT DE LIBERATION DU QUEBEC (FLQ)

What does all this have to do with Canada's Latin American relations? Only this, that deep down in the Canadian psyche the fear lingers that Washington could still countenance some form of military action against Canada, given extreme circumstances affecting the large U.S. interests in Canada. Canadian writers and scholars cite the U.S. intervention in 1954 to unseat the neo-Marxist but nevertheless indigenous Arbenz regime in Guatemala, the American military invasion of the Dominican Republic in 1965, and the activities of the CIA (Central Intelligence Agency) in the internal affairs of several Latin American nations during the mid-1970s.

The urban terrorism in Quebec Province during the so-called FLQ crisis in October 1970, after all, was not so different from urban guerrilla attacks against the social order in Latin America. During the brief FLQ crisis, the Canadian armed forces were called out to police Montreal as well as Ottawa, Canada's capital, and the Trudeau government ordered the temporary termination of civil liberties through the reintroduction of the War Measures Act first passed in 1917. American concern about the huge U.S. direct and portfolio investment in Quebec was understandable: Quebec has more U.S. investment than any single Latin American republic except Brazil or Mexico.

During the 1960s, the FLQ acted in similar fashion as did terrorists in Brazil, Uruguay, and Argentina, carrying out bombings (mainly in post offices and busy supermarkets in Montreal), mail threats, and, finally, in the fall of 1970, political kidnappings and murders. The FLQ had a small membership. But so, it was pointed out, did similar urban terrorist groups in Brazil and Uruguay. The latter country had reached a state of social upheaval by 1970, as a result of incessant attacks against the social order by the Tupamaros urban guerrillas.

The similarity of FLQ and Tupamaro methods for seeking publicity and setting a community on edge came late to the attention of Canadian law enforcement agencies, who had no reason to follow the activities of Latin American urban guerilla movements closely until Canada faced an identical threat. No direct FLQ associations with the Tupamaros were ever found, although it was public knowledge that some FLQ leaders had studied and worked in Cuba during the 1960s.[4] The technique was to kidnap a prominent foreign diplomat or domestic politician and then blackmail the media (newspapers, radio, and TV) into announcing the FLQ manifesto for violent social change as part of the negotiations for release of "political prisoners."

The FLQ crisis produced a new Canadian literature (in both English and French) of nationalist protest against the strong-arm methods used by the Canadian government, and of profound criticism of outside ownership of Quebec's resources, which is considered one of the main reasons for the FLQ's emergence. This new school of protest literature, which has spread to films and the stage, keeps alive the rumor, passed around during the FLQ crisis, that national guard units in states bordering on the province of Quebec had been secretly authorized to "mobilize" if Canada were to experience a "Latin American-type" urban guerrilla upheaval.

This rumor was strongly denied, has never been proven, and probably was unfounded. But given the revelations during 1973-75 of the activities of the CIA, not only in Latin America but also in Canada, the rise of a revisionist school of Canadian opinion that sees the traditional, friendly U.S.-Canada relationship as an American plot to hold Canada in "neo-colonial bondage" to an "imperial America" is to be anticipated. Peter C. Newman, a former editor of the Toronto Star and now editor of Maclean's magazine, the country's two largest and most nationalistic publications, told a Canadian university convocation in the spring of 1975 that Canada "has suffered from a psychology of surrender" (relative to U.S. ownership of Canadian industry). He continued: "Canada is now economically and culturally dominated by the U.S. to a degree by which few nations have ever been controlled without actual conquest and long occupation."[5]

CANADA'S CARIBBEAN INTERESTS

Canadian trade patterns in the hemisphere for a long period were determined by historical links rather than strict economic advantage. During the British imperial era, trade followed the British flag between British North America and the British West Indian colonies, and it continued to do so after Canadian confederation in July 1867. As a result, traditional Canadian exports, such as dried fish and lumber, to what is now the Commonwealth Caribbean, have always been fairly strong. In 1964, for example, total Canadian exports to the West Indies were valued at $70 million, more than Canada's exports the same year to three large Commonwealth nations ($64 million to India, $20 million to Pakistan, and a miniscule $7 million to Nigeria).[6]

In the years before the American Revolution, the English version of the Western European mercantilist system flourished on the staples of the northern and southern colonies. Nova Scotia and Newfoundland supplied dried fish for export; the New England colonies, the essential white oak barrel staves for rum casks; the English homeland, most of the finished goods.

The distinguished Canadian historian Arthur Lower writes in his superb history of Canada:

> All 18th Century roads led to the West Indian islands, those givers of good things, they were the pivots of Empire. The Old Colonial System was a West Indies system, a sugar, rum and molasses system. Regrettably but true, the old Empire was largely built on rum and slaves. But it worked well and brought prosperity all round, except to the slaves.[7]

The American Revolution destroyed the profitable colonial trade triangles, although Canadian east-coast dried fish products remain a staple to this day in West Indian diets, and such far-away markets as imperial and Catholic Brazil, with its many fish-eating holy days, were competing for fish from the Maritime Provinces by the 1850s.

However, Canadian trade patterns in the hemisphere changed substantially during the late 1960s and early 1970s when Brazil, Mexico, Venezuela, and, more recently, Cuba became the major trading partners. Nevertheless, a strong sense of identification continues between Canada and fellow Commonwealth nations in the Caribbean (Jamaica, Barbados, Trinidad and Tobago, Guyana) based on their joint inheritance from Britain, constitutional government, and the English language. The small Caribbean Commonwealth nations take advantage of Canadian industries in their various economies. Trinidad and Tobago, for example, whose economy is on a rebound, is seeking more Canadian business participation in a small national market through its aggressive Industrial Development Corporation.

Moreover, entrepreneurs, railway builders, bankers, and engineers did not only follow the British flag in Latin America. The dynamic William Van Horne, who pushed the transcontinental Canadian Pacific railway through the Rocky Mountains in 1883-84 as its general manager, later worked for British-owned railways in colonial Spanish Cuba.[8] Yet another Canadian, William Reid, worked in the Dominican Republic and married into a prominent local family, who helped him establish the Royal Bank of Canada in that republic. His son, Donald Reid Cabral, one of the republic's largest car dealers, served briefly as president in the 1964 triumvirate immediately preceding the Dominican revolution, by which time the Royal Bank of Canada had become the second largest bank in the Dominican Republic in terms of net assets. (See Appendix Table 4.A.)

It may come as a surprise to both Canadians and Americans to know that 6 percent of the foreign-owned Cuban sugar centrales before the Cuban revolution were Canadian, and that Canadian banks and life insurance companies, such as Confederation Life, Sun Life Assurance Company of Canada, and Imperial Life, did a large business among Havana's prospering bourgeois society of the 1940s and 1950s.[9] Several of today's Canadian-based multinational companies, notably Massey Ferguson Ltd. (farm machinery, in those days known as Massey Harris Ltd.) and the predecessor companies of Brazilian Traction Light and Power (today's Brascan Ltd.), began at the turn of the century from the efforts of Canadian entrepreneurs in Latin America. The late industrialist and cabinet minister, Clarence Decatur Howe, Canada's wartime minister of munitions and supply, who was largely responsible for changing Canada from an agrarian country before 1939 into an industrial state, visited Argentina in May 1931 as head of his own engineering company. Before he left, Howe signed contracts worth $40 million to build 400 Argentine grain elevators. Many of them are still in use. Howe would not return to Argentina until 1953, when he led Canada's second postwar ministerial trade mission to Latin America.

PREJUDICE, PUBLIC OPINION, AND CANADA'S FOREIGN POLICY

The "British connection," which has helped shape so many Canadian attitudes, left both public opinion and policymakers opposed to strong multilateral associations with Hispanic America. Generations of Canadian schoolchildren, some of whom would become diplomats, politicians, business leaders, and opinion makers, were raised on British-oriented history books, which demeaned Spain and the role of

Spanish civilization in history. Their dubious vérités, for example, that the defeat of the Spanish Armada in 1588 precipitated the decline of the Spanish Empire and the rise of the British one, were not likely to encourage fair or objective appreciation of the Hispanic societies of Latin America. It should come as no surprise, therefore, that the frank memoirs of the late internationalist and world diplomat, Prime Minister Lester B. Pearson, reveal his personal doubts about and dislike of Latin Americans. Pearson was the product of a Protestant manse in anti-Catholic southern Ontario and was raised within the Calvinistic tradition that had promulgated the idea, century after century, that Spaniards were cruel and corrupt because they were Catholic. And, in their typically quiet way, Canadians used the leyenda negra (black legend) against Spain.

More important, perhaps, until very recent years, Canadian diplomatic and trade relations with the Latin American republics almost always have been assessed and implemented in the context of Canada's relations with the United States. And perhaps rightly so. There is no advantage in Canada siding firmly with Mexico or Brazil in its differences with the United States if this position is to the detriment of the vital U.S.-Canada relationship.

In the late 1970s, however, a major shift in this view might be seen if powerful Latin American republics, potentially Venezuela, Mexico, Brazil, and perhaps small but bauxite-rich Jamaica, persuade the Canadians to participate in punitive activities against the United States, as the major user-nation, such as the price fixing of their international commodity cartels. Already in the early 1970s Canada supported Mexican and Brazilian opposition to the import surcharges instituted by the Nixon administration. (In this instance, Canada was more severely affected than any Latin American exporter to the United States, since that country was still its largest customer.)

Canada's classic position relative to the hemispheric multilateral agencies was stated almost thirty years ago by the late the Right Honorable Vincent Massey, Canada's first native-born governor general. Massey, a distinguished Canadian of clearly patrician views and with a strong British orientation, wrote in his book, paradoxically entitled <u>On Being a Canadian</u>:

> . . . If we look on the Union's [Pan-American Union] activities with friendly detachment (as I hope we will) and wish to remain outside (as I hope we do) we should make known our views. Otherwise we may well find ourselves manoeuvered towards joining this organization. That would not indicate a very firm conception of Canadian policy.[10]

As a result of these attitudes, many modern Latin American experiments in nation building, which should have interested Canadian policymakers and scholars, have largely escaped them. For example, Canada has ignored the genuine social revolutions in Mexico in the 1930s and 1940s, especially the emergence of a Mexican technocratic elite (tecnicos), and in Cuba in the 1960s, as well as the building of social democracies with Europeanized traditions of reform and state involvement not entirely unlike Canada's (chiefly in the Chile of the 1950s and 1960s and Venezuela at the present time).

More recent instances of Latin American developments relevant to Canada include the decisions of Brazil, Mexico, and Peru on the difficult question of ownership of natural resources, seabed resources, and ocean frontier extensions.

For Canada to have borrowed from any Latin American model in the 1950s and 1960s, from nations allegedly plagued with coups, poverty, revolutions, and instability, would have been considered incongruous; to have compared emerging Canadian institutions with those of another democracy in the hemisphere would have been considered intellectual license. And yet major Canadian foreign policy pronouncements extending territorial water limits and declarations of national sovereignty affecting Arctic waters were made only as recently as 1969-70, long after Latin American countries had taken similar measures, and the Canadian Development Corporation, comparable to those of Chile and Mexico, was not approved by Parliament until a few years ago.

Canadian foreign policy toward the hemisphere often has appeared to be an extension, unconscious or otherwise, of the pietistic and self-assured Calvinism that influenced Canada so deeply during its formative years. It was bound to clash with the parallel value systems of societies where Catholic social dogma based on papal encyclicals predominated.

In 1970, Chile's former Christian Democratic president Eduardo Frei suggested to the author that Canadian Prime Minister Pierre Elliot Trudeau, well grounded in the social doctrine of the Church by his Quebec education, would have been a Christian Democrat in a Latin American political context.[11] But such observations remain at the level of high sophistication. As recently as 1972, an ambassador from a Spanish-speaking Caribbean country in Ottawa despaired openly to the author about the bias against "Latins" that he sensed in his dealings with the Department of External Affairs. Although there are many French Canadian (hence "Latin") diplomats in its senior ranks, department officials feel more at home with a Jamaican or a Dominican diplomat who speaks English than with a Guatemalan, Cuban, or Dominican who speaks Spanish. My reply was that despair is in order. As long as the domestic relationship between English- and French-speaking Canadians has not been resolved, relations with more distant Latin communities will not always proceed smoothly.

NONCOMMITTAL SUPPORT FOR HEMISPHERIC ORGANIZATIONS

With the exception of the brief interlude 1957-63, when a conservative government with strong British Commonwealth ties held power in Canada, Canadian federal governments since 1935 have been liberal. The liberal party produced Lester Pearson and former secretaries of state for external affairs Paul Martin and Mitchell Sharp. Both Pearson and Martin as external affairs ministers and Pearson as prime minister indicated publicly several times that they supported Canadian membership in the Pan-American Union and the OAS, but without ever proposing any firm date for entry. The late prime minister Mackenzie King, in whose administration Martin had held senior cabinet posts, said in December 1939 that Canada would enter the Pan-American Union when he saw enough public support to justify it.[12] Meanwhile, King was applying delaying tactics, as he constantly did in stormy interludes of Canadian politics—what a distinguished Canadian journalist, the late Blair Fraser, long ago called King's "tiptoeing around the sick room."

Nevertheless, statements such as these almost always occasioned optimism in Washington and among American editorial writers. The liberal governments of King and Pearson were continentalist after all, solicitous of "the special relationship" between the two countries, with their intimately intertwined economic, financial, and even cultural relations. The late President John Kennedy must have sensed this optimism personally when he offered Canada a direct invitation to join the OAS during a visit to Ottawa in 1961 shortly after the Cuban Bay of Pigs fiasco. The Canadian reception to the invitation was cool and would get cooler, since the American view seemed to be that Canada would bolster America's position in the OAS, the very function Canada had always wanted to avoid.

Opinion in Mexico, the United States' restive, nationalistic neighbor on its other border, saw Canada's "special relationship" with the United States as a source of opposition to Washington in hemispheric affairs rather than of cooperation. When Canada joined the Inter-American Development Bank (IDB) in May 1972, Mexico's secretary of finance and public credit commented:

> The entrance of Canada into IDB will be fundamental to prevent any single country from control of the Bank. The

> full entrance of Canada will have the effect of neutralizing the U.S. which now controls 42 percent of the Bank's capital.[13]

The distinguished Mexican political scientist Mario Ojeda, of the Colegio de Mexico, saw "Canada and Latin America . . . trapped in the abstractions of 'the special relationship.'"[14]

That "special relationship" of the Pearson years would disintegrate somewhat in the mid-1970s—a result of former President Nixon's import surcharges, DISC proposals, and U.S. dollar devaluation, as well as of domestic pressures in Canada to reduce resources exports during the energy crisis in the United States. At the same time, a new Canadian prime minister with a new style of analyzing and settling foreign policy and trade matters has given a different tone to Canadian relationships with the Third World, including Latin America.

TRUDEAU TAKES COMMAND

Since Trudeau was first elected prime minister on June 25, 1968, Canadian foreign policy has become more "hemisphere oriented."[15] Almost immediately, Trudeau announced a major ministerial visit to most of the leading Latin American countries, to take place in October-November 1968. It included at least four cabinet ministers, representing interests as wide-ranging as trade, cultural affairs, and immigration.[16] The prime minister also announced that two foreign policy seminars would be held between January and March 1969 in which government and private-sector specialists would discuss his policy for Canada's new role in the North American Treaty Organization (NATO) and its relationship with Latin America. At the same time, Trudeau instructed the Department of External Affairs to approach Peking about beginning recognition procedures. This move was made in Stockholm in February 1969 and culminated in the recognition of the People's Republic of China on October 13, 1970.

In all of these areas—NATO, China, the Third World—and in his clarification of Canada's position on sovereignty over coastal waters and Arctic islands, Trudeau drew Canadian foreign policy out of the limbo where it has been suspended for years. Specialists had long discussed these changes, but Trudeau "grasped the nettle," as one relieved official put it and made Canada independent of Washington in foreign policy.

The prime minister's foreign policy statement of early February 1969 gave more emphasis to Canada's interests in the hemisphere and resulted in a downgrading of its NATO military role. This launched a debate that has continued in Canada as to whether Trudeau abdicated some of the international responsibilities guaranteed by his predecessor to Canada's NATO allies. Many of Trudeau's critics could not, or would not, understand a foreign policy articulated in interdisciplinary terms (Latin Americans, on the other hand, would understand it very well), seeing them only as verbal smoke screens hiding an isolationist Canada. Before the October 1972 federal election, Trudeau told a Toronto audience that the three frontiers of Canada would be "technological, geographic and social" and that Canada "must have a will to hold them together." He complemented such philosophical comments with his proposal that "counterweights" be applied at the diplomatic level to reduce Canadian dependence on the United States; hence the move to recognize Peking, which had been delayed since 1950, and the signing of bilateral agreements with the USSR on research sharing, joint discussion of pollution problems, and Arctic development in 1971.

The government's foreign policy review of 1970, issued in the form of six brightly designed paperbacks, discussed nearly all major aspects of foreign policy shifts, but did not devote an entire volume to the Canadian-U.S. relationship.

During the same year, Trudeau made his unilateral declarations extending territorial waters from three to twelve miles and announcing 100-mile-deep "sanitation zones" around the Arctic islands, moves that earlier governments had not made because they knew Washington would have protested. The United States did protest, even though Canada does not consider the Northwest Passage international waters, and is now prepared to police the passage in order to prevent oil spills from supertankers, which ecologists agree could pollute the entire Arctic shoreline. Fishing states like Peru, Chile, Mexico, and Brazil understand the context in which Canada is at last taking these protective measures.

CANADIAN-LATIN AMERICAN TRADE PATTERNS

The 1970 White Paper on Foreign Policy recommended the expansion of Canadian aid and trade to the developing world. Since then, trade with Latin America has, in fact, increased. This has been the result of several rigorous and well-planned trade missions (to Mexico in 1973, Brazil in 1974, and Cuba and Venezuela in 1975) and of the increase in the amounts of Canadian aid and developmental capital available through two Canadian federal agencies, the Export Development Corporation and the Canadian Industrial Development Agency (see appendix tables).

In 1974, Canada's exports to the western hemisphere (minus the United States) reached a record $1.4 billion.[17] This was twice the amount exported in 1970, the year of the foreign policy white paper, and well in excess of the $431 million exported in 1965. Also, in 1974, total Canadian exports to the United States, by far Canada's largest trading partner, were $20.6 billion. The increases in import figures were somewhat less significant. The large jump from the $751 million imported from South American countries in 1973 to $1.6 billion the next year reflects the record increases in the prices of Venezuelan crude oil and distillates, which account for about 55 percent of the oil imported by the province of Quebec and the large Montreal industrial complex. Canadian imports of manufactured goods from complementary Latin American economies, such as Brazil, Mexico, and Argentina, are still low, although car parts made in the Brazilian branch plants of American automakers are currently being exported for assembly in the Canadian plants of the same manufacturers.

Nevertheless, the historic pattern (Canada's exports going predominantly to the Commonwealth Caribbean) has been broken, and four Latin American countries are becoming Canada's major trading partners in the hemisphere (after the United States). Table 4.1 indicates the increase in trade with these four countries between 1973 and 1974.

TABLE 4.1

Canadian Exports to Latin America
(millions of dollars)

Country	Exports 1973	Exports 1974
Brazil	112.2	393.4
Cuba	81.8	144.7
Mexico	118.5	187.1
Venezuela	129.8	203.6

Source: Annual Surveys of Exports (Imports) 1965-1974, Statistics Canada, Ottawa, 1975.

The Canadian government also appears to be engaging in its own brand of export substitution by attempting to cut into some traditional U.S. export markets in Latin America where Canadian products, for example, rail and air transport equipment, are highly competitive with the American product in both performance and price. Alastair Gillespie, the former Canadian industry, trade, and commerce minister who led the three successful Canadian trade missions to Latin America in 1973-75, himself a former Toronto industrialist, is reticent to state publicly that this is a Canadian export goal. Nevertheless, when the Canadian industry minister "hopes" for a $1 billion Brazil-Canada trade pattern by about 1985, it is clear that Canada wants a larger share of the export business that traditionally has been dominated by the close U.S.-Brazilian connection, a north-south, minimilitary-industrial complex if you will, based on World War II agreements of Brazilian lend-lease bases in exchange for American financial assistance to emerging industry.[18]

The Canadians are not averse to selling military equipment to the Brazilians, having had considerable success already in sales of STOL (Short Take-Off Landing) aircraft for infrastructure uses by the Brazilian air force in the Amazon regions. During Gillespie's mission to Venezuela in 1975, a spokesman admitted that the Venezuelan economy is a hard nut to crack, given the number of U.S. branch plants already established there and the extent of American technology already available. Robert L. Grassby, president of MLW-Worthington Ltd. of Montreal, itself a former subsidiary of Worthington Industries in the United States, said Canadian firms like his are "starting from square one" in Venezuela, "riding head on against entrenched American interests here." Nevertheless Grassby's firm (whose sale of thirty locomotives to the Cuban state railways, technically in violation of the U.S. Trading with the Enemy Act, raised a storm in U.S.-Canada relations in 1974) was prepared to bid on both a $50-million locomotive requirement in Venezuela and on new diesel engines for the Venezuelan navy. A. R. McCougan, meanwhile, a vice-president of the Canadian newsprint and pulp giant MacMillan Bloedel Ltd., saw great opportunities in the technical areas in which Canadians claim superiority over Americans, such as pulp and paper and hydropower technology. Since the rich Venezuelans propose to develop an integrated pulp and paper industry, Canadian paper technology will be very welcome.

The Canada-Mexico trade relationship is, in many ways, even more intimate, given the problem shared by these two countries of defining their economic sovereignty in relation to the neighboring U.S. industrial colossus. Indeed, one of the many reciprocal Latin American trade missions that came to Canada in the 1970s was a major Mexican trade delegation that arrived in May 1972 under the Mexican minister of foreign trade. One of its main purposes (which it largely accomplished) was to seek Canadian government support in ending the transshipment of Mexican fresh produce bound for Canadian food terminals into U.S. truck transports at the Texas border.[19] Canadian transportation technology, a very popular commodity in Latin America these days, is the basis for a $200-million "package" of railway cars, steel rails, and railway shop modernization to be supplied by a consortium of Canadian firms in railway transport equipment manufacture to meet the long-range modernization plans of the Ferrocarriles Nacionales de Mexico (the Mexican state railways).

Mexican president Luis Echeverria included Canada in his 1973 world tour, and visited several Canadian cities between March 29 and April 2. But chiefly he came to inspect at first hand the world's largest commercial nuclear reactor at Pickering, Ontario, about twenty-five miles east of Toronto, designed from independent Canadian nuclear research relying on heavy water reactors and operated by the Ontario Hydro Electric Power Commission, a provincial crown corporation. The day he visited the plant, President Echeverria made a speech in Toronto about the danger of technological transfers becoming masters, not servants, to an emerging nation. This was a clear reference to the political strings he believes are attached to any deal to buy U.S. nuclear know-how. Instead, nuclear technology, developed independently of the United States by a friendly middle power in the Americas, appealed to him. Presumably, he also investigated the cost of duplicating in Mexico the proposed nuclear power capability of Ontario Hydro, a staggering $4 billion.

The Canadian industrial presence in Brazil is matched by an emerging Brazilian presence in Canada. In the spring of 1974 an important private mission of Sao Paulo industrialists visited eastern Canada and in December 1973 the Brazil-Canada Information Centre was opened in Toronto (a parallel office was recently opened in Sao Paulo). The growing Canadian involvement in the centrally planned Marxist economy of Cuba is analyzed elsewhere in this chapter. But there are clear indications that Cuba will be one of Canada's largest Latin American customers as a result of an unusual chain of international political and economic events from which Canadian exporters of many kinds are benefiting.

Michael Morris, an American specialist on Canadian foreign policy, writes:

> When Prime Minister Trudeau announced the appointment of E. A. Ritchie, an economist by profession, as Under Secretary of State for External Affairs in early 1970, he remarked that the Department [Canada's foreign ministry] would emphasize "trade and commerce" rather than the "political and metaphysical aspects of foreign policy." . . . This orientation finds expression as well . . . in the dispatch of high-level trade missions to Latin America.[20]

CANADIAN-BASED MULTINATIONAL COMPANIES

This Canadian trade and export push is helped undoubtedly by the fact that several Canadian-based multinational companies are already well established in Latin America. In the Dominican Republic, the lateritic nickel mining operations of Falconbridge Dominicana at Bonao is the second largest producing facility in that nation after the state-dominated sugar industry.

The foremost example, however, is, of course, Brascan Ltd., a $2 billion holding company with head offices in Toronto. Before the change of corporate name in June 1969, Brascan was known as Brazilian Light and Power Ltd. and before that as Brazilian Traction Light and Power. It was incorporated under the laws of Canada in 1912 from several antecedent power, utility, and urban transport companies formed in Brazil by turn-of-the-century Canadian entrepreneurs.

In addition to the considerable Canadian interests it has acquired in the last few years in brewing, food, and Arctic oil and gas explorations, Brascan remains Brazil's second largest foreign-owned corporation and has expanded from its still-profitable utilities services into food processing, development banking, transport equipment manufacture, and general investments in real estate. Brascan also holds a 35 percent interest in the Fabrica Nacional de Vagoes (FNV), the only remaining privately owned manufacturer of railway rolling stock in Latin America.

In early 1975, Brascan Ltd. completed a financial coup in Latin America (where multinational corporations are more often nationalized than assisted financially) by raising a $100-million loan without the assistance of world equity markets or the multilateral funding agencies. *Business Week* reported that "the catalyst for the loan was a Brazilian government guarantee, one of the very few ever granted to a foreign company in Latin America."[21] With gross assets of $1.9 billion and profits in 1974 of $119 million, the company obtained the backing of twenty banks, three of them Arab, in a five-year floating rate Eurodollar loan. What's more, Brascan announced in June 1975 that the loan was "only an initial step" in its plans for massive expansion and diversification in the Brazilian economy for the rest of the seventies.

TRUDEAU'S "THIRD OPTION"

The official Canadian position is that both the capitalistic economy of Brazil and Castro's Marxist Cuba, although bitter ideological enemies, are equally good business prospects for Canada with its changing trade policy. Prime Minister Trudeau has increased the thrust of his foreign policy review proposals of 1970 with his proposed "third option" for Canadian foreign trade. The expression emerged from a policy paper written for Trudeau during the 1972 Canadian federal election, which cloaked the real meaning of his policy in such phrases as giving Canadian foreign trade policy "a comprehensive long-term strategy" and "reducing Canadian vulnerability."[22]

The name of Trudeau's game is the reduction of Canada's reliance on the American export market. And the prime minister defines his three options as follows: (1) maintain the status quo with the United States in trade; (2) make Canada even more reliant on the U.S. market (politically impossible in a country where economic nationalism is rising); or (3) diversify trade with the European Common Market, Japan, China, and the Third World. The place of Latin American markets in Trudeau's third option is obvious. The prime minister's critics suggest that Trudeau's trade diversification is identical to that unsuccessfully attempted by prime ministers in the 1950s and 1960s, and that he is only restating the old and so far unresolved trade problem in his own more confusing behavioral language.

WHEN POLITICS AND TRADE DO MIX

The global energy crisis during 1973-75 and growing economic nationalism in Canada have compelled the Canadian government to investigate and initiate, if not necessarily duplicate, Latin American models for controlling foreign-owned oil industry and branch plants.

In October 1973, Hugo Perez la Salvia, the former Venezuelan minister of hydrocarbons, made clear to visiting Canadian energy minister Donald Macdonald (the first senior Canadian cabinet minister to visit Caracas since 1953) that Venezuela would prefer to deal with Canada on international oil negotiations concerning supply through an agency of the Canadian government similar to the Venezuelan Corporacion Venezolana de Petroleo (CVP), Venezuelan Petroleum Corporation. Not only are Canada and Venezuela the two remaining oil-producing nations in the hemisphere where foreign-owned oil corporations dominate the industry, but about 55 percent of the crude oil used by eastern Canada and the Montreal industrial complex is imported Venezuelan crude. Foreign ownership of the Venezuelan oil industry ended during the summer of 1975 with the passage of a complex oil nationalization bill by the Venezuelan congress. The Accion Democratica party, reelected in the presidential election of December 1973, had promised to advance the date for oil nationalization from the previously planned deadline of 1983. The CVP's participation in integrated petroleum industry operations is small compared to that of the dominant foreign-owned giants, Shell de Venezuela and Creole Petroleum, but it will soon dominate the Venezuelan retail oil and gas industry.

In Canada, where Shell and Exxon (called Imperial Oil Ltd.) have the same major roles in the oil industry as in Venezuela, there will be no nationalization of oil. But there is a new Canadian state oil corporation called Petro-Canada whose formation received parliamentary approval on July 11, 1975 after a lengthy debate. Petro-Canada will meet the requirement of Venezuela for government-to-government negotiation on oil imports, as well as the growing demand by Canadian nationalists that Canada, too, take meaningful measures to control the foreign-owned multinational oil companies that dominate about 70 percent of the Canadian domestic oil and gas industries.

Petro-Canada will be a crown corporation of the type that has intervened in private industry where the political climate has demanded it, or where the private sector has not participated in economic growth.*

Other crown corporations include Air Canada, the government-owned international airline formed during the depression as Trans Canada Airlines when Canada's private aviation industry, in its infancy, was hit hard by the economic slump; Canadian National Railways, formed from the merger in 1920 of bankrupt transcontinental railroads hastily built but undercapitalized during the immigration booms at the turn of the century; and the very recent Canada Development Corporation (CDC). The CDC is an agency for the state's investment and for public participation in purchasing industries that Parliament deems should remain under Canadian control. The CDC functions similarly to Mexico's much more manipulative Nacional Financiera, founded in 1933 originally as an agrarian credit bank.

However, the use of the crown corporation formula has been noticeably absent from the largely foreign-owned Canadian oil and gas industries until now. And, although the former minister of energy Donald S. MacDonald, now Canada's finance minister, insisted that the concept of a Canadian state oil corporation predated his hasty visit to Caracas in October 1973, the similarity of the functions of Petro-Canada to those of the present CVP in Venezuela worries the Canadian petroleum industry. This is especially revealing in a country that once

---

*The royal, or crown, corporation is not alien to Hispanic America, being the major monopolistic vehicle the crown of Spain used to control and develop extractive and limited manufacturing industries in colonial America. The modern Canadian crown corporation, by comparison, functions very much like a modern private company and rarely has a state monopoly over its appropriate fabricating or regulatory field.

shunned Latin American formulas for controlling the foreign-dominated extractive industries.

Petro-Canada has the authority under the act creating it to conduct international oil purchase negotiations for Canada, which the Venezuelans insisted before its establishment could only be done between state oil agencies. Petro-Canada may participate in so-called frontier region oil exploration and extraction, and possibly could build a small tanker fleet if future oil discoveries in remote Arctic locales, such as Ellesmere Island, justify such state-supported sea transport. Venezuela's CVP now operates a modest tanker fleet that it hopes to expand. This offers the possibility for an interesting Canada-Venezuela trade quid pro quo, since the Canadian shipyards that would build new tankers for the future Petro-Canada are interested in bidding on the new tanker fleet proposed by the Venezuelan government.

CANADIAN VIEWS ON FOREIGN-OWNED INDUSTRY

In spite of growing interest in Canada in Mexico's long experience in the control and takeover of foreign investment and industries, and the publication of several serious studies of the Mexican record, there is little public proof that Mexican models have been applied by Ottawa in the formation of the CDC or of a Foreign Investment Review Agency (FIRA) that rules on the sales and takeovers of foreign-owned branch plants.[23] An important investigation of the Mexican experience in local ownership and control was published by two Canadian academics, receiving wide notice and comment in appropriate government and industrial circles in Canada in the early 1970s. Yet the conclusions of this study are not based on a major empirical analysis of the Mexican experience.

But Canadian government policy affecting foreign ownership and control of extractive industries and branch plants has been influenced by the earlier academic studies of a small, active, and very articulate community of Canadian scholars. Three of them, Abraham Rotstein and Mel Watkins, both of the University of Toronto, and the late Steven Hymer, a Canadian who had a short but impressive career at Yale University, were employed in 1966 by the Honorable Walter Gordon, former minister without portfolio and president of the privy council in the Pearson government and Canada's best-known economic nationalist, to prepare a major government study on the status of foreign-owned industries in Canada and to recommend measures to control them.[24]

The interventionist proposals of Gordon and his team, although mild by Latin American standards, were too extreme for the continentalist-minded liberal party with its historic and influential connections among Canada's corporate elite. But they were not too controversial to sink Gordon's ideals of a state development corporation to buy out some existing foreign-dominated industries as prescribed. Admittedly, the CDC did not surface as a crown corporation approved by Parliament until the early 1970s, even though Gordon had placed it on the order paper for passage in the House of Commons as early as 1963.

Since 1966, Watkins has supported extreme socialist ideas, advocating a total takeover of foreign enterprises in Canada, not unlike Fidel Castro's "solution" for Cuba's foreign-controlled industries in 1959-60. Rotstein has remained a moderate, and has helped raise the level of the discussion of economic nationalism.[25] The colorful titles of two of Rotstein's delightfully written books say much about their subject, which has become increasingly popular in Canada in the mid-1970s: Getting It Back and The Precarious Homestead (Canada, of course!).

THE CUBAN CONNECTION

At first glance, Canada's very quickly growing trade and technological assistance connection with Cuba appears to be a side benefit of the long American blockade, one that will quickly wither away when the "natural" Cuban market for U.S. goods and services and the "natural" U.S. market for Cuban sugar are again available to one another. Such a judgment, however, is totally unrealistic. The pre-1959 laissez-faire Cuban market for U.S. goods and services was one of the many reasons for the revolution, and never will be restored, certainly not while the Soviet Union helps call the tune in Havana. The nonideological Canadians are a preferable alternative, with an economy based on the U.S.-style goods and services that are still in demand in Cuba, especially in high technology areas. Moreover, the conservative Canadians, in spite of themselves and their historic reticence to associate closely with Latins, have come a cropper, you might say, in their Cuban connection. Personal friendships are developing between Canadian company presidents, some of them tycoons, and the Marxist bureaucrats who are their customers in Cuba. Canadians clearly like the Cubans they deal with and the island in which they live, and the Fidel Castro technocrats reciprocate accordingly.

The Canada-Cuba trade and aid association appears to have just as many positive cultural benefits for Canada as well as commerical ones. Canadian trade relations with Cuba before Castro were perfunctory, the major trading items being bulk exports of Cuban sugar to Canada and of Canadian newsprint to Cuba. In the early 1950s Canada imposed a tariff against imports of Cuban refined sugar, which was competing with the output of the few, closely integrated Canadian sugar refineries. But Castro's revolutionary regime's need to find substitute markets in which to procure about 70 percent of its finished products, consumer goods, capital equipment, and transport facilities, which had previously come from the United States and had been cut off by the 1961 blockade, was an opportunity for Canada. The close association began with a typical misreading of developments in a Latin American country by a prominent Canadian. This time it was the Honorable George Hees, former minister of trade and commerce in Diefenbaker's conservative government, who said of the first trade delegation to Canada from Castro's Cuba, "you can't do business with better businessmen anywhere!"[26] The Cuban visitors were hardly "businessmen": 1960 was not only the second year of the revolution but the year in which all major U.S. and other foreign-owned businesses in Cuba were nationalized and the flood of real Cuban businessmen into exile began. They were revolutionaries, of course, and included Regino Boti, Cuban economist and faithful follower of Fidel. Son of one of Cuba's classic poets from Guantanamo, Boti arrived as Cuban minister of economics, the head of the three ministerial missions (among the many others) Cuba would send to Canada in the period 1960-75.

The 1960 visit began a Canadian-Cuban trade relationship that has become a phenomenon in Canadian export development. It is quite free of political commitment on either side, but rather emphasizes the pragmatic partnership of a centrally planned Marxist economy and a Western industrial capitalist one. For Canada, with its determination to augment trade with Latin America, the Cuban outlet means another market for selling goods and services, one which Canadian industry minister Alastair Gillespie, during his Cuban trade mission in mid-March 1975, estimated could reach $400 million by 1980 from the $144.7 million in exports in 1974 (see Appendix Table 4.B). It began with the agribusiness needs of the Cuban farm economy in the early 1960s, which led to the development of a new strain of Cuban cattle, partly native Cebu, partly Canadian Holstein Friesian. It has since expanded into such planned capital goods exports as diesel locomotives for the Cuban state railways and three coastal tankers, Canada's contribution to date to a major Cuban global ship-purchasing program through its Ministry of the Merchant Fleet.

IMPLICATIONS FOR THE UNITED STATES

At the same time, growing economic nationalism in Canada had received an unexpected boost from the many wrangles between Ottawa and Washington over sales to Cuba by U.S. branch plants in Canada. These sales are technically still in violation of the U.S. Trading with the Enemy Act, which makes it illegal for U.S. companies and their foreign branch plants to do business under certain conditions with Cuba, even though the U.S. government announced an end to the ban on trade with Cuba in late August 1975.

If licenses of approval to do so are not obtained from the State Department and any efforts are made to export either strategic materials or U.S.-originated technology to Cuba, the prohibitions on Cuban trade allowed in the act will continue to be applied.

Canada has always viewed the legislation as extraterritorial, not enforceable in Canada and an infringement of its sovereignty. The official Canadian response to the easing of the ban, expressed by Alastair Gillespie, not known to be an economic nationalist, continued to be critical. In an interview for the Miami Herald, August 24, 1975, Gillespie, who now heads the powerful Energy Ministry, said, "the U.S. move is a most welcome one, clearly an improvement from Canada's point-of-view." But he still saw the lingering restrictions as, ". . . an intolerable interference in Canadian affairs."

In Canada, test cases of the Trading with the Enemy Act had not resulted in threats of punitive action from Washington. The possible prevention of the sale of thirty new diesel locomotives and of the overhaul of the old ones, all originally U.S.-built, for the Cuban state railways by MLW Worthington Ltd. of Montreal brought a public promise from Prime Minister Trudeau that the sale would go through. The American government apparently did not make an issue of the prime minister's position, and the National Bank of Cuba later signed an agreement for credits with Canada's Export Development Corporation in Ottawa in the fall of 1974.

THE GILLESPIE MISSION, 1975

One of Canada's most successful trade missions to Latin America was that of Industry Minister Alastair Gillespie to Cuba on March 19-24, 1975. It began in Havana with the signing of an agreement for $200 million in credits (which must be applied for by the Cubans within one year), half of the amount to come from Canada's Export Development Corporation, whose own capitalization for such activities has been greatly increased, and half in standby by Canada's private banking system.

The approximately fifty Canadian industrialists in this trade mission included senior executives from hydropower companies, transport equipment manufacturers (STOL aircraft and diesel engines), pulp and paper engineers, agribusiness representatives, and port development consultants. The pulp and paper representatives were interested in ongoing Cuban experiments to develop bagasse (bagazo) as a raw material in the production of newsprint, and offered the Cubans their immediate technical assistance. After more than twenty years of experimentation, the Cubans have not been able to manufacture newsprint from the short-fibered bagasse, which is produced annually in the millions of tons as the chief residue from the grinding of sugarcane.

Some of the visiting Canadian industrialists, well known at home for their public denunciations of "creeping socialism" in the Canadian economy, had found out they could do business very well with Cuba's Marxist technocratic elite. What's more, the timing of the mission was excellent for Canada, with Cuba about to launch a five-year plan (1976-80) in which Cuban President Osvaldo Dorticos promised the former Canadian industry minister that his country would have a growing role.

In referring to the growing Canada-Cuba trade and aid pattern, unbroken since the revolution, Cuban Vice Prime Minister Carlos Rafael Rodriquez, in charge of Castro's program for technological imports, told the visiting Canadians and their minister, "Canada was one of the few countries which took a firm stand in favor of freedom of commerce while others discussed the blockade. This position based on principles of international obligations, we shall not forget."*

Gillespie's trade mission of early 1975 bore later fruit during the same year in the formation of a permanent Cuba-Canada Ministerial Committee, which had been announced during his visit to Havana. Its first meeting was held in Ottawa during the visit of one of the largest trade missions sent by Cuba to an hemispheric trading partner, September 23-26, 1975.

The ministerial committee concept permits cabinet ministers of the two nations involved and their accompanying senior officials to meet on common goals and problems in trade development and technological exchange at a time and place agreed to by both partners. Canada already has two other such ministerial committees formed with Mexico in 1970 and the Soviet Union in 1971.

Carlos Rafael Rodriquez, Cuban Vice Prime Minister, was in charge of the Cuban mission of about thirty-five representatives. It included the minister of industrial development, four vice ministers, and the chiefs or deputy chiefs of state agencies concerned with foreign trade, forestry, tourism, port development, rail and air transport.

This Canada-Cuba trade relationship is an anomaly in Canada's foreign trade pattern that could make Cuba one of its largest continuing

---

*This was said at a meeting between Rodriquez and the Canadian trade delegation on March 21, 1975. Author in attendance.

trading partners in Latin America. It could conceivably make Fidel Castro's Havana a more likely venue for Trudeau's "third option" than the rich but disinterested trading centers of the European Common Market that he visited at about the time of the trade talks with Cuba in search of what he has called "a contractual link" between Europe and Canada.

MULTILATERAL ASSOCIATIONS

While Canada's diplomatic posts in the hemisphere were multiplied and enlarged during the 1950s and 1960s, successive Canadian prime ministers and foreign ministers continued to express cautious opposition to full Canadian membership in hemispheric multilateral structures. Ambivalence appeared to be the official Canadian posture toward the Americas from the 1940s through the early 1960s. But it only mirrored the view expressed in 1948 by Vincent Massey, the creme de la creme of old-school Canadian diplomacy, that Canada should "cultivate good relations with Latin America in our own way and not as a cog of the Pan American machine."[27]

The change came in the mid-1960s, partly as a result of persistent and friendly invitations from many prominent and influential Latin American leaders to participate more directly in the hemisphere through the Pan-American Union, then the OAS, and the Inter-American Development Bank (IADB), and partly by the implementation of global foreign aid and technical assistance policies for Canada under Lester Pearson.

One of these invitations was extended in 1969 by Felipe Herrera, president of the IADB, who was the keynote speaker at the sixty-ninth annual general meeting of the Canadian Manufacturers Association. Herrera proposed to an audience of Canadian industrialists that Canada explore "new forms of cooperation with Latin America," including the possibility of establishing a "more permanent and a more institutionalized association" with the bank; in other words, that Canada join in the IADB.[28] Herrera's invitation was still three years before Canada's formal entry into full membership in the IADB. It came eight years after Canada had made its first contributions to the bank as a nonmember and twelve years after this important agency had been formed to assist Latin American member states in infrastructure and social-sector development.

On joining the bank in May 1972, Canada agreed to subscribe a total of $242.68 million to the bank's ordinary capital resources, $40 million to the paid-in side, $202.68 million to the callable capital, and to contribute a further $60 million to the fund for special operations.

On March 27, 1974, the Canadian government and the IADB agreed to the administration of a special fund of $1.5 million Canadian dollars. It will finance the preparation of development projects, including basic feasibility studies and final engineering design in IADB's Latin American member countries.[29]

Canada's future participation in Latin American development will continue to be governed by both the roadblock of historic and diplomatic restraints, even though Canada now has fourteen missions in the hemisphere, as much as by the new contacts and positive trade drives it has made officially and privately in the region.* Where OAS membership is concerned, the political disadvantages outlined earlier will undoubtedly prevail, given the ongoing internal difficulties of the OAS and the reported efforts of Venezuela, Cuba, and Mexico to form a countervailing organization in the Caribbean area. Official Canadian statements about OAS membership, however, continue to express vague and noncommittal interest. Klaus Goldschlag, former director general of the Western Hemisphere Bureau of the Canadian Department of External Affairs, now in another senior diplomatic post, rephrased the traditional Canadian reticence about full OAS membership at the third conference of the Canadian Association for Latin America on October 18, 1972 in Toronto: "Canadian membership in the OAS is not, however, foreclosed."

Canada's formula for involvement with the OAS through the establishment of a permanent observer's office in 1972 will probably be a semipermanent arrangement.

In 1969, Canadian private companies with major Latin American interests or business responded to the Trudeau initiative in foreign policy and trade diversification by forming their own association, the prestigious Canadian Association for Latin America (CALA), with Michael Lubbock as managing director. Lubbock, a former managing director of the Peruvian state railways and a former director of the Bank of London and South America, is thoroughly experienced in Latin American affairs, and has tripled the corporate membership of CALA since its founding. CALA was largely the brainchild of Grant Glassco, an ex-president of Brazilian Light and Power, and of his successor the Honorable Robert Winters, a cabinet minister in the liberal administration of Louis St. Laurent, one of Canada's outstanding executives and business executives. He, too, was president of Brascan Ltd. at one time.

---

*Canada's fourteen Latin American trade missions include the official observer to the OAS (with the rank of ambassador) and two consulates in Brazil in addition to the Canadian Embassy in Brasilia.

CALA's annual conferences, especially the last one, CALA IV, held in Toronto, have brought together large numbers of senior Latin American and Canadian executives from the public and private sectors for the first time. Its membership has expanded from the obvious giant firms with major hemispheric interest (the Aluminum Company of Canada, Massey Ferguson, and so on) to include smaller Canadian firms in export industries, metalworking, management consulting, mining, transport, food processing, and machinery. CALA now has 114 corporate members.

In the Canadian academic world, a parallel organization with strong Latin American contacts is the Canadian Association for Latin American Studies (CALAS), formed in Toronto at York University in June 1970. Although almost all its members are academics specializing in mainly nonbusiness disciplines, CALAS members include many academics who have worked as consultants to government and industry in the Americas. For them, personal cross-referencing with CALA's corporate members and their management has been mutually useful.

NATIONALISM IN THE CARIBBEAN

During the 1970s, Canadian banks and private industry in the Caribbean have felt the chill winds of nationalism and have experienced attacks all too familiar to U.S. private enterprise in Latin America. West Indian nationalists are more concerned with the "Canadian Empire" than the more familiar American whipping boy, and point to the dominant role in some of their nations of Canadian banks and extractive industries.

No one knows the exact net worth of total Canadian private interests in the Commonwealth Caribbean, since this includes real estate and land properties held throughout the islands by individual Canadian citizens. The Standing Committee on Foreign Affairs of the Senate of Canada conducted a thorough investigation of all Canadian relationships in the Commonwealth Caribbean, and concluded that Canadian private investment in the region stood at about $500 million at the time of their review in 1969-70.[30]

This excellent study by the Canadian Senate also reported on Canada's extensive activities in nonbusiness areas, including the churches, youth groups, university cooperation, and the activities of the Canadian University Service Overseas (CUSO), and of Canada's large aid agency, Canadian International Development Agency (CIDA).

At the beginning of the decade, restrictive local banking laws were passed against Canadian private enterprise. In Trinidad and

Tobago, following riots against Canadian banks in 1970, the National Bank of Trinidad and Tobago was formed from the Bank of London and the Bank of Montreal operations in that country, one third of which had been owned by the Bank of Montreal. Other restrictive measures against the banks are underway in Guyana and the Bahamas.

In 1974, Prime Minister Michael Manley of Jamaica sharply shifted the formula for royalty and tax payments on bauxite exports by all the major producers, American as well as Canadian, to help solve his growing balance-of-payments crisis, aggravated by mounting crude oil prices. The new payment arrangement, estimated on the price of the finished product, changed the formula from the basis of tonnage of bauxite extracted to aluminum ingot. This has meant that all bauxite-producing companies in Jamaica have had to maintain production levels set by the government. As a result, tax payments by the companies have jumped from $80 million to about $200 million. More local control was to come in early 1975 for the American-owned bauxite firms, which, unlike Canadian-owned firms, were not incorporated as Jamaican firms, when the Jamaican government assumed a 51 percent controlling interest in them. Negotiations for an increase from the present minority Jamaican interest in the Canadian firms to 51 percent control are underway.[31]

The big bauxite producers, who account for 60 percent of Jamaica's bauxite exports, are convinced that Jamaica is set on a socialist course not unlike the more intensive one in Guyana, where the Aluminum Company of Canada, also operating in Jamaica, was unable to work out a joint-venture agreement with the Guyanese government. The result was the nationalization in 1971 of its subsidiary, Demarara Bauxite Company, which became the basis of GuyBau, the Guyanese State Bauxite Corporation. In 1974, Guyana also nationalized the local operations of Reynolds Metal Company, a major American bauxite producer.

CONCLUSION

In the future, Canada will continue to become more prominent in the hemisphere, largely in trade and development assistance, with diplomatic activity remaining at a minimum. Membership in the IADB will continue to satisfy both altruistic and business-seeking urges: Canadians will be "helping out" in a needy part of the world (mainly through the bank's strong socially oriented projects), and they will be helping themselves.

Attacks on the "sordidness" of "tied aid" as an aspect of development assistance have never reached a crescendo in Canada, probably because regional economic development financing has been used to persuade industry to settle in Canada's own remote regions, through both federal and provincial government incentive schemes during the 1960s and 1970s.[32] Canada's role in the IADB could almost be seen as an extension of its domestic experience in finding the funds and resources to develop its own substantial frontier regions. On the other hand, one wonders whether Canada's Arctic and far north, one third of its national territory (equivalent in size to Brazil's Amazon or Venezuela's Guyana region), would have been developed more rapidly if a Brazilian or Venezuelan ethic of forced-draft growth had been applied. Inuvik is a Canadian-government-built Arctic town of about 3,000 and the prospective place of departure for the $8 billion Canadian Arctic Gas Pipeline, which, if it is built, will be the largest single industrial project in North American history. The mayor of Inuvik is already complaining about the day close at hand when the population might grow to 25,000, too much for his town to bear, but a good deal less than the 250,000 and more who live in each of the forty frontier urban communities in Brazil.

A. R. M. Lower, Canada's most acerbic historian, reminds Canadians how often their national decisions have been made "around the parish pump," the result of too much old-country methodism in the English colonial system. Bookkeepers do not build Brasilias. Canadians may have a strong aversion to the emotional ideological pronouncements of Latin American leaders about "extending the national will" or defining "national consciousness," but back at home much discussion and government legislation these days are centered around defining once and for all the "Canadian national identity." The CDC and the extension of the newly formed FIRA—all vehicles of a kind familiar to Latin American economic nationalists—are manifestations of this mood.

Because Canada has chosen to increase its involvement in the hemisphere slowly and selectively, Canadians can scarcely show annoyance when an unctuous senior OAS official involved with Canadian negotiations for permanent observer status calls them, "cautious and unadventurous, but on the whole progressive and reliable. . . ."[33] A few years ago, John W. Holmes, director general of the Canadian Institute of International Affairs and a former senior Canadian diplomat, observed about Canada's growing hemispheric awareness that because Canada is situated in the same hemisphere as the Isthmus of Panama, she shouldn't develop "a sense of sanctity" about it.[34] Sanctity, indeed not. But a Canadian identification with our common hemisphere, yes.

TABLE 4.A

Dominican Banking Order

Rank	Bank	Net Assets ($ millions)
1	Banco de Reservas (Dominican-government-supported bank in commercial banking activities)	317.0
2	Royal Bank of Canada (Canadian)	153.6
3	Banco Popular Dominicano C por A (Dominican)	106.8
4	Chase Manhattan Bank (American)	51.8
5	Bank of Nova Scotia (Canadian)	40.3
6	Bank of America (American)	26.1
7	Banco Condal (Spanish)	14.6
8	Banco de Santo Domingo S.A. (Puerto Rican minority interest)	7.6

Source: John D. Harbron, "Chill Grows Colder in Caribbean," *Financial Post* (Toronto), 17 August 1974, pp. 4-5.

TABLE 4.B

Canadian Exports to Cuba, 1970-75
(millions of Canadian dollars)

1974	1973	1972	1971	1970
142,474	81,871	57,613	58,823	58,900

Source: Annual Surveys of Exports (Imports) 1965-74, *Statistics Canada*, Ottawa, 1975.

TABLE 4.C

Survey of Exports, 1965-74
(hundreds of millions of Canadian dollars)

	1965	1966	1967	1968	1969	1970	1971	1972	1973	1974
South America	191,922	232,512	233,416	281,628	291,495	374,184	384,366	404,075	379,671	787,895
Central America and Antilles	238,329	259,856	245,198	257,826	292,375	387,079	349,809	369,282	445,699	611,236
Total	430,251	492,368	478,614	539,454	583,860	761,263	734,175	773,357	825,370	1,399,131

<u>Source:</u> Annual Surveys of Exports (Imports) 1965-74, <u>Statistics Canada</u>, Ottawa, 1975.

TABLE 4.D

Survey of Imports, 1965-74
(hundreds of millions of Canadian dollars)

	1965	1966	1967	1968	1969	1970	1971	1972	1973	1974
South America	364,832	319,041	377,487	465,559	466,322	476,892	530,116	565,418	751,402	1,595,602
Central America and Antilles	183,185	183,557	204,034	215,876	247,397	213,787	224,634	222,279	287,487	418,619
Total	548,017	502,598	581,521	681,435	713,719	690,679	757,750	787,697	1,029,889	2,014,321

<u>Source:</u> Annual Surveys of Exports (Imports) 1965-74, <u>Statistics Canada</u>, Ottawa, 1975.

TABLE 4.E

Export Development Corporation
(millions of dollars)

Country	Amount
South America	
Argentina	184,863
Bolivia	4,200
Brazil	172,666
Chile	33,742
Colombia	3,434
Peru	72,853
Venezuela	28,485
Total	500,243
Central America and Antilles	
Bahamas	17,091
Barbados	8,357
Cuba	41,910
Dominican Republic	25,933
Guatemala	17,250
Guyana	5,200
Honduras	1,500
Jamaica	29,433
Mexico	201,460
Panama	43,500
Total	391,634
Grand Total	891,877

Note: Analysis by country of financing agreements and guarantees signed from 1961 to 1974. (Canadian dollars, million)

Source: Annual Report, Export Development Corporation, 1974, p. 16 (compiled from global total).

TABLE 4.F

Canadian International Development Agency
(millions of dollars)

Country	Amount
South America	
Argentina	756
Bolivia	1,620
Brazil	10,167
Chile	10,357
Colombia	1,080
Ecuador	12,956
Paraguay	800
Peru	540
Total	60,948
Central America and Antilles	
Dominican Republic	7,474
El Salvador	3,240
Mexico	540
Nicaragua	1,900
Total	15,154
Grand Total	76,102

Note: Historical record of loans to Latin America from 1961 to 1974 (Canadian dollars, million).

Source: "Historical Record of Loans, Latin America," vol. 7 (Ottawa: Bilateral Division, Canadian International Development Agency, 1975), pp. 6-41.

NOTES

1. Richard A. Preston, "American Plans for the Invasion of Canada," Canadian Defence Quarterly 3, no. 4 (Spring 1974), pp. 46-48.

2. Maurice Matloff, "The American Approaches to War," in Theory and Practice of War, ed. Michael Howard (New York: Praeger, 1967), p. 218.

3. Preston, op. cit., 47.

4. The FLQ's association with Castro's Cuba and involvement in the former Cuban hemispheric guerrilla training school, Escuela Minas Rio Frio, were well known and documented during the mid-1960s. See John D. Harbron, "Quebec's Guerrillas Learned How in Cuba," Miami Herald, October 14, 1970, p. 7-A.

5. Toronto Star, June 8, 1975. The Quebec film documentary Les Ordres, which won a Cannes International Film Festival Award in 1975 for its sharp attack on Canadian government methods used during the 1970 FLQ crisis, is in this revisionist trend.

6. Karl Levitt and Alister McIntyre, Canada-West Indies Relations (Montreal: Private Planning Association of Canada and Centre for Developing Studies, McGill University, 1966), p. 14.

7. Arthur R. M. Lower, Colony to Nation, a History of Canada (Toronto: Longmans Canada, 1948), p. 93.

8. J. C. M. Ogelsby, Gringos from the Far North: Essays in the History of Canadian-Latin American Relations (Toronto: Macmillan, forthcoming).

9. Twentieth Century Cuba (Garden City, N.Y.: Doubleday, 1966).

10. Vincent Massey, "North American or Pan American?" in On Being a Canadian (Toronto: J. M. Dent & Sons, 1948), p. 153.

11. The author's interview with former President Eduardo Frei Montalva of Chile in the Presidential Palace, Santiago de Chile, 30 July 1970, portions of which were broadcast by the International Service, Canadian Broadcasting Corporation, Montreal, September 1970.

12. John D. Harbron, Canada and the Organization of American States (Washington, D.C.: National Planning Association, 1963), p. 2.

13. El Dia, Mexico City, International Cable of UPI, January 27, 1972.

14. Mario Ojeda, "Latin America and Canada: Mutual Ignorance" (Paper delivered at the Conference on Canada, Latin America and U.S. Foreign Policy, Northwestern University, Evanston, Ill., February 17-20, 1972).

15. Prime Minister Trudeau's second major foreign policy statement before his election June 25, 1968 was entitled "Canada and the World," May 29, 1968, Canada, Department of External Affairs, Statements and Speeches, 68/17, Ottawa.

16. Preliminary Report of the Ministerial Mission to Latin America October 27-November 27, 1968. See especially, "IV: Impressions of the Mission, Some Future Possibilities, Political Affairs, Development Assistance, Trade and Economic Affairs," mimeographed (Ottawa: Department of External Affairs, 1968).

17. For all statistical data on Canadian exports and imports to Latin America, see Statistics Canada (Ottawa, 1975).

18. See John D. Harbron, "Brazil Is 'Buying Canadian,'" Miami Herald, October 29, 1974, opposite editorial page.

19. John D. Harbron, "Mexico Starts Big Effort Here to Sell Itself Industrially," Financial Post, June 3, 1972, p. 13.

20. Michael Morris, "Canadian Foreign Policy and Latin American Politics," unpublished paper, Foreign Policy Research Institute, Philadelphia, Pa., April 1973.

21. "A Financial Coup for Canada's Brascan," Business Week (June 16, 1975): 86, 88.

22. Special United States-Canadian Relations Policy (Ottawa: Department of External Affairs, October 1972).

23. I. A. Litvak and C. J. Maule, Foreign Investments in Mexico: Some Lessons for Canada, Behind the Headlines, vol. 30, nos. 5-6. (Toronto: Canadian Institute of International Affairs, July 1971).

24. Abraham Rotstein, Mel Watkins, and Steven Hymer, Report of the Task Force on the Structure of Canadian Industry (Ottawa: Privy Council, 1968).

25. Rotstein was an important Canadian contributor to the large Conferencia del Pacifico held at Vina del Mar at the end of the Eduardo Frei administration in Chile. His paper "Development and Dependence: The Canadian Problem" was later published in Spain in Estudios Internacionales, journal of the now defunct Instituto de Estudios Internacionales, Universidad de Chile. Other participants included Mexican economist Miguel Wionczek, Chilean economist Osvaldo Sunkel. See Latina vuelve al pacifico, Vina del Mar, Chile, September 27-October 3, 1970.

26. "Trade with Cuba," Canadian Annual Review (Toronto: University of Toronto Press, 1960), p. 137.

27. Massey, op. cit., p. 155.

28. News release from the Inter-American Development Bank, Washington, D.C., June 2, 1969.

29. Booklet, Canada and the Inter-American Development Bank, Washington, D.C., 1974.

30. Report on Canada-Caribbean Relations, Senate of Canada Standing Committee on Foreign Affairs, the Honorable John B. Aird, Q.C., Chairman, in English and French, Ottawa, 1970.

31. Marvin Howe, "Jamaica Trying to Create Her Own Brand of Socialism," New York Times, May 16, 1975.

32. For a general view of Canadian public- and private-sector developmental roles in the hemisphere, see John D. Harbron, "Canada in Caribbean America: Technique for Involvement," Journal of Inter-American Studies and World Affairs no. 4 (July 1970): 475-484.

33. Quoted in a paper read by John W. Holmes, Director-General, Canadian Institute of International Affairs, to the American Historical Association, December 1967.

34. Ibid.

CHAPTER

5

LATIN AMERICAN ECONOMIC RELATIONS WITH WESTERN EUROPE

Lawrence B. Krause

Economic relations between Latin America and Europe can only be understood within a worldwide context. A number of salient points must be kept in mind in this regard. The first is the ebbing of U.S. dominance over economic relations among the world's market economies. This was an inevitable development given the state of these economies after the Second World War. The extent of the change is often exaggerated, but it is real, nonetheless. Second, military security concerns in most parts of the world (with some obvious exceptions) have declined with the movement toward detente and nuclear stalemate between the superpowers. Third, there is growing recognition that the relations between rich and poor countries, the so-called north-south relations, will be the central focus of world politics in the near future and for some time to come. And fourth, some countries have already emerged or are now emerging from the status of developing countries and will have to be recognized as significant powers in their own right. These include such countries as Iran and Saudi Arabia, Nigeria and Zaire, Indonesia, Brazil, and Mexico.

The implications of these developments for Latin America are profound. They suggest that the Latin American countries will have the ability to follow through on their desire to promote all of their national interests through international economic relations.

The national interest goals being pursued by Latin American countries through their international economic relations are not confined to the promotion of economic welfare, although economic welfare

---

The views are those of the author and should not be attributed to the trustees, officers, or other staff members of the Brookings Institution.

remains of great importance. Economic welfare, furthermore, is no longer being considered as identical to increase in per capita national income. The other goals to be served include greater economic security, improved international status, and greater national independence. The desire for greater economic security can be traced at least as far back as the Great Depression and World War II when substantial economic insecurity was created for Latin America as a result of developments abroad.[1] The wish for an improvement in international status, understandable for any group of countries, is particularly poignant for Latin Americans because of their recognition that they were once more important on the world scene than they are today. The strong desire for greater national independence comes from the Latin American perception of the implications of the growing trend toward world interdependence, a subject to be explored later on.

Since they serve several goals simultaneously, international economic relations are not determined solely by what are sometimes called purely economic considerations; instead, these relations are politicized in the most profound sense of that term, that is, determined by the creation and distribution of power and the giving out of rewards and penalties among and within countries. Economic relations, then, are necessarily very complex. The several functional channels through which international relations take place, such as international trade, direct investment, international capital flows and aid, and the policies related to them, constantly overlap and interact rather than remain separate and confined. When it comes to the specific topic being considered here, it must be recognized that Europe is not a monolith, but a collection of countries with similar though somewhat different interests. And what is true of Europe is true in spades of Latin America.* Thus the economic relations between these two parts of the world are very complex indeed.

The very complexity of the international situation warns us that single-channeled or simple policies are unlikely to be responsive to the needs of nations. Furthermore, there will probably be little policy cohesion on the part of Latin America, that is, Latin Americans may well be seeking several policy outcomes that, from the point of view of Europe, will seem to be contradictory. The demand being made by many Latin American spokesmen (and others) for a new international economic order illustrates this point. Each spokesman has a somewhat different plan in mind when making the demand—a plan that may in fact be incompatible with all the others—but the demand is real and important and requires a responsible and sympathetic response. This com-

---

*In a short paper, little attention can be given to the diversity of country interests for which an apology is offered.

plexity may lead to confusion so great that the Latin Americans may believe they are practicing cooperative politics, while the Europeans may interpret the same actions as confrontation politics. Such confusion is undesirable, but probably unavoidable. What is required is a high degree of understanding and patience on both sides until some roots for a new economic relationship have been firmly established.

DEPENDENCIA

The world is becoming more interdependent. This can be observed in the figures for international trade, in the measures recording direct investment, in tests of perfection of capital markets (or lack of imperfections) and recorded flows of funds, and in figures for labor migration. Interdependence means that all countries are dependent on other countries, but there are differences of degree. Some countries such as the United States are dependent, but have a great deal of control over their external economic relations. The Latin Americans feel they are dependent and have no control.[2]

From one point of view, the Latin American countries' concern about dependence is surprising: By most statistical measures, they are less dependent on the international economy than many other areas. For instance, the ratios of exports and imports to gross national products are lower in Latin America than they typically are in Europe. The share of foreign ownership of natural resources is no higher in Latin America than in Canada and Australia, nor is that of manufacturing capacity any higher than in Canada, the United Kingdom, Germany, or possibly France; and Latin America is less dependent on inflows of foreign technology than Japan was a few years ago and Belgium is today.

Furthermore, Latin American countries are less dependent on world capital markets than are the United Kingdom and Italy (although Brazil is approaching those levels) and receive less concessionary aid than other developing countries in view of their relatively advanced state of development. (Compared to Africa and Asia, Latin America is an advanced area.) Moreover the labor markets of most Latin American countries have been less affected by the immigration and emigration of workers than have been those of Europe. (Some immigration has occurred into the southern part of Latin America from Japan and Europe and much emigration from the Caribbean and Central America to the United States.)

From another point of view, however, the Latin American countries' concern over their dependence is not surprising at all. The raw materials and traditional products that Latin America exports have their prices determined in world markets over which they have very little control. For most of the postwar period, they have seen their export prices decline relative to their import prices, and they have felt powerless to reverse this deterioration in their terms of trade. No wonder that the OPEC (Organization of Petroleum Exporting Countries) method of gaining control over prices is so attractive to them. Furthermore, the foreign firms with direct investments in Latin America do dominate the industries in which they operate (although not the entire economies). These are the most dynamic and promising industries for the future. There are few domestic firms with sufficient countervailing power to ensure that local interests are protected. It is this situation that causes Latin Americans to feel that they are too dependent on foreigners for technology and capital. As a result, Latin Americans have felt that they have been subjects of instruments rather than participants in the evolving interdependent world economy.[3]

While there are many dimensions to the economic relations between Latin America and Europe, attention will be directed primarily to international trade. Trade is the most important channel in quantitative terms and permits many of the nuances of the relationship to be examined. It is unlikely that an encyclopedic approach (covering direct investment, capital, aid, and so on) would change the major conclusions of this study, although it would add substantially to its bulk.

EUROPE LOOKS AT LATIN AMERICA

Europe is aware of Latin America, but just barely. Europe's attention span for Latin America and its problems is limited to brief periods of official visits and occasional special conferences. Latin America just isn't very high on the list of European political or economic priorities. The political interests of Europe have been absorbed elsewhere, especially with problems of internal integration and foreign relations with other areas. Recently, the oil crisis and unemployment have been more than enough to absorb all energies.

Europe does have a commercial interest in Latin America, but, as Table 5.1 shows, this interest is declining. In 1960 only 6 percent of European exports went to Latin America, down from around 8.5 percent in 1950. Furthermore, the drop continued, so that by 1970, Latin America absorbed 4 percent of European exports and only 3.3 percent in 1973. This same erosion of the Latin American position is seen in the figures relating the share of European imports coming from Latin America. The decline of Europe's trade relations with Latin America mirrors what has happened elsewhere in the world. In 1950, Latin America exports were 11 percent of world trade. That figure declined to 7.18 percent in 1960, 5.6 percent in 1970, and 4.5 percent in 1973. This suggests that if one wants to discover what caused the relative decline in commercial relations, Latin American variables might be more important than European ones.

When Europeans focus on their commercial relations with Latin America, they generally do find grounds for optimism.[4] First of all, they point to Europe's cultural and historical links with Latin America, in particular the Spanish and Portuguese heritage of most of the area and the important linguistic tie. Furthermore, Britain has had a long history of close commercial relations with Argentina and a few former colonial territories. Second, Europe embarked upon economic integration early in the postwar period and the Europeans believe some of the lessons they have learned can be usefully passed on to other areas. Indeed, the forming of the Latin American Free Trade Association (LAFTA) in 1960 is generally attributed in part to the earlier European example. Third, Europeans often view their economies as being complementary to those of Latin America and the two regions as natural trading partners. They are complementary not only in climate, geography, and natural resources base but also in stage of economic development: Latin America can provide tropical agricultural products, mineral raw materials, and traditional manufactures of a handicraft or labor-intensive nature in return for European advanced manufactures.

In reality, there is little substance to any of the three factors that supposedly promise an expansion of European-Latin American trade. Cultural bonds do not really count for much in commercial relations; sentiment cannot overcome political and economic factors. The lessons of European integration are not easily transferable to Latin America, mainly because the motivation behind the drive for integration was very different in the two areas. Even if there were some lessons to be learned, they could only be passed on effectively if Europe were to supply technical assistance to Latin America, and such a commitment is unlikely without more promising commercial prospects, given the demands on Europe by other countries. Furthermore, the role assigned to Latin America in this supposedly complementary arrangement is neither satisfactory to Latin America as a goal nor in conformity with recent trends in Latin American trade.

As Table 5.2 shows, the most dynamic sector of Latin American exports over the decade of the 1960s has been manufactures. For countries such as Argentina, Brazil, and Mexico, the share of manufactures in total exports has risen manyfold. Moreover, these are not the traditional products of developing countries (like textiles) to which European industry is already adjusting. Rather they are products in direct competition with some parts of the European industrial structure.

TABLE 5.1

European and Latin American International Trade
(exports FOB; imports CIF)

Region, Exports and Imports	Value (in millions of dollars)				Total Trade (percent)			
	1960	1965	1970	1973	1960	1965	1970	1973
EUROPE								
Exports								
Total to world	51,890	79,510	138,090	258,660	100.0	100.0	100.0	100.0
Total to Central and South America	3,120	3,300	5,480	8,448	6.0	4.2	4.0	3.3
Of which:								
EEC:								
Total to world	29,730	47,920	88,510	171,560	57.3	60.3	64.1	66.3
Total to Central and South America	1,730	1,860	3,250	5,310	3.3	2.3	2.4	2.1
EFTA:								
Total to world	19,860	28,020	43,110	73,830	38.3	35.2	31.2	28.5
Total to Central and South America	1,305	1,280	1,890	2,600	2.5	1.6	1.4	1.0
Imports								
Total from world	54,450	84,850	144,880	268,100	100.0	100.0	100.0	100.0
Total from Central and South America	3,220	4,170	5,515	8,043	5.9	4.9	3.8	3.0
Of which:								
EEC:								
Total from world	28,280	46,890	85,260	159,490	51.9	55.3	58.8	59.5
Total from Central and South America	1,720	2,390	3,330	4,920	3.2	2.8	2.3	1.8
EFTA:								
Total from world	22,420	30,850	47,390	85,490	41.2	36.4	32.7	31.9
Total from Central and South America	1,390	1,480	1,630	2,320	2.6	1.7	1.1	0.9
CENTRAL & SOUTH AMERICA								
Exports								
Total to world	9,950	12,620	17,590	25,770	100.0	100.0	100.0	100.0
Total to Western Europe	3,220	4,170	5,515	8,043	32.4	33.0	31.4	31.2
Of which:								
Total to EEC	1,720	2,390	3,330	4,920	17.3	18.9	18.9	19.1
Total to EFTA	1,390	1,480	1,630	2,320	14.0	11.7	9.3	9.0
Imports								
Total from world	9,680	11,550	18,500	28,640	100.0	100.0	100.0	100.0
Total from Western Europe	3,120	3,300	5,480	8,448	32.2	28.6	29.6	29.5
Of which:								
Total from EEC	1,730	1,860	3,250	5,310	17.9	16.1	17.6	18.5
Total from EFTA	1,305	1,280	1,890	2,600	13.5	11.1	10.2	9.1

Source: "General Agreement on Tariffs and Trade," International Trade 1973/74 (Geneva, 1974), Appendix Table E.

TABLE 5.2

Share of Manufacturing in Total Exports of Latin American Countries

Region and Country[a]	Total Manufactures 1959-60	Total Manufactures 1969-70	Textiles and Clothing (in percent of total trade) 1959-60	Textiles and Clothing (in percent of total trade) 1969-70
LAFTA				
Argentina	4.0	13.9	0.0	0.6
Bolivia	0.0	0.0[b]	0.0	0.0[b]
Brazil	1.8	11.4	—	1.0
Chile	1.8	3.9	—	0.0
Colombia	1.5	8.4	0.0	1.9
Equador	1.4	1.3	0.7	0.4[b]
Mexico	12.2	28.9	3.3	2.9
Paraguay[e]	—	8.3[c]	—	0.0[c]
Peru	1.2	0.2[b]	0.1	—[b]
Uruguay	—	8.6[d]	—	3.4[d]
CACM				
Costa Rica	4.2	18.3	—	3.6
El Salvador	5.0	30.0	2.0	11.4
Guatemala	2.7	26.7	0.4	4.4
Honduras	0.8	8.2	0.0	2.0
Nicaragua	0.8	14.3	—	2.1
Other				
Cuba	4.1	—	0.8	—
Dominican Republic	3.1	(3.5)	—	0.0
Panama	—	1.4	—	0.5

[a]Venezuela and Haiti not included.
[b]1968-69.
[c]1968.
[d]1970-71.
[e]Excluding exports of gold.
Note: Figures in parentheses indicate preliminary estimates.
Source: "General Agreement on Tariffs and Trade," International Trade 1973/74 (Geneva, 1974), Table F.

Thus, a traditional complementary relationship—raw material for manufactures—is unlikely to be perpetuated.

Most of the European trade policies that have affected Latin America have resulted from concerns far removed from Latin America, namely, the needs of European integration and the desire to associate certain countries with the European Community. For purposes of trade policy, the European Community is synonymous with Europe now that the community has been expanded to include the United Kingdom. Neither in the original nor the expanded European Community has any explicit attention been directed to the consequences for Latin America—there was no obligation to do so. There was and is an obligation to consider Latin America in the operation of the Common Agricultural Policy (CAP), but little real concern has been in evidence. Argentina, Uruguay, and Brazil (and others) all produce and export temperate agricultural products that are protected by the CAP. When European farmers face difficulty, the CAP forces as much of the adjustment burden as possible onto competing exporters, including Latin America (witness the total meat embargo imposed by the European Community in 1974 in order to help support European meat prices [contrary to expressed concerns about inflation]).

The European associate agreements, the CAP agreements, of which the most recent was the Lome Convention, also hurt Latin American exports because they give preferences to certain African countries whose tropical agriculture competes directly with that of Latin America. Furthermore, this latest treaty has given preferences to certain English-speaking Caribbean countries, splitting them off from the rest of Latin America. Even the trade credits provided by Europe to facilitate trade with Latin America primarily have benefited European exporters and have carried rather onerous terms for Latin American importers. Not all European policies have been adverse, however. The generalized system of preferences implemented to encourage developing countries' exports of manufactures has been beneficial, but most of its gains are yet to be realized.

Over the years the European Community has increased its formal recognition of Latin America. Under some prodding from Italy, the community began regular diplomatic contacts with Latin America in 1970. The Latin American side was represented by CECLA (the Special Commission for Latin American Coordination), which formulated a set of requests (or demands) known as the Buenos Aires Declaration. The requests have not been acted upon, but regular consultations have followed. Three Latin American countries, Argentina, Uruguay, and Brazil, subsequently signed nonpreferential trade agreements with the European Community. These agreements have little economic meaning (they didn't even guarantee the Latin American parties prior consultation before the meat embargo) but they do have some diplomatic content. Joint parliamentary meetings have also been arranged to supplement the economic consultations.

While these improved institutional ties are desirable, it is clear that form cannot replace substance. In March 1974, a joint meeting was convened in Montevideo which ended in what must be called a fiasco because the Latin Americans were interested in concrete economic measures while the Europeans were only prepared to discuss vague generalities. The European attitude toward Latin America is still one of studied indifference.

LATIN AMERICA LOOKS TO EUROPE

The European-Latin American economic relationship is perceived very differently from the other side of the Atlantic. From both an economic and a political point of view, Europe is of great importance to Latin America. As can be discovered from Table 5.1, Europe has been absorbing over 30 percent of Latin American exports, and while the European share of the total has been declining slightly, the portion going to the European Community has been rising. The European Community is the world's largest import market and Latin America is obviously quite anxious to share in its growth. Latin America also obtains about 30 percent of its imports from Europe, including much of the capital equipment so critical for industrial growth. Thus, Latin Americans have reasons for being concerned over their future trading relations with Europe.

Latin America also attaches substantial political importance to its economic relations with Europe. Living in close proximity to the United States causes problems for Latin American countries. Given the disproportionate size of the United States relative to Latin American countries, there is the real prospect that the United States will both overwhelm and forget Latin America. Without either status in the eyes of the United States or independence from the United States, Latin America will be ignored by other areas as well. Thus, Latin America is interested in its relationship with Europe in part as a counterweight to its relationship with the United States.

Latin America is able to promote its broader political goals (in addition to economic welfare) through economic ties with Europe. Latin American leverage, for instance, with private foreign enterprises, is increased through greater competition among firms wanting to do business in the area. For this purpose, of course, Europe is not unique. Latin America is also looking to Japan and Canada and potentially also to socialist countries and the emerging developing countries. In essence, Latin America is seeking to overcome what it believes to be a very unequal bargaining position in the world economy that has worked to its disadvantage.

The international economic relations of Latin America in the main have reflected the evolving growth and trade strategies of the region itself.[5] The Great Depression caused much suffering in Latin American countries because the health of their economies was closely linked to their exports of raw materials, the markets for which collapsed. In response to this calamity, import-substituting industrialization policies were adopted. World War II reinforced this trend since competitive manufactures from Europe and Japan were eliminated and shipments from the United States were not always available. In the postwar period, import-replacing policies were strengthened to spur industrial growth. Tax and credit policies were directed to stimulating investment in industry but, in fact, led to inequitable tax burdens and fragmented capital markets; high tariffs and quotas on imports were instituted, which protected many undersized and inefficient producers; and foreign exchange controls and multiple exchange rate systems were employed, yielding overvalued currencies that discouraged exports.

The import-replacing policies were successful in encouraging industrial growth. Latin American growth rates during this period compare favorably with their own earlier experience and also with the experience of developed countries in previous decades. But the policies failed to free Latin America from external dependence. Latin America still exported raw materials that were subject to the vagaries of world markets. Exports were still critical to domestic growth for they financed imports of needed raw materials and capital equipment. Thus, Latin America remained vulnerable to developments abroad. Furthermore, this industrial growth resulted only in a low level of development since it was limited by the size of domestic markets. Foreign firms were attracted by the high level of protection to make direct investments to serve the local markets. These firms were able to outperform and often to bring out locally owned firms because of superior technology and management abilities. In this way many Latin American industries passed into foreign hands without necessarily bringing the benefits that could flow from foreign investment because of the lack of a competitive environment. At last it was recognized that the end of the road had been reached for import-replacing industrialization policies.

One solution to the dilemma of small markets is the formation of customs unions and free trade areas, and this became the theme of the next phase of Latin American policy. Europe had demonstrated that customs unions were workable and that they could bring substantial economic benefits. But the great promise of the LAFTA was never achieved. Some tariffs and nontariff barriers were reduced and market access expanded, but the sort of commitment that would have accepted short-term losses for the sake of long-range gains was never made. The Andean Group followed in response to disappointments over LAFTA, but it is not certain that the basic problem has been overcome even in this more restricted group. Without completely turning their backs on integration, most Latin American countries decided to seek still other approaches to their dilemmas.

What has followed has been the adoption in some countries of outward looking policies aimed at encouraging large and efficient industries to produce and serve world markets. Various policies, including exchange rate reforms (to correct overvaluation) and specific export stimulants, have been tried. But it is clear that even if these policies are successful, they will not necessarily overcome all of the dissatisfaction surrounding the economic situation of Latin America. The existence, for instance, of German-owned subsidiaries operating in Latin America and exporting manufactured components to their parent firms does not relieve Latin America of external vulnerability, nor give these countries much more control over their external relations. Nor does it promise to correct the inequalities of income distribution that have accompanied growth in Latin America. Expanding employment has gone hand-in-hand with rising urban unemployment as a multitude of people have been attracted to the cities from the countryside. Without going into the totality of the problems of Latin American development, it should be clear that the economic and social problems are complex and that a number of strategies will be required to make inroads against them.[6]

Latin Americans are seeking certain specific objectives from a reorganization of the world economy. They will be looking to Europe for support for these objectives. First, they desire an improvement in the terms of trade for the raw materials they export and will continue to export for some time to come. Second, they desire improved access for their exports of manufactures, which alone promise the growth of earnings that will be required to finance economic and social advance. As seen in Table 5.3, Latin American countries have been making substantial gains in their export performance and are capable of extending them with proper market access. Third, they want assistance in promoting greater Latin American participation in the advanced industries of the world, with substantial Latin American ownership.

POLICY POSSIBILITIES

Europe could be responsive to Latin American needs through multilateral forums or bilateral arrangements or both. A new multinational round of trade negotiations has begun recently under the aegis

TABLE 5.3

Foreign Trade of Selected Countries in Latin America
(millions of dollars and percentages)

	Imports				Exports			
		Annual Rate of Change				Annual Rate of Change		
Country	1973 CIF	1958–60 1969–71	1972	1973	1973 FOB	1958–60 1969–71	1972	1973
AFTA	$(20,200)	5.5	17.2	(31)	$(20,500)	5.1	18.5	(37.5)
Argentina	(2,090)	3.6	2.0	(10)	(3,050)	4.7	11.5	(57)
Bolivia	(240)	7.9	8.2	(30)	277	13.0	14.6	32.5
Brazil	6,855	7.0	29.2	43	6,198	7.0	37.4	55
Chile	(1,500)	7.1	(25.0)	(25)	1,231	8.2	-11.1	44
Colombia	(1,000)	5.5	-2.4	(20)	(1,250)	3.5	8.3	(68)
Ecuador[a]	532	10.2	8.2	68	558	4.0	38.9	66
Mexico	4,146	6.9	21.9	41	2,452	6.1	23.8	34
Paraguay	122	7.6	-0.7	47.5	127	6.3	32.2	47
Peru	(1,000)	6.4	5.8	(26)	(1,039)	9.6	5.8	10
Uruguay	285	1.5	-15.9	52.5	322	5.2	4.1	50
Venezuela	3,602[b]	2.7	17.6	18.5[b]	5,778[b]	1.9	12.6	25[b]
ACM	1,856	9.9	6.5	34	1,634	8.4	18.7	23.5
Costa Rica	459	10.2	6.6	22	339	8.9	24.6	21
El Salvador	377	6.6	10.9	36.5	352	6.0	19.7	17
Guatemala	431	6.3	9.3	33	436	8.9	15.6	33
Honduras	262	10.5	35.7	36	237	9.1	7.1	15
Nicaragua	327	9.5	3.8	50	270	9.7	29.5	14
Other								
Cuba	(1,500)	5.3	-6.7	(16)	(1,000)	2.4	-6.5	(24.5)
Dominican Republic	486	8.2	3.3	31.5	442	3.7	43.0	27
Haiti	(74)	3.0	7.0	(16)	(49)	2.0	-6.3	(15)
Panama	489	12.1	11.3	11	133	12.6	5.0	9

[a]Based on import and export permits.

[b]IMF, International Financial Statistics, March 1975.

Note: Figures in parentheses indicate preliminary estimates.

Source: "General Agreement on Tariffs and Trade," International Trade 1973/74 (Geneva, 1974), p. 115.

of the General Agreement on Tariffs and Trade (GATT). This negotiation could provide a useful beginning. Latin America (along with other developing countries) has insisted that it be included as full participants, which it was not at the Kennedy Round and its predecessors.[7] In particular, the Latin Americans will want to reduce the escalation of the European Community tariff (which raises the effective tariff rate) and should be prepared to make some concessions in return. Whether in the end the Latin Americans will want to bargain for concessions remains to be seen. In the past they have settled for a "free ride" but have received very few benefits as a result.

The Latin Americans will also want an improvement in the European Community generalized tariff preference scheme, particularly because tariff reductions reduce the value of existing preferences. The improvements could come through fewer exceptions, more liberalized quotas, and less stringent escape clauses. Furthermore, the Latin Americans will seek to negotiate commodity agreements on products of particular interest to them, which should at least reduce price and income instability for exporters. Much could be accomplished in such a negotiation.

The European Community could improve its bilateral relations with Latin America, but only by making major changes in the institutional arrangements that exist. The pattern for a new arrangement might be found in the agreement that Mexico is seeking with the European Community.[8] Unlike the Argentina-Uruguay-Brazil trade agreement, the broad agreement Mexico wants would include commercial cooperation, industrial cooperation, and a mechanism for promoting investment and transfer of technological and scientific know-how. Such an agreement would not be in conflict with the European Community's obligations to other countries and could provide real benefit to both Mexico and the European Community.

Europe and all other advanced areas have an obligation to respond sympathetically to the request for a restructuring of the world economic order. It should not be beyond the abilities of man to create a system that more nearly meets the demands for justice without destroying the basis for economic efficiency. The world economy is constantly changing. The older order is never maintained. Change will come; only the new forms are in doubt.

NOTES

1. Adalbert Krieger Vasena and Javier Pazos, Latin America: A Broader World Role (London: Ernest Ben, 1973).

2. Osvaldo Sunkel, "The Pattern of Latin American Dependence," in Latin America in the International Economy, Victor L. Urquidi and Rosemary Thorp, eds. Proceedings of a conference held by the International Economic Association in Mexico City (New York: Wiley, 1973), pp. 3-25.

3. Ibid.

4. Maurice Schaeffer, "The European Community and Latin American Development," Urquidi and Thorp, op. cit., pp. 313-330.

5. Miguel S. Wionczek, "Latin American Growth and Trade Strategies in the Postwar Period," in Structural Adjustments in Asian-Pacific Trade, ed. Kiyoshi Kojima. Papers and proceedings of the Fifth Pacific Trade and Development Conference, vol. 2 (Tokyo: Japan Economic Research Center, July 1973), pp. 191-229.

6. See Victor L. Urquidi, introductory discussion, Urquidi and Thorp, op. cit.

7. United Nations, Economic and Social Council, Economic Commission for Latin America, Latin America and the Forthcoming Multilateral Trade Negotiations (E/CN. 12/955), March 7, 1973.

8. European Report, no. 176, Brussels, October 11, 1974.

CHAPTER

6

SOVIET, EAST EUROPEAN, AND CHINESE COMMUNIST TRADE AND AID WITH LATIN AMERICA: SCOPE AND TRENDS

James D. Theberge

The purpose of this chapter is to examine briefly the scope and trend of recent Soviet, East European, and Chinese communist trade and aid with Latin America, to review some of the factors responsible for the increase in economic relations, and to consider the prospects for an expansion of socialist area trade and aid in the future.

Since Cuba is a socialist state, it is excluded from this review of socialist area trade with Latin America. Latin America includes the English-speaking Caribbean Commonwealth states of Jamaica, Trinidad-Tobogo, Guyana, and Barbados. The term "East European" embraces Bulgaria, Czechoslovakia, East Germany, Hungary, Poland, and Romania.

SOVIET AID AND TRADE

For over two decades the USSR has used foreign aid as an important instrument for promoting its interests in the Third World. Moscow's basic objectives have not changed: to weaken Western influence and substitute its own to counter Chinese challenges to Soviet pretensions to leadership of the national liberation movements, and to persuade Third-World countries that the communist path to development is the only certain one. In Latin America, the USSR also uses its aid program to support the economy of its Cuban socialist client, which has become increasingly dependent on Soviet aid to finance imports essential for its development.

Since 1954, the USSR has provided $8.9 billion in economic aid (Cuba excluded) in pursuit of these objectives. About 80 percent of this economic aid has been delivered to South Asia and the Middle East, followed by Africa and Latin America in order of importance. About two thirds of Soviet economic aid has gone to countries close to its borders: Afghanistan, Egypt, India, Iran, Iraq, and Turkey.

Moscow's economic aid program was largely the creation of the Khrushchev years (1954-64), during which it expanded rapidly but with severe yearly fluctuations. In the post-Khrushchev era, Moscow has exercised much greater caution in extending aid, and more selectivity in its choice of aid recipients. Moscow has become more skeptical about the lasting political gains that can be expected from its aid program.

During the Khrushchev years, Latin America received less foreign aid than other regions of the Third World, including Africa. Soviet economic aid to Latin America was negligible and only amounted to $45 million in the 1954-65 period, or about 1 percent of total Soviet aid. During the past decade, Latin America still lagged behind South Asia and the Middle East, but moved ahead of Africa as an aid recipient, receiving $503 million in the 1966-73 period, or about 11 percent of total Soviet economic aid. (See Table 6.2.)

Although it has risen sharply since the mid-1960s Soviet economic aid to Latin America is still irregular and remains at a low level. During the 1966-73 period, Allende's Chile received $260.5 million, or over half the total Soviet aid to Latin America. Brazil was next in importance, receiving an $85 million credit in 1966. Smaller amounts have been received by Bolivia, Colombia, Peru, and Uruguay. In 1973, no Soviet aid was authorized for any Latin American country.

As for Soviet trade with Latin America, it has changed little over the past decade. Aside from trade with Cuba, Soviet trade with Latin America is insignificant, trailing far behind the Middle East, Africa, and Asia.

Soviet exports to Latin America reached $59.5 million in 1966 and have declined since. Soviet imports from Latin America reached $147.2 million in 1972. Except for Cuba, the Latin American countries regularly enjoy a trade surplus with the USSR. Neither Soviet exports nor imports have shown any clear tendency since the mid-1960s, and total trade turnover during the past decade has remained at about $175 million. Soviet trade is heavily concentrated in two countries, Argentina and Brazil, which together accounted for 70 percent of total Soviet trade with Latin America in 1972. (Table 6.9)

EASTERN EUROPEAN AID AND TRADE

During the last half of the 1960s, East European economic aid declined to $11 million (Ecuador, $5 million and Peru, $6 million) in 1969. In 1970, it increased to $51 million (Peru, $25 million; Uruguay, $15 million; and Venezuela, $10 million), and reached a high point of $174 million (Chile, $95 million; Peru, $44 million; and Bolivia, $25 million) in 1971 (Table 6.3). Throughout the past decade, East European aid, like Soviet aid to Latin America, has been insignificant and has tended to be concentrated in two countries: Velasco's Peru and Allende's Chile.

East European trade with Latin America is also small, but more important than Soviet-Latin American trade. Trade turnover with Latin America reached $434 million in 1972, compared with a Soviet-Latin American trade turnover of $179 million. East European trade with Latin America has been expanding steadily and shows a certain momentum that is lacking so far in Soviet trade with the region. Brazil, Argentina, Peru, and Colombia account for about 90 percent of East European-Latin American trade turnover in recent years. Eastern Europe's imports from Latin America regularly exceed its exports. (Table 6.10)

COMMUNIST CHINESE TRADE AND AID

Peking's only economic aid to Latin America, a total of $133 million, was authorized in 1971 and 1972. In 1971, aid was given to Peru ($42 million) and Chile ($2 million) and in 1972 to Chile ($63 million) and Guyana ($26 million). Chinese communist economic aid has been concentrated in Peru, Chile, and Guyana, and so far has been limited to the 1971-72 period. No aid was authorized for Latin America in 1973. About 85 percent of Peking's aid, which amounted to $3 billion (1956-73), has been allocated to Africa, South Asia, and the Middle East. For Peking's aid program, Latin America has the lowest priority in the Third World. (Table 6.4)

Chinese trade with Latin America, like its aid program, is still modest. Peking's exports fluctuated within a narrow range of $4 to $8 million in the 1968-72 period, with imports from Latin America rising from less than $1 million in 1968 to $191 million in 1972. Chile, Brazil, and Peru are the main trading partners, accounting for about 95 percent of total Chinese trade with Latin America in 1972. Despite the signs of rising levels, Chinese-Latin American trade is highly unstable and subject to severe fluctuations from year to year. (Table 6.11)

RELATIONS WITH THE SOCIALIST STATES

As noted above, substantial trade relations with the socialist states have been established by the larger, more developed countries of Latin America: Argentina, Brazil, Peru, and Colombia. Mexico has not yet established significant trade flows with the socialist countries, although in the past few years, trade and economic missions have been sent to the USSR, Eastern Europe, and China, which may lead to some improvement in trade relations.

Nevertheless, during the past decade, and particularly since the end of the 1960s, an increasing number of South American and Caribbean states have established diplomatic and commercial relations with the socialist countries. This should lead to some expansion of trade relations by the small and medium-sized Latin American countries over the remainder of this decade.

The following factors may be mentioned as contributing to the recent upsurge in Latin America's interest in increasing its economic ties with the USSR, Eastern Europe, and China:

1. The widespread desire to diversify export markets and obtain access to new sources of capital and technology so as to reduce what is considered excessive economic dependence on the United States. This long-term aim of the Latin American countries is now encouraged by East-West detente and the socialist states' increased interest in widening trade relations with the nonsocialist world.

2. A strong anticapitalist and anti-U.S. trend pushes many Latin American governments toward policies of greater autonomy and more balanced relations with the world community, favoring in particular the establishment of economic relations with the socialist world.

3. The protectionist trend in the United States, which has led to trade restrictions that protect domestic labor-intensive industries (such as textiles and footwear) against import competition, has driven some Latin American countries to redouble their efforts to find markets elsewhere, including the socialist countries.

4. Some Latin American governments advertise the establishment of diplomatic and economic relations with the USSR, Cuba, and other socialist states as a sign of "independence" from the United States, which is popular with anti-U.S. nationalist forces at home. In some countries, revolutionary rhetoric and gestures of independence from the United States are convenient substitutes for needed radical reform.

5. More recently, OPEC's (Organization of Petroleum Exporting Countries') ability to raise oil prices fourfold in 1973-74 has contributed to balance of payments problems that press these countries to seek new export markets and explore trade relations with the socialist states.

6. Ideological sympathy has led some Latin American countries (such as Allende's Chile and Velasco's Peru) to open trade relations and to use that in the anti-U.S. struggle.

OBSTACLES FACING TRADE AND AID EXPANSION

These are some of the pressures that have encouraged the expansion of political and trade relations between the South American countries and the USSR, Eastern Europe, and China in the late 1960s and early 1970s. The states bordering on the Caribbean are now beginning the process of trade diversification. Thus, it can be expected that Latin American-socialist area commercial relations will continue to increase over the remainder of this decade.

The economic aid program will remain a major element in Soviet and Chinese policy toward the Third World, but large-scale commitments to Latin American countries are not likely.* After the costly Cuban experience (over $5 billion in aid since 1960 with no end in sight), the USSR is particularly conservative about its aid commitments, even to friendly Marxist regimes, such as that of Salvador Allende in Chile. Nevertheless, the program remains one of the few substantial instruments (the other being military aid) available for expanding Soviet influence in Latin America, weakening U.S.-Latin American ties, and countering Chinese influence. Soviet economic aid authorizations will rise and fall in response to new opportunities and Moscow's short-run economic capabilities.

The low level of trade between the USSR and Latin America is due to the fact that Moscow has little need for many of the raw materials and foodstuffs exported by the Latin American countries. The USSR either exports some of the same raw materials or has more accessible and cheaper sources of supply. However, Soviet imports of manufactured goods from the Third World are on the rise, and there is some room for an expansion of Latin-American-manufactured exports to the USSR.

Thus far, socialist trade and aid agreements with Latin American countries have been partial or limited ones that have not covered a wide area of planned cooperation or included large development projects taking years to complete and involving large numbers of Soviet

---

*The USSR seems to be increasingly interested in providing military aid to Latin American countries (offers having been made to and rejected by Chile and Argentina and accepted by Peru) because of its greater political impact and the immediate dependence it creates.

engineers, technicians, and administrative personnel. The East European states, which prefer to create mixed-stage enterprises financed by local and socialist state capital, recently have begun to explore this trade and aid technique in Latin America. In 1973, for example, the state mining companies of Romania (Geomin) and Peru (Minero Peru) established a jointly owned state mining enterprise to exploit the Atamina copper deposits. Thus far, the USSR seems to prefer to extend long-term commercial credits to finance its machinery and equipment exports rather than to tie up scarce managerial and technical personnel in ambitious development projects.

The trade surplus with the USSR, Eastern Europe, and China enjoyed by the Latin American countries reflects the difficulties of the socialist states in competing in the Latin American market for machinery, equipment, and other manufactured goods. These difficulties stem from several factors: the sluggishness of the state trading bureaucracies; the state five-year plans, which introduce rigidities restricting the expansion of the foreign sector; the unsuitability or high price of socialist manufactured goods (when maintenance is taken into account); unfamiliarity with the Latin American market; and problems of spare parts and component supplies.

Finally, the traditional ties of Latin American countries to U.S., West European, and, more recently, Japanese suppliers of capital, intermediate, and consumer goods and access to their large, dynamic, commodity and capital markets will contrive to exercise a powerful attraction for a long time to come. Considerable economic advantages flowing from these traditional trade and financial ties cannot be easily dismissed.

These are some of the factors that set limits to the expansion of Latin American-socialist area trade. They indicate that a large-scale expansion of trade between the USSR, Eastern Europe, and China and Latin America is unlikely in the near future. Nevertheless, within the socialist camp, Eastern European-Latin American trade will continue to set the pace.

TABLE 6.1

Total Communist Bloc Economic Aid Authorized for Developing Countries, by Area, 1954-73[a]
(millions of dollars)

Year	Africa		Asia		Latin America[c]		Middle East		Total
	Amount	Percent	Amount	Percent	Amount	Percent	Amount	Percent	
1966	118	7	848	53	128	8	497	31	1,591
1967	78	16	22	5	112[b]	23	267	56	479
1968	56	10	240	40	12	2	290	48	598
1969	146	16	72	8	31	3	657	72	906
1970	589	54	233	21	107	10	162	15	1,091
1971	586	32	303	17	280[b]	15	658	36	1,827
1972	419	24	319	18	368[b]	21	621	36	1,727
1973	443	30	593	40	5	3	446	30	1,487
Cumulative									
1954-65	1,367	20	2,748	41	233	3	2,328	35	6,676
1966-73	2,435	25	2,630	27	1,043	12	3,598	37	9,706
1954-73	3,802	23	5,378	33	1,276	8	5,926	36	16,382

[a]Less than 5 percent of economic aid represents grants.

[b]These figures differ from State Department data as a result of upward adjustments in Soviet aid to Chile based on official Chilean figures.

[c]Excluding Cuba.

Note: The sum of the regional percentages may not add up to 100 because of rounding off.

Source: U.S. Department of State, Bureau of Intelligence and Research, "Communist States and Developing Countries: Aid and Trade in 1973" (October 10, 1974).

TABLE 6.2

USSR: Authorization of Economic Aid to Developing Countries, by Area, 1954-75[a]
(millions of dollars)

Year	Africa		Asia		Latin America[c]		Middle East		Total
	Amount	Percent	Amount	Percent	Amount	Percent	Amount	Percent	
1966	77	6	660	53	85	7	422	34	1,244
1967	9	3	5	2	97[b]	31	200	64	311
1968	0	0	194	52	2	1	178	48	374
1969	135	28	20	4	20	4	301	63	476
1970	51	26	11	6	56	29	76	39	194
1971	192	22	214	24	62[b]	7	418	47	886
1972	0	0	195	32	181[b]	29	242	39	618
1973	10	2	422	68	0	0	189	30	621
Cumulative									
1954-65	788	19	1,880	44	45	1	1,513	36	4,226
1966-73	474	10	1,721	36	503	11	2,026	43	4,724
1954-73	1,262	14	3,601	40	548	6	3,539	39	8,950

[a]Less than 5 percent of economic aid represents grants.

[b]These figures differ from State Department data as a result of upward adjustments in Soviet aid to Chile based on official Chilean figures.

[c]Excluding Cuba.

Note: The sum of the regional percentages may not add up to 100 because of rounding off.

Source: U.S. Department of State, Bureau of Intelligence and Research, "Communist States and Developing Countries: Aid and Trade in 1973" (October 1974).

TABLE 6.3

Eastern Europe: Authorization of Economic Aid to Developing Countries, by Area, 1954-73[a]
(millions of dollars)

Year	Africa		Asia		Latin America[b]		Middle East		
	Amount	Percent	Amount	Percent	Amount	Percent	Amount	Percent	Total
1966	0	0	125	55	43	19	60	26	228
1967	47	40	10	8	15	13	46	39	118
1968	56	34	0	0	10	6	100	60	166
1969	11	3	52	12	11	3	356	83	430
1970	84	45	10	5	51	27	43	23	188
1971	99	21	0	0	174	16	195	42	468
1972	209	32	35	5	98	15	313	48	655
1973	98	20	157	32	5	1	226	47	486
Cumulative									
1954-65	279	15	629	34	188	10	756	41	1,852
1966-73	604	22	389	14	407	15	1,339	49	2,739
1954-73	883	19	1,018	22	595	13	2,095	47	4,591

[a]Bulgaria, Czechoslovakia, East Germany, Hungary, Poland, and Romania. Less than 5 percent of economic aid represents grants.

[b]Excluding Cuba.

Note: The sum of the regional percentages may not add up to 100 because of rounding off.

Source: U.S. Department of State, Bureau of Intelligence and Research, "Communist States and Developing Countries, Aid and Trade in 1973" (October 1974).

TABLE 6.4

People's Republic of China: Authorization of Economic Aid to Developing Countries, by Area, 1956-73[a] (millions of dollars)

Year	Africa		Asia		Latin America[b]		Middle East		
	Amount	Percent	Amount	Percent	Amount	Percent	Amount	Percent	Total
1966	41	34	63	53	0	0	15	13	119
1967	22	44	7	14	0	0	21	42	50
1968	0	0	46	80	0	0	12	20	58
1969	0	0	0	0	0	0	0	0	0
1970	454	64	212	30	0	0	43	6	709
1971	295	62	89	19	44	9	45	9	473
1972	210	46	89	20	89	20	66	15	454
1973	335	89	14	4	0	0	29	8	378
Cumulative									
1956-65	300	38	348	44	0	0	143	18	791
1966-73	1,357	61	520	23	135	6	231	10	2,241
1956-73	1,657	55	868	29	133	4	374	12	3,032

[a]Less than 5 percent of economic aid represents grants.

[b]Excluding Cuba.

Note: The sum of the regional percentages may not add up to 100 because of rounding off.

Source: U.S. Department of State, Bureau of Intelligence and Research, "Communist States and Developing Countries: Aid and Trade in 1973" (October 1974).

TABLE 6.5

Communist China's Trade with Cuba: 1962-72

	Turnover[b]	Exports	Imports	Balance[c]
1962[a]	192.2	89.0	103.2	-14.2
1963[a]	163.5	72.7	90.8	-18.1
1964[a]	187.7	81.4	106.3	-24.9
1965	223.0	123.0	100.0	+23.0
1966	173.0	86.0	87.0	-1.0
1967	152.0	73.0	79.0	-6.0
1968	137.0	76.0	61.0	+15.0
1969	146.0	80.0	66.0	+14.0
1970	145.0	75.0	70.0	+5.0
1971	n.a.	n.a.	n.a.	n.a.
1972	n.a.	n.a	n.a.	n.a.

[a]The Battle Act Report (1970), p. 85.
[b]Chinese exports plus imports.
[c]Chinese exports minus imports. Chinese deficit (-), surplus (+).
n.a.: Not available.
Source: A. H. Usack and R. E. Batsavage, "The International Trade of the People's Republic of China," in U.S., Congress, Joint Economic Committee, People's Republic of China: An Economic Assessment, 18 May 1972, p. 351.

TABLE 6.6

Eastern European[a] Trade with Cuba: 1966-72
(millions of dollars)

	Turnover[b]	Exports	Imports	Balance[c]
1966	240.5	123.0	117.5	+5.5
1967	210.8	107.3	103.5	+3.8
1968	250.3	125.1	125.2	-0.1
1969	262.5	139.1	123.4	+15.7
1970	302.1	139.5	162.6	-23.1
1971	293.0	128.4	164.6	-36.2
1972	242.2	119.9	122.3	-2.4

[a]Bulgaria, Czechoslovakia, East Germany, Hungary, Poland, and Romania.
[b]East European exports plus imports.
[c]East European exports minus imports.
Source: U.S. Department of Commerce, Value Series: Communist Area Trade, 1966-72 (May 1974).

TABLE 6.7

USSR Trade with Cuba: 1960-72
(millions of dollars)

	Turnover[a]	Exports	Imports	Balance[b]
1960	176.6	73.9	102.7	-28
1961	592.9	284.1	308.8	-24.7
1962	594.8	363.1	231.7	+131.4
1963	558.6	395.8	162.8	+233.0
1964	647.4	362.3	285.1	+77.2
1965	710.5	371.7	338.8	+32.9
1966	758.1	475.1	283.0	192.1
1967	935.8	563.0	372.8	190.2
1968	902.0	624.2	277.8	346.4
1969	901.8	624.0	231.7	392.3
1970	1161.1	644.4	516.7	127.7
1971	989.9	668.9	321.0	347.9
1972	997.2	774.8	249.4	498.4

[a]Soviet exports plus imports.
[b]Soviet exports minus imports.
Source: 1960-66: U.S.S.R. Foreign Trade: Statistical Handbook, 1918-1966. 1967-72: U.S. Department of Commerce, Value Series: Communist Area Trade 1966-1972 (May 1974).

TABLE 6.8

Total Communist Exports to and Imports from Selected Latin American Countries, 1968–72
(million of dollars)

Communist Trade with:	1968		1969		1970		1971		1972	
	Exports	Imports	Exports	Imports	Exports	Imports	Exports	Imports	Exports	Imports
Mexico	5.5	3.5	14.9	2.4	6.2	3.7	7.1	19.4	7.2	17.9
Caribbean	0.7	—	1.6	1.4	0.8	1.7	1.4	2.9	1.2	1.8
Guyana	0.7	—	1.8	—	0.7	—	1.4	0.3	1.2	0.6
Jamaica	—	—	—	1.4	0.1	1.7	—	2.6	—	1.2
Central America	1.2	9.8	1.6	6.4	2.0	14.2	2.9	4.4	1.5	8.0
Costa Rica	—	1.7	0.6	3.5	1.1	6.7	1.2	3.6	1.4	5.3
Honduras	1.2	—	0.9	0.3	0.8	1.2	1.6	0.3	—	—
El Salvador	—	8.1	0.1	2.6	0.1	6.3	0.1	0.5	0.1	2.7
Andean Pact	43.9	65.4	57.5	65.3	56.2	68.2	41.2	144.2	57.8	211.9
Bolivia	1.6	—	2.1	*	—	—	—	10.0	—	3.0
Chile	5.3	—	5.9	0.6	4.4	0.5	8.8	17.3	15.7	78.8
Colombia	17.0	20.7	17.7	26.0	17.7	26.3	12.3	27.0	22.6	27.4
Ecuador	2.7	23.5	9.7	14.3	7.0	8.3	3.6	13.1	4.9	13.4
Peru	6.0	21.2	9.8	24.1	4.2	32.9	3.8	76.8	5.8	84.2
Venezuela	11.3	—	12.3	0.3	22.9	0.2	12.7	—	8.8	5.1
Other	108.7	179.7	104.4	207.2	89.4	228.9	129.1	259.9	115.2	388.5
Argentina	13.5	51.1	24.6	67.7	22.0	75.7	21.9	74.9	21.6	64.9
Brazil	92.9	121.5	73.2	129.0	58.6	124.8	102.5	175.2	90.6	308.6
Uruguay	2.3	7.1	6.6	10.5	7.8	28.4	4.7	9.8	3.0	15.0
Total	160.0	258.4	180	282.7	154.6	316.7	181.7	430.8	182.9	628.1

* Excluding Albania, Cuba, Mongolia, North Korea, and North Vietnam.

Source: The figures in this table are the sum of those of the previous three and therefore come from the same sources.

TABLE 6.9

Soviet Exports to and Imports from Selected Latin American Countries, 1960-72
(millions of dollars)

	1960	1965	1966	1967	1968	1969	1970	1971	1972	1960	1965	1966	1967	1968	1969	1970	1971	1972
Mexico	0.7	0.7	0.1	0.3	0.6	0.4	0.2	0.4	0.7[a]	3.3	0.1	0.5	0.3	0.4	c	0.1	10.2[a]	9.4[a]
Caribbean	—	—	0.7	0.5	0.4	0.7	0.5	0.6	0.1	—	—	—	—	—	1.4	1.7	2.6	1.2
Guyana	—	—	0.7	0.5	0.4	0.7	0.5	0.6	0.1[a]	—	—	—	—	—	—	c[a]	—	—
Jamaica	—	—	—	—	—	—	—	—	—	—	—	—	—	—	1.4	1.7	2.6[a]	1.2[a]
Central America	—	—	—	c	c	c	c	c	c	—	—	—	—	1.7	3.3	6.3	2.4	3.4
Costa Rica	—	—	—	c	c	c	c	c	c[a]	—	—	—	—	1.7	3.3	6.3	2.4[a]	3.4[a]
Honduras	—	—	—	—	—	c	c	c	c[a]	—	—	—	—	—	—	—	—	—
Andean Pact	0.2	c	1.3	1.8	2.6	8.1	4.1	10.5	18.7	0.2	0.4	2.5	1.2	22.1	11.2	5.5	20.6	23.2
Bolivia	—	c[a]	c	c	c	c	c	c[a]	1.0[a]	—	—	—	—	—	c	c	10.0[a]	3.0[a]
Chile	—	—	0.1	0.1	0.1	0.2	0.6	7.8	14.0[a]	—	—	0.2	0.2	c	0.1	0.3	0.9	8.8[a]
Colombia	0.2[b]	—	1.2[a]	1.7	2.4	3.4	1.3	1.8	3.3[a]	0.2[b]	0.4[b]	2.3[a]	0.8[a]	3.7	4.4	5.0	6.0	1.4[a]
Ecuador	—	—	—	c	c	1.1	0.4	0.4	0.1[a]	—	—	—	0.2[a]	18.2	6.4	0.1	3.5	2.8[a]
Peru	c[b]	—	c[a]	c	c	3.3	2.1	0.1	0.2[a]	—	—	—	—	0.2	—	0.1	0.2	2.2[a]
Venezuela	c[b]	—	c[a]	c[a]	0.1[a]	0.1	0.1	c	0.1[a]	—	—	—	c	—	0.3	c	c	5.0[a]
Other	31.1	48.0	57.5	23.7	21.7	25.9	7.8	7.8	12.2	32.3	127.0	126.2	52.2	44.1	66.6	48.4	78.2	110.0
Argentina	14.0	16.2	16.6	6.6	4.5	8.9	3.1	3.9	2.2[a]	21.7	90.0	88.1	19.5	17.6	21.4	26.8	30.3	27.7[a]
Brazil	15.8	31.5	36.3	16.5	17.0	16.2	3.5	2.2[a]	8.6[a]	9.3	32.2	31.6	28.7	24.9	43.7	21.2	46.3[a]	79.6[a]
Uruguay	1.3	0.3	4.6	0.6	0.2	0.8	1.2	1.7	1.4[a]	1.3	4.8	6.5	4.0	1.6	1.5	0.4	1.6	2.7[a]
Total	32.0	48.7	59.5	26.3	25.3	35.1	13.0	19.3	31.7	35.8	127.5	129.2	53.7	68.3	82.5	62.0	114.0	147.2

[a]U.S. Department of State, Bureau of Intelligence and Research, Communist States and Developing Countries: Aid and Trade, 1967, 1968, 1969, 1970, 1971, 1972, 1973.

[b]U.S. Department of State The Communist Economic Offensive through 1964 (4 August 1965).

[c]Less than 100,000.

Source: With the exception of Chile, the source unless otherwise noted is official trade statistics as compiled by the International Trade Analysis Staff, Bureau of International Commerce, U.S. Department of Commerce. Chilean-Soviet trade figures (excluding 1966 and 1968 Soviet import and 1968 Soviet export figures) are from the cited State Department sources.

TABLE 6.10

East European Trade with Selected Latin American Countries, 1968–72
(millions of dollars)

	1968		1969		1970		1971		1972	
	Exports	Imports	Exports	Imports	Exports	Imports	Exports	Imports	Exports	Imports
Mexico	4.9	3.1	14.5	2.4	6.0	3.6	6.7	4.9	6.4	3.3
Caribbean	0.1	—	0.7	—	c	—	—	—	—	—
Guyana	0.1	—	0.7	—	c	—	—	—	—	—
Jamaica	—	—	—	—	c	—	—	—	—	—
Central America	1.1	8.1	1.6	3.1	1.9	7.9	2.8	1.6	1.4	4.6
Costa Rica	—	—	0.6	0.2	1.0	0.4	1.1	1.2	1.3	1.9
Honduras	1.1	—	0.9	0.3	0.8	1.2	1.6	0.3	—	—
El Salvador	—	8.1	0.1	2.6	0.1	6.3	0.1	0.1	0.1	2.7
Andean Pact	35.1	43.3	42.4	54.1	49.1	62.7	26.4	84.4	34.8	76.0
Bolivia	1.6	—	2.1	c	—	—	—	—	—	—
Chile	4.8	—	5.5	0.5	3.3[a]	0.2	—	0.4	—	—
Colombia	14.6	17.0	14.3	21.6	16.3	21.3	10.5[b]	21.0	19.3[b]	26.0[b]
Ecuador	2.7	5.3	8.6	7.9	6.6	8.2	3.2	9.6	4.8[b]	10.6
Peru	1.8	21.0	2.4	24.1	1.9	32.8	3.3	53.4	5.3	39.3
Venezuela	9.6	c	9.5	c	21.0[a]	0.2[a]	9.4	c	5.4	0.1
Other	86.7	135.0	77.6	140.3	80.6	176.7	119.6	175.2	101.5	206.1
Argentina	8.7	32.9	14.9	46.0	18.2	46.4	17.0	38.1	18.9[b]	35.6[b]
Brazil	75.9	96.6	57.0	85.3	55.1	102.3	99.7	128.9	81.0[b]	158.2[b]
Uruguay	2.1	5.5	5.7	9.0	7.3	28.0	2.9	8.2	1.6	12.3
Total	127.8	189.5	136.8	199.9	137.6	250.9	155.5	266.1	144.1	290.0

[a]Estimates.
[b]Based on partial-year data.
[c]Less than $100,000.

Source: U.S. Department of State, Bureau of Intelligence and Research, Communist States and Developing Countries: Trade and Aid, 1970, 1971, 1972, 1973.

TABLE 6.11

Chinese Exports to and Imports from Selected Latin American Countries, 1968-72
(millions of dollars)

	1968		1969		1970		1971		1972	
	Exports	Imports	Exports	Imports	Exports	Imports	Exports	Imports	Exports	Imports
Mexico	—	—	b	b	b	b	—	4.3[a]	0.1	5.2
Caribbean	0.2	—	0.2	b	0.3	b	0.8	0.3	1.1	0.6
Guyana	0.2	—	0.2	—	0.2	b	0.8	0.3	1.1	0.6
Jamaica	—	—	—	—	0.1	b	—	—	—	—
Central America	0.1	—	b	—	0.1	—	0.1	0.4	0.1	—
Costa Rica	—	—	b	—	0.1	—	0.1	—	0.1	—
Honduras	0.1	—	—	—	—	—	—	—	—	—
El Salvador	—	—	b	—	b	0	b	0.4	b	—
Andean Pact	6.2	b	7.0	b	2.6	b	4.3	39.2	4.3	112.7
Bolivia	—	—	—	b	—	—	—	—	—	—
Chile	0.4	—	0.2	b	0.5	—	1.0[a]	16.0[a]	0.7	70.0[a]
Colombia	—	—	—	—	0.1	b	b	—	—	—
Ecuador	—	—	—	—	—	—	—	—	—	—
Peru	4.2	b	4.1	b	0.2	b	0.4	23.2	0.3	42.7
Venezuela	1.6	—	2.7	—	1.8	—	2.9	0	3.3	—
Other	0.3	0.6	0.9	0.3	1.0	3.8	1.7	6.5	1.5	72.4
Argentina	0.3	0.6	0.8	0.3	0.9	2.5	1.0	6.5	0.5[a]	1.6[a]
Brazil	b	—	b	b	b	1.3	0.6	—	1.0[a]	70.8
Uruguay	b	—	0.1	b	0.1	b	0.1	—	b	—
Total	6.8	0.6	8.1	0.3	3.9	3.8	6.9	50.4	7.1	190.9

[a]Estimate.

[b]Less than $100,000.

Source: U.S. Department of State, Bureau of Intelligence and Research, Communist States and Developing Countries: Aid and Trade, 1970, 1971, 1972, 1973.

CHAPTER

7

LATIN AMERICAN ECONOMIC RELATIONS WITH THE THIRD WORLD

H. Jon Rosenbaum
William G. Tyler

DEFINING THE LATIN AMERICAN AND THIRD-WORLD SUBSYSTEMS

Introductory texts about Latin America often begin with a sterile and unresolvable debate about Latin America's existence as a discernible subsystem in world politics.[1] This debate routinely raises the rhetorical question, "Is there a Latin America?" and then marshals the evidence that attests to both the diversity and the similarity of the Latin American nations. It tends to conclude with the observation that the real common denominator among the Latin American nations is the predominance of the United States in the western hemisphere.

It is tempting to use the same approach here in discussing Latin America's economic relations with the Third World. These relations have received scant attention from North American scholars, despite their seeming importance to Latin American leaders, and the analysis of Latin American-Third World economic relations is complicated by the difficulty of defining the participants.[2] If there is disagreement about which countries comprise Latin America, there is even more uncertainty about the composition of the Third World. If there is doubt about Latin America's geopolitical reality, there is even more skepticism about the Third World's. Clearly, while a discussion of this definitional problem cannot replace a consideration of the substantive aspects of Latin American-Third World economic relations, it cannot be totally ignored.

Although misgivings about Latin America's authenticity as a subsystem in international affairs no longer merit serious consideration, until recently Latin America's subordination to the United States often concealed the subsystem's existence or, perhaps more accurately, nearly engulfed it. In the twentieth century U.S. predominance in the region often has prevented the Latin Americans from undertaking independent initiatives in international and regional affairs. Nevertheless, during the last few years efforts to restore the subsystem's vitality have achieved considerable success, with the emergence of such local powers as Argentina, Brazil, Mexico, and Venezuela, attempts at regional integration, and the partial abdication by the United States of its traditional supervisory role.

The Latin American nations are not united on all issues and ancient rivalries are reviving, but most observers now have little difficulty in determining the membership of the Latin American subsystem. The only dissension concerns the status of the former British colonies in the Caribbean. In spite of their ambition to be accepted as full members of the Latin American subsystem, they are sometimes viewed as intruders by the other nations of the region.

There is less unanimity about which nations constitute the Third World. Poverty, nonalignment, dependency, and other characteristics are frequently attributed to Third-World nations, but analysts disagree about the necessary and sufficient conditions for bona fide membership in the Third World. Certainly the choice of criteria determines how exclusive or ecumenical the group will be. Moreover, the rigidity with which these standards are applied influences the composition of the Third World's constituency.

Until recently, Latin American nations were reluctant to identify themselves too closely with the Third World. "Knowledge of Africa and Asia was negligible among Latin American elites, and what they did know they did not like. They identified their future development with that of Europe and the United States rather than with the seeming backwardness and savagery of Africa and the chilling, overpopulated patterns of Asia."[3] In addition, some Latin American elites felt a racial antipathy toward the Afro-Asian nations. (Argentines continue to be particularly hostile toward people of non-European origin.) They also considered their countries superior, since Latin America achieved its political independence 150 years before most of the Third-World nations. Finally, the Latin Americans did not consider themselves nonaligned since they were signatories to the Inter-American Treaty of Reciprocal Assistance and had entered into bilateral military treaties with the United States.

For these reasons as well as others, Cuba was the only Latin American nation to send a representative to the first Third-World conference held at Belgrade in 1961.* By 1973, however, the Latin

---

*The Belgrade conference made only one reference to Latin America in its concluding declaration, characterizing the U.S. naval

American nations had become much more interested in achieving Third-World status, and several of them sent representatives or observers to the fourth conference of Third-World heads of state held in Algiers.*

Clearly, while all the Latin American countries now believe that at least some of their national interests can be advanced by collaboration with other Third-World states, some are more convinced than others of the value of this relationship. Argentina, Mexico, Panama, Peru, and Venezuela at present seem persuaded that their interests lie primarily with the Third World. On the other hand, Brazil, Bolivia, Chile, and Uruguay are among those that continue to feel that advantages can be obtained from the partial preservation of their traditional relations with the United States as well as from participation in Third-World activities.

The desire to be accepted as part of the Third World does not in itself bring about membership. Peron may have devised the term "Third World" following World War II, but many Afro-Asian nations remain suspicious of Latin America's commitment to the movement. Not only are the Latin American countries more prosperous, in general, than those of Africa and Asia but the fear persists that the Latin Americans may be serving as a Trojan horse for the United States, bent on the subversion of Third-World efforts.

If Latin America becomes more developed economically, it may be more effectively absorbed into the world economy. In this event, it might find integration with the Third World less attractive and its regional consciousness might be weakened, although few Latin American nations could become part of an emerging Fourth World composed of the globe's least developing countries. In the meantime, however, it is likely that the Latin Americans will join other Third-World nations in attempts to obtain favorable agreements in such areas as the price and supply of energy, management of food reserves, access to scarce raw materials, the stabilization of commodity markets, the transfer of technology, and the behavior of multinational firms.

Nevertheless, alignments probably will be quite fluid, and Latin Americans will find it convenient to enter into temporary alliances on specific issues. Ephemeral coalitions almost certainly will characterize the Latin American approach to problems not strictly economic in nature. At times, Latin Americans will no doubt prefer to pursue policies that coincide with those of the developed countries or that ad-

---

base at Guantanamo Bay as an affront to Cuba's sovereignty and territorial integrity.

*In addition to Cuba, Jamaica, Trinidad, Guyana, and Barbados were among the first western hemisphere nations to associate with the Third-World movement.

vance their regional interests at the expense of Africa and Asia. Since Latin American interests are not identical to those of Africa and Asia, there is no reason to expect that the Latin Americans will always conform to the positions taken by other Third-World nations.

However, because Latin America's integration into one unit is far from complete, certain Latin American nations may find collaboration with extraregional Third-World states more palatable than coordination with the policies of other Latin American countries. For example, Brazil and Chile currently might be more comfortable associating with Indonesia and Singapore than with Peru and Cuba because of the compatibility of their political and economic philosophies. Similarly, although the populations of El Salvador and Uruguay, for instance, are both Spanish speaking, the cultures of the two countries are sufficiently dissimilar that El Salvador might have more in common with an African coffee-producing country.

LEVELS OF INTERACTION

Latin American-Third World economic relations still have not taken definite shape. Their dimensions, however, are more distinct. Paradoxically, despite the importance assigned to economic relations with developing countries by Latin American leaders in their public pronouncements, there has been little interaction to date. Moreover, the results of unified action have been largely intangible.

The low level of interaction is due largely to the character of Third-World relations in general. Traditionally, the foreign relations of individual developing countries have been influenced heavily by hegemonic powers that have sought to maintain colonial or neocolonial bonds. This vertical client-patron relationship has been hermetic in character. Consequently, the relative weakness of horizontal economic and political relations among the developing nations has been common.

One economic manifestation of this situation is the Third World's specialization in the production of primary products destined for export to the industrial nations. Rather than being resolved by developing countries themselves, the vital international economic issues that profoundly affect their economies have been the subject of negotiation among the developed countries, or, at best, between the developed and developing countries.[4] To be sure, negotiations of the latter type are conducted from highly unequal bargaining power positions.

During the past few years south-south relations have expanded considerably. In the economic sphere, total trade among developing countries doubled between 1955 and 1971, while developing-country-manufactured exports destined for other Third-World nations more than tripled. Regional trading blocs have been established in Latin America, Central America, West Africa, and East Africa, while regional development banks and United Nations economic commissions have flourished. In addition to the enormously effective Organization of Petroleum Exporting Countries (OPEC), commodity agreements or arrangements among producers (which are usually developing countries) have been initiated or instituted for coffee, tin, cocoa, copper, and sugar. Regular meetings between developing countries' officials in responsible economic-policymaking positions have become common, and many of these have occurred under the auspices of such varied international institutions as the International Monetary Fund (IMF), United Nations Conference on Trade and Development (UNCTAD), and General Agreement on Tariffs and Trade, and the regional and more specialized organizations. Yet, although interaction has been increasing, the sensitivity of economic transactions among the developing countries is still low.

While the resolution of economic issues is the most important dimension of Third-World relations, other types of interaction have also been growing. In the political sphere, relations have been intensified on both the regional and bilateral levels. Within Latin America, not only economic but political transactions are being conducted increasingly through the still somewhat ad hoc Special Commission for Latin American Coordination (CECLA) rather than through the Organization of American States (OAS), which some Latin Americans view as dominated by the United States. Coordination of Latin American policy is likely to be advanced further by the formation of the Latin American Economic System (SELA), an institution championed by Mexico and Venezuela.[5]

On the bilateral level, certain key developing countries have been particularly assertive in dealing with others. Venezuela, for instance, has been using its augmented oil revenues to assert its influence, particularly in the Caribbean and in Central America. Similarly, Brazil has gained power as a result of its phenomenal economic expansion. Argentina, Mexico, and Peru must also be numbered among those Latin American countries with ambitions of regional leadership.

Despite these developments—the partial erosion of the former north-south relationship, largely due to OPEC, and the possibility of a still more profound alteration in coming years—Third-World relations continue to be conditioned by the attitudes and actions of the developed nations. Moreover, although Latin America participates in and even leads some of the new Third-World councils, Latin American countries have proved more interested in intraregional activities than in transactions with extraregional developing countries, which remain extremely limited. This would undoubtedly be confirmed by a study measuring Latin America's contact with Third-World countries outside the hemisphere in such areas as diplomatic representation, telephone, mail, and telegraph traffic, translations of literature, tourism, exports, emigration, foreign student exchange, comembership in international organizations, United Nations voting, and official conflict behavior. The difficulty of obtaining quantified data for more than 100 countries in any of these areas except trade (which is discussed in some detail below) prevents our pursuing such a study here. Nevertheless, it can safely be said that Brazil has been involved in more extraregional developing-country transactions than Latin America as a whole, which is hardly surprising given Brazil's economic power and international ambitions. Even so, having made a prodigious effort to assemble sufficient data, Wayne Selcher found Brazilian flows, as of 1968, to be exceedingly light in most instances.[6]

The economic relations among developing countries, including those of Latin America, take place on two levels, direct and collective. Direct interactions are trade, investment, and aid flows. Collective interactions are often less easy to observe, but whether consensual or conflictual, these interactions usually focus on the developing countries' common or disparate interests vis-a-vis the developed countries. While bilateral relations among the developing countries have been and continue to be rather weak, as has been indicated, the proliferation of international organizations since World War II has afforded them new opportunities to conduct international relations, settle differences, aggregate collective interests, and articulate their positions, and thus make a greater effort to influence the direction and extent of change in the international economic order.

DIRECT INTERACTIONS

Trade

The growth of the world economy and international trade during the last thirty years has been truly dramatic. Between 1948 and 1973, total world exports grew at a compounded annual rate of 9.6 percent in current dollars. Since the early 1960s, the rate has been still more rapid, with world exports growing at 15.4 percent annually between 1962 and 1973. Even if dollar inflation is discounted, the observed growth rates have been substantial. By and large, however, the developing countries have not participated in this world trade boom. Their exports grew at only 8.3 percent annually between 1948 and 1973, although the rate increased somewhat, to 14.4 percent, after 1962.

The developing countries' share of the total world exports has declined from 30.3 percent in 1948 to 20.7 percent in 1973.[7]

Many explanations have been suggested for the relatively poor performance of the developing countries. In particular, the slow growth of demand for many primary products and the inappropriateness of their economic policies seem to be largely responsible.[8] Nevertheless, in recent years, many Third-World nations have demonstrated an interest in the possibility of sustaining economic growth through export-oriented development. There are several reasons for this. Dissatisfaction with economic policies that promote industrialization through import substitution, the boom in commodity prices since 1972, the growing awareness among policymakers of the intellectual deficiency of the so-called Prebisch Thesis, and the recent dramatic export successes of a small number of developing countries have all contributed to a reconsideration of economic policy in the Third World.

Several Latin American nations have shown an interest in international markets and export-promoting policies. Brazil and Mexico, to name only the most important, have reformulated their economic policies in an attempt to expand exports, especially of manufactured items. The success of these two nations, especially Brazil, has been widely discussed in Latin America, and it is likely that more and more nations of the region will follow Brazil's example and try to stimulate economic growth by selling more in the world market. Unlike Brazil and Mexico, however, most developing economies are relatively small and open. Therefore, their success in fomenting growth will depend even more heavily on international market conditions and their progress in penetrating these markets.

At present, international trade is the most prominent factor in direct Latin American-Third World economic relations. A summary of Latin American trade with other developing countries is presented in Table 7.1. This table shows that the Latin American share of total world exports has declined substantially and steadily, falling from 8.5 percent in 1955 to 4.5 percent in 1971. While Latin American exports to all developing countries have grown in absolute terms, they constitute only about 20 percent of Latin America's total exports, and its share does not seem to be rising. Latin America's exports to the Third World, excluding Latin America, have been declining in relation to intraregional exports.

Exports to other developing countries accounted for 10.8 percent of all Latin America's exports in 1955, but had fallen to 8.8 percent by 1971. On the other hand, the exports of Latin American countries to other Latin American countries have been growing, increasing from 9.5 percent of total Latin Americans exports in 1955 to 12 percent in 1971. This growth reflects not only efforts at regional integration (such as the Latin American Free Trade Association [LAFTA], Central

TABLE 7.1

Latin American Exports to Third-World Countries, Selected Years

	1955	1962	1971
Total world exports (millions of $)	93,540	141,410	348,230
Total developing countries' exports (millions of $)	23,730	29,060	61,910
Share of developing countries' exports in total world exports	25.4%	20.6%	18.8%
Share of Latin American exports in total world exports	8.5	6.5	4.5
Latin American exports (millions of $)			
To all developing countries	1,620	1,570	3,230
To Latin American developing countries	760	670	1,860
To other developing countries	860	900	1,370
Share of Latin American exports going to developing countries			
To all developing countries	20.3%	17.1%	20.8%
To Latin American developing countries	9.5	7.3	12.0
To other developing countries	10.8	9.8	8.8
Latin American exports to developing countries as a percentage of total world trade	1.7%	1.1%	0.9%

Source: Calculated from information published in United Nations Monthly Bulletin of Statistics 27, no. 7 (July 1973), pp. xxii-xxxix; and UNCTAD, Handbook of International Trade and Development Statistics-1972 (New York: United Nations, 1972), p. 46.

American Common Market [CACM], and the Andean Pact) but also the marketing policies of multinational corporations located in Latin America and the natural tendency to look first at the Latin American market when beginning to export new products, particularly manufactured goods. For manufactured exports alone (SITC 5-8), which accounted for about 20 percent of total Latin American exports in 1971, the record is somewhat different. In that year the Latin American countries sent 30 percent of their manufactured exports to other developing countries. However, the major developing country markets were in Latin America itself, which absorbed 28.6 percent of all Latin-American-manufactured exports.

In relation to total world trade, Latin American exports to all Third-World countries are minute and their importance is decreasing, accounting for only 0.9 percent of total world exports in 1971. Latin American imports from other developing countries are still less; they accounted for only 0.7 percent of total world imports in 1971. However, for individual commodity imports, a different situation prevails. For example, Brazil's dependence on imports for about 75 percent of its petroleum requirements has caused it to turn to Africa and the Middle East for this indispensable resource.

The reasons for the relative paucity of trade between the Latin American countries and other developing nations are related to economic specialization. Third-World economies are competitive rather than complementary; therefore, the expansion of inter-developing-country trade would require the development of new export lines (such as manufactures) and a lessening of emphasis on primary product production. However, the implicit resource shifts accompanying such export diversification might be less efficient and not necessarily beneficial. It would be a mistake to view increasing inter-developing-country trade as a valuable end in itself.

From the information presented in Table 7.1, it can be concluded that Latin America's trade with other developing countries is not as important as its trade with the developed nations. This is not to suggest, however, that Latin American-Third World trade relations are limited to trade flows. Many developing countries confront similar problems in increasing their exports to the developed countries, and are concerned about these difficulties. But before discussing this and other Latin American-Third World collective economic relations, we must consider the other forms of direct economic relations.

Aid

Some of the wealthier developing countries recently have begun to provide economic assistance to other developing countries as part of their attempts to establish client-patron relationships and spheres of influence. In Latin America, Argentina, Brazil, Mexico, and Venezuela have been the major donors. However, almost all of the assistance provided by these countries has gone to other Latin American nations. With the exception of Venezuela's $875-million contribution to the World Bank, only token donations have been made to extraregional developing countries: Argentina has joined the African Development Fund, is building a soybean processing plant in Liberia, and has presented Libya with $200 million in credits; and Mexico is providing technical assistance for the construction of fishing vessels in India and for henequen fiber farming and cattle raising in Tanzania. Aside from these, only a few isolated cases of direct Latin American support for extraregional Third-World development could be cited. For their part, the Asian and African nations, too, have demonstrated particular concern for the plight of their own neighbors. The oil-producing nations of the Middle East, for instance, have given 80 percent of their assistance to other Arab and Moslem countries.

Perhaps the single most important aid arrangement between an extraregional developing country and a Latin American nation is the $100 million that Iran has provided to help Peru finance the Trans-Andean pipeline. But this, too, is one of only a handful of examples.

Despite claims of Third-World solidarity, the principal aid interactions continue to be along north-south lines, with 80 percent of all assistance given to the developing countries by the noncommunist developed nations. The small percentage provided by the richer developing countries is likely to grow, particularly if the Western industrial nations retaliate against collusive commodity agreements by restricting assistance or if they continue to suffer economic setbacks. However, considering even the most prosperous developing countries' needs in terms of capital and technical skills, most developing nations will have little to offer their more unfortunate neighbors for many years. No doubt, inter-developing-country assistance will grow slowly, but, in the meantime, the developing countries will have to continue depending upon the developed nations for foreign assistance. This will be true particularly for the least economically viable.

Investment

Public and private investment by developing countries in other developing countries is also rare, although it would appear that, at least for some of the more advanced, such investment is growing. A few large Brazilian and Mexican firms have made investments of this kind, but, again, Latin American investments are concentrated almost entirely in Latin America with extraregional investments confined to Asia and Africa. Furthermore, with a few exceptions, such as Braspetro's investment in Iraq's oil industry, the Latin American investments are small.

The Latin American countries, including those that are petroleum exporters, can be expected to invest most of their capital domestically for years to come. What foreign investments they make are more likely to be made in neighboring nations for the purpose of promoting regional integration or developing spheres of influence and in the developed nations for security rather than in extraregional developing countries. (Of course, some Latin American capital no doubt will continue to find its way to safe havens in Swiss banks as well.) Joint ownership probably will characterize most Latin American investments in the Third World. Iran and Venezuela, for example, already have agreed to establish a jointly owned maritime oil transportation company.

COLLECTIVE INTERACTIONS

Trade

The similarity of the problems faced by many developing countries in increasing their exports to the developed countries has led to both consensus and conflict in the relations of the developing countries.

One area in which developing countries have shown an increasing interest is the formation of commodity agreements by primary product producers. The purpose of such arrangements is to establish and exercise monopolistic strength in the international marketplace. Conditions conducive to the formation of commodity arrangements include price inelasticity, growing demand due to high income elasticity, the relative absence of production facilities in the principal consuming countries, and climatic or natural resource limitations on supply expansion. In addition, the fewer producing countries there are the fewer political and organizational difficulties that arise in reaching mutually advantageous restrictive agreements. Much of the spectacular success of the petroleum cartel OPEC can be explained by the ability of the oil-producing nations to satisfy these conditions. However, the replication of the OPEC model, attempted by the producers of coffee, cocoa, tea, bauxite, bananas, and other commodities, so far, has proven unattainable.

The political economy of developing countries' collaboration, while in some respects is conducive to the formation of effective producers' alliances, also presents ample opportunity for conflict among developing-country suppliers. The interactions within collusive organizations occur at the interstate level, and decisions, such as those pertaining to production and export quotas, can provoke antagonism. If this occurs, the producers must be willing to sublimate what may seem to be important national interests in favor of common gains in order for the cartel to thrive.

Only a few primary products are exported exclusively by the Latin American countries or by the Latin Americans and a few minor extraregional developing-country producers. However, even Latin American domination of the market has not resulted in fully successful producers' alliances. The Union de Paises Exportadores de Banano (UPEB) has not had the full cooperation of Ecuador, the largest banana producer, and some of the policies of the Communidad de Paises Latinoamericanos y del Caribe Exportadores de Azucar have been opposed by the Dominican Republic and Brazil, both large sugar producers. When the Latin American suppliers have joined other developing countries, difficulties often have been compounded. For example, traditional Latin American coffee producers have been forced to reduce the relative size of their sales to allow new producers a share of the market.

The import barriers of the developed countries are another trade-related issue that has affected Latin American-Third World economic relations. The protectionism that confronts developing countries wishing to export their products to the developed nations is well documented, and trade restrictions evidently are most severe for labor-intensive items, which developing countries have the greatest comparative advantage in selling. Rather than dealing bilaterally with the developed countries, it is clearly in the interests of the developing countries to work collectively toward the alleviation of trade barriers. The primary institutional setting for collective action by the developing countries in this area has been the UNCTAD, which has been fairly successful in focusing attention upon developing countries' trade problems and negotiating tariff preferences for some of their exports.

Nevertheless, some rancor has attended these collective efforts. The Latin Americans resent the favored treatment that members of the European Economic Community have given to goods imported from their former African and Caribbean colonies. On the other hand, the Latin Americans, while wishing to obtain similar benefits from the EEC, would also like special treatment from the United States.

In addition, the more developed Latin American nations, such as Brazil and Argentina, as well as some other developing countries, have some interests that diverge from those of the smaller developing countries. These more developed nations have proposed a system of general nonreciprocal and nondiscriminatory preferences for all Third-World manufactures and semimanufactures exported to the developed nations. This would benefit the more industrialized developing countries, but would do little for those with less advanced economies. The semi-industrial nations, however, are not convinced that special treatment should be accorded to the poorest aliens, and have been reluctant to support their requests for trade preferences.

Yet, within the UNCTAD there is a growing consensus about the need for special negotiating techniques and ground rules that can ensure maximum benefits for the developing countries.[9] If the developing countries mount a concerted effort in the ongoing multilateral trade negotiations, it may be possible to avoid a repetition of the Kennedy Round, which was less beneficial to them than to the industrial countries.

The presence of multinational firms in much of the Third World has also influenced Latin American-extraregional developing-country relations. The manufacture and export of components involving labor-intensive production have increased substantially in many developing countries during the past few years,[10] and foreign firms are significant exporters of these and other manufactured goods. In Brazil, for example, 43 percent of the manufactured goods in 1969 were exported by multinational firms, a rise from the 34 percent recorded for 1967.[11] Moreover, it seems that inter-developing-country trade still has a greater tendency to be dominated by multinational firms that are usually based, of course, in the developed countries.

To cite the Brazilian case again, in 1969, a full 71 percent of multinational-firm exports went to the LAFTA area, while nationally owned Brazilian firms appeared to concentrate more heavily on the developed country markets.[12] Thus, it would seem that the multinational firm is important for developing-country exports, especially manufactures, and perhaps even more important in inter-developing-country trade relations. Here again, relations between developing countries are tempered by what is essentially a north-south interaction, the operation of developed-country firms in the developing countries.

Other

To attract foreign firms, developing countries have been offering a host of inducements, including tax rebates and exemptions, subsidized credit, and import privileges at overvalued exchange rates. Since competition among them for foreign investments, especially in the export-oriented industries, is unregulated and intense, there is a real risk that the developing countries will sacrifice a considerable amount of the potential benefits they could receive from multinational firms in order to attract investments in the first place.

The advantages to be obtained by the developing countries from a cooperative approach toward dealing with the multinational firms is clear, but the obstacles to agreement are equally apparent. As demonstrated by the UNCTAD III meetings, the growth of multinational firms in the developing countries has produced concern about their behavior and has stimulated attempts to control their activities. Several Latin American countries are in the vanguard of this movement. However, an international organization may be needed to integrate policy in this area; perhaps UNCTAD will prove capable of undertaking this mission, but regional cooperation may be necessary first. The Andean Group's implementation of common ground rules governing the treatment of foreign capital and the activities of foreign firms may be the necessary model.

There is not space here to consider in depth all the economic problems that have stimulated attempts by Latin American and other developing nations to harmonize their policies. However, some Latin American countries have been at the forefront of the Third-World solidarity movement, and the following discussion of Latin American leadership will mention some of the collective relations overlooked in this section.

LEADERSHIP

Algeria, Ghana, India, Indonesia, the United Arab Republic, and Yugoslavia commonly have been touted as leaders of the Third World. The Latin American nations rarely have been in the running. However, their conspicuous absence has not been due to any lack of ambition.

Venezuela, particularly since the election of President Perez, has been trying to obtain a leadership role in the Third World by defending the need for higher prices for the raw materials produced by the developing countries and by vigorously championing the creation of cartels for such commodities as petroleum, iron ore, bauxite, coffee, and bananas.

Mexico, under President Echeverria, has been seeking to mobilize the developing countries by emphasizing the need for a common defense against the developed nations. In a speech delivered at a 1972 UNCTAD meeting, Echeverria outlined the Charter of Economic Rights and Duties of States, which he felt would protect the developing countries. However, the developed and developing countries have not agreed on the charter's details. Many of the developing countries believe that the charter should be accepted as a binding treaty, while the developed nations would prefer to have some of its contents accepted merely as recommendations without the force of international law. Controversy also surrounds five of the charter's clauses, those pertaining to the control of multinational corporations, their nationalization, other foreign investments, permanent sovereignty over natural resources, and certain aspects of international trade.

Brazil also has been encouraging developing countries to negotiate as a group in order to win economic concessions from the developed nations, and has been particularly active within the Group of 77. The Brazilians have pointed to their multiracial society and success in industrializing a tropical nation as examples other developing countries should follow. Yet, despite Brazil's desire to play a prominent role in the Third World, some of its present leaders warn that this can be done only after Brazil has become the undisputed leader of Latin America.[13]

Cuba is another Latin American country that has been eager to guide the developing countries. In an effort to reduce its dependence on the Soviet Union and counter its isolation in the western hemisphere, Cuba began to court the Asian and African nations in 1961. A series of Third-World meetings was held in Havana, among them the Tricontinental Conference of 1966, the OLAS* Conference of 1967, and the Cultural Congress of 1968. Castro seems to have entertained "exaggerated hopes in certain 'neutralist' and 'nationalist' regimes." These were disappointed and, by the mid-1960s, Castro had decided to emphasize his association with the more revolutionary Third-World governments and movements even though Cuba's reliance on the Soviet Union inhibited him from moving decisively in this direction.[14] Nevertheless, Cuba has not abandoned its interest in the Third World and has tried to demonstrate that size, propinquity to a great power, and level of economic development need not prevent developing countries from achieving greater independence.

Finally, Argentina and Peru can be counted among the Latin American nations bidding for Third-World leadership. Both countries claim to be creating societies that will be neither capitalist nor communist and seem to imply that their "unique" developmental models might be adapted beneficially by other developing countries. While the Peruvian revolution is being studied throughout the Third World, the latest Argentine experiment with Peronism appears to have aroused little interest.

The present Argentine regime may venerate Peron, but the incessant allusions to the former president's post-World War II vision of Argentina's "Third Position" between the United States and the Soviet Union in world affairs are only part of a ritual. (Constant references to Argentina's "independent foreign policy" may be the government's attempt to endear itself to the country's left.) Since 1973, Argentina has been following a pragmatic foreign policy with trade promotion the primary immediate goal. At the same time, polemics and symbolic acts have been used by the Argentines in their attempt to present a nationalist image attractive to other developing countries.

Peru claims that it is engaged in an antiimperialist revolution that is an integral part of the Third World's struggle against foreign domination by the developed nations. In a 1971 address to the Group of 77, President Velasco called for the creation of a permanent organization

---

*Organizacion Latino-Americano de Solidaridad [Latin American Organization for Solidarity] always identified by Spanish initials (ed.).

to deal with the Third World's common problems. Peru also has proposed the formation of a new monetary organization in which developing countries would have greater voting power than they have in the International Monetary Fund (IMF). However, it is in the area of natural resource protection that Peru has been most active. The Peruvians believe that the offshore resources of many Third-World nations are vital for successful development and that access to them must be safeguarded. Strong advocates of the 200-mile territorial sea, they have persistently criticized the developed countries at recent international conferences convened to consider maritime disputes and the establishment of a new regime to govern the seas. In preparation for these conferences, the Peruvians expounded their position on the law of the seas at the Kabul and Algiers meetings of nonaligned nations and received significant support for their policy.

Despite their aspirations, the Latin American contenders for Third-World leadership have found it necessary to deny any wish to obtain positions of primacy among the developing countries. They realize that to acknowledge their ambitions would cause apprehension within the Third World and erode their influence. As Guy Poitras has observed, "the image of even modest power does not rest comfortably with a leader of the dependent world."[15] Therefore, the Latin Americans have proclaimed consistently that they are too preoccupied with their own development to have any designs on weaker states.

Among the Latin American contenders, Peru appears to have the greatest interest in Third-World leadership and, at present, the most success. Cuba is currently identified too closely with the Soviet Union to appeal to many Third-World countries, although this image may be altered if Cuba is able to gain more flexibility by reducing its economic reliance on Moscow through the reestablishment of diplomatic relations with the United States and the strengthening of its ties with other Latin American nations.

Brazil's identification with the United States, as well as its authoritarian political system, make it unattractive to some developing countries. Moreover, the anxiety felt by some South Americans about Brazil's expanding power may soon spread to West Africa and other parts of the Third World.

In the past, Mexico has found it beneficial to bargain with the United States on a bilateral basis and has taken care not to be perceived as the leader of a multinational challenge to American power. President Echeverria's travels throughout the Third World and his pronouncements about the need to reform the international economic system may indicate that a profound change in Mexican foreign policy is in the making, but some observers have concluded that most of his initiatives have been for domestic consumption or have been undertaken because of a lack of Latin American receptivity to Mexican overtures. While

Mexico may become more assertive in its economic relations with the United States, it is unlikely that it will risk exposing its economy to American retaliation. Thus, Mexican leadership of the Third World probably would be cautious, and this might alienate those developing countries that seek more radical changes in the international economic system.

Given its traditional political instability and racial attitudes, Argentina probably should not be counted among the serious contestants for Third-World leadership at the present time. (However, the Argentines have been energetic in wooing certain Arab and African nations. Economic ties have been strengthened, but direct economic relations may not be sufficient to earn Argentina a leadership role in the Third World. Peronist ideology certainly has not attracted a great deal of attention; the translation of Peron's collected works into Arabic for distribution in Libya, part of a recent exchange agreement, is a goodwill gesture rather than an indication of Libyan interest in Peronism.) Argentina has craved a leadership role in South America since the nineteenth century but, since it may no longer be able to rival Brazil there, it may continue to search for allies wherever it can find them in a last attempt to outmaneuver Brazil.

As for Venezuela, despite its wealth, for the time being, its ambitions seem limited to increasing its influence in Latin America. However, should Venezuela's aspirations soar, its very wealth, like Brazil's, may prove a mixed blessing, raising doubts about the country's real motives for seeking leadership. Finally, if a Fourth World of the globe's most impoverished nations emerges, several smaller Latin American countries might become candidates for its leadership. At present, Jamaica, Panama, and Guyana would seem to be the most likely Latin American competitors for such a role.

The inclination of some Latin American nations to seek greater influence in the rest of the Third World may produce some negative repercussions. For instance, a contest between two or more Latin American countries for Third-World leadership (or for Latin American leadership, for that matter) could jeopardize the Latin American solidarity movement just as it is beginning to thrive. The zeal of Mexico and Peru, for example, has already strained their bilateral relations somewhat. When Peru proposed the establishment of a new world monetary arrangement, Mexico objected, claiming that a reformed IMF could deal with the international monetary crisis. This insult was compounded when Mexico, rather than Peru, became a developing-country member of the IMF's Committee of 20. Friction between Mexico and Peru has been exacerbated further by Peru's criticism of President Echeverria's Charter of Economic Rights and Duties of States and his SELA proposals.

Of course, more traditional Latin American rivalries also could be inflamed should one party to such a rivalry appear to be currying favor among the developing countries at the expense of the other. In fact, this has occurred. Although Argentina is self-sufficient in petroleum (to be precise, Argentina produces over 80 percent of the oil it consumes, but has enough oil reserves to be completely self-sufficient), the state petroleum company has bought crude oil from the Arab producers, Libya in particular, and some Brazilians have interpreted these purchases as an Argentine attempt to deny Brazil the oil that it must import, despite the fact that Brazil procures much of its petroleum from Iran and Nigeria.* (Although Brazil has large iron ore reserves, it has purchased ore from Bolivia, stimulating Argentina, in turn, to charge it with economic denial.)

In addition, strains in Latin American-Third World relations may be generated by increased trade, aid, and investment flows. For instance, the smaller countries of West Africa conceivably might encourage a greater Brazilian presence in their nations in order to offset their growing dependence on Nigeria. If Nigeria became alarmed by Brazil's encroachment in its local sphere of influence, it might seek to promote Argentine interests in Africa or even reduce its sales of petroleum to Brazil. While a scenario of this sort seems fanciful today, Third-World local leviathans are arising and may not be content for long to restrict their activities to their own regions.

To conclude this part of the discussion, the Third-World solidarity movement has been founded upon the recognition of a common goal: the reform or replacement of the present international economic system. Whatever unity now exists among the developing countries will not be easy to maintain as some Third-World nations become less economically dependent. Balance of power politics are likely to be a feature of inter-developing-country relations unless additional bonds can be forged. Moreover, the search for new goals could produce conflict between Latin America and other developing countries and hinder Latin American nations interested in leading the Third World. Clearly, some objectives that might be attractive to the African and Asian developing countries could prove less appealing to the Latin American countries, some of which have demonstrated their impatience with African and Asian rhetoric on colonialism, racism, and disarmament at recent conferences of the nonaligned nations.

---

*There are indications that Argentine and Brazilian diplomacy in Africa has also been affected by the rivalry, with the black African nations trying to exploit the situation for their own advantage.

If any Latin American countries become too active in helping to define future Third-World objectives, they might sacrifice some of the advantages to be gained from direct economic relations with the rest of the Third World. Along with leadership could come suspicion and a disinclination on the part of the weaker developing countries to become economically entangled with countries that seem to have unlimited ambitions. On the other hand, if direct economic interaction increases and seems to be unfairly benefiting a Latin American nation, that country may lose some of its ability to influence the collective behavior of the Third World.

IMPLICATIONS FOR THE UNITED STATES

Membership in a "western hemisphere community" or "inter-American family" dominated by the United States no longer has a strong allure for many Latin American nations. These countries seem convinced that their interests lie more closely with other developing countries than with the United States. Other Latin American nations, while wishing to expand their relations with the Third World, still seem to believe that their interests coincide, first with those of the other Latin American countries, second with those of the western hemisphere, third with those of the "western community," and finally, with those of other developing countries. Still other Latin American countries, however, are trying to avoid declarations of loyalty to either the Third World or the United States; they are prepared to side with whichever country or countries offer the most at a particular time. The majority probably belong to this category, although the positions taken by all three groups are probably not irrevocable. Therefore, United States policy will be a factor, although not necessarily the only or the decisive factor, in determining whether the Latin Americans become fully integrated into the Third World.

Should the United States oppose the Latin American "opening" to the Third World? Could it do so successfully? Greater Latin American-Third World unity probably would not endanger America's security since Latin America's contribution to this country's security is minimal. The U.S. military presence in Latin America is declining, and Latin American solidarity with the Third World might help to ensure that its territory would not be used by an unfriendly superpower. Given Latin America's low strategic value, Latin American nonalignment might be a cheaper and more certain contribution to American defense than the present undependable alliance.

During World War II, Latin America was regarded as a valuable source of raw materials for the Allies; access to these resources has again become a primary American concern in the era of the petroleum crisis. However, of total world exports of nonfood, nonfuel, raw materials, only 30 percent are produced by Latin America and other developing countries; the industrialized noncommunist countries account for 60 percent and the communist nations 10 percent.[16] Much of the food that is exported comes from the United States and other developed countries.

The preservation of U.S. access to Latin American petroleum is vital if the United States is not to become dependent on Middle Eastern imports. Although production in Venezuela, the United States's leading oil supplier, is declining, Ecuador, Bolivia, Peru, and Mexico are or may become major suppliers, and additional important discoveries may be made in other parts of Latin America.

Although Venezuela was a founder of OPEC and a strong advocate of higher petroleum prices, oil from Latin America continued to flow to the United States during the 1973 Arab boycott. Yet the United States Congress did not bother to discriminate between the Arab oil producers and Latin America's two OPEC members, Ecuador and Venezuela, when framing the new trade act that denies most-favored-nation status to OPEC members. Retaliation of this sort is ill-advised and could eliminate the possibility that the Latin Americans will serve as a moderating influence in Third-World forums.

At least one writer has suggested that it would be more productive for the United States to provide Latin America's nationalized petroleum industries with design, engineering, and capital assistance so that these industries can expand their capacities.[17] In conjunction with these suggestions, it has been proposed that Latin America be provided with facilities for training those who will operate the petroleum industries. While these proposals are preferable to a policy of reprisal, expectations about the leverage produced by foreign assistance must not become too high. Long-term price and supply arrangements with the Latin American suppliers, another proposal based on an earlier Venezuelan overture, might now be perceived as a none too subtle attempt by the United States to destroy the OPEC cartel. Efforts to prevent the Latin American countries from associating freely with other developing countries could damage U.S. interests and buttress Latin American enchantment with the Third-World movement.

Making concessions to the Latin Americans and other developing countries under duress is not a prospect likely to please many Americans, and some, despite the Indo-China debacle, may unwisely advocate direct U.S. intervention rather than mild retaliation, cooperation, or other forms of diplomacy to protect its access to vital raw materials, such as oil. Although in the past U.S. military intervention in Latin America has taken place primarily in the Caribbean, Central America, and Mexico, this does not mean that North American forces could not operate effectively in South America where most of Latin America's oil is located. Logistics would be more difficult than those of previous interventions, but the oil fields might be seized intact; since no threats of military action have been made, the Latin Americans, unlike the Arabs, probably have not made preparations to sabotage their production facilities. Intervention in Latin America would also be less likely to entail the risk of a forceful Soviet response than would such action in the Middle East, since presumably the Soviets have accepted the legitimacy of United States domination of the area—much to the displeasure of some Latin Americans.

Once the oil fields had been gained, however, their retention and operation by the United States would pose grave difficulties and would require the commitment of a large occupation force. Controlling a relatively large South American country such as Venezuela, for example, would bear little resemblance to the minimal effort required to "stabilize" a small island such as the Dominican Republic. Certainly occupation would be costly in terms of men and material since continued resistance could be expected; whether the American public would accept this cost would depend upon whether it had accepted intervention as vital for United States survival.

Clearly, this course of action would drive even the most conservative Latin American countries into the Third-World camp, where, together with other developing countries, they could be expected to resort to terrorism, nuclear blackmail, expropriation of foreign assets, default on debts, and other disruptive actions. The forceful destruction of the cartel strategy, in other words, would not guarantee a return to the world economic order that prevailed before 1973.[18]

Closer relations between Latin America and other developing countries need not mean a Latin American rejection of the United States. Most Latin Americans probably continue to believe that they have a stake in maintaining cordial relations with the United States, and if the United States has patience (something that evidently does not come easily to many Americans) and makes some allowances, a new cold war between the industrial countries and the developing countries, including the Latin American nations, may be averted. All alliances are transitory, and some day the United States might even find itself being asked by the Latin Americans to mediate a Third-World dispute.

SUMMARY AND RESEARCH AGENDA

Latin American economic relations with the Third World are a relatively recent phenomenon, although some important exceptions to this generalization can be cited. These include Brazil's nineteenth-century economic involvement in Portuguese Africa,[19] particularly Angola, and the slave trade between Africa and Latin America, which did not cease until the middle of the nineteenth century.

While contemporary direct economic interactions between Latin America and other developing countries are growing, they are still far less important than north-south interactions. Even in the case of international trade, Latin American-extraregional Third World flows, save for petroleum, are not terribly significant and do not seem to be keeping pace, for example, with the relative growth experienced in intra-Latin American trade.

Direct economic flows, however, constitute only one form of Latin American-Third World economic relations. Many problems of an economic nature have caused concern in Latin America and other developing countries. Most of these relate to the domination of the international economic order by the developed nations. Therefore, in an attempt to cope with their attendant economic problems, the Latin Americans and other Third-World nations have been trying to organize in order to present their demands collectively to the richer nations. This entirely new pattern of south-south interaction has been characterized by both consensus and conflict.

This chapter has dealt primarily with the present state of Latin American-Third World relations. As these evolve it will be possible to examine the topic more comprehensively. Among the many aspects of the Latin American-Third World relationship that will merit analysis are the following:

- Latin American-Third World ideological and cultural affinities
- Soviet and Chinese interest in Latin American nonalignment
- Possibility of the transfer of Latin American technology to other developing countries
- Development of Latin American-Third World transportation and communication links
- Evolution of Latin American-Third World economic organizations
- Competition between Latin America and other developing countries for assistance, loans, and technology
- Latin American attempts to export manufactured goods to other developing areas
- Latin American-Third World cooperation and conflict when dealing with noneconomic issues such as disarmament
- Role of diplomats and transnational institutions in strengthening Latin American-Third World ties
- Third-World interest in Latin American development models
- Domestic politics and the Latin American-Third World relationship

NOTES

1. In fact, entire books have been based upon this debate. See, for example, Luis Alberto Sanchez, Existe America Latina? (Mexico City: Fondo de Cultura Economica, 1945).

2. Very few studies of relations among the Latin American states have been undertaken either. Among the pioneering efforts to understand these relations are David F. Ronfeldt and Luigi R. Einaudi, "Conflict and Cooperation among Latin American States," in Beyond Cuba: Latin America Takes Charge of Its Future ed. Luigi R. Einaudi, (New York: Crane, Russak & Co., 1974), pp. 185-200; Weston H. Agor and Andres Suarez, "The Emerging Latin American Political Subsystem," in Changing Latin America: New Interpretations of its Politics and Society. ed. Douglas A. Chalmers, Proceedings of the Academy of Political Science 30 (August 1972): 153-66; and several articles in the first volume of Latin American International Affairs, Ronald G. Hellman and H. Jon Rosenbaum, eds., Latin America: The Search for a New International Role (New York: Sage Publications/Halsted Press, 1975).

3. "Latin America: Joining the Third World," Latin America 8, no. 9 (March 1, 1974): 278-279.

4. This theme is discussed in greater detail in H. Jon Rosenbaum and William G. Tyler, "South-South Relations: The Economic and Political Content of Interactions Among Developing Countries," International Organization 29, no. 1 (Winter 1975): 243-274.

5. "Latin America: The Launching of SELA," Latin America 9, no. 13 (March 28, 1975): 97.

6. Wayne A. Selcher, The Afro-Asian Dimension of Brazilian Foreign Policy (Gainesville, Fla.: University of Florida Press, 1974). This study is the best of only a handful of American studies of Latin American-Third World relations. Another less ambitious work is Aaron Segal, "Giant Strangers: Africa and Latin America," Africa Report 11 (April 1966): 48-53. A significant number of Latin Americans have written about the topic, however. One of the most recent studies is Carlos E. Perez Llana, "America Latina y los paises no alineados," Estudios Internacionales 6, no. 24 (October- December 1973): 43-65. Almost nothing has been published in other Third-World nations about economic relations with Latin America.

7. The figures were calculated from data contained in various issues of International Financial Statistics. If petroleum exports are considered extraordinary and subtracted from the data, the differences between developed- and developing-country export growth become still more striking. In fact, much of the sluggish behavior of developing-

country exports is disguised by the rapid increase in the value of petroleum exports, especially in recent years. Oil-producing developing countries saw their export receipts grow from $43 billion in 1973 to $133 billion in 1974.

8. Evidence supporting this assertion is available in several forms. For an empirical substantiation, see Ranadev Banerji, "The Export Performance of Less Developed Countries: A Constant Market Share Analysis," Weltwirtschaftliches Archiv 110, no. 3 (September 1974): 447-480.

9. See Sidney Dell, "An Appraisal of UNCTAD III," World Development 1, no. 5 (May 1973): 7.

10. See Gerald K. Helleiner, "Manufactured Exports from Less Developed Countries and Multinational Firms," Economic Journal 83, no. 329 (March 1973): 21-47.

11. Fernando Fajnzylber, Sistema Industrial e Exportacao de Manufaturados: Analise da Experiencia Brasileira, IPEA/IMPES Relatorio de Pesquisa no. 7 (Rio de Janeiro: Ministerio do Planejamento e Coordenacao Geral, 1971), p. 209.

12. Ibid., p. 238. In all fairness it can be argued that the Brazilian example may not be representative since many foreign firms are reported to have initiated or expanded their Brazilian operations with the objective of supplying the LAFTA market at least partially from Brazil.

13. An extreme case for Brazil's being the key country of the Third World is made by Mario Pessoa, Politica Internacional a Tropico (Recife: Universidade Federal de Pernambuco, 1970). A somewhat more balanced treatment is to be found in Jorge Maia, O Brasil no Terceiro Mundo (Rio de Janeiro: Bloch Editores, 1968).

14. Robin Blackburn, "Cuba and the Super-Powers," in Patterns of Foreign Influence in the Caribbean, ed. Emanuel de Kadt (London: Oxford University Press, 1972), p. 145.

15. Guy E. Poitras, "Mexico's 'New' Foreign Policy," Inter-American Economic Affairs 28, no. 3 (Winter 1974): 71.

16. Edwin L. Dale, Jr., "Kissinger's Worldwide Economic Design," New York Times, June 8, 1975, section 3, p. 15.

17. Norman Gall, "The Challenge of Venezuelan Oil," Foreign Policy, no. 18 (Spring 1975): 67.

18. Robert L. Rothstein, "The Rich: They've Got to Give a Little," New York Times, June 6, 1975, p. 31.

19. See Jose Honorio Rodrigues, Brazil and Africa (Berkeley, Calif.: University of California Press, 1965), p. 382.

CHAPTER

8

LATIN AMERICAN ENERGY SUPPLY AND THE UNITED STATES

Philip Musgrove

To consider the place of Latin America in "the world system" is necessarily to overlook many of the vital internal characteristics of this region. To emphasize only those of its relations and possibilities that are of direct interest to the United States is to narrow the field still further. Where energy is concerned, the enquiry is subdivided into two questions: How important is Latin America now as a source of energy for the United States? Is its importance likely to change dramatically in the near future?

In trying to answer these questions, it is appropriate to begin with a summary of the situation of 1971-72, the last relatively normal years before the worldwide disruption of energy markets set in motion by the Arab-Israeli war of 1973 and the ensuing Arab oil embargo. Since this author has analyzed this situation elsewhere,[1] it does not seem necessary to review it in detail here. More to the point is a consideration of how the prospects in view in 1971-72 have been modified by the events of the last two years and especially by the enormous increase in oil prices imposed by the member states of the Organization of Petroleum Exporting Countries (OPEC). Because this sharp change in relative prices affects the competitive position of oil with respect to other sources of energy, it becomes necessary to consider briefly the availability of alternative sources in Latin America, their current and potential levels of exploitation, and their implications for the United States. Oil continues to receive primary attention because nothing is likely to displace it soon from major importance in the Latin American economy and because it is almost the only form in which the region is likely to export energy. Other sources, however, may become increasingly important determinants of the net amount of oil available for export.

In the short run, the greatest effect of the quadrupling of oil prices may be financial: importing countries are faced with greatly increased charges, while many exporters are accumulating revenues for which there is no immediate domestic use. For the most part, this chapter will ignore the financial and balance of payments effects of the energy crisis for Latin America.[2] Our concern here is with the physical availability of oil and alternative energy sources, rather than with the levels of income and total trade likely to be associated with particular levels of production, consumption, and trade in energy.

LATIN AMERICA'S POSITION IN THE EARLY 1970s

In 1971, Latin America accounted for some 5.8 percent of world production of commercial energy (oil, gas, coal, lignite, wood, hydroelectricity, and nuclear power). This figure breaks down into 0.4 percent for coal, 3.7 percent for natural gas, 6.3 percent for hydroelectric power (there is no nuclear power in Latin America), and 10.9 percent for crude oil. Petroleum was exported from the region in large amounts, small amounts of coal were imported, and there was essentially no trade in natural gas or hydroelectricity. Latin America's shares of world consumption for these last two categories, therefore, were the same as its shares of world production. In total, Latin America consumed 3.85 percent of world energy and 6.3 percent of world oil.[3] Of all the energy produced in Latin America, oil accounted for 81.6 percent and natural gas for 13.4 percent; of all the energy consumed, the shares for these fuels were 70.1 and 20.6 percent.

These figures illustrate the position of Latin America in the world energy system: the region was a net exporter of about 4.6 percent of the world's oil, equivalent to 2.25 percent of energy consumption in the rest of the world. All other sources of energy in Latin America were important to other regions only insofar as they reduced domestic demand for oil and therefore made more oil available for export.

In 1972, Latin America produced 4.884 million barrels per day (b/d) of petroleum and consumed 2.544 million b/d, leaving net exports of 2.340 million b/d of crude oil and refined products. Venezuela alone exported directly or through refineries in the Netherlands West Indies 2.993 million b/d, but this was offset by substantial net imports into countries producing no oil or less than their domestic requirements: 458,000 b/d into Brazil, 80,500 into Chile, 100,500 into Cuba, and between 35,000 and 40,000 b/d into Argentina, Peru, and Uruguay. In addition to Venezuela, Bolivia, Ecuador, Colombia, and Trinidad exported oil averaging 214,000 b/d for the entire year and much more at the end of the year. Total imports into the region were 2.127 million b/d, higher than the difference between production and consumption because only 53 percent of total imports came from other Latin American countries and because some 313,000 b/d were imported from outside the region for refining and reexport, principally to the United States.

Two features emerge from this balance. The first is that, although Latin America as a whole is self-sufficient in oil, the region is connected to the rest of the world by imports as well as exports, in consequence of price variations and differences among types of oil and among markets. The second is that so far as the rest of the world is concerned, Venezuela dominated the energy market in Latin America. In 1972, all the other countries together produced some 1.664 million b/d and consumed 2.317 million b/d, forming a market for at most 653,000 b/d, or only 450,000 b/d after deduction of imports from Venezuela.

These levels of production were based on reserves totaling some 30.5 billion barrels of oil: 45 percent in Venezuela, 19 percent in Ecuador, 9 percent in Mexico and almost the same amount in Argentina, 6.5 percent in Trinidad, and 4.9 percent in Colombia, with smaller amounts in Bolivia, Brazil, Chile, and Peru. Of total reserves proved and available in early 1973, perhaps 20 billion barrels could be considered potential exports, with the remainder destined to meet domestic needs in the producing countries. This is not a negligible amount, but it is dwarfed by the exportable resources of the Middle East. The ration of reserves to production varied greatly among Latin American countries because in some (notably Ecuador) large oil resources were only recently discovered, while in others (Colombia and Venezuela) reserves were being drawn down. Latin America also had reserves of some 2,315 billion cubic meters of natural gas, equivalent to some 16 billion barrels of oil, concentrated in Venezuela but with relatively large amounts in Argentina, Bolivia, Chile, Mexico, and Trinidad. Much of this gas was used domestically, particularly in Argentina, Mexico, and Venezuela. None of it was exported.

Latin America's exports of 3.620 million b/d in 1972 were almost evenly divided between crude oil and refined products. The latter, 1.760 million b/d, included some products refined from 313,000 b/d of crude imported from outside the region. If these are excluded, together with exports to Latin American destinations, exports were 2.776 million b/d, consisting of 1.467 million b/d of crude oil and 1.309 million b/d of products. Besides the 15 percent of gross exports represented by intraregional trade, about 58 percent went to the United States, 12.4 percent to Canada, and 10 percent to Western Europe.

Latin America was unusual in exporting large volumes of refined products; about three fourths of world oil trade was in crude. In 1972, half of Venezuela's exports and all those from Trinidad-Tobago were refined. A large share of these exports was in the form of residual fuel oil, which is in heavy demand in the eastern United States for heating and for generating electricity. Of crude oil imports of nearly 1 million b/d (to consuming countries only, excluding imports for refining and reexport), 21 percent came from Venezuela, 10 percent from other exporters in the region, one third from the Middle East, and one fourth from North Africa.

THE PROSPECTS FOR 1973-85

Two years ago, it appeared that Latin America's net exports of oil would be unlikely to exceed 3 million b/d within the next decade. Simply to maintain this level in the face of rapidly growing consumption in the region was expected to require that Venezuela maintain exports of 3 million b/d and that Ecuador and Peru together export another 1 million b/d. These are the two countries in which a rapid expansion of exports seemed most feasible. (In the case of Peru, production would first replace imports and then allow for exports.) No substantial change in the net oil surplus or deficit was expected in any other producing country. Output was expected roughly to keep pace with consumption in Argentina, Colombia, and Mexico or even to lag behind it and no significant increases seemed likely to Bolivia, Brazil, or Chile.

Moreover, even this projection[4] assumed that before 1980 there would be significant output from the faja petrolifera, or heavy oil belt, in Venezuela, to compensate for the expected decline in production in the areas held as concessions by U.S. oil firms. Since only small amounts of oil had been produced along the border of the faja, and since the nationalization of the entire oil industry was expected to take place in 1975,* a great deal of uncertainty attended the attempt to guess how much Latin American oil might be available to the United States in another five or ten years. The same questions arose for both conventional and heavy oil in Venezuela: To what degree would foreign companies be allowed to participate in the oil industry after nationalization, and how might the rate of development depend on their technical and financial resources?

In the other producing countries, the question of national oil policy appeared less uncertain, largely because state monopolies already existed (as in Brazil, Chile, and Mexico) or because the traditional

---

*Nationalization of the industry took effect January 1, 1976, with the former concessionaires to be operated as units of Petroven, the new state oil company.

concession arrangement had been replaced by service contracts with foreign enterprise (as in Argentina, Peru, and Bolivia). (Foreign private firms, chiefly United States, produced about 30 percent of Latin American oil outside of Venezuela and essentially all the oil in that country, or about 75 percent of the regional total. The share of the foreign private firms has been falling slowly as state operations expand in several countries; it will now fall still farther with the nationalization of private firms in Venezuela.)

The chief conclusions that seemed evident before the events of 1973-74 were, first, that Latin America was unlikely to provide oil in the volumes needed to end U.S. dependence on the Middle East for energy imports; and, second, that Latin America was nonetheless important enough to the United States to justify substantial continued investment in the region (where permitted) and possibly to warrant direct understandings between governments to ensure a stable flow of oil in the future. Its importance to the United States lies in the obvious value of diversified sources of supply and in its detachment from one major political problem, the Arab-Israeli confrontation, which threatens to interrupt supplies. In some other respects, Latin America is not so very different from the Middle East: political decisions affect actual supply in the short run, while in the long run they help determine the physical availability of oil.

THE UPHEAVAL OF 1973-74 AND ITS POTENTIAL EFFECTS

We have already referred to one effect of the events of 1973-74: Since Latin American exporters did not participate in the Arab oil embargo, the region became relatively more attractive as a source of energy for the United States. (Venezuela did not interrupt supplies to the United States as a result of the 1967 war either, or when the Suez Canal was closed in 1957; in fact, exports increased to make up for reduced shipments from the Middle East.) The other principal effects are all consequences of the rise in oil prices obtained by OPEC since late 1973. Before considering what actually has occurred in the last two years, it may be useful to indicate the effects that might be expected to follow from such a sharp price increase, particularly in the Latin American countries that are not members of OPEC. The expected changes are the same as in the United States, but their relative feasibility and magnitude may be very different in a region that is much less developed and much more dependent on petroleum. (Of the major regions of the world, Latin America is the most dependent on oil for its energy. This is a consequence of its being much more developed than most of Asia and Africa and therefore using relatively less vegetable fuel, and of its having begun industrial development only after coal had begun to be replaced by oil in the traditional industrial centers of Europe and North America.)

Among the effects to be expected are conservation in the use of oil, either through reduced end use or through greater efficiency; increased current production of oil; increased exploration for conventional oil; development of unconventional sources of oil, such as tar sands and oil-bearing shale; and replacement of oil by alternative energy sources (natural gas, coal, hydropower, nuclear power, and so on).

The net result of these measures should be to make more oil available to other regions, including the United States. However, whether there is any substantial effect on net availability depends not only on the feasibility of reducing demand or increasing supply but also on the actions of other oil exporters. It is this last factor that makes it impossible to predict the course of oil supplies or prices. Because world oil trade is dominated by a producers' cartel, it is not evident that one barrel more of oil exported from Mexico or one barrel less imported into Brazil means one more barrel available to importing countries outside Latin America. (Saudi Arabia alone exports more than twice as much oil as all of Latin America, and can easily raise or lower its exports by more than 1 million b/d in a short interval.) We limit ourselves, therefore, to evaluating the potential for increasing net exports from Latin America, on the assumption that this will have some effect on the total net availability of oil and that there is some benefit to the United States, in the present circumstances, from replacing a barrel of Middle Eastern oil with a barrel of Latin American oil.

A further complication is that only two years have passed since the sharp rise in prices, and the adjustments indicated may take years to complete. Many of them will be economically justified only if oil prices remain high; some changes may be set in motion that will eventually prove uneconomic.

CONSERVATION AND REDUCED DEMAND

In the short run, oil demand may be reduced in Latin America not in response to any policy of conservation, but simply as a consequence of balance of payments problems and the worldwide recession in industrial output. The principal oil-importing countries of the region face greatly increased import charges at the very time when their exports may be diminished by the recession in the industrial countries. (For seventeen importing countries, including Barbados and Jamaica, the increase in the cost of oil in 1974 was expected to amount to roughly one fourth of foreign reserves at the start of the year, the share being especially high in Chile and in several small Caribbean countries that are wholly dependent on imported oil. See Gonzales, op. cit., Table 3.) Since oil is vital to industrial output, equilibrium is reached only by reduced income or slower growth. In the long run, this pressure might be eased by substitution of nonoil imports (which occurred in Latin America in response to supply shortages and balance of payments problems in 1930-45),[5] except that most of the opportunities for import replacement have already been exploited in Latin America. Imports average only about one eighth of gross product in the region and are concentrated on industrial inputs and capital equipment.

In general, Latin America probably has fewer opportunities for conservation of energy than the United States. Less commercial energy is used in frivolous or luxurious consumption and more in industrial production. Also, many measures to reduce fuel use require capital investments that are difficult to achieve in poorer countries. For example, less fuel would be needed for transportation with a newer and more efficient vehicle stock, but it is beyond the region's capacity to replace or modify quickly the many old vehicles still in service.

There are, however, some opportunities for conservation that are worth investigating. One is reducing private vehicular travel by raising fuel prices, which have been subsidized in many countries to cheapen urban mass transport. A striking example is Peru, where gasoline prices were kept low (about twenty cents per gallon), despite the country's need to import one fourth of its consumption, when world oil prices rose. This subsidy to upper income groups is now being reduced.[6] The amount of extra oil made available by more reasonable prices, however, is likely to be slight, given the small amount of fuel affected and its relatively low price-elasticity of demand; at most, perhaps 100,000 b/d might be saved. Larger amounts might be conserved by reductions in vehicular speeds and in electrical service and heat, but the potential saving is unknown. (Emergency conservation measures were adopted briefly in some countries, such as Argentina, in 1974.)

Another possible saving is in reducing transmission losses in electrical systems. These now waste, on average, 16 percent of the energy generated, while a loss of only 10 percent could be reached quickly and with relatively little investment.[7] Again, the saving would be slight, perhaps 50,000 to 100,000 b/d, although the financial saving would be valuable to a number of the smaller countries. Other savings would result from the displacement of private generators with public supply, which is generated more efficiently, and the retirement of the oldest thermal plants.

In the long run, and particularly in association with the installation of new capital in industry, transport, and electrical generation, undoubtedly there is room for significant fuel savings. No sizable effect can be expected immediately, however, and any effect may be submerged in changes on the supply side.

INCREASED OIL OUTPUT

This section refers only to increases from reserves that have already been found, although perhaps not yet exploited much, and accelerated rate of use of resources, as distinct from the increased output to be expected from the discovery of major new resources. It appears that output is increasing, or is to be increased, in a few countries, such as Brazil, Bolivia, and Trinidad. In Trinidad, a production decline has been reversed; in Bolivia, there are plans to increase output even if the lifetime of reserves falls from ten years to seven; and, in Brazil, a major new field is to be exploited in only ten years rather than the twenty that would usually be allowed for maximum eventual recovery.[8] In total, these increments may amount to 250,000 b/d within a few years and to still more in the 1980s if reserves can be expanded sufficiently. Output will also be expanded sharply in Peru in the next two years when a pipeline is completed over the Andes from the producing area in the Amazon Basin, adding another 200,000 b/d or more to regional output.[9] In none of these countries, however, are reserves to be drawn down sharply to meet a temporary crisis or opportunity. Finally, oil production is rising dramatically in Mexico, from 500,000 b/d in 1972 to about 700,000 b/d in 1975, but this increase comes from major new fields discovered in the last few years.[10]

In several other Latin American countries, output has been declining, although for different reasons in each case. Colombian production is shrinking (and exports have ceased) because reserves are dwindling. They were over 900 million barrels in 1961 (some estimates run much higher, to 1.5 billion barrels in 1972) but now may be as low as 700 million, and exploration has been too slow to maintain output. In turn, this situation may result, in part, from high costs in Colombia and the very low price paid to private producers by the government for oil consumed domestically.[11] Output fell by about 50,000 b/d between 1970 and 1974.

Like Colombia, Argentina is almost self-sufficient in oil, importing 10 to 20 percent of its requirements. Production has been declining slightly, despite the large balance of payments savings that more output would bring. The reason appears to be the same one that has caused

Argentine production to fluctuate since the 1950s: political "self-sufficiency," in the sense of relying entirely on a state company, conflicts with the goal of economic self-sufficiency, which is most easily attained with the help of foreign enterprise.[12] Fluctuation in recent years has been less than 20,000 b/d.

Output also has declined in the two major exporters of 1973, Venezuela and Ecuador. Reductions in output in large exporting countries are perhaps to be expected, since reduced demand in the industrial nations has led to a surplus of oil at OPEC prices. However, price maintenance does not seem to have been at issue in Ecuador. The government imposed taxes slightly higher than those agreed to by OPEC, and the private concessionaire responded by cutting production sharply, from 220,000 b/d to only 55,000 b/d.[13] Taxes were reduced in July 1975, but it is too early to tell whether this will lead to greatly increased output.[14] In Venezuela, reductions in output have served partly to maintain prices. (Other OPEC members have also cut production, but the organization has not acted in concert.) Perhaps more important, reduced output slows the flow of windfall income (around $10 billion in 1974) which the Venezuelan economy cannot now absorb. The measure is thus intended primarily to conserve oil and postpone those receipts while the country develops its capacity to invest the proceeds. Output was cut by about 300,000 b/d during 1974.[15]

On balance, supplies available for net export from Latin America have been reduced, since reductions in the exporting countries exceed increases in importing and exporting countries. In the long run, however, net supplies from Latin America may increase. This will depend not only on the immediate technical, political, and financial problems described above but also on Latin America's success in finding more oil or substitute sources of energy.

FINDING MORE OIL

The search for new oil reserves should perhaps be stimulated more by a price rise than by any other means of increasing net supply; it requires large investments but does not require modification or reduced use of existing capital. It also takes time, so that it is not yet possible to attribute any new discoveries to the rise in prices. (It should be remembered that continual discovery of oil is necessary simply to maintain output, since reserves are usually proved for only ten to twenty years ahead. The necessary increase to reserves in each year is that year's output times the reserve lifetime [100 percent plus the rate of growth output]. Only discoveries larger than this permit a long-term increase in the rate of growth of supplies.) Considered here are the resources found in the last few years and the prospects for significant discoveries in the near future.

There have been two substantial discoveries since 1970. In Brazil, reserves have been found on the continental shelf opposite Rio de Janeiro that are believed to hold at least 600 million barrels. This is a small amount by world standards, but it almost doubles Brazil's reserves. Production from the new fields is expected to reach 200,000 b/d quickly, and there is a slight chance that by 1980 Brazil will be self-sufficient in oil, eliminating what is currently the country's largest single import.[16]

Much larger discoveries were made in 1972 in Mexico, in the Reforma field in the southeastern part of the country. It is not yet known how large the find is; some estimates have run as high as 10 to 20 billion barrels,[17] but the fields are more likely to hold 1 or 2 billion barrels. That would almost double Mexico's reserves, with a much greater impact on the volume available for export. The surplus for export is estimated at nearly 1.3 million b/d in 1975, and will undoubtedly increase. This is a more than a one-third increase in the region's net exports. Mexico has not joined OPEC, but has announced that it will sell at or near OPEC prices rather than try to undermine the cartel.[18] Since Mexico's natural markets are in the United States and the Caribbean, it will be competing most directly with Venezuela.

Elsewhere in Latin America there are prospects of discovering much more oil. The Mexican find has revived interest in Central America,[19] where there has been considerable exploration in the past, but no success except for small discoveries in Guatemala. There is active exploration of the continental shelf off Venezuela, along the coast of Brazil, and in Argentina, Uruguay, and Chile. Both the Gulf of Venezuela (north of the Gulf of Maracaibo where production is now centered) and the Gulf of Vela (off the Paraguana Peninsula) in Venezuela appear to hold large amounts of oil; and it is expected also that the oil basin of the upper Amazon, already yielding oil in Colombia, Ecuador, and Peru, extends into western Brazil.[20]

The total amount of oil that eventually may be discovered in Latin America is believed to be very large. Mexico and Venezuela have ultimately recoverable reserves estimated at between 100 and 1,000 billion barrels; Argentina, Bolivia, Colombia, Ecuador, and Peru are believed to have between 10 and 100 billion barrels; and the range for Brazil, Chile, and Trinidad is 1 to 10 billion barrels.[21] Something like 40 billion barrels may lie in fields of between 100 and 500 million barrels each, along the coasts of South America; some 2 billion barrels are believed to exist in several major basins on the Peruvian coast alone.[22] As production increasingly moves offshore, the costs of drilling will rise, but this may be partly compensated for by transport costs lower than those associated with production in the Amazon Basin.

In summary, two observations: (1) There has been one major change in oil availability with the development of the Reforma field in Mexico. Net exports from Latin America can increase by 1 million b/d or more, and the discovery appears large enough to sustain such exports for several years despite rapidly growing domestic use. (2) In the long run, a great deal of oil remains to be found in Latin America. Some of that will come from the southern coasts and the Amazon Basin, but the largest amounts are still likely to be found around the Caribbean. The crucial questions, unanswerable at present, are how quickly this oil can be found and what effect its eventual discovery will have on prices and on actual supplies.

DEVELOPING UNCONVENTIONAL OIL SOURCES

Latin America has two major unconventional petroleum sources. One is oil-bearing shale, similar to that found in the western United States. The shale deposits are believed to hold as much as 820 billion barrels of oil in southern Brazil and much smaller amounts (380 and 125 million barrels, respectively) in Argentina and Chile. Oil has been produced from shale since 1972 in Brazil, at the pilot-plant rate of 1,000 b/d, and there are no plans for expansion to commercial scale.[23] The great increase in oil prices should make shale oil more nearly competitive, but the problems of mining the huge volumes of rock and disposing of the waste have yet to be resolved. Brazil's recent discovery of conventional oil makes development of the shale in the near future even less likely.

There is also a large belt of heavy oil and tar sand in Venezuela, running for 375 miles along the north bank of the Orinoco River in a band some 25 to 50 miles wide. This faja petrolifera is assumed to contain some 700 billion barrels, of which 70 billion could be recovered with current techniques.[24] More recent exploration suggests that the sands are thicker than was previously believed and that the oil is lighter, so that recovery would be higher. Proven reserves ready to produce are now 100 million barrels.[25] Aside from the low gravity, the chief problems with the faja oil are a high sulfur content (about 4 percent) and a relatively large content of such metals as nickel and vanadium. These impurities must be removed, and in order to make light products such as gasoline, the oil must be cracked with large quantities of hydrogen.

The techniques for extracting and refining the heavy oil are fairly well developed,[26] although it remains to apply them on a large scale. The larger economic question of how to finance the very large investments that will be needed to exploit faja oil is intimately connected with the political question of the terms on which foreign enterprise will be allowed to participate in this exploitation.

The advantages to Venezuela of developing this resource are clear. First, the country depends overwhelmingly on oil exports to sustain its high level of consumption and to pay for the capital needed to develop other industries. None of the new industries financed by oil is likely soon to replace it as a source of foreign exchange, nor can the country do without future imports except at a great cost in efficiency. Second, investment in the faja offers a sound domestic use for the reserves now being accumulated. Investment of those reserves abroad may yield a much quicker return, but is politically less acceptable and is regarded as a short-term use of the money.

The disadvantages of investing in the faja are less obvious, but are politically no less important. This policy would commit the country to depending on oil exports for a long time, reducing the chances for eventual diversification, and it would require the participation of foreign expertise at least on a contractual basis.[27] The Venezuelan government therefore has not yet determined its policy toward these investments. Since 1972 it has been discussing with the United States the possibility of a direct agreement covering investment and future supplies, so as to reduce still further the role of private firms and to protect Venezuela against possible future price declines.[28]

It is also clear that, other things being equal, especially prices, the development of the faja is to the United States' advantage since it would ensure a continued flow of oil from Latin America and lessen dependence on the Middle East. (The profits that U.S. firms might earn by participating in this development are a relatively negligible consideration.) The obstacles to any direct arrangement are uncertainty about future supplies and prices from other sources. In most respects, the problem of Venezuela's heavy oil is exactly what it was two or even five years ago, and the need to resolve it becomes more urgent as the country's conventional resources decline.

In one important respect, however, the situation has changed dramatically since 1973. Venezuela now has the money to buy whatever services, foreign and domestic, it needs to develop the faja without having to divert investment from other sectors, or borrow abroad, or make large concessions to private companies in return for their investments. It should now be much easier for Venezuela to decide how to exploit this immense resource and to begin to benefit from it. By 1985, the faja could be producing perhaps as much as 1 million b/d; in fact, output of that magnitude will be needed simply to sustain production of 3 million b/d, unless very large discoveries of conventional oil are made in the new or potential producing areas.

ALTERNATIVE ENERGY SOURCES

Availability

Although Latin America is extraordinarily dependent on petroleum, it is not entirely without other energy resources. In fact, some of these alternatives have been exploited already to a large degree and are increasing their shares of regional energy consumption. The great rise in oil prices gives a further impetus to such replacement, but it does not by itself eliminate the numerous technical and economic obstacles to the wider use of oil substitutes.

We may distinguish four principal applications of energy, which differ in their ability to use different sources: transportation (where, except for electrified railways, there is essentially no substitute for oil products); reducing metal ores, especially in steel making (where coal of coking quality is almost indispensable); heating (where any fuel can be used, but electricity is generally inefficient); and generating electricity (which is virtually the only application of hydro- or nuclear power, but can also employ any fuel).

Two salient facts about energy consumption in Latin America are that the share of electricity has been increasing and that an appreciable share of the region's oil is used to make electricity. The coefficient of electrification (kilowatt-hours consumed, divided by nonelectrical fuel use) rose from 1.07 in 1961 to 1.33 in 1972.[29] Of total commercial energy used in 1973, 64 percent was oil and 16 percent natural gas; hydroelectricity, 15 percent; and coal, 5 percent. Electricity was about 28 percent of the total energy used, the remaining 72 percent being direct consumption of fuel. Hydropower accounted for 55 percent of all electricity generated; oil, 32 percent; and coal and natural gas, the remainder. This means that about 16 percent of the petroleum consumed was used for electrical generation; it is this share that is most susceptible to substitution, although oil may also be displaced from some other uses. Complete substitution of oil in electricity generation would represent a saving of nearly 0.5 million b/d.

Natural gas, coal, and hydropower are likely to replace oil only where they are locally available. Coal can be imported over long distances, but importing from outside the region is less help to the balance of payments. Gas and hydroelectricity can be shipped considerable distances, up to a few thousand miles in the case of gas and some hundreds of miles for electricity; thus, some trade within Latin America is feasible, although significant extraregional trade is not, except in the case of liquefied natural gas.

Nuclear power differs from these sources in being nearly independent of local fuel, since the raw fuel is a small share of the total cost and its volume is small. It happens that the first nuclear station in Latin America is in Argentina, and that others are under consideration there and in Brazil and Mexico; and these three countries also have uranium resources. Possession of domestic uranium may, however, affect the type of reactor installed. Argentina, for example, is using a Canadian system that employs natural uranium, without enrichment. This reduces the market for U.S. designs based on enriched fuel and so affects total U.S.-Latin American energy trade. (These and other issues are more thoroughly explored in this volume in Chapter 11.) Their interest in nuclear power owes more, however, to their large markets for electricity and their need in recent years to import oil than to the eventual development of nuclear weapons.

So long as oil cost a few dollars per barrel, nuclear plants were competitive only at sizes of 500 megawatts or greater, which effectively limited their use to the three largest countries of the region. At current oil prices, nuclear plants may be economical at 150 to 200 megawatts, making their installation feasible in such countries as Chile, Peru, Cuba, Jamaica, Uruguay, and perhaps Colombia.[30] However, other alternatives to oil may become even more attractive, so that a rapid expansion of nuclear energy, while possible, is not a foregone conclusion. (Replacement of oil by nuclear power is also limited by the fact that nuclear plants are suitable only for base-load demand and are extremely inefficient and costly for meeting peak loads.) In the long run, nuclear power may offer considerable import savings, but in the short run, which may be as long as ten years, given the time required to build reactors, much of the capital must be imported.

This last feature makes nuclear power less attractive than hydroelectricity, which also requires much capital and a long development period, but which can be produced with a much higher proportion of domestic inputs. Latin America has a very large hydroelectric potential. Before the rise in oil prices, it was estimated that some 2.8 billion kilowatt-hours could be produced annually from sites that were economically feasible. (This in turn was only 20 percent of the power that might be generated at all sites, including those that would be uneconomic. The proportion that is economic has since risen, but there are no more recent estimates.) About 1 billion kilowatt-hour capacity is ascribed to sites that have been adequately studied or actually developed. These account for half or more of the total potential in Argentina, Chile, Peru, Paraguay, and Uruguay and 40 percent of that in Brazil, all oil-importing countries; elsewhere, detailed knowledge of the hydropower potential is much less advanced.

Total hydroelectric production in the region is now about 110,000 kilowatt-hours yearly; this is only 11 percent of the identified potential and 4 percent or less of what could be produced.[31] In Mexico some 18 percent of the potential has been developed, and in Brazil 6 percent; in no other country does the share exceed 5 percent. If it were possible to produce all the region's electricity from water, only about 7 percent of the resource would be needed. Thus hydroelectric development is held back not by overall resource scarcity, but by consideration of cost, size of markets, and location of appropriate sites, which are often far from the centers of consumption.

Coal is the only major fuel with which Latin America is poorly endowed. Measured reserves are some 4 billion tons, roughly comparable in energy value to the region's oil reserves, and potential resources are estimated as high as 60 billion tons.[32] However, this figure includes much coal that is of low heat value or that is found in seams too thin or short to be economic to exploit.[33] Much of the coal also contains a large share of impurities that must be washed out before use.

Half or more of the regional total is found in Colombia, which is the only country likely to be able to export coal (with the possible exception of Venezuela). Sizable amounts (1 billion tons or more) are found in Brazil, Chile, and Mexico and smaller quantities in Argentina, Peru, and Venezuela. These seven countries also account for almost all imports (of coke and coking coal) and consumption. Total consumption was some 16 million tons in 1972, as against production of 11 million tons. Slightly more than half of their consumption is for metallurgical coke, this being virtually the only coal used in Venezuela. The remainder is used to generate electricity (35 percent in Brazil and Chile and between 10 and 20 percent in Argentina and Colombia) or for heating and domestic use.[34]

Historically, coal has been displaced from all nonmetallurgical uses by oil and gas, and, until recently, it was expected that this process would continue. Coal cost between two and four times as much as these fuels (per unit of energy) in the major consuming countries; and its use as fuel depended partly on the low share of production suitable for coke (leaving much heating coal as a by-product) and partly on balance of payments problems that favored domestic over imported fuel.[35]

With the sharp rise in oil prices, this process might now be reversed. The obvious candidate for substitution is oil used to generate electricity, but here coal must compete with hydropower and natural gas. Coal could also displace fuel oil and kerosene from home uses, but only at a considerable cost in reequipment of capital and in pollution. We suppose, therefore, that coal will replace oil only in large industrial installations, and even there much investment would be required. Natural gas has an advantage over coal in this respect. In the long run, coal can be used to make gas or petroleum products, and thus replace oil over the entire range of uses. However, this process is not commercially very advanced even in the United States. The high capital costs required and the low heat value of much of the coal in Latin America seem certain to delay the process there even more. By the time coal replaces oil in this way in Latin America, it will probably have done so already in the United States. In the short run, the effect of coal on net oil exports from the region is likely to be slight.

Finally, we consider natural gas as a substitute for oil. This differs from all other alternatives in that it is (usually) a joint product with petroleum, and in that it can be pumped back underground to help raise more oil. If gas is used as fuel that would otherwise be flared or vented to the atmosphere, there is a clear savings; in all other cases, using more gas does not necessarily mean making more oil available, over the life of a reservoir. In many cases, reinjection of gas can be replaced by reinjection of water or steam, which makes more of both gas and oil available. Of course, when consuming gas reduces the amount of oil ultimately recoverable, current oil production need not be affected and can be had at lower cost. Thus, we can think of gas as a substitute for oil, at least early in the life of a reservoir. Using the associated gas raises the rate of return on oil-field investment even if it reduces total eventual recovery.

Direct export of natural gas is possible by tanker, if the gas is liquefied. This process has been studied extensively, and its use has appeared imminent several times in Venezuela and in Trinidad, but no exports have yet occurred. This may be in part because both countries have reserved gas exports to the state, banning or limiting participation by private firms. There are plans to export gas from Venezuela equivalent to about 135,000 b/d of oil, and much larger amounts could eventually be traded.[36] Where gas itself is not exported, it can still make more oil available for export.

Natural gas already accounts for about one sixth of the energy used commercially in Latin America, and the share is much higher in those countries that have relatively accessible gas fields and large internal markets. In Argentina, Mexico, and Venezuela, gas is the principal nonvehicular fuel; that is, it has already displaced petroleum for heating and thermoelectric generation. The share of gas that is wasted is fairly low in these countries (between one fourth and one third in Venezuela) and is declining. Waste tends to be very high only where there is no economic way to use the gas, as in the Amazon Basin or at offshore production sites far from consuming centers.* Where there

*The gas produced, together with oil in the Peruvian Amazon, may be piped over the Andes, once an oil line is completed and more reserves are developed.

is an insufficient domestic market, gas may be piped to neighboring countries, as it is from Bolivia to Argentina and Brazil.[37]

If all the gas currently wasted (perhaps half of the difference between production and consumption) could be used as fuel, the effect would be that of replacing some 400,000 to 500,000 b/d of oil. All the gas either wasted or reinjected is theoretically equivalent to nearly 1 million b/d, but, if it were used, production of oil would fall (within a short time, if not immediately). Not all the wasted gas can be used economically, so the actual margin for replacement is probably only about 250,000 b/d, or roughly 10 percent of oil consumption. This is a significant amount of oil, but it is only about one sixth or one seventh of Latin America's net exports to the United States. Thus, while natural gas is contributing to make more oil available, and there are strong incentives to use gas whenever possible, it does not appear that it can dramatically increase net regional supplies in the short run. In the long run, greater use of gas means greater availability of oil by directly lowering oil costs and thus making marginal resources economical.

Prospects

There are no projections for the use of different energy sources and the degree to which they will replace oil in the near future. Given the uncertainty about oil prices and about technological development, it would be hazardous to make any such projections; a few trends can be observed, however, and a few plans have been announced.

It is expected that Latin America's installed electric generating capacity will almost double between the end of 1973 and the end of 1980, from 50 to 98 million kilowatts. Of the net increase of nearly 48 million kilowatts, 32 million are expected to be provided by hydroelectric plants, 7 million by natural gas, 2.3 million by coal, and 2.9 million by nuclear power. Petroleum would provide 3.4 million additional kilowatts, or only about 7 percent of the total (after allowing for the retirement of 2 million kilowatts of obsolete capacity).[38] Oil would still add significantly to capacity in Brazil and Mexico, but not at all in Argentina or Venezuela.

Since these plans were formulated before the 1973–74 price rise, they may overstate both the increase to be achieved and the share of it likely to be provided by oil. It is possible that petroleum will account for only about 5 percent of the added capacity or less, its share of the total installed capacity falling from 37 percent to only 21 percent. Oil consumption for thermoelectric generation is unlikely to decline soon, but it will represent a declining share of the total use of oil. Particularly rapid expansion is expected for hydroelectricity, which will more than double, and coal, which will nearly triple, and both sources are likely to be developed somewhat more rapidly than was foreseen, although the impact of this will be slight before 1980. (It should be noted that steel making will continue to be the major use for coal and to provide most of the impetus for growth; in fact, it is the demand for coking coal that makes it possible to produce, as a joint product, lower grade coal for other uses.)

A detailed energy plan, covering nonelectrical uses as well, was elaborated in Argentina for the period 1974-75.[39] Given the country's extreme political instability, it does not seem likely that the plan will survive unchanged for a decade, but it is an interesting depiction of what might be done to reduce oil consumption. Under the plan, oil and gas together would decline from 90 percent of the energy used in 1971 to 70 percent in 1985. Fuel oil, used principally for electricity, would be replaced almost entirely; hydroelectric capacity would expand sharply; and coal use would increase dramatically from only 357,000 to 3 million tons annually. A rapid program of nuclear installation is also included.

This plan actually goes beyond what would be economically reasonable for the country, since it does not count on the expansion of oil production, which could probably be achieved at a lower cost than some of the alternatives. It illustrates perfectly the political constraints on energy decisions (because greater oil output could most easily be achieved with greater foreign participation); the preference for possibly high cost domestic sources over sources involving payments abroad;* and the dangers of overreacting to a price situation of unknown duration.

IMPLICATIONS FOR THE UNITED STATES

None of the findings or speculations reviewed here appear to alter the fundamental fact that where energy is concerned, the chief concerns of the United States are the behavior of the major Middle East oil producers and the development of domestic resources of both oil and substitutes.

---

*Even domestic oil has a foreign cost component, if foreign enterprises are allowed to participate. Of course, the nuclear program will require heavy foreign payments but may be politically justified by the existence of domestic uranium resources, questions of national security, and so on.

Latin America is unlikely to approach either of these sources in importance as a supplier of energy to the United States. Nonetheless, the region continues to be important to the United States, and over the next decade its importance could well increase. If Latin America does not come to furnish a larger share of total U.S. energy consumption, it might still provide a larger share of U.S. oil imports. Whether this occurs will depend predominantly on the United States success in reducing its total imports, since Latin America cannot displace the Middle East at current levels, but it will also depend on political and economic developments within the region. These developments are, for the most part, not subject to either private or governmental control by the United States, but they will be influenced by U.S. policies on trade and investment and on the degree of U.S. accommodation with Latin American needs and objectives.

The United States, in turn, is important to Latin America not only because it provides a market, important as that is, but because it can also offer technology and funds for investment. For finding and producing conventional crude oil, the United States has no technological monopoly, but it has many firms and large amounts of equipment; for unconventional sources and particularly for tar sands, U.S. technology comes much closer to holding a monopoly.[40] The same is true of some advanced processes for refining and for removing impurities.

The importance of the United States as a source of investment funds has diminished in Venezuela as oil prices have risen (and there are barriers to investment in Brazil, Chile, and Mexico), but the United States still is or can be a major source of capital for smaller exporters or net importing countries such as Colombia, Ecuador, Peru, and Trinidad. (It should be stressed that investment in Latin America is important to the United States primarily insofar as it makes more oil available from the region. The profits to be earned are valuable but should not be a principal objective, because while they can, in principle, offset the costs of importing Middle Eastern oil, they do nothing to reduce dependence on Arab oil.)

It does not seem feasible to outline a Latin American energy policy for the United States, particularly since any such policy should fit into the broader pattern of policy on domestic energy and reliance on other foreign supplies. We can, however, mention again the developments that are of principal importance to the United States where Latin American energy exports are concerned. These include:

1. Expansion of conventional oil sources in all countries (exporters particularly but also importers) where the United States can participate.

2. Development of alternative energy sources, where these can be accelerated by inputs provided by the United States (which may be most important in the case of nuclear power, but which will not free large amounts of oil for export).

3. Exploitation of Venezuela's heavy oil belt to ensure a continued flow of oil beyond what is likely to be available for current conventional reserves.

None of these developments is without political difficulties, but none of them is made impossible by political obstacles; each is amenable to the appropriate choice of policy on the part of the United States over the next several years.

NOTES

1. Philip A. Musgrove, "Latin America," Chap. 5, in Energy and U.S. Foreign Policy ed. Joseph A. Yager and Eleanor B. Steinberg (Cambridge, Mass.: Ballinger, 1974).

2. These aspects have been examined in two recent studies. See Joaquin Gonzalez, with the collaboration of Leonardo A. da Silva, "Latin America and the Oil Deficit: The Long-Term Balance of Payments Adjustment Process" (Washington, D.C.: Inter-American Development Bank, August 1974)(Paper presented at the Latin American Symposium on Energy, Economic Commission for Latin America, Santiago, Chile, September, 1974); "The Petroleum Crisis: Financial and Economic Implications for Latin America" (Washington, D.C.: Organization of American States, February 1974) (Paper prepared for the Meeting of Experts on the Economic and Financial Implications for Latin America of the Oil Crisis, OAS, March 1-2, 1974).

3. Yager and Steinberg, op. cit., Appendix Table A-1, p. 443. All amounts were converted to oil equivalent for comparison.

4. See Musgrove, op. cit., pp. 78-80, 83-86. Official Venezuelan projections assumed a somewhat more rapid increase in output; see Francis Herron, "Latin American Aspects of Energy Policy" (unpublished paper prepared for the Brookings Institution) (July 1973).

5. For a summary of this process and measures of its intensity in certain resource products, including oil, see Joseph Grunwald and Philip Musgrove, Natural Resources in Latin American Development (Baltimore: Johns Hopkins Press for Resources for the Future, 1970).

6. See Ministerio de Economia y Finanzas and Encuesta Nacional de Consumo de Alimentos, Gastos de las Familias en Gasolina Motor y otros Derivados del Petroleo en el Peru (Lima, 1975) (study prepared by Dante Curonisy Lostaunau). Prices are also low in exporting countries, which implies the same cost, but is much more acceptable politically.

7. Economic Commission for Latin America (ECLA) and Instituto Latinoamericano de Planificacion Economica y Social (ILPES), "Los Nuevos Precios del Petroleo y la Industria Electrica en America Latina" (Simposio Tecnico sobre America Latina y los Problemas Actu-

ales de la Energia, Santiago, Chile, September 23-27, 1974), document ST/CEPA L/Conf. 50/L3., pp. 57-58.

8. On Trinidad, see Oil and Gas Journal (February 18, 1974): 42; on Bolivia, ibid. (March 4, 1974): 42; and on Brazil, New York Times, December 23, 1974, p. 43.

9. See Washington Post, September 21, 1974, p. 1. This expectation now seems overly optimistic: several firms that have not recovered their investments in Peru are leaving the country, and a number of once-promising fields are yielding very little oil or have encountered high costs. Peru is still likely to become self-sufficient, but the likelihood of substantial exports is reduced.

10. Oil and Gas Journal (March 31, 1975): 31.

11. The Petroleum Economist (May 1974): 179-180.

12. Ibid. (April 1974): 139. For the history of Argentine oil policy in the last two decades, see Grunwald and Musgrove, op. cit., chap. 8.

13. New York Times, December 9, 1974, p. 57, and February 26, 1975, p. 45. No other foreign companies have entered Ecuador since the original concessionaire was forced to return a large part of its concession and to accept a 25 percent government share in the operation. See also Oil and Gas Journal (March 17, 1975): 60.

14. Dissatisfaction with the government's oil policy was one of the major causes of the attempted coup on September 1, 1975. See Latin America 9 (September 5, 1975).

15. See Wall Street Journal, April 8 and August 23, 1974; New York Times, August 28, 1974; and Oil and Gas Journal (September 2, 1974).

16. New York Times, December 22, 1974, p. 43; Oil and Gas Journal (December 16, 1974): 28; The Petroleum Economist (January 1975): 28; and Brazilian Bulletin (January 1975): 12. Initial estimates, which now appear overoptimistic, put potential production at 400,000 b/d. About three quarters of Brazil's consumption should be met domestically by the end of the decade.

17. Oil and Gas Journal (October 21, 1974): 73.

18. Ibid. (March 31, 1975): 53; Wall Street Journal, October 16, 1974; and Washington Post, October 16, 1974. PEMEX, the state oil monopoly, has not published reserve estimates for the new fields.

19. Wall Street Journal, October 16, 1974, p. 14.

20. See Oil and Gas Journal (June 17, 1974): 94-97; and Musgrove, op. cit., pp. 78-79.

21. U.S. Geological Survey, Summary Petroleum and Selected Mineral Statistics for 120 Countries, Including Offshore Areas, John P. Alben, et al., Geographical Professional Papers 817 (Washington, D.C.: Government Printing Office, 1973).

22. Oil and Gas Journal (October 14, 1974): 141; ibid. (December 9, 1974): 107.

23. Musgrove, op. cit., p. 80.

24. The recovery rate from wells, even when aided by steam injection or in situ combustion, drops sharply as the oil gets heavier. At the northern edge, the faja shades into conventional low-gravity (heavy) crude oil; farther south it becomes tar sand rather like the Athabasca deposits in Canada, and might require open-pit mining to exploit. See Alvaro G. Reyes, "Consideraciones para la explotacion de la Faja Petrolifera del Orinoco," Revista de la Sociedad Venezolana del Petroleo (December 1972): 27-39.

25. Oil and Gas Journal (November 11, 1974): 134.

26. A joint private-state pilot plant is being built to process 3,000 b/d of faja oil. The private partner is Shell, which also operates a pilot plant treating Canadian tar sands. Oil and Gas Journal (December 30, 1974): 93.

27. There is no prospect of traditional concessions being let for heavy oil production; existing concessions would have expired in 1983-84 but for the 1975 nationalization, and no new concessions have been let since 1958. The nationalization law allows for foreign participation in the industry, but there is so much political opposition that the president has promised not to undertake any joint ventures with foreign firms in 1976-77. See Latin America 9 (September 5, 1975).

28. Herron, op. cit., discusses the Venezuelan rationale for such an arrangement, while skirting somewhat the crucial issue of prices. For a very good discussion of the complex interaction of economic and political factors, including the possible repercussions within Venezuela of different outcomes, see Norman Gall, "The Challenge of Venezuelan Oil," Foreign Policy (March 1975): 44-67. See also Washington Post, January 6, 1975, p. 9, for a brief account of the scarcity of trained personnel, which impedes large-scale state development. Until Venezuela surmounts these difficulties, Petroven will sell oil to the foreign enterprises (the former concessionaires) and will in effect control only the price and (to some extent) the quantity of oil exported but not its uses or destinations. Building a complete marketing capacity would be costly and would probably be strongly resisted by the major oil firms; a government-to-government agreement is seen as a way to bypass this competition.

29. ECLA-ILPES, op. cit., pp. 13-15. The index excludes fuel burned to make electricity. It is low in oil-rich countries, such as Mexico, Trinidad, and Venezuela, and also in poor countries that still use much vegetable fuel. It is higher for countries that depend on imported oil.

30. ECLA-ILPES, op. cit., pp. 53-57.

31. ECLA-ILPES, op. cit., pp. 3, 18, 27.

32. Ramon Suarez, "El Carbon Latinoamericano y sus Perspectivas," ECLA (Simposio Tecnico sobre America Latina y los Probemas

Actuales de la Energia, Santiago, Chile, September 23-27, 1974), Doc. No. 3, p. 13. These seemingly large amounts are only about 1 percent of the world total. It is easier to estimate total reserves in a coal field than in an oil field, so measured resources are usually a much larger multiple of annual production.

33. See Grunwald and Musgrove, op. cit., chap. 9. Exploitable reserves were estimated at 17 billion tons in 1960, out of a total of 23 billion; these figures exclude 29 billion tons of lignite in Chile.

34. Suarez, op. cit., pp. 8, 20, 24, 27, 29, 32, 34, 36.

35. See Suarez, op. cit., pp. 10, 16. The comparison covers only Argentina, Brazil, Chile, and Mexico, all in 1972, net importers of oil. Coal was probably relatively cheaper in Colombia.

36. On plans up through 1973, see Musgrove, op. cit., p. 80, and the articles in Petroleum Press Service cited there. Small amounts of gas are liquefied in Chile for shipment from producing to consuming areas.

37. A gas line is planned from eastern Bolivia to the industrial area of Sao Paulo, carrying initially the equivalent of 100,000 b/d of oil. See Oil and Gas Journal (March 4, 1974): 42. (This project has been under discussion for several years.)

38. ECLA-ILPES, op. cit., pp. 32-33. These projections are based on national plans in virtually all countries of the region.

39. "Argentina's Energy Plan," The Petroleum Economist (April 1974): 139-141.

40. The Venezuelan nationalization law provides that "Shell and Exxon have apparently been awarded rights to supply future technology to Petroven." Latin America 9 (September 5, 1975).

CHAPTER

9

LATIN AMERICAN RESOURCES IN THE WORLD ECONOMY: COPPER AND IRON ORE

Joseph Grunwald

THE SETTING

As in any developing region, natural resources have played a critical role in Latin America's economic development. But in Latin America more than other regions, raw material policies have been marked by controversy and the mixing of political and economic objectives.[1] It was in Latin America that the thesis of unequal gains from trade between raw material exporters and industrial nations was first developed.[2] And it is in Latin America that raw material dependency has been most keenly felt, a feeling that undoubtedly has encouraged import-substituting industrialization in the region.

Before the Great Depression of the 1930s, Latin American raw materials dependency was not challenged by government policy. The subsequent two or three decades have often been called the period of neglect of raw material development in Latin America, when governments increasingly turned their attention toward industrialization. If, however, the policy was to free the nations from dependency on raw material exports by manufacturing domestically what previously had to be imported, it did not get very far. The reduction of imports of consumer goods, now produced locally, has been offset by new import requirements for machinery, equipment, spare parts, and industrial raw materials, including fuels. Few new exports have emerged so far, not enough to compensate for the new import requirements, because import-substituting industrialization has been geared to the home market. Nevertheless, the new import requirements have been necessary to keep the new domestic industry in operation and therefore cannot be easily reduced for political as well as economic reasons. Thus the burden for foreign exchange earnings has continued to fall on raw materials, and this dependency may be intensified as the industrialization of Latin American countries progresses.

(According to recent Latin American writings, Latin American countries find themselves facing a new kind of "dependency." Increasingly sophisticated manufacturing requires not only massive infusion of capital but also extensive technology, which must be imported. Even if raw material and other exports could finance this industrialization, which, except for the petroleum-exporting countries, is rarely the case, the industrialized countries become dependent on foreign technology and resources, not to speak of foreign investment. If there is a shortfall in foreign exchange earnings, the usual case with the exception noted, then the "dependency" will be aggravated by foreign indebtedness. A discussion of this new dependency, described and conceptualized by a new school of Latin American intellectuals, falls outside the scope of this chapter.)

At the same time, the availability of raw materials for exports will be restrained by the increasing requirements of the region's expanding industrialization.

Within the global picture, Latin American resources have played an important, although declining, role. Thus the region accounted for 25.5 percent of world trade in fifteen primary commodities in 1960, but only 18.4 percent in 1970.[3] Excluding petroleum, however, Latin America maintains the importance of its main resources in world trade. The exports (excluding petroleum) were 25.8 percent in 1960 and 26.2 percent in 1970. In those commodities Latin America did better than other developing regions, although during the last decade Latin American participation in total world trade declined proportionately more than the share of other developing countries.

As a proportion of total Latin American exports, the fifteen basic commodities, including crude oil, dropped from 70 percent in 1960 to 60 percent in 1970, but, if petroleum is excluded, the share of the fourteen primary goods remains the same, about 47 percent. All primary goods taken together still constitute well over four fifths of Latin America's total exports, despite the region's rapid industrialization since World War II. If refined and semirefined metals, which are sometimes classified as manufactures,[4] are considered in the primary commodity category, the proportion of natural resources in total regional exports would still be about 90 percent at the beginning of this decade.

Among the nonfuel mineral products, copper and iron ore stand out as Latin America's most important resources. The region produces almost one fifth of the world's copper and one eighth of world iron ore output (not including the Centrally Planned Economies [CPES]), and accounts for over one quarter of world exports in each of the two minerals. They are also among the most important single commodities in world trade, copper competing with wheat for second place after petroleum. Over 70 percent of copper and iron ore production enters world trade. As a share in total developing-country export earnings, copper ranks second together with coffee (after petroleum) and iron ore sixth in importance. Copper plus iron ore contribute about 10 percent to the total value of Latin American merchandise exports, a percentage exceeded only by crude oil and coffee.

In the following sections, the role of these resources in Latin America, and the world economy in general and the United States in particular, will be discussed. Particular attention will be given to the prospects for producer arrangements and to the general outlook for Latin American production, exports, and prices of these two commodities.[5]

COPPER

Copper was the second most used metal (after iron) until it was displaced by aluminum during the 1950s. It is also Latin America's most important nonfuel mineral, and, during the 1960s, it became the region's third most important foreign exchange earner (after petroleum and coffee). Copper's share of Latin American exports more than doubled between the early 1950s and the early 1970s.

On the other hand, the share of total world supply (excluding the CPEs) furnished by Latin America declined in the postwar period from about one quarter during the mid 1940s to less than one fifth during the early 1970s, as Zambia, Zaire, and Canada became important copper producers. Also, with expanding industrialization, an increasing proportion of Latin American output has been consumed locally.

Chile, whose production during part of the 1950s and 1960s was exceeded by that of Zambia, regained its position as the world's (excluding CPEs) second largest producer at the end of the last decade, but may well lose it again as Canada has emerged as a principal producer. The United States continues to produce about twice as much copper as Chile.* Until 1960, Mexico was Latin America's second copper producer, but is now far behind Peru, which more than quadrupled its output since the 1950s. There are no other Latin American

---

*In the last century, Chile was the world's leading copper producer, supplying 62 percent of total world output in 1876. Since 1880, the United States has been the world's largest producer, but may have been surpassed by the Soviet bloc during the last few years.

producers of any significance, the small outputs of Brazil and Argentina supplying only part of their domestic needs.

Prior to the 1950s, most of the regional copper exports went to the United States, but since then the direction of trade has turned increasingly toward Europe, as the economic growth of the European Common Market accelerated. By the end of the 1960s, nearly all the copper refined for exports and about one third of the nonrefined, primarily blister, copper was sold to Europe. The increasing quantities of Chilean blister copper exported to the United States have been sent there for refining to be reexported to Europe and, more recently, to Japan. Nevertheless, the share of Peruvian exports destined to the United States is still substantial and much larger than the corresponding proportion for Chile.

The United States is virtually self-sufficient in copper, importing (net) less than 10 percent of its copper consumption. About half the U.S. import requirements are supplied by Latin America, with Peru providing somewhat more than Chile. Almost one third of U.S. imports are furnished by Canada. However, over 90 percent of European and Japanese copper consumption must be imported. Latin America provides about one quarter of Europe's and Japan's imports (including reexports from the United States).

From time to time Latin American copper was sold to Soviet bloc countries. But the Centrally Planned Economies did not turn out to be the substantial and reliable markets for which Latin Americans had hoped. Not only does the socialist bloc appear self-sufficient in copper but it seems to have emerged as a small net exporter. In 1972, about 10 percent of Western Europe's imports were supplied by the Centrally Planned Economies, including 3 percent from Yugoslavia. The World Bureau of Metal Statistics (London) gives the following figures for the CPEs in 1973 (in thousands of metric tons):

	Refined Production	Exports	Imports
Communist countries	1,796	193	120
Yugoslavia	138	73	5
Total	1,934	266	125

Total world production (excluding CPEs) was 6,551; exports, 2,457; and imports, 2,589 thousands of metric tons.

Until recently only a few multinational enterprises accounted for the bulk of the world's copper output, making the copper industry even more concentrated than the oil industry. For example, until the end of the 1960s, Anaconda, Kennecott, and Phelps Dodge were the principal U.S. producers, accounting for over three quarters of mine and 90 percent of smelting capacity. The first two companies also accounted for over 90 percent of Chile's output, even though there were, and still are, about 3,000 small and mostly independent mines in that country. The increasing nationalization of the natural resource industries in the developing countries is one reason for the recent dilution of industrial concentration in copper. In many instances private companies have kept de facto control after nationalization through management and technical assistance contracts, and especially through distribution and marketing arrangements. Another is U.S. government policy that encouraged the expansion of small producers and the formation of new companies for national security reasons (Defense Production Act of 1950). Also, some copper-consuming companies acquired mines, and some multinational companies diversified into copper, including the exploration of new sources of supply. Copper fabricators, particularly in Japan and West Germany, financed new copper mines in order to become less dependent on the giant copper producers for an assured supply.[6]

Copper, generally, has been sold on the basis of long-term arrangements between producers and consumers. In the past, the private producer companies set prices that did not fluctuate widely over the business cycle, but which would be adjusted moderately to take into account changed market conditions. The London Metal Exchange (LME) handled only a marginal volume of copper sales, serving not only marginal consumers but also speculators, with the result that LME prices tended to be above Chilean producer prices much of the time. This often gave the impression in Latin America that the large foreign copper-producing companies wanted to benefit the highly industrialized foreign consumers at the expense of the Latin American producing countries.

In the immediate postwar period, the U.S. government set the price of copper, as one of the "strategic materials," at a level far below the world market prices. (Military needs have required between 10 and 20 percent of total U.S. consumption. A copper stockpile, which in some years exceeded total U.S. yearly output, was maintained by the U.S. government until recently.) The U.S. companies operating in Chile followed this level until the mid-1950s when a "new deal" was negotiated between the companies and the Chilean government. (The "new deal" provided for improved rate of exchange and tax treatment for the U.S. companies in return for expanded production and new investment.) Since then, the price of Chilean copper has more than doubled, but in real terms (in constant values, adjusted by inflation) there has been relatively little change over the long run, although there have been sharp fluctuations from year to year. (In mid-1975 the "real" copper price, measured in constant values [adjusted by inflation] was below the values in the mid-1950s, and also below the pre-World War I levels. According to World Bank estimates, copper prices in constant dollars fluctuated more on the average than most other 35 raw materials studied [the coefficient of variation averaged 0.26 during 1955-74].)

At the initiative of Chile, an Intergovernmental Council of Copper Exporting Countries (CIPEC, after its French and Spanish acronyms) was established in 1967, comprising the world's four major copper exporters, Chile, Peru, Zambia, and Zaire. Its aim is to coordinate production decisions with a view of restricting output in order to raise prices and revenues. The underlying assumption is that the price elasticity of demand is less than unity, so that a given percentage reduction in quantity will be more than offset by a more than proportionate increase in price. (The price elasticity of demand is the ratio of the relative change in the quantity demanded over the relative change in price. The ratio will be negative because the two changes are in opposite directions.) The measured price elasticity for copper is very low, less than (-) 0.2. But the long-run elasticity is believed to be high because of the delayed effects of price increases on demand as consumers turn to substitutes if higher prices persist.

Despite the fact that CIPEC comprises the world's lowest cost copper producers, it has not succeeded in operating as a cartel. First of all, copper consumers can turn to new sources of supply or help expand output from existing non-CIPEC sources. Second, if relative copper prices become too high, consumers can substitute copper in many uses with other materials, primarily aluminum and plastics. Also, the CIPEC share of the world supply has fallen. The CIPEC countries accounted for about 44 percent of total world production (except CPEs) in 1960, 43 percent when CIPEC was established in 1967, and only 36 percent in 1973. (The CIPEC share of world production, including the CPEs, declined even more, from 38 percent in 1960 to 29 percent in 1973, as the output of the socialist countries increased faster than that of the rest of the world during the period.) CIPEC's share of world exports, which was more than half when CIPEC was formed, fell to about 46 percent in 1973.

More than half of CIPEC production and most of the marketing of copper is now in government hands. The two U.S. copper companies (Anaconda and Kennecott) that operated in Chile and accounted for about 90 percent of that country's production, were expropriated in the early 1970s. Peru nationalized the U.S.-owned Cerro de Pasco Corporation in 1974, yet a major share of Peru's output is produced by the private Southern Peru Copper Corporation, which is still entirely U.S. owned. The Zambian government owns 51 percent of the copper mining industry, and in Zaire, the government owns more than 90 percent of the mines.

In Africa, the copper industry is more integrated than in Latin America. In Zambia, the copper industry encompasses the entire range from mining to refining, but there is almost no local fabricating.

In Zaire, industry integration is somewhat less but stronger than in Chile, where, in 1970, almost 30 percent of the copper production reached only the blister stage (semirefined). More copper, however, is fabricated in Chile for domestic use than in any of the other CIPEC countries. Integration of the copper industry in Peru only recently has begun. Most of Peru's copper output and exports until now have been in the form of concentrated ore.

The CIPEC countries contain the world's richest copper ores, with the copper content of African ores far exceeding those of Latin America. (The copper content of the ore now mined in Zaire is between 4 and 5 percent and in Zambia, about 2.5 percent; in Chile, it is somewhat more than, and in Peru, somewhat less than 1 percent.) Nevertheless, while Zaire has the richest ore and cheapest labor force, the transportation costs of the metal from the mines to the ports are enormous. A similar situation prevails in Zambia, where copper has to be transported through other countries to foreign ports. Thus, in Africa, up to 80 percent of total costs are incurred in transportation (presumably costs will be lowered with the completion and use of the railroad from Katanga to Dar-es-Salaam), making copper more costly there than Chilean and Peruvian output at the port.

In recent years, a substantial portion of the increase in copper output has come from new mines. The Philippines and Papua New Guinea have become important copper-producing and -exporting countries. In the developed world, output and exports also increased faster than for the CIPEC countries. Canadian production almost doubled between the early 1960s and early 1970s, and it is now the most important exporter outside the CIPEC bloc, followed by Australia and South Africa.

Outlook

Supply

Despite increasing production and exploitation of new ore deposits elsewhere, Latin America is expected to reverse the postwar decline in its world output share for the remainder of the decade. Substantial capacity expansion is foreseen in the region, primarily in Mexico and Peru. Although the major part of the increase in Mexican output will be absorbed by sharply rising domestic consumption, Mexico is expected to become a significant copper exporter.

The new Mexican mine will be run by a Mexican company in which the government has plurality ownership, 46 percent, and, therefore, control. Mexican private capital owns another 44 percent and U.S.

banks, 10 percent. The project is financed in part by a consortium of U.S., Canadian, and European banks. The company will work ore of 0.6 percent copper content and is expected to produce 140,000 metric tons of copper by 1980. If the plans materialize, Mexico will become the world's sixth largest copper producer.[7]

The largest rise in Latin American copper production is anticipated in Peru. The huge Cuajone open pit mine of the U.S.-owned Southern Peru Copper Corporation is expected to come on-stream by 1980 and will almost double the country's copper capacity. In addition, the Cerro Verde project of the government's Mineroperu Company will be in production before 1980, adding another 10 to 20 percent to 1973 capacity.

Cerro Verde will mine oxide ore of an average of 0.7 percent copper content. Adjacent are the much larger, but lower grade, Santa Rosa deposits (0.55 percent average copper content). Santa Rosa is not likely to be in significant production by 1980. Negotiations are underway to finance other copper projects with Canadian, Rumanian, and Japanese participation, with the government retaining 51 percent control. Most of Peru's output is still in private hands, but Mineroperu is the sole exporter of the country's mineral production.

Possibilities of new mining prospects in Chile are uncertain in the medium term. The El Abra deposits near the Chuquicamata mining complex has the potential of increasing current Chilean production by almost one half, but is still a long time off from coming into operation.

One of the greatest copper potentials in Latin America are the rich Cerro Colorado copper deposits in Panama, discovered recently by a Canadian company. Negotiations are still in progress for the private development of these deposits, which, because of political complications, will not come on-stream by 1980. The Panamanian government, conscious of its experience with the Panama Canal, is not willing to grant concessions on natural resources beyond twenty years. Canadian Javelin, the company that discovered the deposits, claims that this period, given present copper prices, is too short to recover its investment plus a reasonable profit. The Cerro Colorado project is expected to require a total capital investment of $800 million, 15 percent of which must be contributed by the operating company.[8]

Argentina also plans to expand its significant copper deposits, but production before the 1980s is unlikely.

The most important capacity increases in Africa during the rest of this decade will be in Zaire. A two-third increase in output is projected. Zambia plans to increase mine capacity to 900,000 metric tons, more than one quarter above 1973 production (based on estimates by World Bank staff). Among the other developing-country producers, capacity will increase in the Philippines, Papua New Guinea, and Indonesia, and Iran, which had no production in 1973, will emerge as a major producer. Yet the combined capacity of these four countries in 1980 is expected to be less than that of Chile.

Developed country capacity is expected to increase at most by one third, with the major increases concentrated in the United States and Canada. Copper mine output of the industrialized countries, which was more than 12 percent higher than developing-country production in 1973, will most likely be below developing-country output in 1980. Mine capacity in Latin America will grow faster than in other regions, so that the Latin American share of world production will probably rise from less than 18 percent in 1973 to over 20 percent by 1980.

Demand

Copper demand is very sensitive to the business cycle. Demand weakened in mid-1974 with the downturn of world economic activity, but is expected to strengthen during the remainder of the decade with the economic recovery of the industrial countries. On the basis of national income projections, refined copper consumption is estimated to grow by less than 4 percent during the second half of the 1970s, reaching about 8.5 million metric tons in 1980.[9]

Since World War II, Latin American copper consumption has increased at a higher rate than consumption in other developing areas. The region now consumes about 12 percent of its production, compared to about 7 percent in 1960. This trend is expected to continue, so that the Latin American share of world consumption will rise from about 3 percent in 1973 to about 5 percent in 1980.

A substantial portion, about 14 percent, of world consumption has been satisfied by secondary copper, the recovery of scrap. While most developing countries' consumption has been virgin or primary copper, up to 40 percent of the industrial countries' demand has been supplied through the recovery of scrap. (The current recovery rate for heavy electrical conductors in the industrial countries is about 90 percent.)

A major factor in the demand for copper over the longer period is the substitutability of the metal by other materials. When the relative price of copper rises and remains high, demand in some uses will be lost to aluminum and in others to plastics. Aluminum is lighter but bulkier and less efficient as a conductor. (Aluminum has about 60 percent of the electrical and thermal capacity of copper, but weighs only one third as much. Aluminum also tends to corrode.) The demand lost to aluminum during the 1950s and 1960s cannot be easily reversed because of engineering costs. The substitution of aluminum for copper was relatively greater in Europe than in the United States. No further substitution is foreseen because the sharply increased price of petroleum will be reflected in higher relative prices of aluminum and plastics (the production of aluminum has large energy and therefore petroleum requirements, and petroleum is the major input in the production of plastics), thus improving the competitive position of copper.

The price of copper adjusted by inflation is lower in mid-1975 than anytime since the early 1960s. According to World Bank projections, the price will rise slowly, reaching 64 cents per pound in 1978-80 (in 1973 dollar terms). This level is still far below the more than 82 cents per pound average over the 1965-74 decade. Based on average capital costs (from mine through refinery) of at least $4,000 per ton of annual capacity, the projected price of 64 cents per pound is only slightly above the minimum price necessary for an average new mine to be profitable.[10]

Cartel Possibilities

The previous discussion indicates that copper capacity will be ample within the foreseeable future. The demand projections compared with the capacity projections estimated by World Bank staff imply a capacity utilization rate as low as 80 percent in 1980. This is a clear indication of a potential surplus unless some of the plans for new capacity are postponed.

There are other factors that do not make for a propitious environment for a cartel arrangement, at least not for developing countries. The price elasticity of copper, although low in the short run, seems fairly high over the long period, primarily because of the already mentioned substitution possibilities. Primary copper must also compete with secondary copper, the output derived from scrap. When primary copper prices are high, a greater effort will be made to increase the recovery rate of scrap.

Furthermore, there is no shortage of known exploitable deposits. Proven world reserves have more than tripled since 1950. Although most new reserves have a much lower copper content than those being worked now in Latin America and Africa, and the capital costs for a new mine are very high,* marginal costs of production are low. Thus ample, though low grade, reserves in the United States and Canada, where tax laws favor mining investment, could be exploited and compete favorably with existing production, if copper prices should rise significantly.

With considerably less than half of world copper output and trade accounted for by the CIPEC countries, CIPEC controls a much smaller

---

*Capital requirements, based on the estimates of the Copper Cost Study, op. cit., are about 460 million (in 1975 prices) for a mine of 100,000 metric ton yearly capacity.

proportion of copper than OPEC does of petroleum. If the two other major developing-country producers, Papua New Guinea and the Philippines, would join CIPEC, the group would account for less than 60 percent of world exports. Given the magnitude of copper production in the industrial countries and the possibilities of increasing output there, CIPEC would need the cooperation of these countries in order to influence prices.

In November 1974, the CIPEC countries agreed to cut back shipments by 10 percent in an attempt to reverse the rapid downward slide of copper prices. While this was the first combined action taken by CIPEC in its entire history, the cutback was not large enough to prevent a further decline.[11] Only when other producers joined CIPEC by cutting production back voluntarily in early 1975 did copper prices start to level off. As of March 1975, the world supply cutback was running at an annual rate of 900,000 tons, or about 15 percent of 1973 world production (excluding CPEs). (In addition to CIPEC, this includes the cutbacks in refined production by Canada, the United States, Australia, as well as the reduction in the output of concentrates in Canada, the Philippines, Papua New Guinea, and Indonesia requested by the Japanese refining industry because of reduced domestic demand.) Therefore, as world economic activity recovers, copper consumption can expand without sharp price rises in the immediate future.

According to internal World Bank estimates, if producers succeeded in deliberately curtailing production by 3.5 percent of the projected output during the remainder of this decade, the 1980 copper price would be about 13 percent higher than the projected 64 cents per pound (in constant dollars; implied price elasticity of supply is 0.27).

IRON ORE

More than other important minerals, iron ore deposits are more widely distributed in the earth's crust; yet, after crude oil, iron ore is by far the major commodity in the volume of world trade. Similar to crude oil, iron ore is closely tied to economic activities and growth. About 95 percent of the world's production of iron ore goes directly into the making of steel.

While, on the average, about 1.1 tons of iron ore is needed to make 1 ton of steel, the mineral constituted only about 9 percent of the total price of steel in 1974.[12] Compared to crude oil, which comprises about 40 percent of the price of gasoline and 85 percent of heavy fuel, iron ore has more linkages to other raw materials and economic activities. On the other hand, a change in iron ore prices will have a much smaller effect on the price of steel than the effect of oil price changes on fuel prices.

The Latin American contribution to total world supply of iron ore increased sharply after World War II. The region accounted for less than 2 percent of world production (including CPEs) during 1945-49 and almost 11 percent during 1970-73. (Excluding the CPEs, which produced about one third of world output in 1973, Latin America's share in the recent period was over 14 percent.) Latin America's share in the world market for iron ore increased from about 8 percent in 1950 to 28 percent in 1960 and then declined somewhat, fluctuating between one fourth and one fifth of total world export volume.

Iron ore is Latin America's third most important mineral and contributes about 8 percent to the region's export earnings, excluding petroleum, a substantial increase since 1950 when it contributed less than 1 percent. Until the mid-1950s, about 90 percent of the region's exports went to the United States. Since then, the U.S. share of Latin American exports declined to less than 40 percent, as an increasing proportion of Latin American ores have been shipped to Europe and Japan.

Almost all of Latin America's iron ore production is concentrated in five countries: Brazil, Venezuela, Chile, Peru, and Mexico. Brazil and Venezuela alone accounted for almost 80 percent in 1973, with neither having had any substantial production before the early 1950s. Chile was the only major producer before World War II, but was surpassed by Brazil and Venezuela in the mid-1950s. From 1954 to 1963, Venezuela's output was significantly larger than Brazil's, but since then Brazilian production quintupled, accounting for over half of Latin American output in 1973.

Brazil contributes somewhat less than half of Latin American iron ore exports, Venezuela somewhat more than one quarter, and Chile and Peru together about one quarter. Mexico's iron ore production, about 5 percent of the regional total, is entirely consumed domestically. The market for Brazilian ore exports shifted primarily to Japan and Peru's almost entirely to Japan.

Japan has become by far the world's largest iron ore importer, absorbing over 35 percent of total world imports during 1971-73; imports constituted about 94 percent of that country's consumption. Other major importers are West Germany and the United States. Almost half of Japan's imports are supplied by Australia, which has recently emerged as the world's largest iron ore exporter. Latin America now supplies over one fifth of the Japanese market. Western Europe imported 37 percent of its requirements and the United States 32 percent in 1972. More than three quarters of European imports came from Latin American and African countries in about equal shares.

U.S. dependence on iron ore imports increased from about 5 percent of consumption in 1950 to about 30 percent during the early 1970s. About half the U.S. requirements are imported from Canada and about 40 percent from Latin America, mostly from Venezuela. In 1973, iron ore constituted by a wide margin the second most important product in U.S. imports in terms of value.

Iron ore, less so than most other raw materials, does not have a representative world market price. At the end of the 1960s, about one third of all ore traded originated in "captive" mines, owned or controlled by steel companies in developed countries. For example, until the end of 1974, 86 percent of Venezuelan ore output was produced by U.S. Steel and 10 percent by Bethlehem Steel Corporation; and half of Canada's iron ore production is controlled by U.S. steel producers through captive mines. Another third of world iron ore sales was under long-term contract, leaving only one third to be traded in the "free market." To a large extent, even the free market transactions are sold basically under short-term contracts. There are no representative free market quotations for iron ore such as exist for nonferrous metals on the LME.

A large part of the CIF price of iron ore consists of transportation costs. In the case of Japan, the freight costs constituted over 40 percent of the delivered price during the early 1960s. This declined to about 30 percent at the end of the decade. Technological improvements in shipping, particularly the introduction of ore bulk carriers, reduced freight rates dramatically.* This was reflected in the fall of import prices between 1957 and 1971. The benefits of lower transport costs are not fully shared by the exporting countries, because the importing countries control the shipping capacities and therefore can negotiate deliveries on FOB terms.

In addition to greater efficiency in transportation, the general long-term decline of iron ore prices between 1957 and 1971 was due to capacity expansion and the exploitation of new high grade deposits, particularly in Australia, Canada, Liberia, and Brazil, multiplying the sources of supply. (In 1970 there were about fifteen more iron-ore-producing countries than twenty years earlier.) Furthermore, the degree of beneficiation—the concentration of the ore at the mine—rose, so that ore of higher iron content was shipped, increasing the

---

*Most modern bulk carriers are convertible for shipping oil or ore. According to a private estimate by the Japan Iron and Steel Federation, freight rates for Japanese imports dropped from 0.14 cent per ton mile in 1960 to 0.06 cent per ton mile in 1968.

value/weight ratio and therefore reducing the incidence of transportation costs in the price of the ore.

Since the early 1970s, iron ore prices moved upward with inflation, but during the general upsurge of raw material prices in 1973 and the first half of 1974, they increased less than the prices for any other Latin American commodity.

Japan purchases iron ore under medium to long-term contracts. In some cases the contracts are based on Japanese financing of the mines and receiving long-term ore deliveries in repayment. Long-term contracts are also used in trade between centrally planned economies. Before 1975, the U.S. market was largely isolated from world market influences because most U.S. imports originated in the Canadian and Venezuelan captive mines. Since the nationalization of U.S. mines in Venezuela on January 1, 1975, most U.S. imports from Venezuela are based on long-term contracts (fifteen years). Western Europe is a "spot" market, which means that sales are made under short-term contracts, usually one year. Special trade arrangements link Swedish and Liberian ore to the Western European market. (Such sales are made through Malmexport, a joint sales company for two Swedish and one Liberian iron ore producer.)

Thus the iron ore market has been dominated by the buyers, and the exporting countries have been in a relatively weak bargaining position. Japanese steel companies, the world's most important iron ore importers have formed a joint purchasing agency, which can influence the world market substantially. The possible exception on the producer side is that of Malmexport, which, however, has only limited influence on the Western European market. At the end of 1974 an organization of Iron Ore Exporting Countries (IOEC) was formed by some developing-country producer countries, with Algeria, India, and Venezuela taking the lead. Brazil and developed country exporters (Australia, Canada, and Sweden) made their participation conditional on consideration of the interests of iron ore consumers. (Other IOEC members are Chile and Peru in Latin America, and Liberia and Mauritania in Africa.)

Outlook

Supply

During the rapid expansion of iron ore capacity ores during the last two decades, production has utilized between 80 and 90 percent of capacity. Therefore production could increase quickly during the recent demand upsurge in 1973-74. The comparatively low capacity utilization combined with the fact that about 85 to 90 percent of the world's iron ore is mined in open pit operations means that quite large, short-term increases in ore production can be achieved relatively fast. New mine production needs at least two and one-half years lead time.

Known expansion plans indicate a mining capacity growth of almost 300 million metric tons between 1975 and 1980, which is more than half the current capacity (excluding CPEs). Financing already has been arranged for more than 60 percent of these expansion plans. Nearly one third of the capacity increase is expected to take place in the developing countries, one third in Canada and the United States, almost 30 percent in Australia, and the rest in other industrialized countries. It is assumed that the CPEs will increase capacity as they need it, although, if they were interested, they could raise capacity for exports.

The planned projects will exploit higher grade ores than those under production now. (The average iron content of iron ore mined is estimated to rise from 56.5 percent in 1970 to almost 60 percent in 1980, according to projections by the International Iron and Steel Institute and the World Bank staff.) Current explorations are for deposits of over 60 percent iron content compared with much of Western European ore being at 30 percent iron content.

Most of the expansion in Latin America is concentrated in Brazil. The biggest project there is the exploitation of the vast iron ore deposits at Serra dos Carajas in the middle of the Amazon region. Proven reserves are 18 billion metric tons of 66.1 percent iron content. Costs are enormous, because men and equipment have had to be airlifted into the jungle, and roads and a railroad are necessary. Current cost estimates approach \$2.5 billion not including steel making, which is also planned near the site. As recently as 1973, total costs were estimated at less than \$1 billion.[13]

The project is being developed by a Brazilian company, 51 percent state controlled, with participation of U.S. Steel, British Steel Corporation, and a consortium of Japanese companies. Annual production of almost 20 million metric tons is expected by 1980. Another large Brazilian project with Belgian and U.S. control, will exploit the large deposits at Guimaraes in the state of Minas Gerais; expected production is 10 million metric tons per year before 1980. While Brazil's domestic consumption will rise sharply, the country's capacity will be large enough to allow for a huge increase in its exports, which, by 1980, may even surpass those of Australia.

Most of Venezuela's new mine production will be for its own existing and new steel mills, whose capacity is expected to quadruple by 1980. Chile's capacity is anticipated to rise by about 7.5, Mexico by 5, and Argentina by 2 million metric tons by 1980. Mexico's and Argentina's output will be absorbed by their domestic steel industries, as will any increase in the presently low Colombian production. (Currently, 60 percent of Mexico's steel production uses ore from local mines.) Peru's capacity is not expected to increase substantially before 1980.* Latin America appears to have almost one fifth of the world's presently known reserves of iron ore. Argentine and Colombian deposits are of low grade and contain more impurities than those in other Latin American countries.

Demand

Demand for ore is derived almost entirely from demand for steel. Since about 70 percent of steel is used in manufacturing and the rest in construction industry, nearly all import demand for iron ore has come from the highly industrialized countries, including the Soviet Union and Eastern European countries. In the future, the distribution of demand in the world is expected to change, as the consumption requirements of the more industrial of the developing countries will rise relatively more sharply than those of the developed world. (According to internal World Bank estimates, the income elasticity of demand for steel varied from 0.64 for the United States to 3.20 for China and North Korea in the period 1955-70. Latin America had an elasticity of 1.48.) Latin America's steel consumption between 1960 and 1973 grew faster than any other region in the world except Japan-Oceania.[14]

There are likely to be some structural changes in the demand for steel of the developed countries, primarily due to changes in transportation modes. Automobiles will tend to be lighter. Private car production will probably grow at a lower rate than during the past few decades. The trend is toward public transportation, away from highway construction.

It is unlikely, however, that the rate of substitution of aluminum and plastics for steel will change. The high petroleum prices not only affect aluminum and plastics costs but also the cost of coal and therefore steel production.† The main competition of iron ore as an input in steel production is scrap metal. Their substitutability, however, is limited by the technology of steel making. The relative stability and

---

*The U.S.-owned Marcona Mining Company was expropriated in July 1975. Marcona asked for nationalization a year ago, but expected compensation, which the government did not grant because of charges of tax evasion and other irregularities.

†The relative position of plastics vis-a-vis steel, however, is expected to worsen somewhat. The cross price elasticity between steel and aluminum was estimated by World Bank staff to be 0.4; for example, a 10 percent increase in the price of steel will increase demand for aluminum by 4 percent (over several years).

moderate fall in iron ore prices over a long period contributed to a decline in the use of scrap in steel production.[15]

About two thirds of the expected increase in world consumption of iron ore between 1975 and 1980 has already been provided for by new capacity for which financing has already been arranged. Although there is competition in investment funds between Western Europe and Japan, it is reasonable to expect that capital will be forthcoming for the remaining third of capacity needs.

Trade

North America (Canada and the United States combined), which has been a net importer of iron ore in the past, is expected to become self-sufficient in 1980 if there are no major production restrictions because of pollution and environmental controls. (After 1980, however, North America is expected to become again a substantial net importer.) This does not mean that the United States will not purchase iron ore from countries other than Canada, because Canada will continue to export to Western Europe and Japan. It does mean, however, that the U.S. market for Latin American ores will not grow very much over the next few years.

Western European import requirements will rise faster than that region's growth in consumption because of the limitation on the expansion of its production due to low grade ore deposits. Therefore Western Europe will provide a larger market for Latin American ores, but Latin America will have to compete in that market primarily with African countries. The Japanese market will probably recover vigorously between 1976 and 1980, although its growth rate will be considerably less than that during the 1960-73 period. Australia is Latin America's main competitor in that market.

Iron ore prices are expected to remain roughly constant in real terms for the remainder of the decade, but are projected to increase after 1980. As many links in the vertical integration of the steel industry are broken because of nationalization of captive mines and other factors, a substantial increase in long-term contractual arrangements between exporters and importers is foreseen. In that sense, free market competition for iron ore will continue to be greatly circumscribed.

Probably a greater proportion of the export value of the product will accrue to developing-country exporters than in the past because of improved transportation systems and greater control over the means of transportation by the exporters, and also because of a greater level of beneficiation of the ore in the LDCs. The degree to which the LDCs can appropriate the value of their natural resources will be limited by the enormous investment requirements needed by shipping, port, and railroad development. India, for example, has spent large amounts obtained through external financing on ore beneficiation processes and the acquisition of ore bulk carriers. Brazil's rapidly expanding shipping industry, on the other hand, has concentrated primarily on specialized oil carriers.

Almost half of iron ore exports have been provided by developing countries in the recent past. Their proportion is expected to decline during the next few years. The Latin American share of the world market, however, will increase primarily because of the huge Brazilian capacity expansion. Although Brazilian production will probably remain below total Australian output by 1980, Brazil's exports are likely to surpass in volume those of Australia. Most of the Latin American export expansion will be for the European and Japanese markets. Latin America is expected to gain almost one third of the world market in iron ore.

CONCLUSION

The rather favorable outlook for an expanded role of Latin America in the world market for nonfuel minerals will not detract the region from its goal of industrialization. More than ever raw material earnings will be looked on as a means of helping to finance the industrialization process. Because of the enormous import needs of capital, technology, and producer goods, such as petroleum, the region will increase its efforts to develop its natural resource base and export capacity. On the basis of recent trends, one can predict that in making these efforts, Latin American countries will try to obtain not only greater control over their raw material production but also greater value for their exports.

The development of nonfuel minerals will require huge capital investments, a major part of which would have to be financed externally. Different uses compete for such funds, and Latin American countries will have to make difficult choices as to whether to invest in the resource base or directly in manufacturing industry. One of the major problems here is that the infrastructure and technology developed in Latin America in the recent past were geared primarily to manufacturing or to the end use of minerals rather than to their production. This implies investment not only in physical infrastructure but also in the training of new scientific cadre.

Latin American efforts to appropriate more of the economic rent from its natural resources follow three avenues:* policies that aim at

---

*It is obvious that, in this and other discussions in this chapter where the term "Latin America" is used, the generalizations cannot

getting greater control over resource production through nationalization or majority ownership of mining and shipping operations; policies to increase the degree of processing of natural resources for exports; and policies to obtain better and/or more stable prices of resource exports through commodity arrangements of various types.

Almost every Latin American country recently has followed policies of at least majority, if not complete, ownership of the mining of major minerals (including Brazil, in its exploitation of the Amazon resources). This is in line with policies in the least developing countries around the world. Developed countries also have begun to insist on reducing foreign control of their minerals. Among the developed country mineral exporters, Australia is probably the most militant, followed by Canada. Insofar as the militancy of these countries increases and they begin to circumscribe their mineral production and exports, more room for developing countries' exports will be made.

The control by Latin American countries of the means of transportation in order to raise their share of the value of their mineral exports is more difficult to achieve. While most countries attempt to increase their merchant fleet, the acquisition of bulk carriers necessary for the shipment of ores and the development of adequate port facilities are usually still beyond their financial means.

The objective of raising the degree of processing of minerals before they are shipped abroad will probably meet with some success in Latin America. Greater processing will increase the value added accruing to the country; widen and intensify the linkages of the mining sector with the industrial sector of the economy (for example, the local manufacture of steel balls for the crushing mills in Chile's copper industry); and lower the transportation costs per unit value exported. There are, of course, economic and social costs involved. Ore processing, from concentrating to refining, requires large investments. Furthermore, it may be difficult to compete with efficient existing plants. For example, Peru's plans to greatly increase copper refining by 1980 may meet with severe obstacles; world copper refining is controlled by the Phelps Dodge and Anaconda companies, and developed country refineries can utilize all by-products more efficiently. Developing countries' refineries may have to discard by-products for lack of ready use. Therefore, it may be difficult to break into the market unless copper prices rise significantly.

---

possibly apply to all the countries within the region. Natural resource policies vary from country to country. At one end of the range are the Andean Group countries (but even within this group there are significant differences) and at the other there is Brazil. But the general thrust of the generalizations appears valid.

On the other hand, industrial country societies have become more pollution conscious. Iron ore beneficiation and smelting are particularly dirty, and developed countries have begun to regulate such activities. This fact may make it easier for smelting and refining operations to be established in Latin American countries that are more willing to bear the social costs for economic (and political) reasons. (Because Latin America's iron ore is of high grade, beneficiation is not necessary for technical reasons.) The ultimate objective of Latin American mineral producers is to establish integrated industries with a view to exporting final products: steel by the iron ore countries and fabricated copper products by the copper mining countries.

In respect to commodity prices, it is quite unlikely that any arrangements among developing-country producers of nonfuel minerals could function as cartels. These minerals are ubiquitous and will become more so as explorations continue and new technologies are developed. A large number of countries share the markets for both copper and iron ore, and a major proportion is controlled by developed countries. CIPEC, for example, cannot defend a bottom price for copper without the cooperation of Canada. IOEC cannot negotiate favorable long-term iron ore export contracts without the collaboration of Australia and Canada. The substitution possibilities with other products, discussed previously, signify that in order to achieve a higher price for copper, CIPEC would not only need the cooperation of Canada but also a collusion with bauxite producers. Leaving aside substitution possibilities, a case could be made that producer arrangements in nonfuel minerals could function as long as they could keep the price situation uncertain. If, however, they should succeed in raising high elasticity of supply in the long run, new investments will be forthcoming in nonmember countries, thus breaking the cartel.

In nonfuel-mineral-producing countries, the common economic and political interest necessary for cartel action appears to be lacking. Brazil, for instance, has little interest in supporting any militant move by IOEC, because Brazil has massive iron ore development plans and wants to have flexibility. It is also less dependent on iron ore for its export earnings than other countries.

Recent shares of the value of iron ore exports in total export earnings varied from about 5 percent in Venezuela to almost 90 percent in Mauritania. In general, Latin American shares were lower than in Africa (Brazil and Chile about 7 percent; Peru, 8 percent; Liberia, about 75 percent). The copper earning shares were over 80 percent in Chile and Zambia, between 50 and 60 percent in Zaire, and 30 percent in Peru. Nevertheless, one could claim that even a low earnings share in Latin America signifies a higher degree of dependency than a similar share in Africa, because of the vital import requirements of the higher level of Latin American industrialization.

Copper may lend itself more to concerted producer actions, particularly if CIPEC could be expanded to include new developing-country producers. (It is interesting to note that in the past the United States had more control over copper prices than CIPEC is likely to have; the U.S. government imposed price controls, tariffs and quotas, stimulated production, and maintained stockpiles.)

There are possibilities for commodity agreements between producers and consumers. CIPEC could enter into long-term contractual relations with Western European countries and Japan, along similar lines that now exist between Japanese companies and iron ore producers. However, this may raise the specter of new dependency relationships unpalatable to developing-country producers.

The more useful approach would be for producer organizations, such as CIPEC for copper and IOEC for iron ore, first, to help producing countries in technical cooperation; to coordinate negotiations of long-term contracts; to provide marketing information and general statistics; and, second, to cooperate with consuming countries for the establishment of an orderly market with relatively stable prices and an assured supply for the industrial countries. This may require buffer stocks or similar types of arrangements. Proposals by developing-country mineral producers to link prices to some index, such as the suggestion by developing-country iron ore exporters to link their export prices to an index of steel prices, are often unrealistic and inefficient, but reasonable versions deserve serious considerations by developed-country consumers.

With the cooperation of the industrialized countries, Latin American nonfuel mineral resources will become more important for the region as well as for the world. They will play a more important role not only in world markets but also in intra-Latin American trade as direct inputs in the region's growing manufacturing industries. As export earners they will continue to help finance the region's industrialization process, even though their share of total regional export value will tend to decrease, slowly giving way to rising nontraditional exports.

NOTES

1. For a review of raw-materials issues and problems in Latin America, see J. Grunwald and P. Musgrove, Natural Resources in Latin American Development (Baltimore: Johns Hopkins Press, 1970), particularly chapters 1 and 2.

2. For an early statement of the Prebisch Thesis, named after its author, Raul Prebisch, the former head of the United Nations Economic

Commission for Latin America, see the Economic Survey of Latin America, 1949 (New York: United Nations, 1950), a relevant part of which was reprinted as an article, "The Economic Development of Latin America and Its Principal Problems," Economic Bulletin for Latin America 2, no. 1 (February 1962).

3. The fifteen commodities constitute Latin America's major natural resource exports, including only those basic products that constituted at least 1 percent of total regional commodity exports in at least one year during 1970-72. The total export value of the fifteen products constituted 56.3 percent of the region's total earnings from merchandise exports during that period. The following are the fifteen basic commodities in order of their importance for Latin America: crude oil, coffee, copper, sugar, beef, iron ore, cotton, bananas, corn, fish meal, wheat, crustaceans, cocoa, soybeans, and wool. See Inter-American Development Bank, Latin America in the World Economy, March 1975, pp. 46-47 and Table III-7, p. 58. If refined petroleum exports, which were about 70 percent as large as crude oil exports, were included, the drop in the region's export share would not be nearly as large.

4. Inter-American Development Bank, op. cit., Table I-7.

5. For a detailed pre-1970 analysis, see Grunwald and Musgrove, op. cit., chaps. 4 and 5.

6. See Theodore Moran, Multinational Corporations and the Politics of Dependence (Princeton, N.J.: Princeton University Press, 1974).

7. Latin American Economic Report 3, no. 2 (May 1975).

8. Ibid., no. 13 (May 1975).

9. Estimates are made on the basis of income and price elasticities of demand. The income elasticity is the relative change in quantity demanded compared to the relative change of income. The income elasticity of demand for copper is estimated to range between 0.5 and 0.9 for individual countries, depending on their level of economic development. For a discussion of income and price elasticities, see F. E. Banks, The World Copper Market: An Economic Analysis (Cambridge, Mass.: Ballinger Co., 1974); Charles River Associates, Economic Analysis of the Copper Industry (Boston: Charles River Associates, 1972); F. M. Fisher, et. al. "An Econometric Model of the World Copper Industry," Bell Journal of Economics and Management Science 3, no. 2 (Autumn 1972).

10. "Copper Cost Study," Metal Bulletin (February 18, 1975). Dollar costs refer to 1974 prices.

11. Some sources indicate that a 20 percent cutback would have been necessary to halt the price slide. See Latin American Economic Report, op. cit., no. 2 (January 1975).

12. Critical Imported Materials, Special Report, United States Council on International Economic Policy, December 1974, p. 25.

13. Latin American Economic Report 1, no. 5, no. 73.

14. UNCTAD. Recent Developments in the World Market for Iron Ore, TD/B.C.I., February 1972; and American Metal Market (February 14, 1975).

15. Iron and Steel Statistics Bureau, Iron and Steel Industry: Annual Statistics for the United Kingdom 1970 (London, 1971); and Japan Iron and Steel Federation, Statistical Yearbook (Tokyo, various issues). In the United Kingdom the use of scrap declined only slightly, from somewhat more than the pig iron input to somewhat less, between the early and late 1950s. Since then, the lower proportion has remained roughly constant. In Japan, however, because of the shift from "open hearth" to the "oxygen process" of steel production, scrap declined from constituting nearly two-thirds of the total inputs of scrap and pig iron to about one-third of the total between 1951 and 1970.

CHAPTER

10

CONVENTIONAL ARMS TRANSFERS TO LATIN AMERICA

Norman M. Smith

PERSPECTIVE

Magazine articles, television specials, congressional bills, and newspaper headlines have highlighted the burgeoning worldwide trade in armaments. Large-scale sales of modern weapons to Middle Eastern countries have become almost commonplace. Latin American specialists tend to transfer the deplorable consequences of the arms race in the Middle East to Latin America and criticize U.S. arms shipments to nations in the hemisphere.

Latin America's arms imports have been exceedingly modest compared with those of nearly all other regions of the world. To place Latin America's arms trade in perspective, an international comparison may be helpful. The level of Latin American arms imports is miniscule compared with, for example, one Saudi Arabian order to the United States in 1974 amounting to about $588 million—20 percent greater than the $476 million norm of arms delivered to all twenty-three Latin American nations combined in 1973.[1] Figure 10.1 depicts arms imports by developing countries in five different geographic areas. Evidence of the Indochina war and the 1973 Arab-Israeli conflict stands out. In contrast, the figure depicts a relatively constant level of spending for arms imports by Latin American nations over the past ten years

Other indicators tend to verify that observation. The regional ratio of military expenditures (MILEX) to gross national product (GNP) in Latin America has remained basically constant during the decade, hovering near 2.0 percent, the lowest of any geographic region. Per capita military expenditures in Latin America have never exceeded $12.00 a year; this is in contrast to the world average of $68.60 and

FIGURE 10.1

Arms Imports of Developing Countries by Area, 1963-73

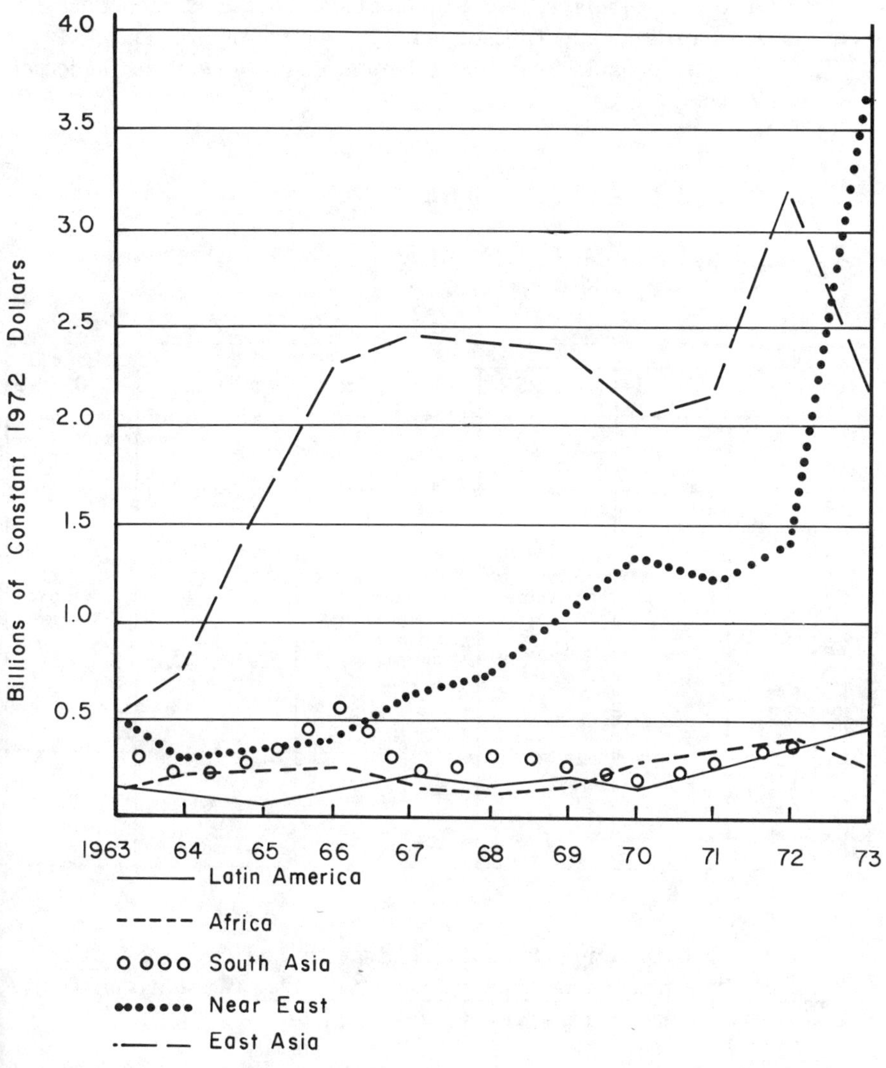

Source: U.S. Arms Control and Disarmament Agency, World Military Expenditures and Arms Trade 1963-1973 (Washington, D.C.: U.S. Government Printing Office, 1975), pp. 72-77.

the developed countries' average of almost $223.00. The amount spent per soldier in Latin America is less than 30 percent of the world average of almost $10,000 per man. Latin American countries average four military personnel per 1,000 population; the Warsaw Pact figure, the world's highest, is approaching 14 per 1,000.[2]

Figure 10.2 displays the Latin American countries according to two ratios: military expenditures as a proportion of GNP and GNP per capita using 1972 data. This is one indicator of the relative burden of military expenditures.

FIGURE 10.2

Relative Burden of Military Expenditures, 1972

MILEX as percent of GNP	GNP Per Capita				
	100-199	200-299	300-499	500-999	1000-1299
5-10%				Cuba	
2-4.9%	Bolivia		Ecuador	Brazil Peru Uruguay	
1-1.9%	Haiti	Honduras	Colombia Dominican Rep. El Salvador Guatamala Guyana Nicaragua Paraguay	Chile	Argentina Venezuela
Less Than 1%				Costa Rica Jamaica Mexico Panama	Trinidad-Tobago

Source: U.S. Arms Control and Disarmament Agency, World Military Expenditures and Arms Trade 1963-1973 (Washington, D.C.: U.S. Government Printing Office, 1975), p. 5.

Figures 10.3 and 10.4 show the Latin American percentage of world arms imports during 1963 and 1973: 4.4 percent in 1963 and 5.1 percent in 1973.[3]

FIGURE 10.3

Arms Imports by Region, 1963

FIGURE 10.4

Arms Imports by Region, 1973

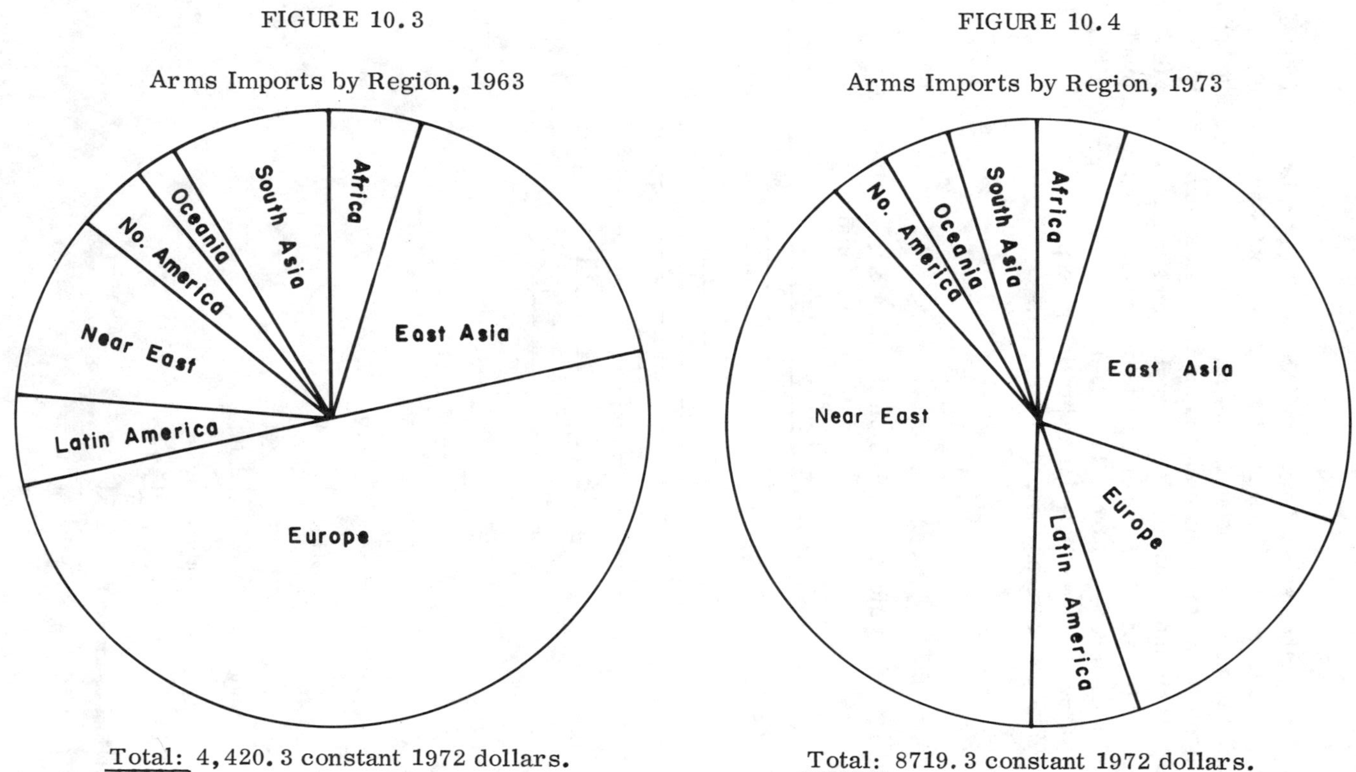

Total: 4,420.3 constant 1972 dollars.

Total: 8719.3 constant 1972 dollars.

MAGNITUDE OF ARMS TRADE

Nevertheless, in Latin America, which is relatively free of international tensions but burdened with many social and economic problems, arms transfers take place with great regularity. The bar graph in Figure 10.5 shows the major arms recipients during the 1964-73 period. (This information, like other data on arms imports in this chapter, refers to deliveries rather than to orders or items in the pipeline. Deliveries received from the United States include grant Military Assistance Program material and training, supply and service costs, as well as government and commercial sales.)

FIGURE 10.5

Major Arms Recipients, Cumulative, 1964-73
(in millions of current dollars)

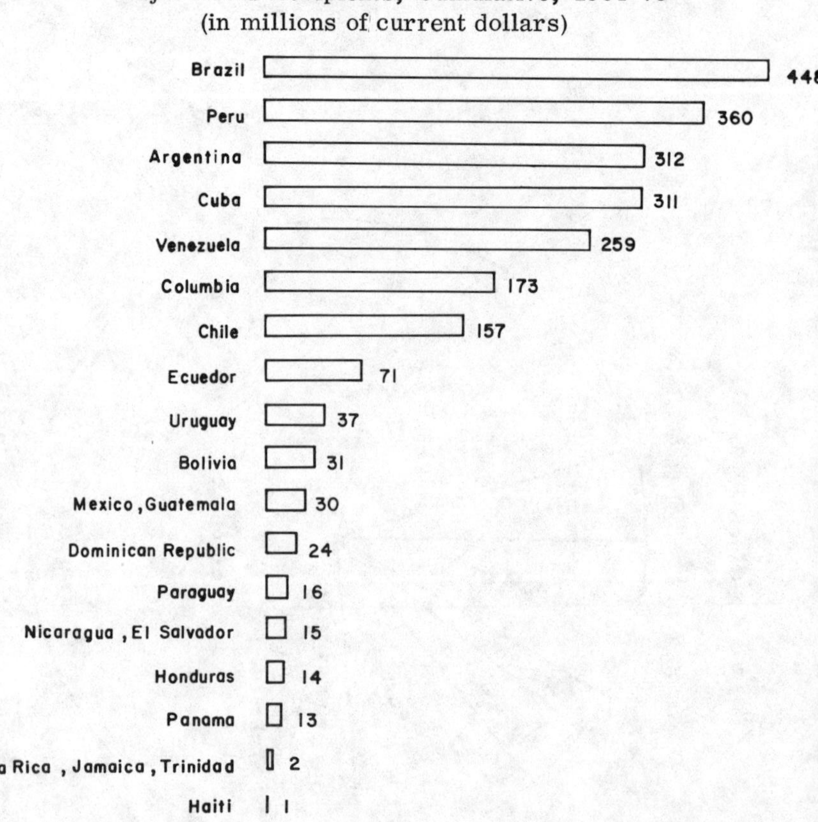

FIGURE 10.6

Major Arms Recipients, 1973
(in millions of constant 1972 dollars)

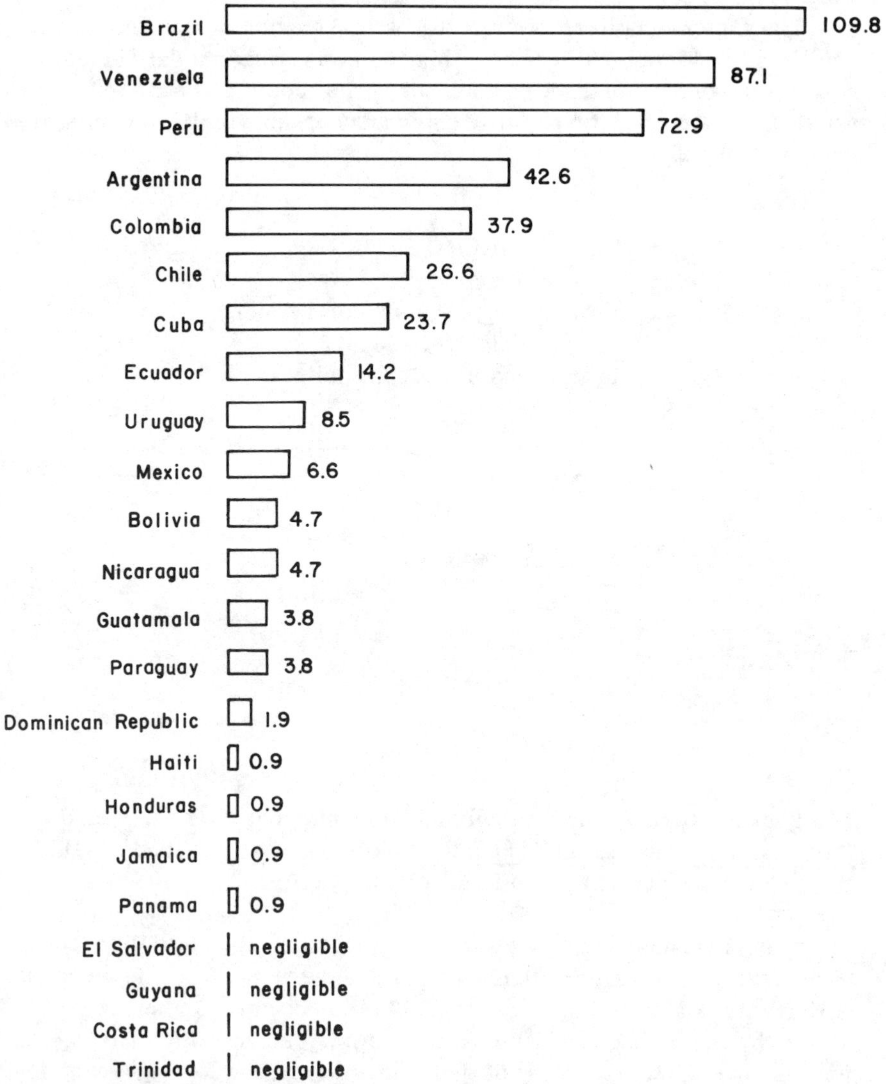

Brazil	109.8
Venezuela	87.1
Peru	72.9
Argentina	42.6
Colombia	37.9
Chile	26.6
Cuba	23.7
Ecuador	14.2
Uruguay	8.5
Mexico	6.6
Bolivia	4.7
Nicaragua	4.7
Guatamala	3.8
Paraguay	3.8
Dominican Republic	1.9
Haiti	0.9
Honduras	0.9
Jamaica	0.9
Panama	0.9
El Salvador	negligible
Guyana	negligible
Costa Rica	negligible
Trinidad	negligible

Source: U.S. Arms Control and Disarmament Agency, World Military Expenditures and Arms Trade 1963-1973 (Washington, D.C.: U.S. Government Printing Office, 1975), pp. 74-120.

Figure 10.6 shows estimated arms imports by Latin American nations for 1973 only. Cuba's relative position is lower here than in Figure 10.5 because of lower imports from the Soviet Union. Venezuela's higher relative position in 1973 may be the beginning of the trend that will soon be evident in the data for other OPEC (Organization of Petroleum Exporting Countries) countries.

The major suppliers of arms to Latin America during the decade are listed in Figure 10.7. Since this figure is based on deliveries rather than orders placed, it does not reveal completely the extent to which Latin America turned to Western European suppliers during the period 1969-72.

FIGURE 10.7

Major Arms Suppliers to Latin America, Cumulative, 1964-73 (in millions of current dollars)

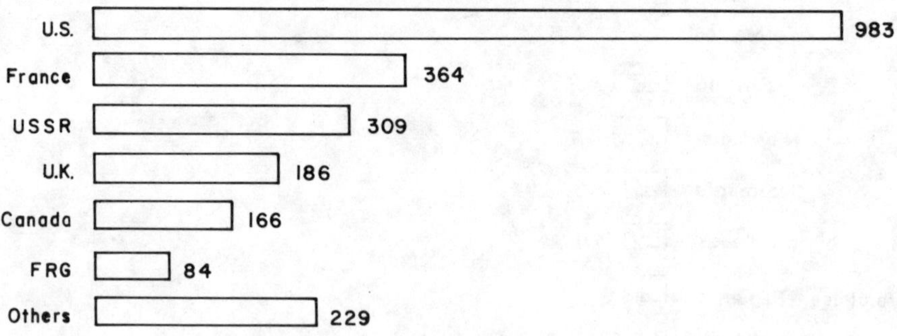

Source: U.S. Arms Control and Disarmament Agency, World Military Expenditures and Arms Trade 1963-1973 (Washington, D.C.: U.S. Government Printing Office, 1975), p. 70.

(Arms purchased or ordered during this period, but delivered after 1973, will swell the figures for subsequent years. The increased dollar value of arms imports after 1973 is accounted for by large orders by the west coast South American states and inflationary costs for weapons systems. Most of the orders have been for high-unit-cost aircraft and naval vessels, followed by surface-to-air and antitank missiles. Peru and Ecuador have placed the most substantial orders. Brazil's purchases have declined as a result of the energy crisis and stringent economy measures by the government.)

Rating	Country	Average Annual Growth
1	Peru	6.95
2	Brazil	6.69
3	Venezuela	5.82
4	Argentina	5.28

Conversely, Cuba having received massive doses of Soviet aid in the early 1960s, reached a saturation point and showed a negative growth rate for arms imports during the decade.

Perhaps equally significant is a general comparison of the average per capita cost of arms imports to each Latin American country during the decade.[4] Prior to calculating this per capita figure, known grant aid was subtracted from the total arms imports listed during the cumulative period 1964-73. The results are as follows:

Over $35:	Cuba
$20-25:	Peru, Venezuela
$10-15:	Chile, Argentina
$5-10:	Ecuador, Uruguay, Panama, Colombia
$1-5:	Brazil, Guatemala, El Salvador, Paraguay, Bolivia, Dominican Republic, Nicaragua, Honduras, Trinidad-Tobago
Less than $1:	Costa Rica, Jamaica, Mexico, Haiti, Guyana

DIRECTIONS OF ARMS TRADE

In the 1961-65 period, the United States was the sole supplier of arms to eleven of the Latin American countries. As Table 10.1 shows, it no longer plays this unique role in any of the hemispheric nations.

During the 1961-65 period, fifteen suppliers provided arms to Latin America. This number has grown to twenty-seven in the last decade. Significantly, some of the sister hemispheric republics have joined the list of suppliers, as indigenous or coproduction facilities have been established. Table 10.2 shows the number of Latin American recipients supplied by the twenty-seven arms exports.

The fact that arms transfers go to developing countries is understandable in terms of their inability to produce their own arms. During the period 1963-73, arms imports by Latin American republics were about 15 percent of military expenditures, a figure not out of line with military outlays in developed countries. The high percentage of arms supplied by the United States is not surprising, since the United States accounts for an even higher fraction of exports in high technology fields,

TABLE 10.1

Number of Arms Suppliers,
Cumulative, 1964-73

15 Peru	4 Bolivia
14 Chile	4 Guatemala
10 Argentina	4 Honduras
8 Colombia	4 Panama
7 Brazil	3 Cuba
7 Ecuador	3 Dominican Republic
6 Mexico	3 Jamaica
6 Paraguay	3 Nicaragua
6 Uruguay	2 Costa Rica
6 Venezuela	2 Guyana
5 El Salvador	2 Haiti
	2 Trinidad-Tobago

Source: ACDA Worksheets.[5]

TABLE 10.2

Supplier-Recipient Relationship,
Cumulative, 1964-73

22 United States	3 Argentina
14 Belgium	3 Brazil
10 Federal Republic of Germany	3 Israel
10 United Kingdom	2 Denmark
8 Canada	2 Australia
8 Spain	2 Japan
8 France	1 Norway
7 Italy	1 Portugal
4 Switzerland	1 Turkey
3 Netherlands	1 Czechoslovakia
3 Soviet Union	1 Venezuela
3 Sweden	1 Chile
3 Yugoslavia	1 Nicaragua
	1 Australia

Source: ACDA Worksheets.[6]

such as civilian aircraft. The United States is an attractive supplier because of its traditional commerical ties with Latin America. In no Latin American country is arms supply the mainstream of U.S. interests, and the United States does not attempt to monopolize arms supply.

In an attempt to isolate somewhat more homogeneous groupings than Latin America, four basically geographic subgroupings are introduced in some of the following figures. They are: Big Six: Argentina, Brazil, Chile, Colombia, Peru, Venezuela; Other South America: Bolivia, Ecuador, Guyana, Paraguay, Uruguay; Middle America: Costa Rica, El Salvador, Guatemala, Honduras, Mexico, Nicaragua, Panama; and Caribbean: Cuba, Dominican Republic, Haiti, Jamaica, Trinidad-Tobago. For purposes of comparison these groups' shares of the total Latin American GNP and population are as follows (in percent):[7]

	GNP	Population
Big Six	64	62
Other South America	4	6
Middle America	26	24
Caribbean	6	7

For the analysis of arms transfers, the inclusion of Cuba and Mexico in this grouping introduces a serious distortion. The exceptionally large Soviet imports to Cuba in the 1961-67 period tend to obscure some of the characteristics of the transfers to the other nations. Similarly, despite Mexico's long-standing deemphasis of military affairs, its military budget and armed forces are much larger than those of the Central American republics and Panama.

Despite this problem, the use of subgroups permits a more detailed analysis of the direction in which arms imports are going. In this regard, Figure 10.8 points up the fact that the larger South American nations are leading the trend to internationalism in arms trade. Middle American and Caribbean countries (except Cuba) have continued to rely on their geographic and historic affinity to the United States in meeting their perceived security needs.

As noted in Figure 10.8, the majority of the arms are imported by the Big Six. Figure 10.10 provides a closer inspection of the suppliers of these arms shipments. The length of each bar is proportional to the corresponding country's share of the arms delivered by the supplier to all of the Big Six republics. The value of that share, in millions of current dollars, is expressed at the end of each bar. (For example, the $78 million of arms shipped by Canada to Peru represents 46 percent of the total arms exports by Canada to the Big Six during the period 1964-73.)

Figure 10.11 shows the percentage of total arms deliveries to the subgroupings over the decade. To eliminate the distortion caused by the large Soviet arms shipments to Cuba in the early period, the top line shows the percentage of the Latin American total that the Big Six would have represented if those Cuban imports had not taken place. It

FIGURE 10.8

Relative Distribution of Arms Imports by Recipients, Cumulative, 1964-73
(in millions of current dollars)

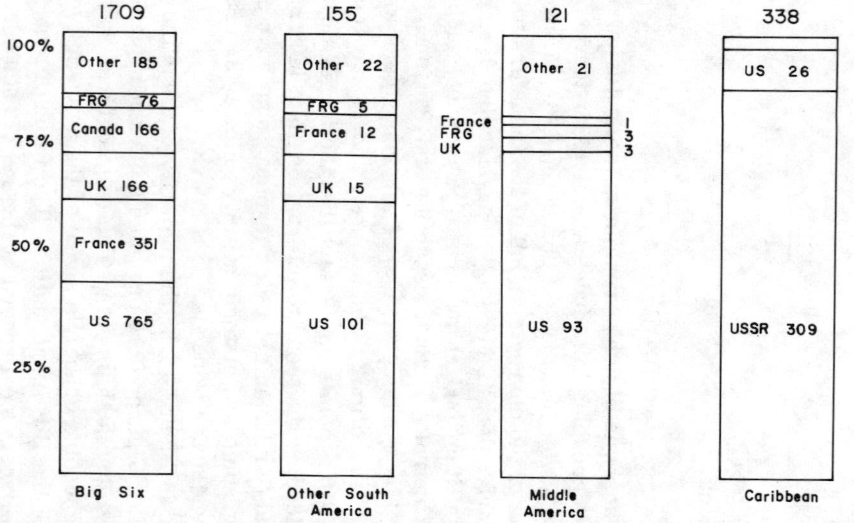

	Big Six	Other South America	Middle America	Caribbean
Total	1709	155	121	338
	Other 185	Other 22	Other 21	
	FRG 76	FRG 5	France 1	US 26
	Canada 166	France 12	FRG 3	USSR 309
	UK 166	UK 15	UK 3	
	France 351	US 101	US 93	
	US 765			

100%, 75%, 50%, 25%

Note: The above findings tend to be confirmed if the same data are transposed to illustrate the supplier relationship (see Figure 10.9).

Source: U.S. Arms Control and Disarmament Agency, World Military Expenditures and Arms Trade 1963-1973 (Washington, D.C.: U.S. Government Printing Office, 1975), p. 70.

FIGURE 10.9

Relative Distribution of Arms Exports by Suppliers, Cumulative 1964-73
(in millions of current dollars)

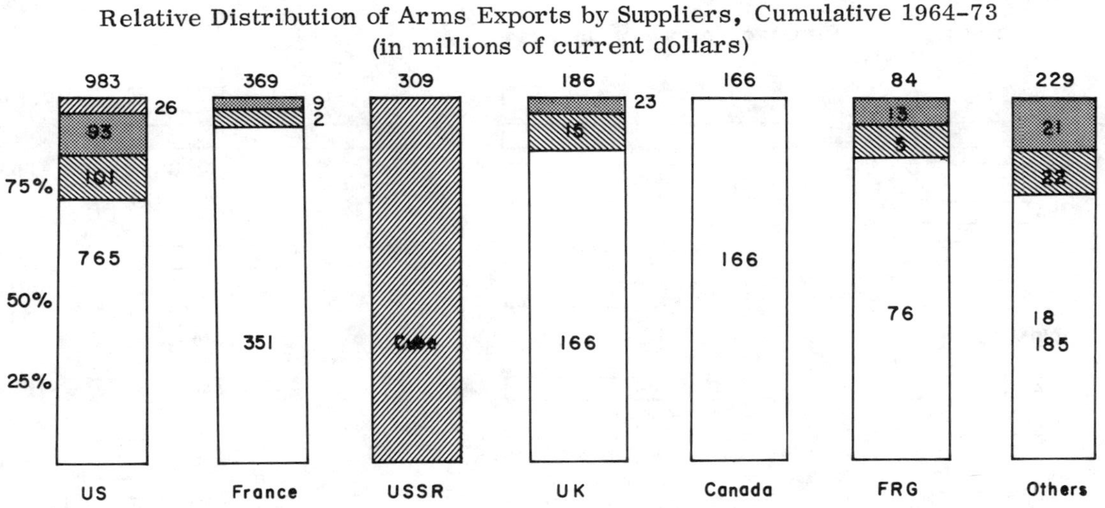

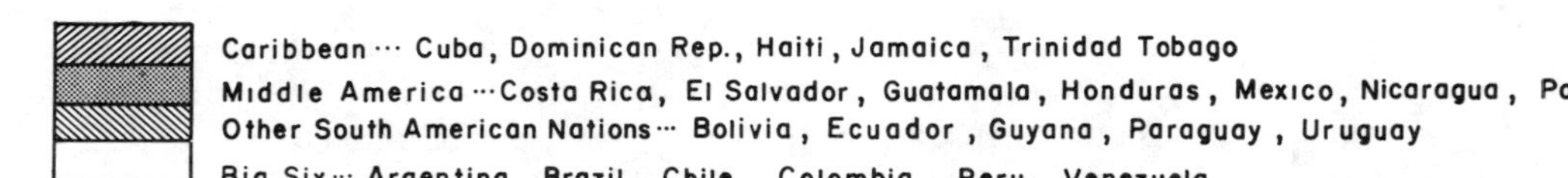

Source: U.S. Arms Control and Disarmament Agency, World Military Expenditures and Arms Trade 1963-73 (Washington, D.C.: U.S. Government Printing Office, 1975), p. 70.

FIGURE 10.10

Distribution of Exports to Big Six by Major Suppliers, Cumulative, 1964-73
(percentage indicated by length of bar; figures at end of lines
in millions of current dollars)

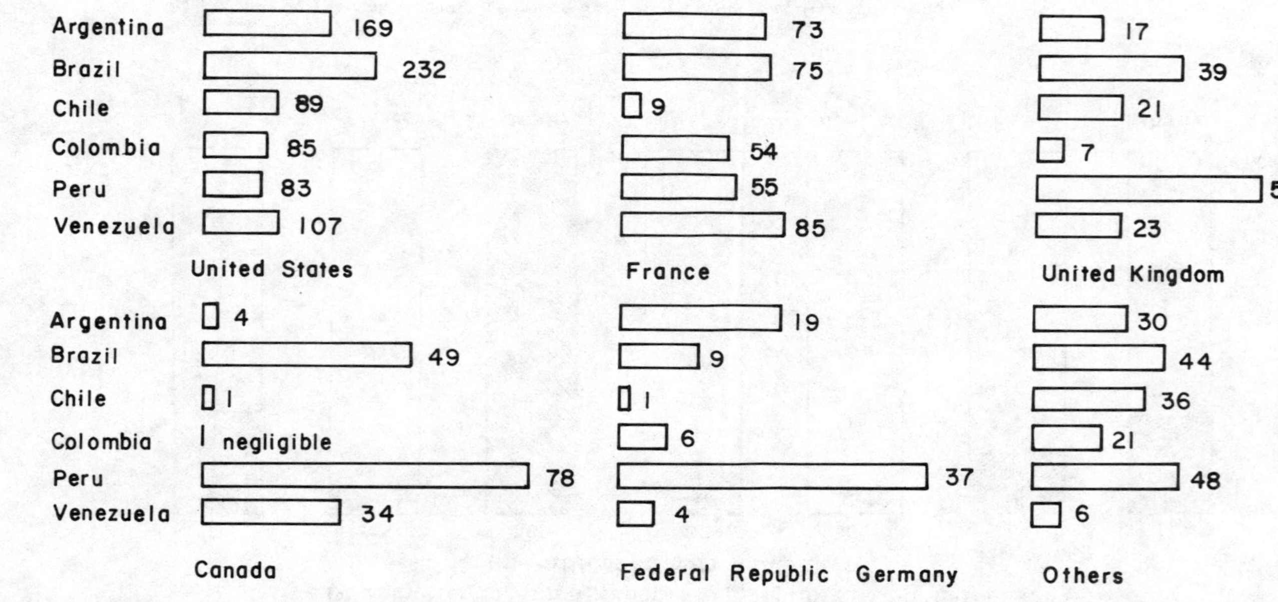

Source: U.S. Arms Control and Disarmament Agency, World Military Expenditures and Arms Trade 1963-1973 (Washington, D.C.: U.S. Government Printing Office, 1975), p. 70.

FIGURE 10.11

Distribution of Arms Imports by Group
(in percent)

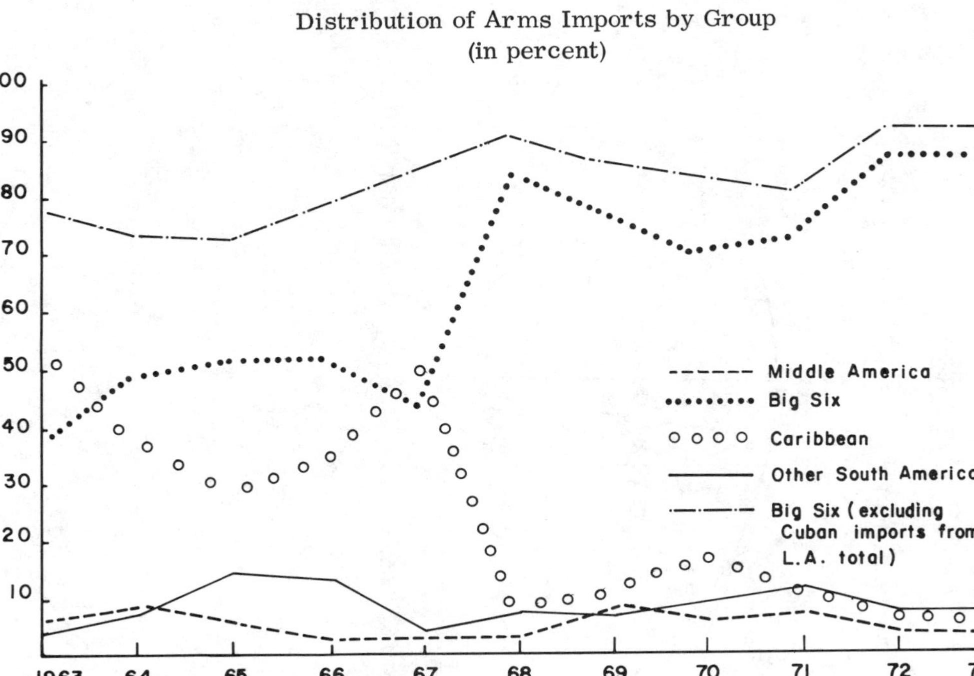

Source: U.S. Arms Control and Disarmament Agency, World Military Expenditures and Arms Trade 1963–73 (Washington, D.C.: U.S. Government Printing Office, 1975), pp. 79–120.

thus becomes evident that the major South American countries normally import about 80 percent of the total arms sent to Latin America.

In the first half of the decade, the USSR introduced massive amounts of military equipment into Cuba, more than twice the amount the remainder of the world exported to Latin America. The magnitude of the Soviet-Cuba transfers in the 1961-65 period is reflected in Figure 10.12. For comparative purposes, this bilateral trade was

FIGURE 10.12

Distribution of Major Arms, Exports by Supplier, Cumulative, 1961-1965

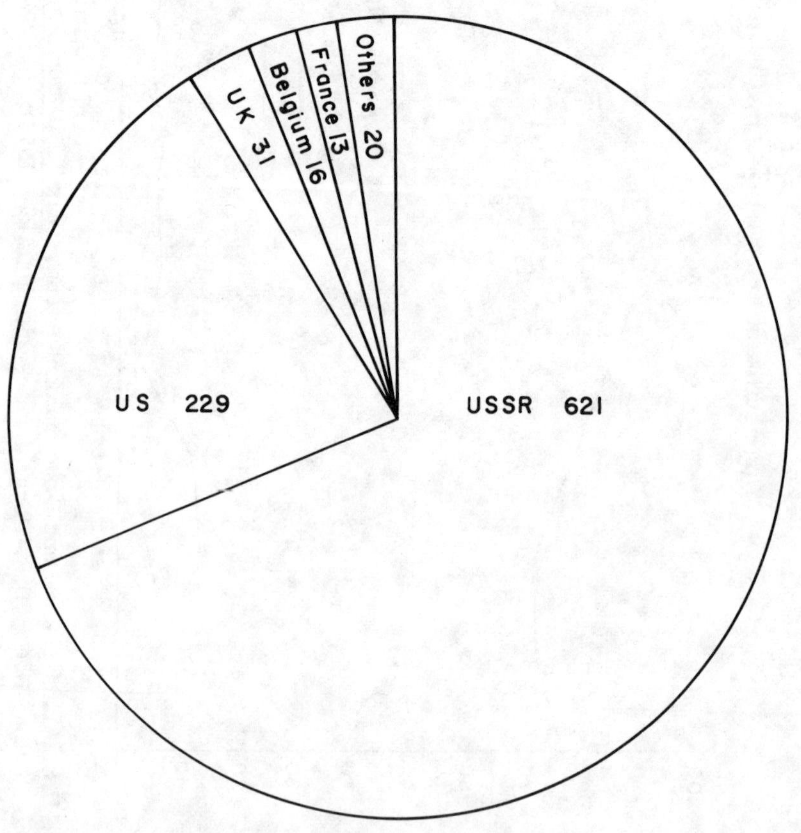

Total: 930 million current dollars.
Source: ACDA Worksheets.[8]

excluded from the total for Figure 10. 8, pointing up the heavy reliance of the other Latin American countries on the United States in that span of years.

Beginning in the mid-1960s, this trade pattern began to change for many reasons (see Figure 10. 13 and 10. 14). Congressional restrictions limited total U.S. sales to Latin America; other legislation, by interpretation, inhibited sales of "sophisticated" weapons; certain U.S.

FIGURE 10. 13

Distribution of Major Arms, Exports by Supplier, Excluding USSR, Cumulative, 1961-1965

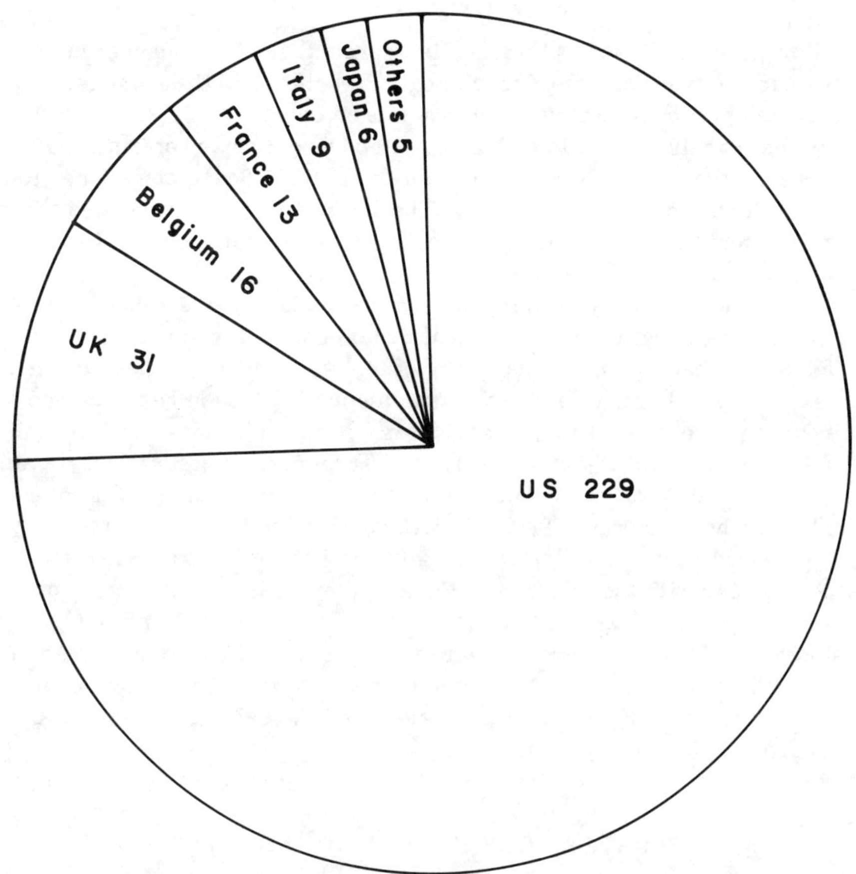

Total: 309 million current dollars.
Source: ACDA Worksheets.[9]

surplus equipment was not available due to worldwide demands; technological additions made the cost of some models noncompetitive; and, at times, the United States did not have the items desired by the Latin American nations, such as new construction submarines, gas-turbine destroyers, or light tanks. But the Latin Americans had the money and were ready to buy, and aggressive Western European salesmen moved into the region with competitive offerings. Our restrictions thus did little to limit imports. Some of this non-U.S. equipment was less than ideal for Latin America: too expensive, too difficult to provide with spare parts and trained operators, too sophisticated for local needs, and so on.

As shown in Figure 10.14, which includes all major suppliers, the growth in the percentage of arms transfers by France, the United Kingdom, West Germany, and Canada reflects the trend toward internationalism.

Figure 10.15 shows the supplier percentage of the market in several weapons system. The French began to sell the AMX-30 tanks, armored personnel carriers, and armored cars to Latin American armies. Their 1967 sale of Mirage introduced a supersonic aircraft to the continent during a period when the U.S. F-5 was considered too sophisticated for Latin America. The Latin Americans went to a more international market in all major categories of weapons except for helicopters.

A general survey of arms orders subsequent to 1971 shows that the market continues to have an international bent. France and the Soviet Union have been primary suppliers of tanks. The British have concentrated on providing naval vessels and aircraft. Canada has received a greater percentage of the subsonic combat aircraft market. U.S. sales of F-5, A-37, and C-130 aircraft have surged. Despite a widespread sales campaign for the French Alouette, the United States still dominates the helicopter market. West German sales have been primarily in armored vehicles and naval vessels. In both dollar value and units, the Big Six, with the addition of Ecuador, now have the preponderate share of sales market, particularly with the lower level of Soviet assistance to Cuba.[10] Recent congressional action lifting certain restrictions placed on the Latin American region, availability of equipment, and competitive prices have again reversed the sales trend, this time in favor of U.S. equipment.

CORRELATION OF U.S. MAP AND SALES

Figure 10.16 depicts the U.S. share of imports by each recipient country, including grant aid under the Military Assistance Program

FIGURE 10.14

Distribution of Major Arms, Exports by Supplier, Cumulative, 1964-73

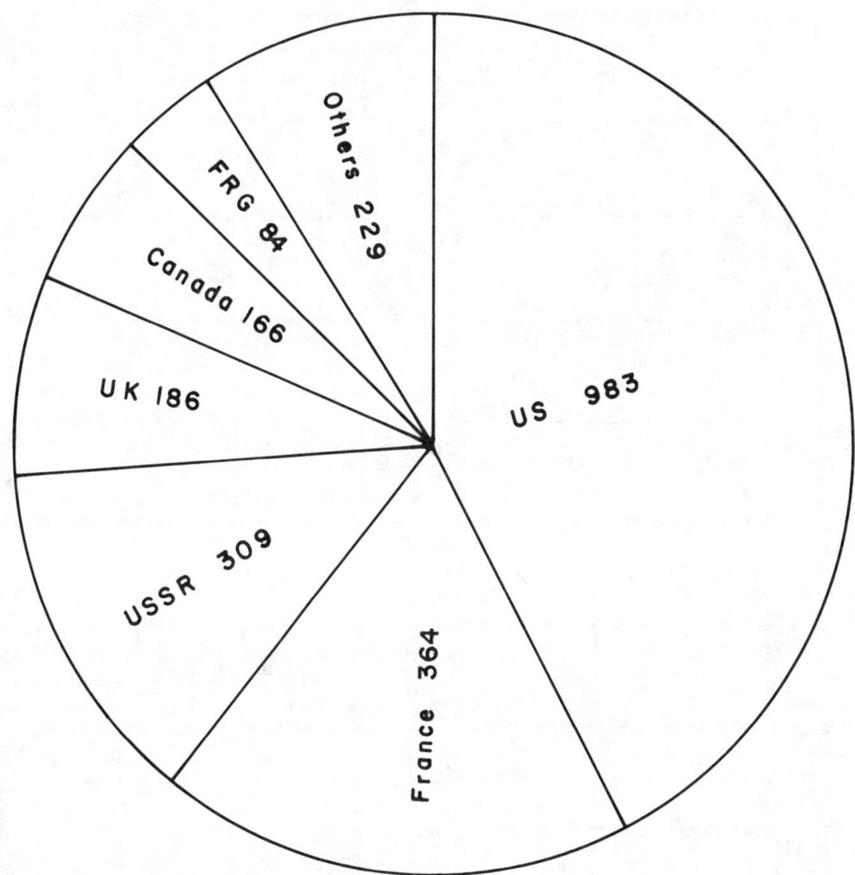

Total: 2,323 million current dollars.

Source: U.S. Arms Control and Disarmament Agency, World Military Expenditures and Arms Trade 1963-1973 (Washington, D.C.: U.S. Government Printing Office, 1975), p. 70.

(MAP) in the form of equipment, supply operations, or training. The figure shows a heavy reliance by Caribbean and Central American nations on the United States for their arms imports. In the Big Six, reliances range from 40 to 60 percent except for Peru. Those countries below 50 percent still have more trade with the United States than with any other arms exporter. They include Colombia: France 31 percent,

FIGURE 10.15

Major Weapons by Major Suppliers, Cumulative, 1967-71

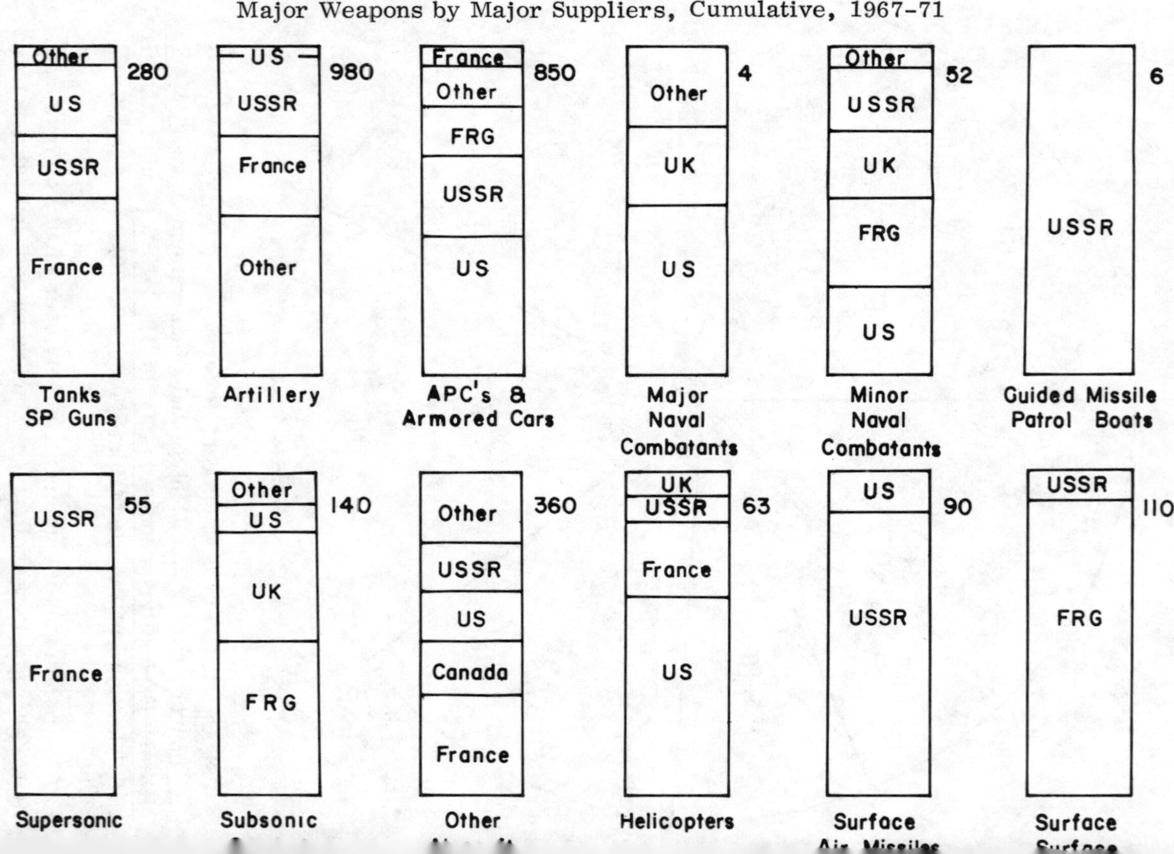

FIGURE 10.16

U.S. Share of Imports, Including MAP

US Share of Imports	Cumulative 1964-1973			
	Big Six	Other South America	Middle America	Caribbean
85-100%		Paraguay Bolivia	Costa Rica Guatamala Nicaragua	Jamaica Dominican Rep.
75-90%	Chile Argentina Brazil	Uruguay	Mexico Panama El Salvador Honduras	
40-49%	Columbia Venezuela	Ecuador		
Less than 40%	Peru			
None or negligible				Cuba Guyana Trinidad Tobago

Sources: U.S. Arms Control and Disarmament Agency, World Military Expenditures and Arms Trade 1963-1973 (Washington, D.C.: U.S. Government Printing Office, 1975), p. 70; and U.S. Department of Defense, Fiscal Year Series (1975), pp. 107-117.

United States 49 percent; Ecuador: United States 45 percent, United Kingdom 21 percent, France 17 percent; Venezuela: United States 41 percent, France 33 percent, Canada 13 percent, United Kingdom 9 percent; Peru: United States 23 percent, Canada 22 percent, United Kingdom 16 percent, France 15 percent, West Germany 9 percent.

MAP is funded by the United States and is therefore counted as a military expenditure of the United States and not of the recipient. Although the market value is included in the respective export and import data, as a grant it is not in reality a direct economic burden on the importer. Therefore, a country that obtains most of its arms imports via MAP may expend a relatively small percentage of its own financial resources for arms. Figure 10.17 lists MAP as a percentage of the total U.S. imports to the various countries. Honduras, Bolivia, and the Dominican Republic rely on MAP to provide for most of their needs. Conversely, throughout the decade, Venezuela and Mexico have used

MAP funds only for training. All their U.S. arms purchases were paid for through some type of sales arrangement.

FIGURE 10.17

MAP as Percent of Arms Imports from the United States

	Cumulative 1964-1973			
	Big Six	Other South America	Middle America	Caribbean
75-88%		Bolivia	Honduras	Dominican Rep.
50-74%	Colombia	Paraguay Uruguay Ecuador	Nicaragua Panama El Salvador Guatamala	
25-49%	Peru Chile Brazil Argentina		Costa Rica	Jamaica
0-10%	Venezuela*		Mexico*	Cuba** Guyana** Haiti** Trinidad-Tobago**

*Training only throughout period.

**No MAP.

Sources: U.S. Arms Control and Disarmament Agency, World Military Expenditures and Arms Trade 1963-1973 (Washington, D.C.: U.S. Government Printing Office, 1975), p. 70; and U.S. Department of Defense, Fiscal Year Series (1975), pp. 107-117.

By deducting MAP from total U.S. arms imports by each country, we can determine which nations traditionally have turned to the United States as an arms supplier to satisfy the remainder of their perceived security requirements. Figure 10.18 shows that only three countries have spent more than 50 percent of these military equipment outlays in the United States. Five of these purchasing nations turned to other areas of the world with more than 75 percent of the funds which they expended on arms.

FIGURE 10.18

U.S. Share of Imports, Excluding MAP

	Cumulative 1964-1973			
	Big Six	Other South America	Middle America	Caribbean
50-75%			Costa Rica Mexico	Jamaica
25-49%	Argentina Brazil Venezuela Chile	Paraguay Uruguay	Nicaragua El Salvador Panama	Dominican Rep.
7-24%	Colombia Peru	Ecuador Bolivia	Honduras	
None or Negligible				Cuba Guyana Haiti Trinidad-Tobago

Sources: U.S. Arms Control and Disarmament Agency, World Military Expenditures and Arms Trade 1963-1973 (Washington, D.C.: U.S. Government Printing Office, 1975), p. 70; and U.S. Department of Defense, Fiscal Year Series (1975), pp. 107-117.

COPRODUCTION

Although attention has been focused on major supplier-recipient relations, mention should also be made of Latin America's growing indigenous defense production capability—coproduction and licensed production as well as the homegrown variety. Brazil and Argentina lead, followed by Peru and Colombia. Under coproduction or licensing arrangements, such items as jet aircraft, helicopters, destroyers, submarines, tanks, and missiles are manufactured or assembled locally. In the indigenous production field, Brazil has emerged as a competitor with the United States for the export of armored personnel carriers to Canada.[11] Brazil has a major development program to enable it to become an independent arms producer. This is only the beginning of Latin America's emerging role as an arms supplier in the world market. Although there has been some intrahemispheric arms trade, direct and indirect revanchist problems will probably limit transfers among neighboring states.

CONCLUSIONS

This review of arms acquisitions by Latin American states makes clear that the dominant post-World War II position of the United States as an arms supplier to Latin America gave way in the late 1960s to an internationalism of arms trade. This shift resulted from U.S. restrictions combined with extensive promotional campaigns by European producers. Congressional supervision and restriction of U.S. arms transfers are exercised through three basic acts: the Foreign Assistance Act of 1961, as amended, controlling the grant aid Military Assistance Program; the Foreign Military Sales Act of 1968, as amended, providing authority for government-to-government credit and cash sales; and the Mutual Security Act of 1954, as amended, covering commercial sales. With the removal of the regional ceiling on grants and credits for Latin America in December 1974, there are no longer legislative restrictions aimed specifically at Latin America. This is not to deny the willingness of the Congress to impose specific country restrictions, as illustrated by the suspension of military assistance to Chile.

However, transfers to Latin America continued to be governed by a number of other more general restrictions contained in the Foreign Assistance Act and Foreign Military Sales Act. For example, provisions of these acts ban the transfer of "sophisticated" weapons systems to least developing countries unless specifically waived by the president; they ban FMS sales to any developing country when the president finds that it is diverting resources to unnecessary military expenditures, to a degree that materially interferes with its development; they require that before furnishing economic aid, the president take into account the amount of resources being expended by a recipient for military purposes. Restrictions also apply to countries that seize U.S. fishing vessels or expropriate U.S. property.

There are other legislative constraints that also have impact on transfers to Latin America. For example, in recent years, legislative emphasis has been placed on the reduction and eventual elimination of the MAP. Worldwide funding limitations have reduced the amount of grant aid available to Latin America. During the peak year, 1968, nineteen Latin American countries received over $70 million in MAP grant material and training. By fiscal year 1975, total MAP grant aid had been reduced to $16.2 million. Of this total, grant material was provided to only nine countries in the amount of $5.5 million. Other Latin American countries were limited to grant training, mainly in the Canal Zone or the continental United States.

In addition, congressional concern with U.S. sales of arms generally is increasing. The executive branch has been directed to reduce government-to-government sales under the FMS program as rapidly as possible in favor of a return to commercial sales under the USG lissense. FMS sales of $25 million or more are now subject to congressional veto by joint resolution. Furthermore, bills have been introduced that would give the Congress the same degree of program review over FMS cash sales as it has exercised over MAP and FMS credit sales in the past. Congressional concern, while focused primarily on sales to the Near East, could have an effect on the scale of U.S. arms transfers to Latin America.

Within the broad constraints established by the Congress, U.S. policy of arms transfers to Latin America has undergone a shift over the past decade. The highly restrictive policy of the 1960s has given way to a policy that seeks to be responsive to reasonable requests for military modernization. In recent years, as earlier generations of military equipment have attrited, the United States has been prepared to meet modest replacement requirements. Thus F-5 aircraft, denied to Latin America in mid-1960s, are now available for purchase by the larger Latin American countries. This is not to say, however, that the United States pursues a free market policy on arms to Latin America. Arms transfers must still meet general criteria established by the Congress and they must meet the test of reasonableness applied by the executive branch. Thus, the United States does not offer to Latin American countries much of the advanced weaponry in its own inventories.

The dominant motivation of other noncommunist arms suppliers to Latin America is economic. As a result, arms are offered on terms that will make them commercially competitive, and few if any complaints are placed on transfers. Because its motivations are primarily political-military, the USSR has made large quantities of arms available to Cuba on favorable terms or on barter arrangements. Similarly, in its recent transfers to Peru, the USSR offered arms at discounted prices and low credit rates.

With the loosening of U.S. restrictions, however, Latin America has again turned to the United States for its weapons systems. But Latin Americans desire independence from the United States, and another trend toward internationalism in arms transfers, regardless of Latin preference for U.S. equipment, seems likely.

While conventional weapons have long been sought by Latin American nations for a variety of reasons, a new element has been injected into the Latin American portion of the hemisphere. Both Brazil and

Argentina are rapidly expanding their nuclear energy programs. Neither has ratified the Non-Proliferation Treaty or the Latin American Nuclear Free Zone Treaty (the Treaty of Tlatelolco). Latin Americanists who have long devoted great attention to the conventional arms trade in the hemisphere have yet to focus on the potential significance of these new developments.

NOTES

1. U.S. Arms Control and Disarmament Agency, World Military Expenditures and Arms Trade 1963-1973 (Washington, D.C.: U.S. Government Printing Office, 1975), p. 75.
2. Ibid., pp. 14-19.
3. Ibid., pp. 72-77.
4. Ibid., pp. 21-62, 79-120.
5. ACDA Worksheets. These worksheets are developed from many sources. Primary among these are The Arms Trade with the Third World (Stockholm: Stockholm International Peace Research Institute, 1971); Arms Trade Registers (Stockholm: Stockholm International Peace Research Institute, 1975); Jane's Fighting Ships, Jane's All the World's Aircraft, Jane's Weapons Systems (London: Sampson Low, Marston & Co., annuals); The Military Balance (London: International Institute for Strategic Studies, annual); Market Intelligence Reports, Military Aircraft, Missiles and Spacecraft (Greenwich, Conn.: Defense Market Service, updated monthly). In addition, data are developed from numerous periodicals and government sources.
6. Ibid.
7. U.S. Arms Control and Disarmament Agency, op. cit., pp. 21-62.
8. ACDA Worksheets, op. cit.
9. Ibid.
10. Ibid.
11. Ibid.

CHAPTER

11

NUCLEAR PROLIFERATION IN LATIN AMERICA

John R. Redick

Among the growing list of important interfaces between Latin America and the world system is nuclear energy. In its positive sense, nuclear energy is envisioned by Latin American states as a means to stimulate national and regional development primarily through generation of power and by so-called "peaceful" nuclear explosive technology. In its negative sense, nuclear energy could expose certain Latin American states to a heightened scale of domestic terrorism, stimulate wasteful military competition, and generally subject the region to accelerated pressure by nonregional nuclear weapon states. This chapter considers the potential for nuclear proliferation in Latin America and its implications for hemispheric peace and security. The prime focus is upon those Latin American nations possessing the most advanced nuclear energy programs: Argentina, Brazil, and Mexico. In addition, nations with less advanced programs, including Chile, Cuba, and others, are evaluated. Finally, the prospects for preventing the proliferation of nuclear weapons in Latin America, through either regional or global mechanisms, are briefly discussed.

NUCLEAR TECHNOLOGY

Nuclear Fuel Cycle

It is estimated that after 1980 there will exist approximately 400,000 megawatts (mw) of installed electrical capacity generated by about 400 nuclear power plants in thirty-five different countries.[1] This will represent an annual output of hundreds of thousands of kilograms of plutonium. Approximately 5 kilograms of plutonium is adequate for construction of a nuclear device sufficient to obliterate a medium size city or, for example, a high population density portion of a large city such as New York's Wall Street. A small natural uranium research reactor in Israel produces annually plutonium equivalent to that utilized in the explosive device detonated in India in May 1974.[2] But the important point, for the purposes of this chapter, is that the production of fissionable material necessary for the construction of a nuclear explosive device, is the unavoidable by-product of nuclear power production.

The current generation of nuclear power reactors is based on the uranium-plutonium fuel cycle.* However, there exists considerable variety in the military implications of differing reactor types. The majority of the power reactors currently in operation are light water reactors, which utilize slightly enriched (2 to 5 percent) uranium-235 as fuel (generally obtained from the United States and to a lesser degree by the Soviet Union). A second type, the heavy water reactor, utilizes natural uranium as fuel and heavy water as a moderator. It has been estimated that a 1,000-mw power reactor using slightly enriched fuel will produce 200 to 300 kilograms of plutonium in a year.[3] Natural uranium reactors will produce plutonium at twice the above rate. Natural uranium reactors also lend themselves more readily to military objectives relative to light water reactors due to the greater quantity of plutonium produced and the comparative ease of insertion and removal of fuel loads without a shutdown of the reactor pile. Natural uranium reactors also permit utilization of domestic uranium reserves and avoid dependence on foreign enrichment services. However, the initial capital investment is somewhat higher than that for light water reactors and a heavy water manufacturing plant is necessary for complete independence.

A third type of reactor, the high-temperature gas-cooled reactor, is in the process of being introduced into the programs of some of the more advanced nuclear powers. This reactor utilizes highly enriched uranium as fuel and the resulting by-product is uranium-233 rather than plutonium. As is true of plutonium, uranium-233 may be separated and utilized in a nuclear explosive device. At least one Latin American nation, Brazil, hopes to introduce this type of reactor into its nuclear program in the future.

---

*Uranium is mined, enriched, and fuel elements produced for the reactor by a fuel fabrication facility. After irradiation in the reactor, the resulting plutonium is separated by a chemical reprocessing (plutonium separation) plant. Natural uranium reactors utilize heavy water as a moderator and the complex enrichment process is omitted.

With respect to the military implications of light water reactors, a critical factor is access to enriched uranium fuel. Production of enriched uranium by the United States pioneered gas diffusion process is not a realistic possibility for most least developing states due to the complexity of the technology, costs (estimated between $1 and $2 billion), and the massive quantity of electricity needed. However, alternative methods of uranium enrichment exist, including the gas centrifuge laser isotype separation, and nozzle process, which may eventually bring the technology within the reach of many new countries.[4]

For both light water and heavy water reactors, a chemical reprocessing (plutonium separation) plant is necessary in order to extract the produced plutonium from the irradiated nuclear fuel. A country desiring to develop an independent nuclear weapons option will undoubtedly seek to develop its own reprocessing facility. A small plant can be built with the declared public intention of gaining experience for subsequent expansion of the nation's nuclear power program. However, even a small plant can separate a militarily significant amount of plutonium.

There is no clear indication that any Latin American state has embarked on a deliberate program to develop nuclear weapons. However, several Latin American nations have had sophisticated research efforts for many years and possess accelerating nuclear power programs. Furthermore, a growing involvement with steps in the nuclear fuel cycle (derived from research programs and as a spinoff from power programs) has enabled certain Latin American nations to become increasingly familiar with technology necessary in any construction of nuclear explosive devices. Brazil and Mexico should each have operating light water power reactors within several years, producing hundreds of kilograms of plutonium annually. Argentina has an operating heavy water reactor and a small plutonium separation plant. All three nations are well advanced in other aspects of the fuel cycle. Brazil and Argentina have made clear their intention to develop so-called peaceful nuclear explosives for a variety of civilian uses.

While none of this directly supports the existence of a nuclear weapons program, the political climate within a nation can change rapidly: intentions can be altered with a shift in governments, in response to a perceived external threat, or other factors. But the momentum of nuclear technology in Latin America is having (and will have) a great effect on the timing and nature of future political decisions regarding nuclear weapons. In short, as has been aptly noted elsewhere "It is certainly not meant to suggest—that what is technically possible could easily occur, but it is useful to know the limits within which political decisions can be made."[5]

Peaceful Nuclear Explosives (PNEs)

"Peaceful" nuclear explosives warrant particular attention inasmuch as they represent the most likely avenue, rather than a deliberate military program, for the development of nuclear weapons in Latin America. Most authorities believe the term PNE to be a misnomer as there is no practical difference between nuclear explosive devices developed for peaceful or military objectives. The important (and only) distinguishing factor between weapons and peaceful instruments is the intent of the user, according to an argument first advanced by Argentina in the negotiating sessions of the Treaty for the Prohibition of Nuclear Weapons in Latin America in 1967.[6] Both Argentina and Brazil have expressed intentions to develop PNEs and both have refused to become parties to the Tlatelolco Treaty and to the Non-Proliferation Treaty (NPT) in part because they view the agreements as inhibiting their option for PNEs.

The principal opportunities for the peaceful uses of nuclear explosive devices are in deep mining and major earth-moving (excavation) projects. In over sixteen years, the U.S. Atomic Energy Commission (AEC) spent over $160 million through its project Plowshare on a host of inconclusive experiments designed to develop the peaceful uses of nuclear explosive technology.[7] The most recent deep mining experiments in the United States have been in the area of natural gas stimulation (Project Gas Buggy, Rulison, and Rio Blanco). These self-contained fission (as opposed to thermonuclear) explosions take place in the deep underground and generally preclude venting of radioactive materials into the atmosphere, which, if it can be detected beyond national borders is a violation of the 1963 Limited Test Ban Treaty. Sophisticated technology is necessary to develop extremely small diameter nuclear explosive devices and then place the charges thousands of feet in the earth. In such deep underground detonations, there is a danger of contamination of underground waters, and it is generally estimated that thousands of explosions may be required to derive significant economic advantage.[8] In addition, it should be noted that alternative non-nuclear methods do exist for most deep mining projects. The U.S. deep mining program continues on a low priority, fueled more by pressure of the energy crisis than practical results.

The second main area of PNE utilization, nuclear excavation, requires "clean" thermonuclear explosions of massive size utilized in moving vast quantities of earth for canals, harbors, etc. Several large-scale excavation experiments (Project Sedan) were undertaken by the AEC in the 1960s, and serious study was given to the creation of a new canal across the Isthmus of Panama. Several factors, including a fear of radioactivity release, have served to undercut the attractiveness of nuclear excavation in the United States.

The Soviet Union is still giving serious study to possible excavation projects, although Soviet spokesmen stress the uncertainty of the technology.[9] Successful Soviet utility of PNEs has been demonstrated in extinguishing fires in runaway gas wells, and several excavation-type experiments (detonations) have been undertaken to reroute rivers and to create a canal system in northern Russia. Soviet authorities recently have reported to the IAEA (International Atomic Energy Agency) that experiments, undertaken in 1971, have yielded preliminary results demonstrating the feasibility of the idea and that costs should be one third that of conventional methods.[10]

India, in the wake of its May 1974 detonation, has been quite vocal in outlining future potential uses for PNEs. Those frequently mentioned include oil stimulation, recovery of nonferrous metals, dam building, and the creation of vast underground reservoirs.[11]

Development of nuclear excavation technology requires an extremely sophisticated and expensive nuclear program, including many thermonuclear tests. It also requires a vast unpopulated geographic expanse, such as in northern Soviet Union or portions of Brazil. The limited progress that has been achieved in the United States and the Soviet Union has been primarily a spinoff of their extensive weapons programs.[12] In the opinion of most experts, such a program is beyond the ability of most non-nuclear weapon states for the foreseeable future.

The United States and the USSR have pledged in Article 5 of the Non-Proliferation Treaty of 1968 to make available the benefits of PNEs on a nondiscriminatory basis. In addition, in its interpretive declaration accompanying ratification of Additional Protocol II of the Treaty of Tlatelolco, the United States reaffirmed its willingness to collaborate with other nations for the purposes of carrying out peaceful nuclear explosions under appropriate international (IAEA) control. Some procedural progress has been achieved by the IAEA toward the creation of an international service, but further progress is dependent upon greater support from the United States and the Soviet Union.[13] Several nations have made informal requests to the IAEA for PNE services. However, PNEs utilized by the IAEA would most certainly have to come from the United States or the Soviet Union and neither seems at this time predisposed to offer such devices. Despite suggestions from non-nuclear weapon states that the United States and the USSR should "cooperate in PNE technology as they do in space," no high level program of bilateral cooperation on PNEs now exists.

Ironically, the U.S.-Soviet Threshold Test Ban Treaty signed in July 1974 may serve to heighten pressure among non-nuclear weapons states for PNEs. Under the terms of the treaty, underground tests beyond 150 kilotons were prohibited after early 1976. However, on Soviet insistence, PNEs of any size were not restricted. Thus, through the Threshold Treaty, the two superpowers have given new credence to claims of non-nuclear weapon states regarding benefits of PNEs. While U.S.-Soviet negotiations continue in early 1975, in response to a renewed U.S. effort to eliminate PNEs under the treaty, the Soviet Union showed little inclination to shift on this topic.

As with other aspects of nuclear energy, the promised impressive benefits of PNEs have been oversold. But leaders of many developing nations, including those in Latin America, are no doubt sincere in their belief that peaceful nuclear explosions are destined to be of great importance to their future development.

LATIN AMERICAN NUCLEAR ENERGY PROGRAMS

Argentina

The Argentine National Commission of Atomic Energy (CNEA) was created May 31, 1950 by the decree of Juan Peron. Very quickly the CNEA became embroiled in controversy primarily arising out of the actions of the Austrian World War II immigrant Ronald Richter. Richter, who had carried out nuclear research in Nazi Germany, convinced Peron to name him director of an Argentine facility on remote Huemul Island in Lake Nahuel Huapi. The effort was initiated with considerable publicity implying future Argentine production of nuclear power and perhaps even an explosive device. Gradually the expensive and exotic facilities became the butt of many Argentine jokes. Richter's laboratory on the island of Huemul was dubbed "Huele a Mula" by a national magazine, which translates colloquially to "to pull a fast one."[14] Eventually opposition within the CNEA to Richter's completely unrealistic scheme prevailed, and he was dismissed in 1952.

Events have progressed rapidly in Argentina from this inauspicious beginning. If the Richter episode was a sham, it nonetheless had the result of developing national interest in an Argentine nuclear energy program. This was given added momentum by the Atoms for Peace agreement signed with the United States in 1955. Today, Argentina has developed the most advanced nuclear power program in Latin America. Argentina possesses five research reactors, four of which were designed and constructed by the CNEA. These reactors are fueled by enriched uranium obtained from the United States and subject to IAEA safeguards. There are six major centers for nuclear research, and many Argentine scientists are receiving advanced nuclear training in the United States, Great Britain, France, and West Germany.

Argentina also possesses far more uranium reserves than any other Latin American country (although this may change as the scale of recent Brazilian strikes is revealed). Its "cheap recoverable" reserves are estimated at between 13,000 and 21,000 tons with another 18,000 tons available at a higher recovery price.[15] This is an ample supply for its own needs while allowing some for occasional exportation. (In the past, Argentina quietly has exported uranium to Israel for use in that nation's supersecret Dimona reactor.[16])

On February 21, 1968, the CNEA announced that the German firm Siemens AG would construct South America's first nuclear power plant at a site near Buenos Aires. Work has begun on the 320-mw natural uranium Atucha plant in 1968 and the facility commenced operation in mid-1974. The uranium utilized by the Atucha station is obtained domestically, and Argentine personnel were fully involved in the installation process. Heavy water was purchased from the U.S. AEC in what represents the only U.S. commitment of heavy water to any foreign power at present. The AEC's reluctance to sell this sensitive element in the nuclear fuel cycle was apparently overcome when the Argentines threatened to go elsewhere for their purchase. (Ironically the United States also sold India heavy water that was utilized in that country's natural uranium [Cirus] research reactor that apparently produced the plutonium utilized in the May 1974 explosive device. Thus the United States shares the blame with much criticized Canada for helping facilitate India's device, and may be contributing to a similar Argentine device.)

The Atucha contract was given to West Germany after intense international competition in which U.S. firms actually underbid the German offer. It is notable that the U.S. enriched fuel based reactors have had a better performance record and involve significantly lower initial capital outlay than those utilizing natural uranium, and the German reactor was a relatively unproven mechanism. However, the choice of a natural uranium power plan allowed the Argentines to utilize their own plentiful uranium reserves while avoiding dependence on U.S. enrichment services. In the words of a former high CNEA official "the fundamental disadvantage of the enriched uranium design is that at the moment only one country [the United States] provides commercial uranium enrichment."[17] (Author's parenthesis.)

In April 1973, Argentina placed an order with a Canadian-Italian consortium for a second 600-mw natural uranium reactor (Rio Tercero) to be built near Cordoba and come into operation in 1979. As with the Atucha plant, there were apparently lower bids from U.S. concerns (Westinghouse) with the eventual decision being based on Argentina's desire for complete independence of fuel supply. Bidding is currently underway for a third 600-mw plant (Atucha II) to be located in proximity to the existing Atucha facility and to commence operation in 1981. A fourth 600-mw facility should begin operation prior to 1987 and will probably be located in the Cuyo region.[18] The recently proposed "Argentine Nuclear Program 1975-1985," prepared by the CNEA for consideration of the Argentine congress, envisions a slightly different time scale with installation of at least four Candu-type 600-mw power reactors in 1980, 1982, 1983, and 1985. Clearly, and despite continued internal political turmoil, Argentine leaders are determined to pursue an ambitious nuclear power program.[19]

Argentina possesses a small fuel fabrication facility with a larger unit under construction. The 1975-85 program envisions development of large-scale fabrication capacity by 1978. In 1972, Argentine spokesmen stressed that "every stage in the fabrication of their fuel elements [for natural uranium power reactors] can even now be carried out in Argentina."[20] In addition, the CNEA has announced its intention to construct by 1980 a heavy water production plant in order to domestically produce this essential moderator for the nation's power plants.[21]

Argentina also has the only publically known plutonium reprocessing plant in Latin America. The stated objective of the "pilot plant" (Ensamble de Reprocesamiento Experimental), which has been in operation since 1969, is to reprocess plutonium from some of the nation's research reactors. It will also apparently be used to reprocess some of the plutonium produced by the Atucha power reactor. The separated plutonium is subject to accounting procedures under the IAEA safeguards system. A large industrial-scale reprocessing plant capable of separating plutonium from existing and forthcoming power plants is under serious study, and the 1975-85 program envisions completion of a larger plant by 1980.

It is quite apparent that over six years of operating experience with the small pilot plant has provided sufficient opportunity for Argentine personnel to master the technology of small-scale plutonium separation. In mid-summer 1975, sources in the U.S. Senate's Government Operations Committee reported additional information pointing toward development of an indigenous Argentine plutonium separation capability. It was reported that, with French assistance, Argentina was constructing a pilot plutonium separation plant and rebuilding and expanding a "British style" reprocessing plant.

Considerable attention has been drawn to a recent agreement between Argentina and India for cooperation in the peaceful uses of nuclear energy. Included in the agreement (not yet in effect) are exchanges of both information and scientists. Argentine spokesmen also have stated that, under the agreement, India could cooperate in construction of the nation's third power plant. The agreement, which was announced less than two weeks after India's detonation, served to spotlight certain clear similarities between the nuclear energy programs of the two nations.[22] The Indian explosive device utilized plutonium produced by a Canadian-built, natural uranium research reactor. However, technological expertise was developed primarily as a spinoff from the nation's highly ambitious nuclear power program. India's power program, like that of Argentina, is based primarily on natural uranium power reactors purchases from Canada (and, more recently, France). As was true with India, the Argentine nuclear energy energy program has been carefully sheltered from domestic politics while relying on cooperation with foreign expertise. Cooperation with India, which shares Argentina's opposition to the NPT, is undoubtedly viewed as a means to guarantee continued access to advanced nuclear technology as other countries (Canada, the United States, West Germany) tighten their requirements for cooperation.

The potential significance of Indian-Argentine cooperation is difficult to assess. Argentine nuclear experts stress that the timing of the agreement was circumstantial and that the Indian bomb has "complicated our lives terribly."[23] Indian spokesmen are even more explicit in stressing privately that there is absolutely no intention to export nuclear technology, including PNE technology, to nations that might be tempted to develop nuclear weapons.[24] Nonetheless, Canada, reacting to internal and international criticism, is demanding explicit assurances from Argentina that no Canadian equipment would be utilized in the development of a nuclear explosive device. The Canadians are negotiating for the specific Argentine pledge far more explicit than received earlier from India in connection with Argentina's second natural uranium power reactor now under construction. Reportedly, Canada's bilateral safeguards will be more stringent than those of the IAEA. IAEA inspection of plants and fuel is a mandatory part of the Canadian plan.[25]

Plutonium produced by Argentina's research reactors is stored in Argentina and subject to IAEA safeguards as required under the terms of the U.S.-Argentine agreement for the supply of enriched uranium. Argentina has also volunteered to place the Atucha power reactor, which which produces approximately 100 kilograms of plutonium per year, under safeguards. The current U.S.-Argentine bilateral agreement for cooperation in the civil uses of atomic energy was signed July 25, 1969 and extends to July 24, 1999. Under the agreement, the United States committed itself to supply enriched uranium for Argentine research reactors and a fixed amount of heavy water. However, the agreement does not specifically prohibit Argentina from using U.S.-supplied fissionable material for "peaceful" nuclear explosives. Thus, as Argentina is party to neither the Tlatelolco Treaty nor to the NPT, technically speaking an Argentine PNE would not be in violation of any bilateral regional or international accord.

Argentina continually and publicly has shared the Brazilian view on the viability and desirability of PNE technology. And, while strongly denying any desire to develop nuclear weapons, Argentine spokesmen now publicly admit that a PNE is but a matter of time. Argentina's ability to develop a nuclear explosive device is probably the least debatable aspect of this question. Unfortunately, the construction of a small explosive device is no longer a particularly difficult undertaking. Argentina appears to have the means to obtain fissionable material and the technological ability to construct and detonate a device well before the end of this decade, if it so desires. Barring some new unforeseen initiatives at the regional or international level, the likelihood that Argentina will follow the Indian example is very high.

Brazil

Brazil's initiation into the nuclear energy field, like that of Argentina, began at a low ebb in the early 1950s. In 1951, a high Brazilian official surreptitiously purchased in West Germany secret equipment supposedly designed for the enrichment of uranium by the gas centrifuge process. The operation was discovered by British occupation officials, and transfer of the costly equipment was delayed for some period. Eventually the equipment was shipped to Brazil and today resides unused in the Institute of Technology in Sao Paulo.[26]

Stimulus initially was provided to the Brazilian program with the signing of a bilateral Atoms for Peace agreement with the United States in 1955, which was followed a year later by the establishment of the Comissao Nacional de Energia Nuclear (CNEN) by former President Kubitschek. The CNEN coordinates all national policy in nuclear energy and is subordinate to the Ministry of Mines and Energy. However, in late 1975, President Ernesto Geisel brought to the urgent attention of the Brazilian Congress a bill to create the Empresa Nuclear Brasilena (Nuclebras) from the Compania Brasilena de Technologia Nuclear (CBTN) founded in 1970.

Nuclebras, envisioned as a counterpart to the national oil company Petrobras, was given a complete monopoly in the nuclear industry for building and operating nuclear power stations, research centers, and exploration for uranium deposits. Of most importance, however, was the fact that private foreign investment and shareholding was to be permitted in Nuclebras on a minority basis. This has prompted considerable speculation in the Brazilian press of forthcoming series of contracts with foreign interests in nuclear technology. Another explanation advanced for the hurried action regarding Nuclebras is a possible government intention to pave the way for participation by foreign interests in the Brazilian oil industry.[27]

Brazil has an extremely varied and sophisticated nuclear research program which includes four operating reactors. These reactors, manufactured by Brazilian companies, are fueled by enriched uranium obtained from the United States and subject to IAEA safeguards. Brazil's nuclear power program has lagged relative to that of its neighbor to the south, due to the nation's vast hydroelectric potential. However, prompted in part by the rise in international oil prices (Brazil must import over two thirds of the oil it consumes, representing 40 percent of the energy used)[28] a massive national commitment to nuclear power now appears to be in the making.

The nation's first power plant, a 626-mw enriched uranium based (Angra dos Reis) facility obtained from the United States, is now scheduled for completion in 1977. Companies from Canada, West Germany, and the United Kingdom submitted bids in addition to the United States. Shortly before the actual awarding of the Westinghouse contract, the British Nuclear Power Group and the German firm Siemens (which constructed the Argentine Atucha facility) combined forces to submit a three-way bid for the Brazilian order. One of the options offered by the Brazilian German combine was a natural uranium plant.

As a former secretary general of the Ministry of Foreign Relations, Correa da Costa has stated that the choice facing Brazil at that time was as much political as economic. In effect, a choice of an enriched reactor would, according to the official, put Brazil in the unfortunate position of being dependent upon one supplier, the United States.[29] Several factors including (at that time) inadequate uranium reserves and a close relationship with the United States apparently affected the Brazilian policymakers in selecting the enriched uranium based U.S. plant. In addition, as officials of the Brazilian nuclear energy commission later states, the U.S. reactor is a proven mechanism, from experienced suppliers, and would permit maximum participation by Brazilian organizations in the construction, engineering, and manufacturing.[30]

Previously, Brazil's known uranium reserves were believed to be far short of its eventual needs. Only 5,400 tons of high recovery cost uranium had been discovered despite intensive exploration efforts strongly supported by the Brazilian government. However, in midsummer 1975 the discovery of extensive new uranium deposits was confirmed by French geologists. Although the extent of the deposits was not revealed at that time, the amount was considered sufficient to meet national requirements for decades into the future, while still permitting exports (to West Germany.)[31]

Brazil possesses large deposits of the fertile material thorium and consequently has a distinct interest in development of thorium technology, especially in the eventual development of a thorium breeder reactor. Brazilian cooperation with France in the development of thorium technology has been underway for several years. More recently, Brazil has signed an agreement with Gulf General Atomic Company for cooperation in research and development of a gas-cooled fast breeder reactor that will use thorium as fuel.[32]

A small fuel fabrication facility exists in Sao Paulo, with current plans calling for completion of a facility with a capacity of 200 to 400 tons per year before 1980.[33]

Considerable debate has occurred within Brazil in the early 1970s concerning the desirable nuclear technology to be adopted as a national program. As reported by the prestigious columnist in the Jornal do Brasil, Carlos Castello Branco, some critics called for investment in heavy water natural uranium technology in order to achieve total energy independence and to avoid the necessity of submitting to international safeguards.[34] Defenders of the current policy pointed to the Second National Development Plan, 1975-79, which envisions massive uranium exploration efforts, commitment at the present time to enriched uranium technology, cooperation with foreign (European, U.S., and Japanese) enterprise, development of total mastery of the uranium-plutonium fuel cycle (fuel fabrication and enrichment ability), a massive commitment to nuclear power, and investment in diverse reactor types. The decision to opt for light water enriched reactors for the nation's next phase in nuclear technology was taken, according to the Brazilians, because "not only is this type of reactor already opted for in more than 85 percent of existing plants but, furthermore, because of the current dissemination of technology dealing with fuel enriching; this technology is indeed being made available to private companies in the United States, in Europe and in Japan."[35]

Brazil has programs of cooperation in the peaceful uses of nuclear energy with Japan, Italy, Euratom, Paraguay, France, Switzerland, Portugal, the United States, Bolivia, Israel, Peru, Chile, India, and the Federal Republic of Germany. The most important agreements, however, are with France, the Federal Republic of Germany, and the United States. The French-Brazilian program, signed in May 1967, includes cooperation in the development of research and power reactors, joint research in thorium technology, French assistance in uranium exploration, and cooperation in the construction of a fast thermal factor. In summer 1975, the Brazilian-French agreement was amended to include purchase by Brazil of a French experimental nuclear reactor to be used in research leading to later construction of a full-scale breeder reactor.[36] A further agreement, updating earlier

French-Brazilian agreements for uranium exploration and production, was also signed.

A U.S.-Brazilian agreement was signed in September 1972 and extends until 2002. As part of the agreement, the United States has contracted to supply enriched uranium for the 626-mw Angra dos Reis plant. In 1974, Brazil also formally requested that the United States supply enrichment services to the Angra 2 and 3 plants upon their completion, an arrangement that ultimately fell through. As with the 1969 U.S.-Argentina agreement, there was no specific prohibition regarding a Brazilian PNE written into the U.S.-Brazilian agreement. Subsequently, the United States communicated to Brazil an interpretive note outlining the U.S. view regarding this issue. However, the Brazilians may also recall a statement made by former AEC chairman Glen Seaborg in a 1967 visit in which he promised that enrichment services would be continued unconditionally even if Brazil refused to abandon plans to develop PNEs. In July 1975, Brazilian sources stated that a contract with the United States would soon be forthcoming for cooperation in development of high temperature gas-cooled reactors.[37]

Brazilian nuclear cooperation with other Latin American countries is also increasing. Recently, it was announced that Brazil will construct a nuclear research center in Paraguay to undertake investigatory work in medicine, agriculture, and industry. The center, to be constructed outside of Asuncion, will also include a subcritical reactor and other equipment given by Brazil.[38]

On June 27, 1975, West German Foreign Minister Hans-Dietrich Genscher and his Brazilian counterpart, Antonio Francisco Azerido da Sildeira, signed a massive commercial agreement for nuclear cooperation that was to have profound effects upon prospects for nuclear arms control, as well as on peace and security in the Latin American region.[39] Under the terms of the $4- to $8-billion contract, a West German consortium will build four 1,300-mw enriched uranium power reactors in Brazil by 1986, and another four plants by 1990. (To be precise, the West German consortium has a firm Brazilian commitment for two 1,300-mw power reactors, while Brazil has taken an option for six more. The nuclear power plants will be constructed by the German firm Kraftwerk Union AG, which will join with Nuclebras to guide the nuclear power program through 1985.)

In addition, West Germany agreed to supply Brazil with a complete nuclear package of fuel fabrication, plutonium separation, and a "nozzle" type enrichment plant. This represented the first sale of a complete fuel cycle to any nation. A separate portion of the agreement, as noted earlier in this chapter, provided for partial Brazilian payment by exportation of uranium to West Germany. Brazil reportedly gave assurances that it had discovered sufficient uranium to meet the projected requirements of both nations through 1990.[40]

In 1974, Brazil approached the U.S. firm Westinghouse (which is constructing Brazil's first nuclear power plant) for a large-scale nuclear power plant order. However, Brazilian representatives were insistent that, as a part of the agreement, enrichment and reprocessing technology be included. The U.S. government, following well-established policy, refused to issue Westinghouse licenses for exportation of enrichment or reprocessing technology on the grounds that to do so would be tantamount to granting the recipient nation nuclear weapons capability. The timing of the Brazilian request was a definite complicating factor, as it occurred during a period of rising debate within the U.S. Congress and the administration over nuclear export policies.

Yet another factor may have influenced the Brazilians to seek access to a complete nuclear fuel cycle from a non-U.S. source. This is the inability of the United States (at that time) to guarantee long-term enrichment services. Due to protracted disagreement between the leadership of the Joint Committee on Atomic Energy and the administration, crucial decisions pertaining to the expansion of U.S. enrichment capacity had been delayed continually. Wholly aside from military considerations, Brazil was sincerely dedicated to developing rapidly a dependable source of power to feed its expanding economy, already experiencing significant balance of payments strains because of the rise in world oil prices. Consequently, the ongoing reassessment of U.S. nuclear export policies and prevailing doubts as to long-term U.S. enrichment capability apparently gave the upper hand to those elements in Brazil long desirous of an independent nuclear capability.

The West German decision to supply Brazil with access to the complete nuclear fuel cycle was greeted with concern by some elements within the Ford Administration, and attempts were made by what was described as low-level State Department representatives to block that portion of the arrangement granting Brazil enrichment and reprocessing technology. However, the failure of the Ford Administration to risk a rift in bilateral relations with West Germany over the issue was apparent in the words of Chancellor Helmut Schmidt following the signing of the agreement: "The American Government, which understands the matter better than some senators, has not directed criticism at us, so I concluded that the criticisms in some parts of the American press goes back to industrial interests."[41]

An interesting and possibly significant footnote to the West German-Brazilian agreement was the apparent effort by the Bechtel Power Corporation to sell the Brazilians a uranium enrichment process. Occurring at the same time ACDA and the U.S. Department of State were attempting to dissuade the Germans from proceeding, the Bechtel initiative lent to the interpretation that the U.S. government was simply seeking to assist U.S. nuclear industry in obtaining a major sale, rather than expressing honest concern in regard to nuclear proliferation. Apparently, those elements of the U.S. government charged with the responsibility of discussion with the West Germans were unaware of the Bechtel effort, whereas Dixie Lee Ray, former assistant secretary of state for Oceans, International Environmental and Scientific Affairs, may have given it tacit support.[42]

Criticism was, however, voiced by Dr. Fred Ikle, director of the U.S. Arms Control & Disarmament Agency, who stated U.S. opposition was not derived from commercial jealousy and did not apply to the sale of the nuclear power reactors themselves:

> Our problem is with the reprocessing equipment which in treating the spent fuel of reactors, can produce plutonium for weapons. We also have a problem with the uranium-enrichment equipment, which can make weapons-grade uranium. American firms have not been permitted to sell this type of equipment abroad.
>
> In the United States, at the present time, there are over 50 nuclear power reactors in operation but not a single commercial reprocessing facility in operation or likely to be in the near future. . . . American industry has not been permitted to promote reactor sales abroad by offering also to provide as a "sweetener" enrichment and reprocessing facilities.[43]

However, the harshest criticism of the West German-Brazilian agreement was expressed in the U.S. Congress. The words of the respected chairman of the Joint Committee on Atomic Energy, Senator Pastore of Rhode Island, were illustrative of the agreement's serious implications:

> The proposed sale by West Germany to Brazil adds, however, a completely new dimension to the non-proliferation problem. West Germany is going to provide essentially a complete fuel cycle which could assist Brazil in making a nuclear bomb if it so desires. . . .
>
> I think this is an extremely important fact because no matter what arrangements are made with the West Germans, even if they were completely effective, there is nothing to preclude the Brazilians from building separate and indigenous reprocessing and enriching facilities simply by copying what the West Germans have given them and then deciding to build a nuclear explosive device, unless all

such reproduced facilities are specifically subject to adequate IAEA safeguards. . . .
And what concerns me to no end is the fact that this is a likely peril being instituted by an ally in our own back yard, so to speak, while at the same time the U.S. Government is heavily committed in West Germany's back yard to defend them against a likely peril.[44]

The West German-Brazilian agreement did include significant international safeguards somewhat more extensive than any previously negotiated nuclear commercial arrangement. The Federal Republic of Germany is a recent party to the NPT and consequently was required to subject the arrangement to IAEA safeguards. Upon U.S. insistence, the agreement was formulated so as to allow the IAEA to act, in effect, as a third party. All equipment, installations, and material supplied under the auspices of the cooperative agreement are to fall under IAEA safeguards. As a party to the three-party agreement, it is anticipated that West Germany will participate in the inspection controls in Brazil.[45] Other aspects of the agreement emphasized by German authorities are:

The commitment by Brazil not to use any of the nuclear equipment, installations and materials, as well as the relevant technological information for the production of either nuclear weapons or other nuclear explosives.
The commitment to re-export such equipment, installations and materials as well as relevant technological information only if the recipient has also concluded an agreement on safeguards with the IAEA.
The commitment to apply the agreed safeguards indefinitely beyond the period covered by the agreement (which in any case can only be terminated after fifteen years).
A provision on physical protection, i.e. protection of the installations and material etc. against third parties.[46]

An additional significant factor is the time scale for delivery of crucial enrichment and reprocessing equipment for Brazil. The nozzle enrichment plant will be constructed "by 1981" and the delivery of the reprocessing facility will not occur prior to that time or later. Before exportation of this equipment, West German officials emphasize, separate agreements must be signed by Brazil with the IAEA: "there will be no export licenses issued unless complete safeguards are assured."[47]

However, despite the aforementioned safeguard mechanisms built into the agreement, there can be no bypassing the central fact that

Brazil will not have to submit to international supervision any material or equipment developed indigenously as a result of knowledge gained from cooperation with West Germany. An independent program developed parallel to the West German-Brazilian cooperative program is a clear possibility.

Ultimately, the West German-Brazilian agreement is significant because it represents a definite breach in the informal policy among nuclear exporters regarding sale of enrichment and plutonium separation equipment. In addition, it will, no doubt, give a significant boost to the development of a more sophisticated and fully independent Brazilian nuclear program. However, in terms of Brazilian development of a nuclear explosive device, it is likely that the nation need not await German equipment in the early 1980s and the construction of a native imitation. Brazil has the capability now for the construction of a small but militarily significant plutonium separation plant if the decision is made. Fissionable materials sufficient for an explosive device are believed to exist now in Brazil, and more will quickly become available in 1977 when the nation's first power reactor commences operation.

In addition, Brazil explicitly has announced its intention to develop peaceful nuclear explosives, either unilaterally or in concert with other nations. No country other than India has taken a stronger and more public stance regarding the validity of PNE technology. Also, as has been true of India, Brazil has offered various arguments in support of its position. During the Tlatelolco Treaty negotiations, Brazilian representatives sought to mark a clear distinction between PNEs and weapons by arguing that a nuclear weapon possesses "special attributes" not common to peaceful nuclear explosive devices. Brazil also supported the Argentine proposal of "intent" as a factor distinguishing weapons from peaceful devices.[48] On other occasions Brazilian spokesmen have admitted the identical nature of PNEs and weapons technology, while arguing that weapon production necessitates several steps beyond explosives investment in polemics (both domestically and internationally) that several Brazilian administrations have in the issue of PNE technology, the effect of the Indian explosive device has been particularly intense in Brazil. The Indian PNE has reinforced the Brazilian leaders' predisposition to believe that the technology can be of great assistance in stimulating the economic development of the country. In addition, as a country acutely sensitive to factors of international prestige, the lure of joining that new international category, "the PNE state," is considerable.[49] Ultimately, Brazil's ambitions to become a major world power, coupled with its fear of falling permanently behind in technology relative to the advanced industrialized nations, are both potent factors pushing the nation toward an indigenous PNE capability.[50]

The extensive Brazilian commitment to nuclear power is revealed in official projections settling a goal of 10,000 mw by 1990 and up to

70,000 by the year 2000. The $4- to $8-billion to be invested in the nuclear fuel cycle through purchase of German equipment will swell to $27 billion for capital investment, operation, and maintenance of nuclear power plants by the year 2000.[51]

It is anticipated that Brazil will situate the commercial enrichment plant (to be constructed in the early 1980s after completion of the pilot plant) in close proximity to its extensive hydroelectric projects in order to satisfy the immense electrical demands of the nozzle enrichment process.[52] The resulting enriched uranium fuel would then be transported to nuclear power plants, most of which will be located in southeast Brazil in close proximity to major population and industrial centers.

The West German agreement for a complete nuclear fuel cycle, now spearheading a growing national commitment to nuclear power, gives the Brazilian nuclear program a clear military potential. When coupled with Brazil's posture regarding PNEs and its adamant refusal to cooperate with global (NPT) or regional (Tlatelolco Treaty) nuclear arms control efforts, this potential seems even more pronounced. Furthermore, it must be noted that Brazil has been governed for a decade by a military regime, and the foundation for the nation's ambitious nuclear policy was initially set in 1967 by a military figure turned president, Costa e Silva. And while the ongoing economic miracle has been essentially engineered by civilian allies, the military has retained close and careful control of the nation's nuclear energy program. And, finally, the extreme secrecy that increasingly has (particularly in the last several years) cloaked nearly all aspects of the Brazilian nuclear program (that is, their recent uranium strike) lends credence to a military interpretation. As was stated earlier in regard to Argentina, a Brazilian nuclear explosive device appears quite likely unless major new international or regional initiatives are taken.

Mexico

Mexico's civilian-dominated nuclear energy program is directed by the Instituto Nacional de Energia Nuclear (INEN), which succeeded the earlier Comision Nacional de Energia Nuclear (CNEN). The INEN cooperates closely with the national electric monopoly (Comision Federal de Electricidad) (CFE) in directing the nation's accelerating nuclear power programs. The INEN's civilian director has described the goals of the nation's nuclear program as a low cost production of nuclear power, the production of drinkable water, and the production of radioisotopes for use in agriculture, industry, and medicine.[53]

Mexico's nuclear program was initiated in 1955 with the creation of CNEN, but, unlike Argentina and Brazil, it did not benefit from participation in the U.S.-sponsored Atoms for Peace program. Also, in contrast to the two aforementioned nations, Mexico lacks formal bilateral nuclear cooperative agreements with the United States or any other country. Technical assistance for the nation's nuclear energy program has been drawn primarily from the IAEA. However, many Mexican nuclear scientists receive training in the United States and elsewhere, and there does exist certain ad hoc cooperative arrangements (that is, between the U.S. Argonne National Laboratory and Mexico's Salazar Nuclear Energy Center.)

Mexico possesses four small operating research reactors with fuel obtained through the auspices of the IAEA and subject to safeguards. A small fabrication facility exists with current plans calling for the construction of a larger facility in the next several years. There are small reserves of uranium adequate for national purposes, including meeting the needs of the nation's forthcoming power reactors. All uranium is the property of the state with exportation forbidden by law.

Considerable interest exists among Mexican policymakers concerning nuclear power employed for production of fresh water from salt. A 1969 tripartite study (U.S.-Mexico-IAEA) recommended that a series of large nuclear power stations each producing 2,000 mw and 1 billion gallons of fresh water daily be constructed in the southwestern section of the United States and northwest Mexico.[54] Mexico remains quite interested in this project, but interest has lagged in the U.S. Congress. Mexico has continued close cooperation with the IAEA in this area.[55]

Currently under construction are twin 660-mw enriched uranium (Laguna Verde, Ver) power reactors scheduled for completion in 1977 and 1978. The units are being supplied by the United States and financed through loans provided by the Export-Import Bank. Enriched uranium fuel will be provided by the United States, but under a trilateral (U.S.-Mexico-IAEA) arrangement with reprocessing done in the United States. In addition, discussions are underway with Canada for the future purchase of a multiple unit (Candu) natural uranium facility, although Mexico is some time away from a final decision on this matter.[56] Recent oil discoveries making Mexico a net exporter may reduce pressure for nuclear power in the years ahead.

International competition for the Laguna Verde, Ver power plant, which will serve the Mexico City area, was particularly intense with bids received from Japan, Sweden, Germany, France, Great Britain, Canada, Italy, and the USSR. Upon choosing a U.S. supplier (GE), Mexican officials applied directly to the IAEA for enriched uranium fuel rather than choosing the more traditional bilateral route (from their reactor supplier). This represented the first formal request in history to the IAEA of fuel for a power reactor. The IAEA offered the Mexican enrichment contract to all available suppliers and there was "very heated competition" between the United States, France, and the Soviet Union.[57] Mexican policymakers clearly chose to obtain fuel through the auspices of an international authority in order to avoid having to enter into bilateral arrangements in nuclear matters with the United States (or any other country). This Mexican action generated considerable anger among certain leading congressional members of the Joint Committee on Atomic Energy,[58] but it was also a tangible illustration of Mexico's dedication to international control of nuclear energy for peaceful purposes.

Although on occasion Mexican officials claim "the nation has the scientific and technical capacity to construct a nuclear bomb,"[59] there is ample direct and indirect evidence to support the peaceful commitment of the Mexican nuclear energy program. Mexico's postrevolutionary success in achieving a relatively depoliticized military is a definite factor weighing against the development of a nuclear energy program that, from the outset, has been civilian controlled and oriented. In addition, broad foreign policy delineations between Mexico and Brazil and Argentina are significant.

Mexican diplomacy has been in the forefront of regional and international efforts to prevent the proliferation of nuclear weapons. Under the leadership of the able Mexican diplomat, Alfonso Garcia Robles, Mexico spearheaded the Latin American denuclearization movement, which eventually resulted in the Treaty for the Prohibition of Nuclear Weapons (Treaty of Tlatelolco) in 1967 and the Organization for the Prohibition of Nuclear Weapons in Latin America (OPANAL) in Mexico City. (It is notable that internally Mexico's leadership in the denuclearization effort received strong support from all elements, including minority parties of the left and right.) Mexico was an early and consistent supporter of the NPT of 1968, and its U.N. delegation has continued to exercise a leadership position in ongoing disarmament forums (Conference of the Committee on Disarmament) (CCD) and in developing new initiatives (World Disarmament Conference)(WDC). Significantly, Mexico is the only nation with a nuclear weapons potential that has chosen to submit its entire nuclear program to the safeguard procedures of the IAEA. In addition, President Echeverria recently has taken the initiative with the Mexican Congress to seek an amendment to Article 27 of the federal constitution that would specify that "the use of nuclear energy would be limited to only peaceful purposes in accordance with the Treaty of Tlatelolco."[60] In summary, while its nuclear capabilities are indeed progressing, Mexico has taken strong initiatives both nationally and internationally to orient its nuclear energy program to peaceful ends.

Other Latin American Nations

Chile

Chile's nuclear energy commission (CNEC) is seeking, with limited funds, to develop eventually an extensive nuclear capability. In 1969, Chile purchased a 5-mw research reactor from a British firm. Enriched uranium is supplied by the United States under IAEA safeguards. The Chilean army operates a nuclear energy center (Junta de Energia Nuclear)(JEN), which houses the 5-mw facility. Under a Spanish-Chilean agreement, Spain is to build an experimental reactor also to be installed at the army's nuclear energy center. Personnel from JEN will collaborate in the construction of the reactor (as well as the training of personnel and prospecting for new uranium deposits).[61] Also, intensive government-sponsored prospecting efforts for uranium ore are currently under way after a U.N. study predicted that certain sections of Chile may have extensive reserves.[62]

There is considerable interest in Chile with respect to the construction of a nuclear agroindustrial complex creating power, water, and fertilizer in Anto-fagasta, a seaport in the northern copper-producing area. Several U.S. firms have carried out feasibility studies, and in March 1970, the national electric monopoly announced plans to seek funding for a 100-mw facility.[63] However, the project has been shelved temporarily due to the political turmoil of the last several years. Recently, the executive director of the Chilean Atomic Energy Commission has announced that Chile will complete prior to 1984 a nuclear power plant of no less than 300 mw. It is generally considered that in South America Chile trails only Argentina and Brazil in the level and sophistication of its nuclear energy program.[64] Chile has neither signed nor ratified the NPT, ostensibly because Argentina has refused to adhere to the agreement. However, according to one source, Chile has recently ratified the Treaty of Tlatelolco but without waiving the requirements of Article 28. Thus neither the Tlatelolco Treaty nor the NPT is currently in force for Chile.

Colombia

Colombia possesses a very small research reactor, subject to IAEA safeguards. Thus far, there are no announced plans for construction of militarily significant research facilities or a nuclear power plant. Although there is abundant hydroelectric potential in proximity to the three principal cities (Bogota, Medellin, and Cali) and plentiful deposits of coal and petroleum exist, current energy shortages could cause a turn to nuclear energy. Recently, a deposit of uranium ore was discovered that, if recovery costs prove manageable, may be the largest in Latin America. Colombia has signed and ratified the Treaty of Tlatelolco with reservation, although it has not yet completed action on the NPT.

Peru

Peru possesses no research reactors and has no publicly announced plans regarding nuclear power. There is considerable interest in the coastal development of a nuclear energy center, but plans have not advanced beyond the talking stage. There also exists some hydroelectric potential in Peru's Amazonian region. Peru has signed and ratified both the Treaty of Tlatelolco and the NPT.

Uruguay

Uruguay has one small research reactor subject to IAEA safeguards. No national nuclear power facility is anticipated, although Uruguayan policymakers have discussed the possibility of some form of linkage with the nuclear power programs of Argentina and Brazil. Uruguay has signed and ratified both the Treaty of Tlatelolco and the NPT.

Venezuela

Venezuela, since 1962, has possessed a 3-mw research reactor. However, for several years after its initial construction, the facility was not operating because of lack of personnel resources or a program of research. Currently, research is being undertaken with fuel supplied by the United States under IAEA safeguards. With vast petroleum reserves and considerable hydroelectric potential, Venezuela, until recently, has not demonstrated any interest in nuclear power. However, the current Venezuelan administration, realizing the need for a self-sustaining energy source after the depletion of existing oil reserves, is now considering a turn to nuclear power in the near future. Talks began in 1974 between Venezuela and several foreign suppliers regarding the installation of several nuclear power plants.[65] In addition, a potentially significant amount of uranium exists in an area subject to a long-standing territorial dispute between Venezuela and Guyana. Venezuela has signed and ratified the Treaty of Tlatelolco, but has not yet completed action on the NPT.

Cuba

Cuba possesses one research reactor constructed by the Soviet Union and of unknown power. Recently, Premier Castro announced that Cuba would construct its first nuclear power reactor by 1980 and complete a second in the period between 1981 and 1985.[66] Subsequently, the Soviet Union formally announced plans to assist Cuba in constructing by 1980 two 400- or 500-mw nuclear power reactors of unknown design.

Cuba has neither signed nor ratified the Tlatelolco Treaty or the NPT. It is a member of the IAEA but has not chosen to subject its research reactor to international safeguards. Cuba's opposition to any cooperation with the Treaty of Tlatelolco has not altered appreciably since the early phases of the negotiating process, despite the concentrated efforts of the one Latin American nation (Mexico) that refused to terminate bilateral relations.

While welcoming the denuclearization effort, Cuban leaders have continued to demand the return of Guantanamo and the removal of all U.S. nuclear weapons from the Caribbean area. (The U.S. has offered to include Guantanamo within the treaty's zone of application if Cuba ratifies the agreement.) It is clear that Cuba's participation in the treaty is improbable prior to accommodation with the United States. Without some genuine accommodation, quite obviously the Cubans are reluctant to yield the last vestige of threat (however transparent) growing out of the 1962 missile crisis by formally assuming a non-nuclear weapon status as required by the treaty.

The relationship of the Soviet Union to Cuba's failure to cooperate with regional or international nuclear arms control arrangements is difficult to evaluate. The USSR is the only nuclear weapon state that has failed to ratify Additional Protocol II of the Treaty of Tlatelolco, and Soviet spokesmen have maintained that Cuba's opposition is not a factor. This issue (Cuba's opposition), it has been stated, should not be permitted to divert attention from genuine Soviet difficulties with the treaty (principally the favorable advantages that the treaty is perceived to give the United States vis-a-vis other nuclear weapon states). However, it cannot be presumed that the Soviets desire a Cuban ratification of the Tlatelolco Treaty. They may believe that an inclusion of Cuba in the zone would further inhibit them with respect to an unofficial avenue for nuclear weapons into the western hemisphere. In the years following the Cuban missile crisis, nuclear weapons have continued to be introduced into the western hemisphere on Soviet submarines. The apparent U.S.-Soviet "understanding" reached by secret negotiations in the fall of 1970 appears to limit only the use of Cuban bases by Soviet missile-carrying subs as well as their servicing from Cuban-based tenders.[67]

Whether Cuba's position regarding cooperation with the Tlatelolco Treaty will be modified as relations improve with the United States and Cuba is reintegrated into the hemisphere is a matter of conjecture. So, too, is the question whether the USSR will require Cuban participation under international safeguards as a price of its continued nuclear assistance. After having its fingers burned in China, the USSR historically has been far more circumspect than other nuclear suppliers in terms of exportation of nuclear technology. The Soviets have seen it to be to their advantage to require their European allies (Poland, Czechoslovakia, Hungary) to ratify the NPT and subject their nuclear facilities to IAEA safeguards. Their future posture with regard to Cuba should provide a small but interesting illustration of Soviet dedication to world peace and security.

NUCLEAR THEFT AND TERRORISM

The previous sections have focused almost exclusively on the possibility of deliberate government programs in Latin America to develop nuclear explosive devices (whether termed PNEs or weapons). However, nuclear theft and terrorism may ultimately pose a more grave danger to hemispheric peace and security. There is a growing realization among experts concerning the danger of possible theft of nuclear materials by nongovernmental organizations. The simple fact is that sufficient unclassified information exists to permit competently trained individuals to construct a relatively portable nuclear weapon once fissionable material is obtained.

Successful nuclear theft, as has been pointed out in a recent study, "could enable a small group to threaten the lives of many people, the social order within a nation, and the security of the international community of nations."[68] In addition, the vulnerability of nuclear installations, particularly in unstable nations, to terrorist activity is a growing concern.

It is an unfortunate fact of life that the present era is witness to an unparalleled spread of fissionable material and a dramatic upsurge in international terrorism. Recent AEC studies have identified more than 400 cases of international terrorism in the six years ending December 31, 1973, and a continued yearly rise in total incidents.[69] According to these studies, there are over fifty well-financed and well-armed international terrorist groups, including five in Latin America. Thus far there has yet to be a recorded case of a successful nuclear blackmail or act of nuclear violence. However there have been enough disquieting minor incidences and outright threats to lead many to believe such an occurrence is inevitable.

The recent intense discussion within the United States concerning nuclear theft and terrorism has led to strict new requirements concerning shipment of fissionable material and security of nuclear installations. New regulations provide for armed guards for sea, rail, and truck transportation and unarmed guards on airplanes. Guards for nuclear weapons have been given "shoot to kill" orders and security of civilian nuclear power plants has been significantly upgraded throughout the country.[70]

Welcome as such improvements are, the problem is far from resolved due to the continued widespread dissemination of information regarding the construction of nuclear explosive devices and the continued movement of personnel into and out of weapons design and production. This is particularly evident in light of the fact that it is estimated that between 1 and 2 million individuals have been trained by the U.S. government in the handling, moving, and operation of nuclear material.[71]

Thus far, except on a technical level, little has been done internationally concerning the significant implications to world peace and security that will result from the vast forthcoming flow of fissionable material (principally plutonium). Yet the seemingly irreversible global commitment to nuclear power (and particularly to the next generation of plutonium-producing breeders reactors) may demand significant alterations in the internal, social-political fabric of nations (including abridgement of civil liberties).[72] Prodded in part by the criticism of nongovernmental experts, the U.S. Energy Research and Development Administration (ERDA) has begun to move vigorously to hasten the development of advanced and sophisticated equipment to detect, prevent, and/or hinder the theft of nuclear weapons; and to stimulate increased consultation with other governments in means and methods to meet the challenge posed by possible nuclear theft and terrorism.

It is notable that U.S. nuclear export policy has now been revised whereby no future licenses, or authorization for the export or retransfer of significant quantities of fissionable material, will be granted by the U.S. government unless the government of the recipient country has established a system of physical security measures acceptable to the United States. "Adequate" physical security measures would have to be applied before the United States will ship so-called "trigger amounts of material," that is, amounts above 5 kilograms of highly enriched uranium and 2 kilograms of plutonium. Amounts below that, it was stated, are not capable of being made into a bomb.[73] However, whether such stipulations apply to shipments of material to other countries when part of a long-standing arrangement for enriched uranium services (signed as part of a previous bilateral program of nuclear cooperation) is less than clear. ERDA officials are also candid in their assessment of the difficulty of requiring parallel systems from countries with differing constitutional provisions.

In this regard, the United States has initiated a series of bilateral meetings on physical security of nuclear material. Such meetings, carried out with a minimum of publicity (and in part classified often due to the wishes of participating foreign governments), have included visits to the United States by predominately civilian, technical, and working level delegations from both nuclear and non-nuclear weapons states (including some Latin American nations).[74] The bilateral meetings, entitled "Physical Security Concepts and Technology Discussions," are sponsored by ERDA and the Nuclear Regulatory Commission. Typical agendas will include mutual explanations of the nature of security programs, an explanation of the U.S. physical protection and control systems, and joint discussions on international physical security matters. The program may also include on-site tours and in-depth discussions on programs and practices employed at major U.S. nuclear laboratories.

Through this program, and in cooperation with the IAEA, the United States is working toward realization of a proposal initially advanced by Secretary of State Kissinger to the 29th U.S. General Assembly calling for an international convention that could be adopted by all states for use in developing or strengthening physical security systems against a nuclear theft or a diversion of nuclear material. This initiative, which would in effect set up an international standard, could hopefully lead to a more binding international agreement under an international regime, granted authority to level penalties at noncomplying nations.

For Latin America, containing many countries that historically have experienced considerable internal dissension and division, the spread of nuclear technology may pose particular demands in the years ahead. Argentina's current agony, which has become further exacerbated since the death of Juan Peron, is an unfortunate case in point. There has been at least one reported earlier loss of fissionable material in Argentina, and in March 1973 an armed terrorist group attacked and briefly held a portion of the Atucha nuclear power plant.[75]

Only Mexico, as the region's titular leader in the "peaceful" control of nuclear energy, seems to be publicly emphasizing the technology's inherent and growing dangers. In a recent, well-publicized speech, Arseino Farell, director of Mexico's Comision Federal de Electricidad, stated that while the danger of nuclear accidents is minimal it is nonetheless imperative "that all countries move quickly to create effective systems of safeguards over fissionable material to protect the general public, and in order that they may receive the benefits of the peaceful uses of nuclear energy."[76]

REGIONAL NUCLEAR ARMS CONTROL

The discussion of possible nuclear proliferation in Latin America is of particular interest in part due to the existence of the first example of a military denuclearized zone in an inhabited region of the world. The creation of a Latin American nuclear-weapons-free zone in the late 1960s comprising over 8 million square kilometers and 150 million inhabitants is an accomplishment of considerable significance. It also represents a rare working example of the application of legal norms in advance of technological momentum. However, due to several factors, including the nonparticipation of significant Latin American nations and inadequate support from external powers, the agreement cannot yet be said to have ensured the goal of preventing the proliferation of nuclear weapons in the Latin American region.

The Treaty for the Prohibition of Nuclear Weapons in Latin America (Treaty of Tlatelolco)[77] was signed February 14, 1967, following several years of negotiation among Latin American nations. The Tlatelolco Treaty prohibits the development or production of nuclear weapons by any Latin American nation. It also prohibits the receipt or installation of nuclear weapons by any Latin American country from a nuclear weapons state. The Tlatelolco Treaty is a regional version of the NPT, but its demand of abstinence is even more complete than the latter agreement in its prohibition of nuclear weapons bases. The Tlatelolco Treaty also embraces its own control mechanism, the Organization for the Prohibition of Nuclear Weapons in Latin America. Established in 1969 with headquarters in Mexico City, OPANAL is composed of three principal organs, the General Conference, Council, and Secretariat.

At present, twenty-two of twenty-four major Latin American nations have signed the treaty, with only Cuba refusing. Participation by the other nonsignatory, Guyana, has been frustrated by long-standing boundary disputes with Venezuela.

The treaty has been ratified and is currently in force for eighteen Latin American nations.[78] Argentina has signed but not ratified the treaty, whereas Brazil has signed and ratified it. However, the latter nation did not choose to waive the requirements of Article 28, Paragraph 1, and therefore the Tlatelolco Treaty is not in force for it until certain requirements are fulfilled. These include ratification of the treaty by all Latin American nations as well as ratification of additional protocols by all nuclear weapons states and nations having territorial interests in the Americas.

The principal holdouts continue to be Argentina and Brazil. Brazil was an early leader in the denuclearization effort,offering a draft U.N.

resolution in October 1962, prior to the Cuban missile crisis (which ultimately provided the necessary catalyst). With the 1964 military revolution, Brazil's stance at the Tlatelolco Treaty's preparatory commission (COPREDAL) shifted to an obstructionist position, particularly with respect to the question of PNEs. Unlike Brazil, Argentina was not involved in the early stages of the denuclearization efforts. However, Argentina generally shared Brazil's objections to certain sections of the treaty.[79] Argentina has demonstrated on various occasions its profound disinterest in the treaty (even relative to that of Brazil). There appears little likelihood of an early move by Argentina or Brazil to accept the Tlatelolco Treaty.

A recent seven-nation Latin American tour by President Echeverria of Mexico produced strong bilateral declarations of support for the Tlatelolco Treaty from every country on the itinerary (Ecuador, Peru, Venezuela, and so on), but no reference at all in joint communiques from Buenos Aires and Brasilia.[80] Without the participation of Argentina and Brazil, the denuclearized zone is incomplete and OPANAL is denied the benefit of the hemisphere's most able diplomatic and advanced scientific talent. However, Argentine and Brazilian support remain unlikely without full support for the zone by all nuclear weapons states and a clear perception by the two Latin American states that exploitation of PNE technology would not be inhibited.

International support for the Tlatelolco Treaty is outlined under two additional protocols. Protocol 1 is designated for those nations having territorial responsibilities in the Americas (Great Britain, France, Netherlands, and the United States) whereby they pledge "to apply the status of denuclearization" to their territorial possessions falling in the denuclearized zone. Protocol 2 focuses on the nuclear weapon states who are to pledge "not to use or threaten to use nuclear weapons against the contracting parties of the Treaty for the Prohibition of the Nuclear Weapons in Latin America."

Additional Protocol 1 has been signed by Great Britain and the Netherlands, but not by France and the United States. Both France and the United States have objected to forswearing any intentions to store or maintain nuclear weapons in certain of their territorial possessions in the Americas.[81] Great Britain has ratified both protocols while including its interpretation that the Tlatelolco Treaty prohibits detonation of PNEs.[82] The United States has signed and ratified Additional Protocol 2,[83] thus binding the nation "not to use or threaten to use nuclear weapons" against all Latin American parties to the Tlatelolco Treaty. This "nonuse" pledge induced considerable discussion and controversy within the Departments of State and Defense as it represented a self-denying obligation that hitherto the United States had avoided. Other areas of concern particularly to the U.S. Joint Chiefs of Staff were retention of transit privileges for U.S. warships carrying nuclear weapons and the prohibition of PNEs.[84] Such questions were covered under an interpretive declaration accompanying the U.S. ratification.

Both France and the People's Republic of China have ratified Additional Protocol 2, bowing to significant Mexican diplomatic pressure. China's ratification in 1973 represented its first commitment to an international arms control agreement since the establishment of a communist regime.[85] Chinese ratification accompanied by an earlier communication (which committed China not to transport nuclear weapons through the zone) represents a significant commitment, although it could be argued that China possesses far less ability at the present time to violate the zone than other nuclear weapons states.

In early 1975, the Soviet Union remains the only holdout among the nuclear weapons states in its refusal to ratify Additional Protocol 2. The three principal Soviet objections to the treaty concern PNEs, the zone of application, and the question of the transportation of nuclear weapons through the zone.[86] Opposing any loophole for PNEs, the Soviets object to the fact that the treaty's wording permits different countries to interpret provisions pertaining to PNEs in different ways. The extensive territorial expanse to be included when the full zone comes into force is also a difficulty to the Soviets. However, the most troublesome aspect to the Soviets is the treaty's provision that permits a Latin American party to grant or deny permission for transit of such weapons "in the free exercise of its sovereignty." In the view of Soviet policymakers, to allow each Latin American state the right to permit the transit of nuclear weapons through its territory gives the United States, in present-day political conditions, an inherent advantage verging on a virtual monopoly. (The Soviets have, however, in effect committed themselves to a "nonuse" pledge with respect to Mexico and other Latin American nations that may take substantive actions to convert their national territory into a denuclearized zone.) The Soviets continue to view their objections to the entire treaty as substantive, particularly the special privileges they perceive the United States to have been granted with respect to retention of weapons bases in the zone. Soviet adherence will undoubtedly not be forthcoming prior to further improvements of U.S. relations and perhaps detente between the U.S. and Cuba.

The current situation regarding the Latin American denuclearization agreement can be summarized as follows: an established nuclear-weapons-free zone plus machinery enjoying the support of the majority of Latin American nations. However, the agreement is not in force for the two most likely Latin American candidates, Brazil and Argentina. Ratification of Additional Protocol 2 is completed by four of the five nuclear weapons states, but the accompanying interpretations are clearly unacceptable to some Latin American nations. For the

Tlatelolco Treaty to become truly successful in its goal of preventing the proliferation of nuclear weapons in Latin America, there must be a far greater degree of accordance among both states within the zone and significant nonzonal states as to the intent and meaning of important provisions of the agreement. It seems unlikely that this harmony of views will prevail in the near future without significant new initiatives.

PREVENTING NUCLEAR PROLIFERATION IN LATIN AMERICA

A policy preventing the spread of nuclear weapons to the Latin American region may yet be attainable. Indeed, such a policy is a highly desirable objective, not only as an end in itself but also as an example worthy of emulation in other regions. And for Latin America, the regional approach, as opposed to global efforts, may provide the most feasible and desirable means for preventing proliferation. This is suggested by the important but incomplete success of the current nuclear-weapons-free zone, the stringent opposition of the region's principal threshold nations to the NPT, and possibly the nature of nuclear technology itself. Three interrelated policy considerations follow that could contribute to the prevention of nuclear proliferation in Latin America.

Enhancing the Effectiveness of the Latin American Nuclear-Weapons-Free Zone

There are several possibilities for enhancing the attractiveness and thereby the effectiveness of the Treaty of Tlatelolco and its control organization, OPANAL. These actions all center upon upgrading OPANAL's involvement in the peaceful uses of nuclear energy and possibly other energy sources as well. OPANAL's evolution from an organization involved solely in the area of control to one with the added dimension of coordinating the peaceful uses of nuclear energy in Latin America has been foreseen by its supporters and some limited progress achieved. Such an occurrence would serve to make cooperation with the zone more palatable to certain Latin American nations not currently disposed to cooperate. Among possible roles envisioned for OPANAL are the development of a regional radioactivity measurement program, nuclear fellowships, a regional nuclear information clearinghouse, high level conferences, and the establishment of several nuclear research centers for the benefit of the region.[87] However, progress has been limited by inadequate financial support from OPANAL's membership and the lack of participation by Latin America's two most advanced nations in nuclear energy, Argentina and Brazil.

In order to elevate OPANAL's involvement in this area, nations possessing advanced nuclear technology and research programs and are supportive of nonproliferation should consider initiating a program of significant nuclear sharing with OPANAL. In addition to the United States and Canada, others might include Great Britain, Japan, the Federal Republic of Germany, Sweden, and Italy. It is suggested that bilateral cooperation programs in the peaceful uses of nuclear energy be deemphasized in lieu of a policy whereby information is routinely transmitted to OPANAL limited for use of the contracting parties to the Tlatelolco Treaty. Information could involve such areas as nuclear reactor safety, environmental considerations, biomedical research utilizing nuclear materials, and information relating to agroindustrial complexes for desalting of seawater. In addition, consideration might be given to sharing information on alternative energy sources.

A second related consideration might be a merger between OPANAL and the OAS's Inter-American Nuclear Energy Commission (CIEN). CIEN was created in 1959 as a technical organ of the OAS in support of the peaceful uses of nuclear energy in agriculture, industry, and medicine. There is an obvious affinity of interest between CIEN's work and that of an evolved OPANAL in the peaceful uses of nuclear energy, and there would appear to be strong merit to the outright merger of the two organizations. Arguments voiced earlier during the Tlatelolco Treaty's negotiating sessions, advocating strict separation of OPANAL from the OAS, seem far less valid in the mid-1970s as the inter-American system continues to evolve.

Such a merger, necessitating a move by CIEN to OPANAL's headquarters in Mexico City, and possibly an alteration in the name of the organization,* could greatly benefit the objectives of both organizations. For the CIEN, linkage with OPANAL would greatly maximize its ability to promote the peaceful uses of nuclear energy in Latin America while preventing abuses. For OPANAL, a merger would represent greater budgetary support from Latin American countries currently being asked to support two organizations operating on parallel lines. However, the principal advantage derived by OPANAL would be heightened contact and involvement with many of the region's leading experts in nuclear research.

---

*OPANAL's current name has an unfortunate negative context. A new title such as "organization for the peaceful uses of nuclear energy in Latin America" could prove a definite advantage.

A third consideration is the development of close cooperation between an evolved OPANAL-CIEN organization and the newly created Latin American Energy Organization. Analogous to OPANAL as an indigenous Latin American (as opposed to inter-American) effort, the objective of the energy organization is to achieve an unified Latin American energy policy and to protect the region's natural resources.[88] A close liaison between the energy organization and OPANAL for the maximization of regional energy sources would seem not only logical but also extremely beneficial.

Coping with the PNE Problem

A second essential to preventing nuclear proliferation in Latin America is coping with the difficult problem of PNEs. PNEs are likely to provide the most convenient backdoor to a nuclear weapon's option for developing countries in the years ahead. As noted earlier in this chapter, both Argentina and Brazil clearly have demonstrated their intent to develop PNE technology, following the Indian example, and genuinely believe it may promote national economic development. Both have interpreted the Tlatelolco Treaty as permitting such explosions (while declining to adhere to the treaty) and both have refused to sign or ratify the NPT. Supporters of the Tlatelolco Treaty, on the other hand, have maintained their belief in the lack of meaningful distinction between a PNE and a nuclear weapon. This point was graphically illustrated by a formal request from OPANAL's secretary general to India to ratify Additional Protocol 2 of the Tlatelolco Treaty following that nation's detonation of a PNE in May 1974. India, as might be expected, declined, in a note of April 1975, to adhere to the protocol on the grounds that its nuclear device was entirely for peaceful purposes.[89]

PNE development by Argentina and Brazil and many other developing countries seems inevitable unless dramatic initiatives are undertaken in the near future, principally by the two superpowers. It is therefore vitally important, not only to the Latin American scene but also to the larger international situation, that the United States and the Soviet Union move quickly to develop a coherent and coordinated PNE policy.

As a first step there is a necessity for the U.S. government to be of one mind and to speak with one voice regarding the outlook for PNE technology. Such nations as Argentina and Brazil have most certainly noted previous examples in which officials of the (former) AEC and State Department have stated contrary views regarding the promise of PNE technology. Thus, it is suggested that the United States undertake a concentrated effort to publicize fully its experience and view of PNE technology. All information, including an explanation about Plowshare's continued miniscule budget, should be shared with potential nuclear weapon states and the IAEA and OPANAL. Similarly, representatives from the aforementioned countries and organizations should be invited to witness future U.S. PNE experiments.

Second, consideration should be given to a high level international study (including nuclear weapons states and threshold countries), culminating in an international conference on PNEs and their implications for arms limitation and disarmament.

Third, depending upon the results of the aforementioned study, the United States and the Soviet Union should cooperate closely with ongoing IAEA efforts and move expeditiously to establish an international PNE service. All explosive services undertaken within Latin America should be under joint IAEA-OPANAL control and limited to contracting parties of the Tlatelolco Treaty. This formula is foreseen and detailed in Article 18 of the Tlatelolco Treaty. If implemented, such a policy would have the added benefit of enhancing the attractiveness of OPANAL to Latin American holdouts. Most importantly, however, it would allow for the orderly development and legal control of technological processes that seem inevitable within a short time.

Regional Competition and Cooperation

Nuclear proliferation in Latin America is most likely to occur via an Argentine or Brazilian PNE. Detonation of a PNE by either will produce an irresistible pressure for an immediate response by the other. An imperfect but nonetheless relevant analogy can be drawn to the anxiety currently being experienced by Pakistan since India's detonation of a PNE. Furthermore, an Argentine and Brazilian PNE would inevitably fuel historical rivalries and ignite a chain reaction throughout the South American continent. PNE races would occur analogous to the hopeful effort initiated in 1974 by eight Latin American nations with the Declaration of Ayacucho. But as the PNE is potentially a weapon of mass destruction, the consequence of such an occurrence would be highly detrimental to peace and security in the entire region.

Competition between Argentina and Brazil is an important dynamic affecting the possible development of nuclear explosive devices in both countries. The most persistent dispute, which has defied numerous bilateral attempts at resolution, centers upon Brazil's ambitious hydroelectric program in the Rio de La Plata area. Other potential areas of friction are trade discrimination, rivalry in Antarctica, and competition for Bolivian natural gas and iron ore.[90] Brazilian concern also has been expressed in the past regarding possible rekindling of the Peronist goal of unity of Spanish-speaking Latin American countries, or that Argentina might become a haven for Brazilian revolutionary elements.

In the area of nuclear policy, competition between the two powers is resulting in an exceptionally fluid, complex, and potentially serious situation. The current Brazilian leadership previously had felt considerable chagrin (augmented by internal criticism) at the apparent Argentine lead in nuclear power. Prior to the recent signing of the West German contract for a complete fuel cycle, there was much internal disagreement with respect to the dependence of the Brazilian nuclear energy program on foreign (enrichment) technology relative to the independent Argentine program.

Similarly, some Argentines have expressed fear of the consequences on Brazilian policy of their nuclear superiority. An Argentine nuclear explosive device, it was argued, could stimulate a bilateral arms race in which Brazil, with its larger resource base, might ultimately excel. It was argued that an Argentine nuclear explosive device could push Brazil into a close alliance with the United States, leading to a heightening of U.S. influence within Brazil and in Latin America in general (highly undesirable to Argentina). It was also felt that Brazil might be impelled immediately to accelerate its own nuclear weapons program accompanied by a diplomatic offensive throughout Latin America against the "Argentine threat."[91]

However, the West German-Brazilian agreement, augmented by the chaos and political breakdown in Argentina,* may be serving to reinforce some Argentines who view the development of a nuclear explosive device as a "quick fix" to redress their dwindling power relative to Brazil. Even prior to the public announcement of the Brazilian-West German agreement, a Peronista legislator, Edgar Cossy Isasi, requested the passage of a resolution asking the Argentine chief executive to take measures to organize the appropriate scientific and technical talent "to proceed with the development of an atomic bomb for the purposes of national defense."[92]

At present, on the eve of Brazil's apparent massive stride in nuclear technology, a scenario whereby an Argentine chief executive might view detonation of a nuclear device as a means to rally internal

---

*Yet the scale and seriousness of the internal discord within Argentina may be impeding the national nuclear energy program for the first time. Long insulated from internal politics, there are indications that many scientists employed by, or associated with, the CNEA are leaving the country to work in foreign nuclear programs. Many, including a former CNEA president, have gone to Iran.

support (as did Prime Minister Gandhi in India) is not unrealistic. That such an occurrence might actually be in process was suggested in July 1975 by the chairman of the Committee on Government Operations, Senator Abraham Ribicoff, commenting on a reported diversion of 50 kilograms of plutonium from the Atucha power station without detection by the IAEA. It was stated, in a letter from Ribicoff to ERDA Administrator Robert Seamans, that the former U.S. AEC had contracted on a government-to-government basis to supply 661,000 pounds of heavy water for the Atucha reactor. Consequently, it was questioned whether the arrangement would fall under the authority of the newly created Nuclear Regulatory Commission, which must routinely approve all shipments of sensitive material, or under ERDA. While it was noted that Argentina was in the process of expanding its reprocessing plant, it was believed that no plutonium had been separated as yet from the irradiated material.[93] (Whether the purported diversion occurred or not, it nonetheless highlights the apparent ease with which it could take place and the extremely limited recourse retained by the United States to affect such situations.)

While in general Argentine-Brazilian relations in nuclear matters are characterized by elements of competition and suspicion, there have been, in the past, isolated instances that suggest the possibility of a very different relationship in the nuclear area. During the administration of former Argentine President Ongania, close Argentine-Brazilian cooperation in nuclear policy, particularly in shared positions regarding nuclear arms control measures, suggested an emerging Argentine-Brazilian condominium.[94] Similarly, the past existence of a secret Argentine-Brazilian treaty for nuclear sharing has also been suggested.[95] However unlikely, the possibility that compatible leadership might foster substantive bilateral cooperation in the nuclear area remains. In a recent article, which stimulated considerable interest in Brazil, a retired Argentine general advanced a significant proposal for bilateral nuclear sharing. It was suggested that Argentina's current advantage in nuclear technology should be viewed as an opportunity to offer an agreement in information, consultation, and technical cooperation in nuclear matters, subject to the resolution of other outstanding bilateral problems. Such an agreement, it was believed, should include cooperation in the fabrication of PNEs and could benefit the development of the entire Latin American region.[96]

The possibility of nuclear cooperation between the two countries most likely to introduce nuclear weapons into the Latin American region could provide yet another approach to preventing proliferation in Latin America. In this approach the mechanics of the nuclear fuel cycle are the important factor. That is, when a nation develops an independent capability in all elements of the nuclear fuel cycle (raw material, fuel fabrication facilities, chemical reprocessing, and so on), then the development of a nuclear explosive device is a relatively simple accomplishment using information publicly available. In order to prevent nuclear proliferation, as has been pointed out recently by several experts,[97] it is therefore highly desirable that the critical elements of the nuclear fuel cycle should not be under exclusive national control of individual states. Preferably, nuclear power should be developed on a basis of interdependence in the future.

In the case of Argentina and Brazil, colocation of key facilities in the nuclear fuel cycle would greatly reduce the possibility of multilateral ownership with control by a regional organization. In addition to reduced opportunities for diversion, creation of a situation of interdependence has the following advantages:

1. A reduction in mutual suspicion. By joint or multilateral control over the critical elements of a nuclear fuel cycle, there is far less uncertainty over motives and intentions of a potential nuclear rival. It could also promote a climate of confidence facilitating cooperation in other technical and nontechnical areas.

2. Reduced possibilities for nuclear theft and terrorism. Colocation of facilities (with regulation by a regional or international agency) would decrease opportunities for theft arising during transportation of fissionable material, while providing enhanced physical security for fewer nuclear installations.

3. Economies of scale. The economics of the fuel cycle argue strongly for international sharing of facilities. The most economic size of an industrial reprocessing plant, for example, is a very large facility far beyond what is needed to service the nuclear power plants projected for Latin America over the next decade. Thus, regional reprocessing plants, regional waste disposal facilities, and possibly regional enrichment plants are economically the rational choice.

It may of course be argued, with considerable justification, that the trend of nuclear technology (not to mention political factors) in the two countries does not support such a cooperative program. Indeed, the two nations seem to be firmly wedded to differing approaches to the nuclear fuel cycle (Argentina with natural uranium heavy water reactors and Brazil with light water reactors moving toward high temperature gas-cooled reactors). Furthermore, the discovery of significant uranium deposits in Brazil has eliminated one possible incentive for cooperation with its southern neighbor.

However, certain possibilities do still exist for mutually advantageous cooperative measures. For example, Brazil's forthcoming industrial scale enrichment facility, to be constructed in cooperation with West Germany, could be situated in Paraguay in proximity to the vast Itaipu Hydroelectric Facility, which, like the enrichment plant, is scheduled for completion in the early 1980s. Location of such a facility in what has traditionally been a buffer country, and under some type of regional control mechanism, could promote the stability and economic development of the entire region, rather than raising walls of suspicion and mistrust as seems certain to be the case if a purely national route is followed. Eventually, the facility could offer enrichment services to all nations in the Latin American region.

In a similar fashion (perhaps as an informal quid pro quo), Argentina could consider constructing an industrial scale reprocessing plant outside its borders in Uruguay or Paraguay. One such plant, under a regional control mechanism, could (as noted above) serve the needs of the entire region, thus negating the need for Brazilian purchase of a West German unit. Similarly, Argentina and Brazil could cooperate in the development of a regional radioactive waste disposal system.

In conclusion, it may be observed that nuclear energy and in particular nuclear power is destined to become of ever greater importance to Latin American nations in the years ahead. But this need not lead to the development of nuclear weapons. An analysis of ongoing trends suggests that if proliferation is to be prevented in Latin America, it will be through creative leadership on the regional level. Linkage between the existing nuclear-weapons-free zone and bilateral and multilateral cooperative efforts in nuclear energy and other energy sources may prove a feasible and desirable approach. Nonetheless, this chapter has suggested, as it must, the near-term likelihood of nuclear proliferation in Latin America. Ultimately, the last best hope for avoiding this unfortunate development may lie with far-sighted Latin American statesmen, of which the region is uniquely blessed. Historically, Latin American leaders have been in the forefront of advocacy of the rule of law in relations among nations and, relative to other regions, there are few examples of direct armed conflict between Latin American nations. With this in mind, perhaps is is not unrealistic to hope that the Latin American region can be instrumental in stimulating, in the words of one of Latin America's leading statesmen, "a gradual broadening of the zones of the world from which nuclear weapons are prohibited to a point where the territories of powers which possess these terrible tools of mass destruction will become something like contaminated islets subjected to quarantine."[98]

NOTES

1. Dr. Theodore B. Taylor, U.S., Congress, House, Committee on Foreign Affairs, hearings before the Sub-committees on International Organizations and Movements and on the Near East and South Asia, 93rd Congr., June 25, 1974, p. 9.

2. Mason Willrich, U.S., Congress, House, Committee on Foreign Affairs, hearings before the Subcommittees on International Organizations and Movements and on the Near East and South Asia, 93rd Congr. July 18, 1974, p. 171.

3. United Nations Association, "Safeguarding the Atom, A Soviet-American Exchange," UNA-USA Policy Panel Report, 1972, p. 15.

4. There is considerable interest on the part of some Latin American countries for cooperative efforts with West European nations regarding enrichment via gas centrifuge. Laser enrichment, currently being perfected in the U.S. weapons laboratories at Livermore, California, and Los Alamos, New Mexico, has significant implications due to the apparent simplicity of the equipment necessary and lack of expense relative to other enrichment processes. See New York Times, 27 April 1975. The nozzle enrichment process has certain advantages of comparative engineering simplicity, but a major disadvantage of requiring nearly double the electrical requirements of the gas diffusion method. The attractiveness of various enrichment methods will differ as to the particular circumstances of countries.

5. Bennett Boskey and Mason Willrich, Nuclear Proliferation: Prospects for Control (New York: Dunellen, 1970), p. 42.

6. COPREDAL/AR/41/PROV., Preparatory Commission for the Denuclearization of Latin America (February 8, 1967), pp. 5-6.

7. U.S., Congress, Joint Committee on Atomic Energy, AEC Authorizing Legislation 1975, 93rd Congr., p. 1078. For a general discussion, see Mason Willrich, Global Politics of Nuclear Energy (New York: Praeger, 1971, chap. 9.) For a current authoritative U.S. view of PNEs, see "An Analysis of the Economic Feasibility, Technica Significance and Time Scale for Approval of PNEs in the US with Special Reference to the GURC Report Thereon," final report to the U.S. Arms Control and Disarmament Agency from the Program on Science, Technology and Society, Cornell University, 1975; and PNEs (peaceful nuclear explosives) Activity Projects for Arms Control Planning, vols. 1 and 2, Gulf Oil Research Consortium, 1975.

8. Herbert Scoville, Jr., "Peaceful Nuclear Explosives, An Invitation to Proliferation" (Paper prepared for Arms Control Association, Carnegie Endowment, The Non-Proliferation Treaty: A Preview of the 1975 Review Conference, September 9-11, 1974, Divonne, France).

9. See V. S. Enelyanov, "On the Peaceful Uses of Nuclear Explosions," in Nuclear Proliferation Problems (Cambridge, Mass.: MIT Press, 1974).

10. New York Times, 16 February 1975.

11. "India's Aims after the Nuclear Test," Energy International (February 1975); New York Times, 22 August 1974.

12. Scoville, op. cit.

13. See Dr. Sigvard Eklund, director-general of the IAEA. Statement to the 29th Session of the U.N. General Assembly, in IAEA Bulletin 16, no. 6 (1974).

14. Related to the author by Fernando Ortez, Argentine engineer.

15. Nuclear Engineering International (February 1975): 99.

16. Washington Post, 9 May 1969.

17. J. A. Sabato, "Energia Atomica en Argentina," Estudios Internacionales (Santiago)(October-December 1968): 353.

18. Gral. Div. (R) Juan E. Guglialmelli, "Argentina, Brasil y La Bomba Atomica," Estrategia (September -October, 1974): 8. For an earlier Argentine view of the national nuclear energy programs, see Oscar A. Quihillalt, "Desarrollo de Los Reactores Nucleares en La Decade de 70," ibid. (September-December 1970, January-February 1971).

19. See "Proyecto de Ley, Programa Nuclear Argentino, 1975-1985," Camera de Deputados de la Nacion. For a recent analysis of the Argentine and Brazilian nuclear programs and their military implications, see "Argentina-Brazil: La Pusa del Atomo," Informe Economico Latino-Americano (Buenos Aires) 1, no. 5 (March 1975). However, ambitious projections of Argentine nuclear power expansion are challenged by other sources that portray Argentina's total nuclear power component as a small percentage of its total energy output for decades to come. These sources note that the recently announced 1974-85 energy plan relies heavily on an expansion of untapped hydroelectric sources and, to a lesser extent, coal. See "Argentina—The Energy Sector," Bank of London and South America Review (April 1975).

20. "Development of Nuclear Energy in the Republic of Argentina," IAEA Bulletin 4, no. 6 (1972): 8.

21. Bank of London and South America Review 8 (July 1974): 412.

22. See John R. Redick, "Argentina's Nuclear Connection," Washington Post, 30 September 1974; see also Robert Gillete, "India and Argentina: Developing a Nuclear Affinity," Science (June 28, 1974).

23. Washington Post, 26 December 1974.

24. This view was also reportedly stressed by Prime Minister Indira Gandhi to Secretary of State Kissinger during a recent visit to India. Washington Post, 29 October 1974.

25. Nuclear Engineering International (February 1975): 74. New York Times, 29 June 1974.

26. As related in Guglialmelli, op cit., p. 2. It is of note that both Argentina and Brazil have expressed great interest in the purchase of centrifuges and the construction of a gas centrifuge enrichment plant. As a lure toward purchase of a power plant, a German company involved in the construction of the European Trilateral Centrifuge Plant has

briefed Argentine officials on centrifuge technology. There are persistent but unverified reports of German-Brazilian cooperation in this area. See Nuclear Industry (February 1973): 52.

27. Hispano (Mexico City)(December 9, 1974): 39-40.

28. "Second National Development Plan, 1975-1979," Embassy of Brazil, Brazil Today (September 24, 1974). For an early but quite comprehensive description of Brazil's nuclear energy program, see "Politica Brasileira de Energia Atomica," Revista Brasileira de Politica Internacional (Rio de Janeiro)(September 1968).

29. "Politico Brasileira de Energia Atomica," op cit.

30. F. H. Lyra, D. N. Simon, and H. A. Ferreira, Jr., "The Angra Nuclear Power Plant" (Paper presented to the Fourth UN Conference on the Peaceful Uses of Nuclear Energy, September 1971).

31. New York Times, 27 June 1975.

32. Nuclear Engineering International (March 1974): 8-9.

33. Ibid. (February 1975): 99.

34. Guglialmelli, op cit., p. 6.

35. See "Nuclear Programme," in Brazil's Second National Development Plan, 1975/79 (complete English version, April 1975).

36. New York Times, 6 July 1975.

37. Washington Post, 8 July 1975.

38. Nuclear News (December 1974).

39. The Brazilian-West German agreement was widely covered in the world press. See New York Times, 4 June, 10 June, 12 June, 27 June, 28 June 1975; Washington Post, 1 June 1975; International Herald Tribune, 28-29 June 1975; plus voluminous editorial comment.

40. Nuclear Industry (June 1975). Under the agreement, Germany will also assist Brazil in further exploration. See also Brazilian Bulletin, published by Brazilian Government Trade Bureau, July 1975.

41. New York Times, 28 June 1975. However, administration spokesmen testifying before the Senate Foreign Relations Subcommittee on Arms Control and Security Agreements in July 1975 defended their efforts to dissuade the West Germans from proceeding. Nonetheless, Senator Humphrey concluded that rather than using its full influence, the Ford Administration "sort of blinked its eyes." See Washington Post, 23 July 1975.

42. See Senator Abraham Ribicoff, U.S., Congress, Senate, Congressional Record, July 21, 1975, p. S13231; and Robert Gillette, "Nuclear Exports, U.S. Firm's Troublesome Flirtation with Brazil," Science (July 1975).

43. New York Times, 29 June 1975.

44. Congressional Record, June 3, 1975, p. S9313.

45. New York Times, 4 June 1975.

46. See letter from Dr. Niels Hansen, Charge d'Affaires, Embassy of Federal Republic of Germany, to the New York Times, 7 July 1975.

47. A high German official as quoted in Wall Street Journal, 2 July 1975.

48. COPREDAL/AR/41/PROV. (February 8, 1967), pp. 5-6; COPREDAL/AR/47/PROV. (February 12, 1967), p. 7.

49. As stated by the current Foreign Minister Azeido da Silveira as ambassador to the Eighteen Nations Disarmament Committee, March 14, 1967 in Documents on Disarmament, 1967, p. 141, U.S. Arms Control and Disarmament Agency.

50. For an excellent discussion of this aspect of Brazilian foreign policy, see Roger Fontaine, Brazil and the United States (Washington, D.C.: American Enterprise Institute for Public Policy Research, 1975).

51. New York Times, 12 June 1975.

52. See Robert Gillette, "Nuclear Proliferation: India, Germany May Accelerate the Process," Science (May 30, 1975).

53. Hispano (Mexico City)(February 22, 1971): 20.

54. Nuclear Engineering International (March 1969): 8.

55. See Hispano (Mexico City)(September 23, 1974): 52.

56. Nuclear Engineering International (July 1974): 547.

57. U.S., Congress, hearings before the Joint Committee on Atomic Energy, AEC Omnibus Legislation-1974, April 30, 1974, p. 11.

58. See comments of Senator McIntyre and Representative Holifield in AEC Omnibus Legislation-1974, op. cit., pp. 7, 8, 46.

59. Statement by Arnulfo Morales Amado, president of the Mexican Academy of Sciences and Nuclear Technology, Hispano (Mexico City) (November 4, 1974): 49.

60. Hispano (Mexico City)(December 30, 1974): 6.

61. Nuclear Engineering International (February 1970): 16; (March 1972): 11.

62. Hispano (Mexico City)(November 11, 1974): 47.

63. Bank of London and South America Review (April 1970): 151.

64. See Hispano (Mexico City)(November 11, 1974): 47; (March 24, 1975): 52-53; (March 31, 1975): 42-43.

65. Bank of London and South America Review (October 1974): 625.

66. The Times of the Americas (December 25, 1974).

67. For a thorough discussion of this topic, see James D. Theberge, Russia in the Caribbean, Special Report Series No. 13, Pt. 2, the Center for Strategic and International Studies (Washington, D.C.: Georgetown University, 1973).

68. Mason Willrich and Theodore B. Taylor, Nuclear Theft: Risk and Safeguards (Cambridge, Mass.: Ballenger, 1974); see also D. Krieger, "Nuclear Power: A Trojan Horse for Terrorists," in Nuclear Proliferation Problems (Stockholm International Peace Research Institute)(Cambridge, Mass.: MIT Press, 1974); Mason Willrich, "Terrorists Keep Out," Bulletin of the Atomic Scientists (May 1975).

69. Nuclear News (August 1974): 46; Washington Post, 26 May 1974.

70. New York Times, 16 October 1973.

71. Washington Post, 27 May 1974.

72. For perceptive treatment of this topic, see J. Gustave Speth, Arthur R. Tamplin, and Thomas B. Cochran, U.S., Congress, House, Committee on Foreign Affairs, "The Plutonium Decision: A Report on the Risks of Plutonium Recycle," hearings before the Subcommittees on International Organizations and Movements and on the Near East and South Asia, 93rd Congr., 1974, pp. 308-320.

73. Comments by General Edward B. Giller, deputy assistant administrator for National Security, U.S. Energy Research and Development Administration, U.S., Congress, Senate, Committee on Government Operations, hearings April 24, 1975. See also statement by Dr. Robert C. Seamans, administrator, Energy Research and Development Administration, before the Committee on Government Operations, April 30, 1975.

74. Letter to the author from General Edward B. Giller, deputy assistant administrator for National Security, U.S. Energy Research and Development Administration, July 10, 1975.

75. Nuclear Industry (April 1973): 49. A somewhat similar incident occurred at a nuclear power station under construction in Strasbourg, France, in May 1975.

76. Hispano (Mexico City)(December 30, 1974): 6.

77. For a recent discussion of this topic, see John R. Redick, "Regional Nuclear Arms Control in Latin America," International Organization (Spring 1975). See also Hector Gros Espiell, En Torno al Tratado de Tlatelolco y La Proscripcion de Las Armas Nucleares en la America Latina (Mexico: Publicaciones del Opanal, 1973). Many of the principal documents pertaining to the treaty's negotiation can be found in Alfonso Garcia Robles, El Tratado de Tlatelolco (Mexico: El Colegio de Mexico, 1967).

78. Letter to the author from Hector Gros Espiell, secretary general of OPANAL, July 17, 1975.

79. For an Argentine view of the treaty authored by a military member of the Argentine delegation to the COPREDAL sessions, see Roberto M. Ornstein, "La Desnuclearizacion de America Latina," Estrategia (September-December 1970, January-February 1971).

80. Hispano (Mexico City)(July 22, July 29, August 5, 1974).

81. For the most current French statement regarding Protocol 1, see United Nations (A/C.1/PV2018), November 18, 1974, pp. 32-41.

82. United Nations (A/C.1/PV1508), October 26, 1967, p. 8.

83. U.S., Congress, Senate, Message from the president of the United States transmitting Additional Protocol 2 to the Treaty for the Prohibition of Nuclear Weapons in Latin America, 91st Congr., 1970.

84. U.S., Congress, Senate, Committee on Foreign Relations, Additional Protocol 2 to the Latin American Nuclear Free Zone Treaty, 1971.

85. For Chinese statements regarding the Tlatelolco Treaty, see United Nations (A/C.1/1028), November 5, 1972; Hispano (Mexico City) (April 30, 1973): 17.

86. For a complete statement regarding Soviet objections to the Tlatelolco Treaty, see the addresses by Ambassador Roshchin (USSR) to the Conference on the Committee on Disarmament, CCD/1358, March 2, 1972; CCD/PV. 553, March 28, 1972; and M. Petrov, "Denuclearized Zone in Latin America," International Affairs (USSR) (August 1974).

87. OPANAL 22, September 1970.

88. See International Legal Materials 13, no. 2 (March 1974): 377-390.

89. OPANAL CG/126, April 2, 1975.

90. See H. Jon Rosenbaum, "Argentine-Brazilian Relations: A Critical Juncture," The World Today (December 1973).

91. Guglialmelli, op. cit., p. 13.

92. See Camara de diputados de la Nacion, Secretaria, Tramite Parlamentario No. 142 (March 26, 1975) for the full text of the resolution and the accompanying speech by Cossy Isasi. See also New York Times, 2 April 1975.

93. U.S., Congress, Senate, Senator Abraham Ribicoff, Congressional Record, July 8, 1975, p. S12046.

94. David C. Jordan, "Argentina's Bureaucratic Oligarchies," Current History (February 1972).

95. H. J. Rosenbaum and G. M. Cooper, "Brazil and the Nuclear Non-Proliferation Treaty," International Affairs (London)(January 1970): 46.

96. Guglialmelli, op. cit., p. 15.

97. See, for example, Mason Willrich, "Perspective on the NPT Review Conference," Occasional Paper 7, Stanley Foundation, 1975. See also the Stanley Foundation, "Conference on the NPT and World Security," January 31-February 1, 1975, Global Issues Conference Report No. 2, 1975.

98. Alfonso Garcia Robles, United Nations (A/C.1/PV2018), November 13, 1974, p. 32.

CHAPTER

12

QUO VADIS, LATIN AMERICA? REFLECTIONS ON LATIN AMERICAN SOLIDARITY

Paul N. Rosenstein-Rodan

LATIN AMERICA OR LAS AMERICAS? LATIN AMERICAN NATIONALISM OR LATIN AMERICAN NATIONALISMS?

At two symposia held by the Center for Latin American Development Studies at Boston University on "Quo Vadis Latin America?" and on "Quo Vadis the Inter-American System?" the relationship between the United States and Latin America was discussed, stressing the problems of regional cohesion and power asymmetries in Latin America. One extreme view suggested that a U.S. policy toward Latin America does not exist but that there is a series of inconsistent or certainly unsustained drives toward this end. There are thirty different countries that have one common denominator: resentment of the United States. If the United States did not exist, relations among them would be even worse than they are today. The problem of the relationship between the United States and Latin America seems to be the difficult one of how to establish a dialogue between two nonexistent entities.

This is an exaggerated description, but not necessarily a complete distortion of reality. Latin American nationalism may be confined to a narrow circle of intellectuals; "Latin America" may have been a Cepalino abstraction, but it does not make the masses tick. Solidarity built on resentment may be very strong, however, even if it is not based on any positive supernational feelings. In time, myths create

---

Paper prepared for the Conference on Latin America in the World System Williamsburg, Virginia,April 11-13, 1975. Sponsored by The Center for Strategic and International Studies, Georgetown University.

reality; a flag may create a nation. There is no Latin American flag, incidentally, but neither is there a European one.

An impressionist contrast between the Pan-European and Latin American ideal might be useful here. The European patriotism of a Pan-European movement began as a positive emotion, remembering Charlemagne, and stressed common European civilization values, but it was not defensive in character. The United States was very far away and did not count. England and Russia were different and exotic countries and did not, either in the nineteenth century or before the first World War, constitute a tangible sense of threat. The nostalgia for common European values had a positive and not defensive accent, which may perhaps explain its various weaknesses. The Latin American ideal was, at its beginning, a search for liberation and was not only defensive against the Spanish Crown but also had vibrant positive ideals about the common future. These ideals faltered and half vanished after the impact of bitter experiences. Bolivar's tragic dictum "to govern Latin America is like trying to plow the sea" is his expression of it.

What seems to have happened is that the search for a Latin American identity has given way to an intense search for thirty different Latin American identities. "Las Americas," not Latin America, became more and more a reality. In the nineteenth century, nationalism was a constructive and a progressive force. It led to the formation of larger and more viable political and economic units and was beginning to form outward-looking policies. Nowadays, nationalism, while very vital and strong, is most frequently a retrogressive force maintaining small and nonviable units with inward- rather than outward-looking policies; ultimately, these are not progressive even though their intentions sound otherwise.

Let us consider the contrast between the formation of the European and Latin American common markets. The European Common Market was formed between six countries that were already developed, that had a high proportion of trade among them, and that were complementary rather than competitive. Income differences among them were smaller than in Latin America. The first main impact was to increase the flow of an already high intertrade and the secondary effect was a more rational and better organized investment. Even so, two years of negotiations was needed, and it was uncertain for a long time whether agreement would be reached. The motivations were in part defensive, that is, the attempt to keep a major role in world power, and in part dictated by an urge to avoid further internal quarrels and to strengthen common European values.

That thirty countries in Latin America with great differences in income and development level, with competing rather than complementary economies, and with very little intertrade, should succeed in forming a common market has proved so far to be an illusion. The bonds of a common historical and cultural past and the same language for two thirds of them (a similar but not identical language as between England and the United States can often be an obstacle rather than an asset) do not give sufficient basis for success. While the threat and resentment of U.S. dominance might provide the basis for a solid cohesion, a Latin American common market can at best be reached only in 1990 instead of the 1970s or 1980, and it might be achieved by the formation of a series of Latin American BENELUXs, that is, of subregional groups such as the Andean Group, the Central American Group, CONOSUR, etc., which could integrate later on. The central question is whether these subregions may be able to develop sufficient cohesion and solidarity to overcome the centrifugal single nationalisms of its nation members. It is a vital problem for judging the future development of Latin America.

In one respect the political spectacle of a noncohesive Latin America has been simplified for the present. During the last few years the main problem in the United States has been ABM (antiballistic missiles). The main obstacle to Latin American unity and cohesion has also been ABM (Argentina, Brazil, and Mexico). Each of the large units—each one poorer than one member of the European Common Market like France—believes that it alone is enough to secure the basis of national growth and development and pays, at best, lip service to Latin American economic integration. This situation has improved somewhat for the time being.

Out of the three ABMs, two may have a much lesser voice in Latin American affairs. In Argentina there is a surrealist situation that only Salvador Dali could describe. The contrast between individual and collective psychology (individual and collective Argentinians are two completely different beings) and a pronounced political "antitalent" of being unable to arrange social coexistence will necessarily reduce the Argentine voice in the Latin American concert. In Mexico, in spite of all the revolutionary language and great rhetorical extravaganza, the mystique of the revolution is gradually weakened if not exhausted. New internal dissensions and problems confront Mexico, which so far has successfully overcome them. These may also reduce Mexico's real weight in Latin American affairs, however vibrant and loud be its voice. Let us realize what is often only hinted at, that Mexico really considers itself a great power—but not part of Latin America—a great power that is willing to offer its services as a more or less honest broker between the United States and Latin America. Mexico may become more concerned with internal problems unless the oil discoveries restore its dynamism and potential. So Latin America today consists very largely of two units, the Andean Group and Brazil. If the Andean Group maintains its mystique and cohesion, the outlines of Latin American development could become less obscure.

BRAZIL

Brazil is, or seems to be, a continent on its own—in, but not really part of, Latin America—with great patriotism (all the greater because it is not vocal), not in search of but sure of its national identity. Its "psychological integration" means that there is little difference between the individual and collective Brazilian, imbued with biological vitality groping toward manifest destiny. The opening of Amazonia may not satisfy any rational cost-benefit ratio but it has a romantic appeal. The economic dynamism overcoming the oil depression seems to warrant sustained growth.

It is feared that Brazil, without any imperialist push, like a river fed by too many streams, may eventually inundate the surrounding countries just as Russia did in the seventeenth and eighteenth centuries. Its neighbors' anxiety over this builds the image (even if unjustified) of the "ugly Brazilian" substituting for the "ugly American." Brazil does not respond to any Latin American vibration; it accepts participation in the Latin American concert but with as little enthusiasm as England in the European Community. Its population, gross national product, and elan vital would create an imbalance if it were not met by countervailing power of similar dimension.

ANDEAN GROUP

The Andean Group may become the second center of economic and political power. It has only two thirds of the population of Brazil, a gross national product similar to (or only slightly lower) than Brazil's, and still less industrial power. (See Table 12.1) It has, however, an excellent economic potential and has reached a viable dimension with the access of Venezuela. The secretariat of the Acuerdo de Cartagena in Lima is the only unit in Latin America with a sense of mission and a mystique that the U.N. Economic Commission for Latin America (ECLA) had in the 1950s. An Andean spirit of solidarity is emerging that may overcome the many difficulties of its ambitious program and provide the cohesion necessary within a pluralistic group of different political systems. It is too early to speak of an Andean patriotism, but there is an Andean spirit.

THE ROLE OF VENEZUELA

The doctrine of ideological or political pluralism is inherently a commonsense compromise. It cannot create enthusiasm and drive that alone could compel public opinion to overcome the normal inertia and resistance to change; it strengthens divisive inward-looking nationalisms and necessarily weakens the process of continental Latin American cohesion. The myths of the Alliance for Progress and of the Castro, Allende, and Peruvian systems have lost their appeal. A new vision is needed to proceed from nation building to the building of an international community. Above the struggle ("au-dessus de la melee") of different ideological systems there are common values that are the basis of harmonious coexistence.

Today, Venezuela has the unique opportunity to speak with a Latin American voice "above the struggle." Its orderly democratic system, different from the military regimes, and its new economic, but not political, power generates a sense of responsibility to use its wealth with great generosity for proclaiming "new order" values and foregoing Latin American unity. Venezuela is above suspicion of having doctrinal or power ambitions; it is also a natural bridge between South and Central America and the Caribbean world, assuring an outward-looking orientation in the Andean Group. It undoubtedly has the ideal and the means to break a new path toward Latin American unification. It is uncertain as yet whether the means are going to be used for a coherent program instead of a series of isolated actions; whether it will radiate effectively a new long-time vision or get entangled in a series of short-run measures. Supporting some basic commodity agreements and financing ad hoc projects do not add up to a coherent development philosophy and program. The ideological and intellectual means may not necessarily match the material ones.

THE INTER-AMERICAN SYSTEM AND LATIN AMERICAN INSTITUTIONS

To build up a coherent policy and to strengthen Latin America's voice and solidarity are the generally proclaimed aims. Not only what is to be done but also how it is to be done is the problem. What kind of organizations and institutions can implement this policy? There is a bewildering variety of inter-American institutions, but neither OAS, nor the IDB, nor Inter-American Committee of the Alliance for Progress (CIAP) (now Inter-American Economic and Social Council, CIES), nor CEPAL as yet can be said to have a recognized mandate to speak in the name of Latin America. They speak indeed, but hardly anybody listens. The OAS is a ponderous organization difficult to live with and to live without. Its structure—with the General Assembly, the Council, CIES, and so on—is an organizational monstrosity showing the sterilizing force of Roman law in Iberian interpretation. The process of building a national sense of identity is not just a matter of building institutions. It is a conscious assertion of the things that separate the nation (or region) from others. The CECLA (Consensus of Vina del Mar) was a step of self-assertion, but without a secretariat it is just a caucus of occasional meetings of foreign secretaries with less echo than an occasional caucus of political parties (democrats or republicans in the United States, labor-conservatives in England, and so on). The present program of a separate SELA (Latin American Economic System), a Latin American not inter-American organization, may not function better, but worse, without the presence of the United States, which provides the common denominator of resentment, and would only add to the duplication of simplification of institutions.

A functional reorganization and multiplication is needed separating issues of international law and political matters, on the one hand (like the Security Council of the UN), and functional economic and technological matters on the other hand (like a better ECOSOC of the UN). Economic and technological issues form the majority of urgent international problems. They require professional expertise that normal foreign service of juridical experience does not provide. But precisely because these problems are growing in importance, the vested interest of foreign services and their ambassadors (to the governments, to the OAS, to the UN, and so on) want to preserve the prerogative of the "senior service" and oppose a sensible restructuring of an inter-American (or Latin American) system. A constructive functional discussion of economic social and technical problems in a "decarburetted" and depoliticized atmosphere is impossible without a thorough reorganization of the inter-American system.*

---

*This is not the place to discuss it thoroughly. A report on the Reorganization of the Inter-American System (Proceedings of a Symposium held at CLADS Boston University in October 1974) was published in the spring of 1975.

PROSPECTS OF LATIN AMERICAN INTEGRATION

Prospects of Latin American integration and political cohesion cannot be said to be excellent, in spite of a better economic performance than other developing countries. This is not peculiar for Latin America, however, which is part of the world and has inherently the same problems. Progress toward an international community is either at a standstill or is receding. A sense of alienation, disorientation, and weakening of moral values is all-prevading. International cooperation and solidarity are cracking at their seams. Europe is in disarray; in the United States there seems to be neither a well-functioning presidential nor parliamentary democracy. International aid to developing countries is a moral scandal. The lights all over the world are not going out but are being dimmed. It is difficult to preserve one's congenital optimism in the absence of ideals and leadership. The bewilderment is universal, but it is perhaps somewhat less in Latin America than in the rest of the world.

Ten years ago we had at least six people to whom the whole world listened: Pope John XXIII, John Kennedy, Jawaharlal Nehru, Adlai Stevenson, Nikita Khrushchev, and Charles de Gaulle. Today we have technocratically more or less efficient managers of important provinces of the world—the United States, England, and so on—but nobody outside the parochial limits of that province has any reason to listen, and nobody does. This is unbearable. We do not know what made such leaders appear and what made them disappear. As they emerged in the past, so may they emerge again.

TABLE 12.1

Latin American Population and GNP, 1972

	Population (million)	GNP per Capita	GNP (Billion $)
Central America			
Mexico	54.15	750	40.30
Cuba	8.80	450	4.00
Guatemala	5.60	420	2.34
Haiti	4.40	130	0.56
Dominican Republic	4.20	480	2.00
El Salvador	3.70	340	1.25
Honduras	2.70	320	0.86
Nicaragua	2.15	470	1.02
Costa Rica	1.82	630	1.15
Panama	1.52	880	1.34
Total	89.04		54.86
Caribbean			
Jamaica	1.93	810	1.56
Trinidad-Tobago	1.05	970	1.02
Martinique	0.34	1,050	0.36
Guadelupe	0.33	910	0.30
Barbados	0.24	800	0.19
Netherlands Antilles	0.23	1,500	0.35
Belize	0.13	670	0.09
Bahamas	.171	2,240	0.38
Bermuda	.055	4,190	0.23
Puerto Rico	2.86	2,050	5.86
Virgin Islands	0.68	3,590	0.24
Canal Zone	0.65	2,870	0.19
Other[a]	0.52		0.17
Total	9.09		10.94
South America			
Brazil	98.12	530	52.00
Argentina	24.00	1,290	31.00
Colombia	23.14	400	9.27
Peru	14.12	520[b]	7.40[b]
Venezuela	11.10	1,240[c]	13.80[c]
Chile	10.04	800	8.03
Ecuador	6.50	360	2.37
Bolivia	5.20	200	1.03
Uruguay	3.00	760[d]	2.24
Paraguay	2.35	320	0.74
Guyana	0.75	400	0.30
Surinam	0.42	810	0.34
French Guiana	0.05	1,170	0.06
Total	198.69		128.58
Andean Group			
1972	70	600	42
1974	72	708.3	51
Total	142		93
Brazil			
1972	98.10	530	52.00
1974	104.00	586	61.00
Total	202.10		113.00

[a]St. Lucia, Grenada, St. Vincent, Dominica, Antigua, St. Kitts-Nevis Anguilla.

[b]This appears to be an overestimate; a more plausible figure would be GNP per capita, $390; GNP, $5.51 billion.

[c]Venezuela's GNP in 1974 (owing to oil prices) can be estimated at about 2,000 per capita, with a GNP of around $23 billion.

[d]May be a slight overestimate.

Source: World Bank Atlas, 1974.

Summary (rounded figures)

	Population (million)	GNP (Billion $)
Central America	90.00	50.00
Caribbean	4.70	4.00
South America	200.00	129.00
Latin America	295.00	188.00
Latin America without Caribbean	290.00	180.00

	Population (millions)	Percent of Total	GNP (Billion $)	Percent of Total
I. High income countries	35.00	11.8	44.00	23.4
II. Middle income countries	72.00	24.4	56.00	29.7
III. Middle-low income countries	167.00	56.6	78.00	41.4
IV. Low income countries	20.40	6.9	6.25	3.3
V. Haiti	4.40	1.5	0.56	0.24

I. High Income Countries (above $1,000 per capita)

	Population (million)	GNP per Capita	GNP (Billion $)
Argentina	23.95	1,290	31.00
Venezuela	11.11	1,240*	13.80
Frency Guiana		1,170	0.61
Total	35.06		44

II. Middle Income Countries ($600-$1,000 GNP per capita)

	Population (million)	GNP per Capita	GNP (Billion $)
Mexico	54.15	750	40.30
Jamaica	1.93	800	1.56
Costa Rica	1.82	630	1.15
Panama	1.52	880	1.34
Trinidad-Tobago	1.04	970	1.02
Chile	10.04	800	8.03
Uruguay	2.96	760	2.24
Surinam	0.43	610	0.34
Total	71.90		56.00

*(2,000 = 1974)

III. Middle-Low Income Countries (GNP per capita $400-$600)

	Population (million)	GNP per Capita	GNP (Billion $)
Cuba	8.75	450	3.97
Guatemala	5.62	420	2.34
Dominican Republic	4.23	480	1.98
Nicaragua	2.15	470	1.02
Berlize	0.13	670	0.09
Brazil	98.20	530	52.01
Colombia	23.04	400	9.27
Peru	14.12	520	7.38
Guyana	0.75	400	0.30
Total	167.00		78.1

IV. Low Income Countries (below $400 GNP per capita)

	Population (million)	GNP per Capita	GNP (Billion $)
El Salvador	3.67	340	1.25
Honduras	2.69	320	0.86
Ecuador	6.51	360	2.37
Bolivia	5.19	200	1.03
Paraguay	2.35	320	0.74
Total	20.41		6.25

V. Special Case:

	Population (million)	GNP per Capita	GNP (Billion $)
Haiti	4.38	130	0.56

INDEX

ABOUT THE EDITORS AND CONTRIBUTORS

ROGER W. FONTAINE is the director of Latin American Studies at the Georgetown Center for Strategic and International Studies. He received a Ph.D. from the Johns Hopkins School of Advanced International Studies. He has taught at Middlebury College and has done research for the Research Analysis Corporation and the Institute for Defense Analyses, among others. His publications include *Brazil and the United States: Toward a Maturing Relationship* and *On Negotiating with Cuba*, both published by the American Enterprise Institute for Public Policy Research in Washington, D.C.

JAMES D. THEBERGE is currently the U.S. Ambassador to Nicaragua. He was the director of Latin American Studies at the Center for Strategic and International Studies at Georgetown University. He holds degrees from Columbia, Oxford, and Harvard universities. He has taught at Oxford, UCLA, the University of Ceara in Brazil, the Catholic University, and National University in Buenos Aires, among others. He has been a foreign service reserve officer for the State Department and a senior economist for the Inter-American Development Bank. His publications include *The Soviet Presence in Latin America* (Crane, Russak & Co.) and *Russia in the Caribbean* (Georgetown University), and his articles have appeared in *Foreign Policy*, *World Affairs*, *Soviet Analyst*, *American Economic Reveiw*, *Vision*, and other journals.

JOHN R. REDICK has a Ph.D. from the University of Virginia, and is research director for the Stanley Foundation, Muscatine, Iowa.

NORMAN M. SMITH is a lieutenant colonel in the United States Army, and is a military staff assistant for the U.S. Arms Control and Disarmament Agency.

JOSEPH GRUNWALD is a senior fellow at the Brookings Institution, and teaches at the Johns Hopkins School of Advanced International Studies and at Georgetown University.

H. JON ROSENBAUM is an associate professor of political science at the City College of New York.

LAWRENCE B. KRAUSE is a senior fellow at the Brookings Institution and teaches international economics at the Johns Hopkins School of Advanced International Studies.

HIROYA ICHIKAWA currently is an economics research consultant at the U.S. -Japan Trade Council in Washington, D.C. and is an economist with the Keidanren, the Japanese Federation of Economic Organizations in Tokyo.

PAUL N. ROSENSTEIN-RODAN is now director of the Center for Latin American Development Studies, Boston University, and is one of the founding fathers of development economics.

WILLIAM G. TYLER is an associate professor in the department of economics at the University of Florida.

MIGUEL S. WIONCZEK is the director of the technical secretariat, National Science and Technology Council, Mexico City.

JOHN D. HARBRON is a senior foreign affairs analyst for Thompson Newspapers Ltd. in Toronto, Canada.

PHILIP MUSGROVE is a research associate at the Brookings Institution and has taught in the department of economics at the University of Florida.

RELATED TITLES
Published by
Praeger Special Studies

ALLENDE'S CHILE
edited by Philip O'Brien

BRAZILIAN ECONOMIC POLICY: An Optimal Control Theory Analysis
Gian Singh Sahota

CHINESE TECHNOLOGY TRANSFER TO THE THIRD WORLD: A Grants Economy Analysis
Janos Horvath

COLONIAL EMANCIPATION IN THE PACIFIC AND THE CARIBBEAN: A Legal and Political Analysis
Arnold H. Leibowitz

THE ECONOMIC DEVELOPMENT OF PANAMA: The Impact of World Inflation on an Open Economy
Robert E. Looney

THE ECONOMIC DEVELOPMENT OF REVOLUTIONARY CUBA: Strategy and Performance
Archibald R. M. Ritter

ECONOMIC GROWTH AND EMPLOYMENT PROBLEMS IN VENEZUELA: An Analysis of an Oil-Based Economy
Mostafa F. Hassan

ECONOMIC NATIONALISM IN LATIN AMERICA
Shoshana Baron Tancer

FAMILY AND OTHER BUSINESS GROUPS IN ECONOMIC DEVELOPMENT: The Case of Nicaragua

Harry W. Strachan

LEGAL ASPECTS OF THE INTERNATIONAL TRANSFER OF TECHNOLOGY TO DEVELOPING COUNTRIES

Charles Chukwuma Okolie

OIL IN THE ECONOMIC DEVELOPMENT OF VENEZUELA

Jorge Salazar-Carrillo

THE STATUS OF BOLIVIAN AGRICULTURE

E. Boyd Wennergren and Morris D. Whitaker, foreword by G. Edward Schuh